Politics, Nature, *and* Piety

Politics, Nature, and Piety

On the Natural Basis of Political Life

LAURENCE BERNS

Edited by Alex Priou

PAUL DRY BOOKS
Philadelphia 2022

First Paul Dry Books Edition, 2022

Paul Dry Books, Inc.
Philadelphia, Pennsylvania
www.pauldrybooks.com

Printed in the United States of America

Library of Congress Control Number: 2022941277

ISBN 978-1-58988-169-3

Contents

Politics, Nature, *and* Piety

Photo by Sandra J. Cohen

Foreword

For Laurence Berns, born in Newark, New Jersey, in 1928, the burning question of his life was and remained the question of *justice.*

In 1946, right out of high school, he enlisted in the army, where he hoped to find his own Platon Karataev, the wise peasant from Tolstoy's *War and Peace.* Due to his early experience in his mother's photo studio, he was sent to Korea as official photographer for Kimpo Air Force Base. One of Laurence's stories from the months when he was stationed there before the Korean War was about Kim, the house boy who, after reading *The Boys' Life of Lincoln,* exclaimed: "*You,* Abraham Lincoln—same same!"

In 1948, with the help of the G.I. Bill, Laurence went to the University of Chicago, at first to study law, but soon thereafter political science. The decisive influence from those years of studies, which lasted for the rest of his life, was the encounter with Leo Strauss. His longtime student, his research assistant, his friend, Laurence never tired speaking of Strauss as the greatest teacher and thinker he ever knew. It is touching to remember that, of all Strauss's students, Laurence was the only one that, in later years, Strauss called by first name. Laurence was fond of telling the story of Strauss's reaction to the first time he turned in his dissertation on Francis Bacon: "Think about it some more, Mr. Berns!" And so he did, a few years more. Taking all of Strauss's courses, even beyond his

Ph.D. in 1957, Laurence also extensively taught in the university's downtown Basic Program of Liberal Education for Adults.

To improve his knowledge of German, with a view to reading Kant, Hegel, Nietzsche, and Heidegger in the original language, Laurence spent 1959–1960 at the University of Heidelberg and studied with Strauss's old friends Karl Löwith and Hans-Georg Gadamer. In Gadamer's seminar on Plato's *Phaedo*, he met his future wife, Gisela.

From 1960–1999 Laurence taught at St. John's College in Annapolis, Maryland.

Interrupted only by a 1966–1967 Guest Professorship at Rosary College outside Chicago and a 1971–1972 sabbatical at Cambridge University in England, these years at St. John's College, with its required program in sciences and humanities, for students and faculty alike, were very fruitful ones in Laurence's scholarly life. Reading and writing lectures and essays up to his sudden death in 2011, he never stopped thinking about the great questions of philosophy, especially those raised and engaged in by Socrates. Together with his lifelong friend George Anastaplo, Laurence published a translation of Plato's *Meno* in 2004. At his death, he left an almost completed translation of and commentary on Aristotle's *Politics*. Returning once more to the University of Chicago's Basic Program, Laurence gave his last lecture, in November 2010, on "Plato's *Meno* and Aristotle's *Nicomachean Ethics*."

Over his desk hung a saying by Demokritos (247B), in Greek: "Ἀνδρὶ σοφῷ πᾶσα γῆ βατή· ψυχῆς γὰρ ἀγαθῆς πατρὶς ὁ ξύμπας κόσμος." ("To a Wise Man the whole earth lies open before him; for the home of a Good Soul is the entire universe.")

Gisela Berns
St. John's College, Annapolis, MD

Introduction

I.

When Laurence Berns passed away in 2011, he left behind two proposals for a collection of essays, the later of the two having updated titles and an expanded chapter on Kant. This collection is based on that second proposal, save in one respect. He had also planned to write an introduction for this "unified collection of essays." The topic was to be "the unity of the essays," including "brief remarks about what each essay aims at accomplishing and how it relates to the others." Unfortunately, he did not write it before he died.

Though emphasis on unity is common in such collections, here it is rather puzzling. What unity can there be among essays written over nearly forty years? Not arranged chronologically, their unity cannot be developmental. Did he simply not change his mind over the course of his intellectual life? Or did he have the good sense to notice what questions he had yet to consider and so table them for a later time? That is, did he know what he didn't know?

That the latter is the case is clear from the many allusions, repeated examples and arguments, and unattributed quotations scattered throughout these pages. In the present introduction, I offer my understanding of the unity of the book, based on some of these indications. My hope is that readers will approach this volume by taking seriously each essay in itself and as a part of a whole.

II.

The collection breaks into two parts of seven chapters each. The task of the first is to recover the Aristotelian understanding of nature as intelligible to *nous*, the intellect, against its rejection in the "modern natural sciences" and "the social sciences that model themselves on them" (4–5). Berns thus begins and ends the first part with the various articulations of the pre-philosophic or pre-scientific worldview, according to the most significant philosophers of the twentieth century: Edmund Husserl, Martin Heidegger, and Leo Strauss. The first part thus aims to overcome modernity and settle the disputes among its leading contemporary critics.

In the first chapter, Berns argues, following Strauss (305 n. 7), that the return to ordinary, pre-scientific experience entails a return to the political philosophy of Plato and Aristotle. According to Aristotle, man "is required by nature, by his nature as a thoughtful, speaking, and political animal, to form conventions, the most important of which are those conventions that designate certain definite combinations of sounds as representative or significant of certain definite notions of the mind" (15). Reliance on such conventions rests on "the assumption . . . that when men talk to one another they are talking about the same things," so that things have an "intelligible character" (16). On this account, the fulfillment of man, the rational and political animal, would appear to be the philosopher in conversation with another about what can be known.

Yet, as the second chapter, on Aristotle's *Poetics*, shows, the legislator and poet stand between any particular man and his perfection in the philosopher, so that the mythic and the conventional stand between the philosopher and the intelligible character of things. Likewise, the mutual understanding of philosophic conversation has a political and religious corollary in the pity and fear we have for the tragic hero. Poetry, however, also induces the philosophic passion of *wonder*. "The best plots, wondrous, though tragic, are also pleasant, because they offer a promise of and invitation to further learning" (28). On this account, poetry, in its highest form, would point beyond itself to *to noēton* and so be guided by *nous*.

The rift between the political and the philosophic is further developed in the third chapter, on Shakespeare's *King Lear*. Though written eight years before the second, the third is very much anticipated by it, picking up on the twin roles of poetry as religious or political, on the one hand, and philosophic or educative, on the other.[1] Poetry fulfills its educative purpose by presenting the hero's mistakes, but in the realm of politics such mistakes are so consequential as to constitute tragic falls. "The price of sufficiently educating authority in mercy or equity" is thus "hopelessly high" (56). This difficulty is apparently surmounted by "the educator Shakespeare, who by his art, his presentation of feigned experiences, has made it possible for some to feel, without fully suffering, what they might need to feel in order to see" (56). As an illustrative example, Berns offers Edgar, who in the guise of a mad beggar educates his father. The necessity of this guise suggests the extent of the rift between philosophic education and political power, and so the rift between the poet Shakespeare, in his wisdom, and those who have political authority. There seems, therefore, to be no reconciliation for man the political animal and man the rational animal (see 66–67).

By populating his play with the "worldly wise" and the "honest fools" they manipulate, Shakespeare suggests that an oversimplified Christian ethos engenders a dangerous *realpolitik*, suppressive of the longing for excellence and perfection championed by Aristotle. Berns thus turns in the next two chapters to Bacon and Hobbes, founders of the aforementioned "modern natural sciences" and "the social sciences that model themselves on them." The sixth chapter details how Kant brought together the Baconian and Hobbesian threads into a single system based on the rejection of the possibility of knowing things in themselves. The Kantian unknowable noumenal realm thus took the place of the Aristotelian *noēton*. Kant thereby set the stage for the crisis addressed by Husserl, Heidegger, and Strauss, and which Berns himself addresses in chapters seven and eight.

Chapters four through six illustrate the gradual alienation of man from ordinary experience over the course of modernity. The Baconian project of conquering nature requires first the refutation of what Bacon calls the idols of the mind, that is, "the 'refutation of the natural human understanding.' This culminates in the refutation of those philosophies that have been based upon this understanding. These are, most notably, the philosophies of Plato and Aristotle" (71). Hobbes, in turn, envisioned his work attaining the same certitude in political philosophy as found in mathematics and geometry. In this way, "Hobbes's emphatic break with the tradition was decisively prepared by Machiavelli and, following Machiavelli, Bacon" (96). Hobbes' "understanding of common prescientific experience" sets aside the longing for excellence in favor of our equality in fear of violent death (98). Such equality turns men into political atoms, the basis for a geometrically precise science of politics, which is impossible given a hierarchy of heterogenous human types, as found, for example, in Plato's *Republic*. These parallel trends come together in Kant, for whom "reason . . . is not intuitive . . . but legislative: it provides rules for the meaningful organization of sense experience" (134). Reason as legislative, for the one reasoning and for the world, unites the realms of morality and nature "in one and the same world" (129, 147).

The rejection of intellection in favor of self-legislation makes a properly cultivated moral feeling necessary to the modern project, whence the importance of "religion within the limits of reason alone" to Kantian moral education (see 149–50). By lowering the ambitions of reason, so as to make it efficacious, the moderns restricted it to the moral realm, specifically insofar as it coincides with the religious realm governed, for Aristotle, by fear and pity. Wonder is demoted.[2] Berns can therefore conclude that modern philosophy is marked by an incorporation of religion. This he does in chapters seven and eight.

III.

The central two chapters belong together. Each was written with the other in mind (see 329–30 n. 48), and both were published in 1991. They act as a hinge, bound to one another even as they are joined to their respective parts.

Chapter seven completes the inquiry begun in chapter one, settling the lingering question as to how Strauss' response to the crisis of modernity ranks relative to those of Husserl and Heidegger (152). His own version of Strauss' history of philosophy complete, Berns now criticizes Husserl (following Heidegger) for failing to recognize "the fundamental attitude of religiosity permeating the perspective of the life-world" (153). Yet he also finds inadequate Heidegger's examination of the primary prescientific mood or passion; in his work, "religious sentiments are presented in more or less respectable academic garb ('existential analytic'), without the academically less respectable theological presuppositions that might ground those sentiments" (153–54). Heidegger thus continues modern philosophy's tendency "to incorporate religious notions into itself" (155). Assuming his Aristotelian position, Berns identifies the predominant passion in Heidegger's thought as *thumos*, spiritedness:

> Many factors conspire to indicate that spiritedness is the dominant power for Heidegger. There is the emphasis on "mineness," "ownness," and anxiety, a radicalized fear. If resoluteness approaches any Aristotelian virtue, it would seem to be courage, the virtue that refines spiritedness. (160)

Heidegger does not acknowledge that prescientific experience is "constituted at its core by a tension between the demands of piety and the divination of an impersonal nature that leads to philosophy and science" (161). Berns asks,

> What is God? Is it the loving, caring God of justice, for whom righteous action is the one thing needful, or impersonal intelligence, self-sufficient in its intellection, the model and ground of the human capacity to understand things as they are? (164)

There are two ways: that of Aristotle or that of the Bible. Modernity is a third, but only in that it attempts to resolve this more fundamental tension.

In the next chapter, "The Relation Between Philosophy and Religion," these three ways constitute, as the new subtitle puts it, "three fundamental alternatives." These three "permanent alternatives" are those advanced by ancient, medieval, and modern philosophy, which have as their respective centers nature, God, and man (171–72). What is fundamental? Is it what is intelligible to *nous,* so that "it is impossible for any particular or contingent event to be absolutely sacred" (175)? Or is it rather God, "the ultimate principle" that "reveals itself in personal address to *particular* men, *particular* families and nations, on *particular* occasions" (179, emphasis added)? The third, modern alternative offers "a new basis, that is, man: the ultimate source of meaning for humanity's understanding of the world is the human understanding itself" (181). But this only ends up "rationalizing and secularizing revealed religion's sanctification of individuality" (182). Consequently, "the attempt to dispense with or transcend the ancient and medieval alternatives is highly questionable" (190). But how are we to navigate the tension between the ancient and medieval? This would require thinking through the tension between *thumos,* in its allegiance to particulars, and *nous,* in its quest for universals. Chapter nine, whose subject is *thumos,* set us down this path.

IV.

Like the first six chapters, the last six break into two sets of three: chapters nine through eleven have the common theme of Aristotle, while twelve through fourteen all relate somehow to Xenophon and, ultimately, Socrates. As a whole, they continue the recovery of the Aristotelian position, while also raising the question of its connection to Socratic knowledge of ignorance.

The ninth chapter explicates the tension between *thumos* and *nous* on a number of levels, but most relevantly on the question of the greatest of external goods. For the great-souled man, it is honor; but because he is so great, his honor must come from his inferiors, and "honor is [only] as valuable as the cognitive capacities of its bestowers" (200). The alternative is "the friendship . . . based on understanding, understanding virtue and understanding one another" (200). We have moved beyond the mediating influence of the political and religious, so prominent in the first half of the collection, to the anticipated philosophic friendship. But isn't *thumos*, which treats the particular as sacred, still present in friendship? Aren't friends irreplaceable? Or are friendship and philosophy simply incompatible?[3]

Chapter ten focuses on freedom and equality. The modern understanding of freedom includes "an exaltation of human 'creativity,' coupled with despair of finding a rational source of ends to guide that creativity" (214). For Aristotle, however, "freedom gets its character from the end it serves, virtue, that is, "the sharing of a good life, a communion of mutual concern for one another's well-being, which means primarily a concern for one another's qualities, one another's character" (215). Such virtue could be political, but "political virtue is not complete virtue or virtue unqualified" (215). Political virtue finds its basis in justice or the regime, which those seeking philosophic virtue subject to critique.

In this spirit, Berns turns to the American polity and a disagreement with his own friend, George Anastaplo. For Anastaplo, prudence and magnanimity, or greatness of soul, can be combined, as with the example of Lincoln. In contrast, Berns offers a "Xenophontic, that is, elementary and nonideological, approach" to the character of justice in liberal democracies, according to which prudence makes a decision in favor of the lesser of two evils, in favor of the "cheating" that comes with freedom over the "bullying" that comes with "concentrating too much power in the hands of our governmental protectors" (224). This disagreement among friends ultimately concerns whether there necessarily exists a tension between prudence and magnanimity, philosophic and political virtue, and so *nous* and *thumos.*

Chapter eleven focuses on a possible "cooperation," even friendship, between Aristotle and Adam Smith on the question of *philanthrōpia* or fellow-feeling. On Berns' reading, Smith and Aristotle are rather close on this question, though they depart on "the status of reason" (245). "Following his mentor Hume," Smith rejected "the possibility of intellectual intuition, . . . of *nous,*" as is characteristic of the moderns (246). Smith followed "his good friend" Hume, since he is "the one man who more than any other approached his standard of perfect virtue" (230, 247). In a closing dialogue, Berns defends Aristotle and attempts to persuade Smith that his admiration for Hume had to have its source in what Hume *saw* (36–37 n. 22). Smith's system, in its rejection of *nous,* can't make sense of his own fellow-feeling for Hume. Philosophic friendship must have a basis in the intellect, if not also the intelligible, *to noēton.*

By adding "(A Dialogue)" to the subtitle of chapter twelve,[4] Berns emphasizes the connection between the style of this chapter and the close of chapter eleven. This dialogue concerns Anastaplo's famous case before the Supreme Court. Anastaplo invoked "principles which would justify the alteration or abolition of any government which does not measure up to those principles" (254), and so opened up an "abyss" before the Court, much as Socrates did before Anytus; both tribunals had no choice but to condemn the accused (254). This tragic outcome is not without its redeeming lessons. Anastaplo's error seems to have been that "he, as a young man might, esteemed his chosen profession a bit too highly" (255), eventually admitting that "he might be wrong about his high expectations for lawyers" (257). This result is rather less tragic. Toward the end of the dialogue, one interlocutor remarks, "The case, especially near its end, begins to look like the story of one rather uncommon man's search to find out where he rightly belongs," to which the other responds, "It's a funny way to get an education" (257). Comic, even.

Chapter thirteen treats at length the humorous dialogue, from Xenophon's *Memorabilia,* between Alcibiades and Pericles on what law is, a shortened version of which served as the epigraph to chapter twelve. Alcibiades expects the law to be good and thus reasonable. But "the law is to be reasonable in that it is deliberate, in that it intends to promote the common good" (262). Accordingly, law can tend toward the bad, since "it is not reasonable to expect perfect reasonability from human legislators" (262). From this, Berns arrives at his "unified definition": "Law . . . would be a persuasive ordinance for the political community that good things be done and bad things not done, made, and prescribed, after deliberation, by the controlling power of the city" (267). Coercion is necessary, since we live with "non-saints, non-angels, rational *animals*" (267). Alcibiades, like Anastaplo, seems to have had too high expectations of his political community. Rational reflection exposes the limits, specific to one's regime, to being both prudent and great-souled (see 256–57). Our youthful high hopes often occlude these limits.

Thus far, Berns has labored carefully to establish the Aristotelian position over against the modern rejection of *nous* and the occluding power of *thumos* in everything from religion to friendship. But what does *nous* intellect? In the final chapter, Berns juxtaposes Socratic philosophy to various "extreme attitudes" guided by fear, shame, and piety (274). "By exposing the mad-like extremes, Xenophon indicates what, for Socrates, the sober theoretical means are" (275). The intellect, on this account, has less to do with intuiting sempiternal or eternal essences, per dogmatic Aristotelianism, if not per Aristotle, than with intuiting fundamental alternatives or problems. Such theoretical moderation was often mistaken for an immoderate despising of, or looking beyond or above (*huperoran*), the things above (*ta huperthen*) or divine things (*ta daimonia*), when in reality Socrates, much more humbly, looked only at what was before him (*prooran*) (249, 251). He seems, therefore, to have attained a rare reconciliation between the ancient and medieval positions in chapter eight.

V.

I hope the above shows that the unity of the essays lies in the various tensions explored: between ancients and moderns, religion and philosophy, magnanimity and prudence, justice and friendship, and, most fundamentally, spiritedness and the intellect. This collection is thus a testament to the Socratic spirit in which Berns thought and wrote. One tension remains, however: between Aristotle and Socrates. In the first half, Aristotle serves as the representative of the ancients, as is also the case through much of the second half. Toward the end, however, the intellection of essences gives way to the articulation of problems in light of a political psychology. Likewise, the essays become increasingly dialogic in character. How are we to reconcile this tension? I don't think an answer is to be found in the collection as proposed. I surmise, however, that it is to be found in an essay he wrote in the years between the development of his proposal and his passing, "Plato's *Meno* and Aristotle's *Nicomachean Ethics*." He begins the essay with a focus on the relationship between *nous*, *phronēsis*, and virtue, and ends with a reflection on Aristotle's Socratism. That essay has been included as an appendix.

Alex Priou
Boulder, CO

Acknowledgments

I would like first to thank Gisela Berns for the opportunity to bring her husband's vision for a collection of essays into print; I am grateful, too, for the kindness she has shown me over the years, both when I was a student at St. John's and in the years that have passed since. She also offered helpful advice in the editing of the manuscript. I owe much, too, to the advice and help of Nathan Dinneen and Martin Yaffe, who are currently seeing that Laurence's dissertation finds its way to print. Martin Yaffe was especially generous with his time and careful eye in looking over the entire manuscript. The greatest debt of gratitude of course goes to the author of these essays, Mr. Berns (as I always called him), for his friendship. Reading so much of his work, and so closely, has given me the opportunity to visit him again, as it were; I have also come to appreciate much more his talent for putting things simply and clearly yet subtly. I am pleased to be able, with the help of all those named above, to bring the fruits of his thinking to a new generation of scholars.

Thanks are owed, finally, to the various presses and editors for kindly granting permission to reprint these chapters. Chapter 1 was originally published as "Rational Animal-Political Animal: Nature and Convention in Human Speech and Politics," *The Review of Politics* 38 (1976), 177–89; chapter 2 as "Aristotle's *Poetics*" in Joseph Cropsey (ed.), *Ancients and Moderns: Essays on the Tradition of Political Philosophy in Honor of Leo Strauss* (New York, NY: Basic Books, 1964), 70–87, but includes Berns' own corrections and additions, handwritten on a copy made available to me by Martin Yaffe; chapter 3 as "Gratitude, Nature and Piety in *King Lear*," *Interpretation: A Journal of Political Philosophy* 2 (1972–73), 27–51; chapter 4 as "Francis Bacon and the Conquest of Nature," *Interpretation: A Journal of Political Philosophy* 5 (1978), 1–26; chapter 5 as "Thomas Hobbes" in Joseph Cropsey and Leo Strauss (eds.), *History of Political Philosophy*, 3rd ed. (Chicago, IL: University of Chicago Press, 1987), 396–420; chapter 6 as "Putting Things Back Together in Kant," *Interpretation: A Journal of Political Philosophy* 28 (2000–2001), 201–18; chapter 7 as "The Prescientific World and Historicism: Some Reflections on Strauss, Heidegger, and Husserl" in Alan Udoff (ed.), *Leo Strauss's Thought: Toward a Critical Engagement* (Boulder, CO: Lynne Rienner Publishers, 1991), 169–81; chapter 8 as "The Relation Between Philosophy and Religion: Reflections on Leo Strauss's Suggestion Concerning the Source and Sources of Modern Philosophy," *Interpretation: A Journal of Political Philosophy* 19 (1991–92), 43–60; chapter 9 as "Spiritedness in Ethics and Politics: A Study in Aristotelian Psychology," *Interpretation: A Journal of Political Philosophy* 12 (1984), 335–48; chapter 10 as "Aristotle and the Moderns on Freedom and Equality" in Kenneth L. Deutsch and Walter Soffer (eds.), *The Crisis of Liberal Democracy: A Straussian Perspective* (Albany, NY: SUNY Press, 1987), 148–66; chapter 11 as "Aristotle and Adam Smith on Justice: Cooperation Between Ancients and Moderns?," *The Review of Metaphysics* 48 (1994), 71–90; chapters 12 and 13 as "Two Old Conservatives Discuss the Anastaplo Case" and "Xenophon's Alcibiades and Pericles on the Question of Law, with Applications to the Polity of the United States" in John A. Murley, Robert L. Stone, and William T. Braithwaite, *Law and Philosophy: The Practice of Theory—Essays in Honor of George Anastaplo*, 2 vols. (Athens, OH: Ohio University Press, 1992), 1:456–77; and chapter 14 as "Socratic and Non-Socratic Philosophy: A Note on Xenophon's *Memorabilia* 1.1.13–14,"

The Review of Metaphysics 28 (1974–75), 85–88. As noted in the introduction, the titles of some of these essays have been changed, in accordance with Berns' original proposal.

Politics, Nature, *and* Piety

CHAPTER ONE

The Natural Basis of Political Life

NATURE AND CONVENTION IN HUMAN SPEECH AND POLITICS

With all your traveling, trying every road, you could never find the limits of the soul; so deep a *logos* does it have.

—Herakleitos (45 DK)

Could any mortal lip divine
The undeveloped freight
Of a delivered syllable,
'Twould crumble with the weight.

—Emily Dickinson

I

In the beginning of his *Politics* Aristotle argues that "man is by nature a political animal." In fact man is more a political animal than any herding animal, for "man alone of the animals has speech," "man alone of the animals has reason," "man alone of the animals has *logos*." In other contexts the word *logos* can also be translated as word, meaning, account, argument, sentence, or ratio. *Logos* is connected with the verb *legō* which means to speak and to gather, to pick out, to select, to count. The English words collect, select, and elect are related to the same verb. *Logos* is selected, elected, and chosen speech, meaningful speech, thoughtful speech. The traditional definition of man as the rational animal, stemming from Aristotle, goes back to this statement, that man alone of the animals possesses *logos*, possesses thoughtful speech. Aristotle goes on to say:

> Now voice functions as a sign of pain and pleasure and therefore is possessed by the other animals too (for their nature has gone as far as having sensation of pain and pleasure and signifying these things to one another). But *logos* is for making clear the advantageous and the harmful and therefore also the just and the unjust. For this is special to man alone compared with the other animals; he alone has sensation of good and bad and just and unjust and the like. And the community of these things makes a household and a *polis* . . . (1253a9–18)

—a political community. *Logos* makes clear the advantageous and the harmful, which presupposes an awareness of what is good for men and what is bad, which for Aristotle means what is in accord with nature, man's nature, and what is contrary to nature. This awareness is shared through speech, and thoughtful sharing entails thinking about how what is shared is to be distributed; hence the sharing of this awareness makes it possible for men to consider how the advantageous and the harmful ought to be distributed, shared, and apportioned, it makes it possible for them to consider the just and the unjust. The community, or sharing, of good and bad, just and unjust makes a household and a *polis*: that is, what makes a community, and a political community primarily, is the shared awareness of having a *common* good; that good is justice, namely, what is conceived of as the right distribution of advantages and harms. Political societies can then be characterized in terms of the conceptions of distributive justice, the conceptions of the right distribution of advantages and harms, operative or authoritative, in each.[1]

But what has nature to do with good and bad, justice and injustice? Is not the Aristotelian conception of nature obsolete? Do we not learn what nature means from modern natural sciences, and from the social sciences that model themselves on them? Why concern ourselves with Aristotle at all? Before taking up the theme of nature and Aristotle's understanding of nature, let us consider this prior question. Five interconnected responses, in increasing order of importance, can be distinguished.

1. Aristotle's approach to nature and philosophy was the approach opposed by the founders of modern science. By seeing what they were reacting against, what they rejected, we come to understand better the dominant thought of our own times; we come to understand ourselves better. From this point of view Aristotle's philosophy is approached as a historical datum.

2. According to the view which tries to understand modern life in a way appropriate to what it claims is the uniqueness of the modern situation—the Existentialist, or Historical Relativist, or Radical Historicist, or Heideggerian view—world views are primarily creative projects of different ages, or of different men in different ages. True openness, openness to determine the way which would be the authentic way for us, requires freedom from the blinders imposed upon us by our tradition. Aristotle was among those who were most decisive in forming the tradition. Liberation from the tradition, since it is a tradition of thought, requires understanding it. Liberation from the tradition, based on understanding it, is required in order to open ourselves to the broader perspectives that a unified planet requires.

3. Science was originally pursued and regarded as a most important component of the perfection of human life. The crisis of modern science consists, in Husserl's phrase, in "the loss of its meaning for life." From within the perspective of modern science, the modern view of nature, the things which are most important to most human beings seem to make little sense, e.g., goodness and badness, fairness and unfairness, nobility and baseness, beauty and ugliness; and scientistic

social science reports that scientific reason cannot substantiate "value judgments." Instead of rational principles of action, guidance for life is abandoned to various forms of unreason or, at best, to principles of expediency. Within Aristotle's view of nature and human nature those distinctions which are found to be most meaningful for prescientific practical life, distinctions like the distinction between good and bad, make sense. For the sake of a sound view of human life we seek what may still be valid in the Aristotelian understanding of nature.

Another aspect of the crisis of modern science is the problem of the intelligibility of modern mathematical physics, of understanding what it means, how it relates to fundamental human experience. A sign, but only a sign, of what we refer to might be found in considering the classical Greek word for science, *epistēmē*. *Epistēmē* means science and knowledge, but it also means understanding. Classicists hesitate now to translate *epistēmē* as science, because science now usually means modern science, preeminently mathematical physics, and this science does not seem to be necessarily accompanied by understanding.[2]

4. Some look to Aristotle with a view to the need for a comprehensive natural philosophy which could make sense out of the separation of modern science from the world of human meaning by relating both within a unified view of the natural world.[3]

5. Understanding a tradition of thought entails, at least, understanding its constituent parts in their own terms. This, in turn, seems to require an openness to the possibility that the truth itself may have been discovered in the past, since past thinkers have made this claim. Thought dominated by modern science seems to be most in need of the truth about the sphere of human meaning that apparently precedes or lies beyond scientific thinking: that sphere is evidently the sphere of prescientific or prephilosophic experience and discourse. In different ways and for apparently different reasons

a variety of contemporary schools of philosophy have been trying to meet that need: phenomenology, existentialism, ordinary language analysis and pragmatism. Yet all contemporary schools labor under a peculiar difficulty: the difficulty of trying to uncover the meaning of prescientific experience and discourse in a technological society where the ordinary work-a-day world of "prescientific" experience and discourse is itself shaped and dominated by science.

The foregoing considerations lead us to approach with new seriousness those premodern philosophies (most notably the philosophies of Plato and Aristotle) which have taken as one of the fundamental tasks of philosophy the articulation and clarification of the presuppositions and principles of the "natural human understanding." This prescientific or prephilosophic understanding, the beginning of all thinking, is revealed through our discourse about the objects of ordinary experience. The different kinds of scientific thinking are necessarily modifications of this order of understanding.

That men are compelled by nature to think about things in certain ways does not establish that the things thought about in themselves are, or are not, as they are thought to be. It seems that both dogmatic fideism (the unphilosophic faith that things are just as we experience them) and that much more powerful dogma among the learned of our times, dogmatic skepticism (the dogma that we know that things in themselves cannot be as we experience them) should be avoided. This implies that man may be open to the whole and to the essences of things, and that the way of the natural human understanding and human discourse might be indispensable for learning, understanding, and communicating what man can know. Aristotle takes human speech very seriously because the meaning and implications of ordinary speech, properly refined, according to him, more than anything else may lead to the fundamental principles of all things.

The idea of nature has always occupied a key position, if not the key position, in what is called the Western tradition of thought. Throughout the long development of Western thought the fundamental issues were argued in terms of oppositions between Nature and something else: between Nature and Grace (natural and supernatural, natural and divine); between Nature and Art; between Nature and Convention; between Nature and Freedom; between Nature and Spirit; and between Nature and History.[4]

In fact Aristotle, among others, suggests that philosophy and science themselves come into the world with the discovery of nature.[5] There were and still are people who have no distinct idea of nature. The words nature and natural do not occur in the *Old Testament*, or in the *Gospels*. They occur thirteen times in the letters of the most sophisticated of the *New Testament* writers, the Apostle Paul, and only in five other places in the *New Testament*.[6]

Before nature was discovered, when thoughtful men wondered and discoursed about why things are the way they are, they talked about the gods. The *theologoi*, the *mythologoi*, preceded the *physiologoi*. The gods ordered and commanded things to go in their customary ways. The Hebrew word for "way" (*derek*) occurs over 1,700 times in the *Old Testament* and the Greek word (*hodos*) at least 83 times in the *New Testament*. The gods ordained that fire should burn, clouds give rain, that the earth should bring forth crops, that women should bear children, that some should not eat swine and others should not kill cows, that murderers should be put to death, or that they should pay their victim's relatives at least one ox. The commands of the gods were delivered to the ancestors who were closer to them and transmitted by elders to their offspring by word of mouth or by written reports. Authority went with age, with nearness to the sources of authority.

At a certain point some curious and thoughtful man must have noticed that some things and some ways are always the same no matter what anyone does about them, and others vary from time to time and still others would vary from time to time more if men did not make them happen the same way.

He begins to become aware of the distinction between the necessary and the accidental, the necessary and the customary, and the necessary and the artificial.

If the same man or one like him were to become a traveler, like Herodotus, he would then also notice how some ways are the same everywhere, for example, fire burns the same way both here and in Persia, and other ways vary from place to place and from tribe to tribe.

The ways that vary from tribe to tribe, the ways that depend most on decisions and opinions of men, must have been most striking at first because they most contradict "our way." The opinions men hold about the ways that vary from place to place contradict each other: for example, the dead must be buried; they must not be buried, but burned. These contradictions are connected with even more fundamental contradictory opinions, concerning the very origins of the gods.

From one point of view one learns the truth about such matters by listening obediently to the authoritative voices of the elders, from another one learns the truth by seeing for oneself. Men must always in some matters have made a distinction between hearsay evidence and seeing for oneself. The suspicion begins to arise that what one can see to be everywhere the same is primary, permanent, and fundamental and that the other things are secondary, transient, and derivative. Further, one sees that man-made things owe their existence to forethought: if the non-man-made things are so different, perhaps they do not owe their existence to forethought. Those ways which are everywhere the same, which do not evidently depend upon decisions of men, seem to occur by themselves, through some internal power of the things characterized by them. The man who has become aware of these distinctions begins to distinguish between our way and *the* way, the way according to nature, that which is right and good in itself because it is in accord with nature and that which is right and good because it has been instituted, legislated or commanded by our authorities.

Therefore, to summarize, on the basis of the distinctions between that which is everywhere the same and that which varies from place to place and from time to time and from tribe to tribe, between what one can see for oneself and what one hears from authorities, between what seems to grow and move by itself and what depends on decisions and actions of men to come into and remain in being, between our old way and the right way simply—on the basis of these distinctions "the primeval notion of custom or way is split up into the notions of 'nature,' on the one hand, and 'convention,' on the other."[7] Certain men, then, who came to be called philosophers and scientists, begin to think that knowledge of this apparently impersonal necessity, nature, is the one thing most needful.

The distinction between what is good by nature and what is good by law, or by convention, good because it is posited, or legislated, becomes crucial for political and ethical philosophy. In Plato's *Republic,* in the great debate about the nature and worth of justice, despite great disagreements about what is truly good and what truly bad, all the chief interlocutors share the premise that the good, whatever it may be more particularly, is that which is in accordance with nature, or good by nature. Human conduct, conventions, and laws from this point of view are evaluated not in terms of whether they conform or not to divine law, but whether they are in accord with, or against, nature; sin becomes perversion.

Philosophy, from this point of view, becomes the most serious of all human pursuits. But wherever there are philosophers, a class which can include erring philosophers, there seem to arise imitators, or images, of philosophers, men who are aware of the distinction between nature and convention, but who never sufficiently reflect on the reasons for the conventions; who fail to understand how it can be natural for men to live in accordance with conventions. Such men, called sophists or intellectuals, abuse the distinction between nature and convention so as to undermine all conventions, so as to undermine ordinary decency. One permanent task of philosophy, understood in this way, the Socratic way, I believe, would be to defend ordinary prephilosophic practical wisdom from sophistical attack, to prepare, if necessary, a theoretical defense of ordinary decency against sophistical scientism. Plato's dialogues would seem to suggest that where there is "corruption of youth," sophists produce it, but both sophists and philosophers pay for it. One task of political philosophy then would be to extricate philosophy from the opprobrium brought upon it by its imitators.

II

We return to our theme: the connection between man's rationality, his having *logos*, and his being by nature a political animal. In his discussion of the social and economic preconditions of political life Aristotle refers to the story of the Cyclopes in Book 9 of the *Odyssey*.[8] The Cyclops story might be thought of as Homer's anticipation of Karl Marx.

> Thence we sailed on, grieved at heart, and we came to the land of the Cyclopes, an overweening and lawless folk, who, trusting in the immortal gods, plant nothing with their hands nor plough; but all these things spring up for them without sowing or ploughing, wheat, and barley, and vines, which bear the rich cluster of wine, and the rain of Zeus gives them increase. Neither assemblies for council have they, nor appointed laws, but they dwell on the peaks of lofty mountains in hollow caves, and each one is lawgiver to his children and his wives, and they do not trouble themselves about one another. (105–15)[10]

Odysseus, not knowing all that yet, wants "to go and make trial of those men, to learn whether they are both insolent and wild and not just, or whether they love strangers and are god-fearing in thought" (174–76).[10] The Cyclops, Polyphemus, was a monstrous man, "who shepherded his flocks alone and afar, and mingled not with others, but lived apart with his heart set on lawlessness" (187–89).

Odysseus with twelve of his best comrades enters the Cyclops's cave. He supplicates the Cyclops in the name of Zeus, the god of strangers and guests.

> So I spoke, and he straightaway made answer with pitiless heart: "A fool are thou, stranger, or art come from afar, seeing that thou biddest me either to fear or to shun the gods. For Cyclopes take no trouble for Zeus, who bears the aegis, nor for the blessed gods, since verily we are better far than they. No would I, to shun the wrath of Zeus, spare either thee or thy comrades, unless my own heart should bid me." (272–78)

Soon thereafter, after blocking off the cave exit, the Cyclops kills and eats two of Odysseus's comrades. He makes clear that he intends to do the same to all of them. Odysseus and those of his men who remain carry out a plan to put out the Cyclops's one eye while he is in a drunken sleep.[11] The Cyclops cries out and calls to all the Cyclopes living nearby in their caves. They throng about outside his cave and ask what ails him, whether some man is killing him by guile or by force. Since Odysseus had told him that his name is No-one, he replies, "Friends, No-one is killing me by guile, not by force." They answer: if no one is doing you violence, perhaps it is Zeus, so pray to our father, Lord Poseidon. And then they leave. Odysseus later contrives his escape from the cave.

The economic needs of the Cyclopes are provided for by the gods. Consequently economic pressures do not prod them, as primitive men are usually prodded, into forming larger communities for the sake of mutual aid, cooperation, and exchange. Because they are never moved to form a larger society, they never develop any arts or crafts beyond the minimal skills needed for a shepherd's life. They live in caves, not houses, and, Homer specifically mentions, they have no ships, and no men to make ships, so that they might cross the sea and visit the cities of other folk as other men do. But most importantly, by never forming cities, *poleis*, political societies, they never develop the arts of civilized discourse, the arts of communication.[12] The Cyclopes are fooled by a man skilled in the art of using words. Their lack of skill, their lack of any art with words makes it impossible for them to cooperate, to aid their fellow in his time of need. Not only are the Cyclopes brutal, lawless, and uncultivated, but even though they owe their material plenty entirely to the gods, they are impious and, incidentally, conceited. As the Cyclops says, we "pay no heed . . . to the blessed gods, since truly we are better by far than they" (275–76).

In his *German Ideology* Marx gives an all too brief glimpse at his picture of the final communist society, where not the Olympian gods, but machine technology and communist organization will provide every man with all his economic needs, thereby making possible the final freedom, freedom from the division of labor, or, better, division of function, or division of nature itself. It will be "possible for me to do one thing today and another tomorrow, to hunt in the morning, fish in the afternoon, rear cattle in the evening, criticize after dinner, just as I like, without ever becoming a hunter, fisherman, a herdsman or a critic."[13] Homer, on the contrary, suggests: Liberate all men from the pressure and discipline of economic necessity and the result will not be a new higher, humanly fulfilled breed of man, but a race of Cyclopes. In one of the many places where Aristotle touches on the relation between economic necessity and the development of man's higher faculties, he argues that the *polis*, the political community, is the complete community, the community which, after the family and the village, has come to the point of full self-sufficiency: He then remarks "indeed it has *come into being* for the sake of life, but it *is* for the sake of the good life" (1252b30).[14]

III

The "logical" writings of Aristotle received that name because they are, in general, devoted to the understanding, the discipline, and the perfection of *logos*.[15] In the first chapter of *On Interpretation* Aristotle explains that (1) written words are symbols of voiced or spoken words; (2) spoken words are symbols and signs of experiences, or passions, of the soul, that is perceptions, thoughts, and sensations; and (3) the experiences of the soul are likenesses of things. The word symbol comes from two Greek words meaning "to throw" or "to put" and "together." Symbols are always made, or put together, by men. The first thing Aristotle notes about written and spoken symbols is that they are not the same for all men, whereas the experiences of the soul and the things themselves are the same for all. One needs only to think of what happens each time one understands something written or spoken in a foreign language. That sounds referring to the same things differ from tribe to tribe or nation to nation points to the fact that the sounds do not of themselves signify, or refer to, the experiences and things they are signs of, that is, they are not significant, or meaningful, by nature, they are significant by agreement, by compact, by convention. Contrariwise, the experiences of the soul, the perceptions, thoughts, and sensations, are the same for all and do not depend upon human agreement for their meaning; they refer to what they signify by themselves, not through the mediation of anything else; they are significant, or meaningful, by nature.[16]

Let us analyze the spoken symbol more closely. The medium or material of the symbol is voiced sound, which is produced naturally by man. The peculiar combination, organization, and formation of the voiced sounds so as to signify a definite experience, the taking of certain particular sounds to signify a certain specific experience, the forming of the material of the symbol, depend upon human institution, upon convention. Other sounds could do as well, but once the sounds for a particular conception are agreed upon, once the decision is settled, it becomes a mistake to use those sounds another way, to point to something else. Unlike groans of the sick, screams of terror or laughter, speech sounds acquire their signification through human institution. The impulse to form and to share speech symbols arises naturally among men wherever they are found to exist. This natural impulse to develop the instrumentalities that allow for the communication and sharing of thoughts and feelings, of experience, is perhaps the most decisive of those phenomena that point to man's being by nature a social and political animal. This natural impulse coupled with the desire for mutual understanding, among other things, points to the ends or functions of the speech symbol: living together, learning together and mutual understanding. In sum, three of the four causes accounting for the symbol are natural: they are the material cause, vocal sound; the efficient cause, the natural impulse and the men within whom it is found; and the final cause, the end, living and learning together. The formal, or organizing, cause which gives each symbol its distinctive character as a sign is conventional.

Man, then, is required by nature, by his nature as a thoughtful, speaking, and political animal, to form conventions, the most important of which are those conventions that designate certain definite combinations of sounds as representative or significant of certain definite notions of the mind. Human nature is so constituted as to require the formation of conventions for its fulfillment. The same kind of analysis pointing to the need for the cooperation of nature and convention might be used to clarify Aristotle's view of the *polis*, of the political community, itself. Nature provides the material, men, naturally differentiated in their capacities to fulfill their own and each others' needs; nature also provides the efficient cause, the political and social impulses within the men; and the final cause, the good life, the life according to nature. The formal causes, however, the laws and governmental institutions which arrange, organize, and order the men towards the end, are supplied by art, the legislator's art, and by convention. This, however, as our previous discussion of distributive justice indicates, does not go deep enough. For laws are made by and are reflections of legislators. Who, or what kind of men, are to be legislators and governors is determined by the more fundamental order of distributive justice, the polity or regime. The word legislator, then, is ambiguous. For he who shapes the opinions, beliefs, and sentiments on which the order of distributive justice depends is also, in a deeper sense, a legislator. The more fundamental form of the political community, to the extent that it has a definite form and is not shaped solely by circumstances, is derivative from such a legislative art, an art which it might be said is practiced primarily by means of *logoi*.[17]

According to the passage we have been analyzing, the experiences or passions of the soul referred to by the speech symbol are likenesses and thereby natural signs of things. What is understood, what is actualized, when one understands and does not merely hear what someone else says? The experiences of the soul, Aristotle says, are the same for all. In most practical discourse the assumption is made that when men talk to one another they are talking about the same things. If this assumption is correct, there must be something about things which can be the same for all men: that would be, according to Aristotle, their intelligible character. Words then signify or refer to the likenesses or actualizations in men of the intelligible characteristics of things. Or, put somewhat differently, if talk about what is known about unknowable things in themselves is to be avoided, if there is genuine knowledge of things in themselves, then things must possess intelligible characteristics, which characteristics, or their likenesses, can be actualized by all well-functioning human intellects.[18] The intelligible, because it can be truly the same in all men, from this point of view, is the most common, most sharable thing accessible to animate beings. For this reason mutual understanding of the things signified by our words makes the human community a communion more intimate that that of any other animal.[19] More than one romantic novel, or domestic tragedy, not to mention domestic comedy, relies for its effect upon that essentially human awareness that the deepest intimacy can only come from mutual understanding.

CHAPTER TWO

Tragedy and Religion in Aristotle's *Poetics*

> . . . tēn de tou merous pros tēn tou holou dei blepein aretēn . . .
>
> —Aristotle, *Politics* 1260b14–15

I

Henry Jackson, the highly respected classical scholar, an editor of some texts of Aristotle, paid the following compliment to Aristotle's *Politics*. "It is an amazing book," he said. "It seems to me to show a Shakespearian understanding of human beings and their ways. . . ." Aristotle, the philosopher, is praised because his understanding of human beings approaches or matches that of Shakespeare, the poet. The poet's understanding is the standard. In this remark, Jackson seems to take it for granted that the poet's understanding of human beings and their ways is somehow the most adequate and most profound understanding. This is not hard for us modern men to understand. For one thing, the poet's picture of the world preserves that wonder and mystery which seem to dissolve and disappear in the accounts of the philosophers and scientists. Furthermore, the great poet convinces us of his knowledge in a much more powerful way than bare argument and reasoning can ever do. His conceptions are constantly put to the practical test—a test of their ability or inability to move men through their emotions.

What kind of power or understanding is it that the great poet possesses? What is it that makes a great work of art so convincing and moving? It could not have been very long after men were first moved by great works of art that they began to reflect on the nature of art and the artist. This is intelligible, for great art fills us with a sense of wonder, wonder about the artist's subject and the artist himself, and, Aristotle informs us, "in wondering is the desire to learn." Today, too, the enormous amount of literature devoted to literary and artistic criticism testifies to the fact that the desire to understand and learn about great art and artists is just as strong. However, the purpose of art criticism is not only theoretical, to understand the mysterious power of great art, but practical as well, to help artists improve their works and to help us enlarge our capacities to appreciate and enjoy great art.

With such expectations in mind, we turn directly to Aristotle's *Poetics*. What we might provisionally call the fine arts are defined by Aristotle as forms of imitation. The words "creativity," "aesthetics," and "self-expression" do not occur in Aristotle's definition. "Imitation" is the key term. The idea of art as imitation immediately creates a problem for us. It seems to depreciate art. Imitations are secondary or derivative: one need only think of imitation leather, or imitation flavor. Imitations immediately refer us to those more fundamental things of which they are imitations. If art in general is imitation, what does it imitate? Nature is the traditional answer. The phrase "imitation of nature" does not occur in the *Poetics*, but I shall explain later why I think it is what Aristotle meant.

Imitation of nature is often misunderstood, because what Aristotle means by nature is often misunderstood. Imitation of nature does not mean a simple copying of what we happen to find actually existing. Natural things, according to Aristotle, possess certain capacities for development. A thing realizes its nature more, the more it fulfills these capacities, the more it approaches its own specific perfection. Nature, as

Aristotle uses the term, includes what ought to be, and imitation of nature means not mere copying of things, but also the imitation of things in their perfection. The artist is enjoined by the doctrine of imitation of nature to look carefully at the real world about him, not in order to copy it, but in order to see that the ideal characters or perfections that he will portray have some basis in the real world, that they are developments of truly existing possibilities and, hence, more convincing. Santayana wrote of Aristotle's conception of human nature: "Everything ideal has a natural basis, and everything natural has an ideal development." Art imitates not only what is actual in nature, but also what is potential in nature.[1]

From this point of view, many of the arguments directed against the doctrine of imitation of nature from the point of view of creativity lose their force. The artist, according to Aristotle, certainly can and ought to portray things which have never actually been known to exist, but to be convincing as works of art, they ought to be things which we know could possibly exist.

We have an indication of what Aristotle means by nature in the brief history of tragedy which he sketches out in the *Poetics*. He speaks of how tragedy first grew out of crude, improvised imitations and slowly developed and advanced as each of the things which added to its perfection became known. Then he says: "And having gone through many changes, tragedy stopped when it attained its own nature." The perfection, or full development, of the thing is identical with its nature. This understanding of things can still be found implicit in ordinary language; for instance, one can say of a very good play, "Now that really *is* a play," meaning it contains all of what we expect from a play. And we can say of a very bad play, "Do you call that a play?" Or we have to add qualifications like "bad," saying, "That is a bad play," meaning that it lacks those qualities we expect to find in a play. It does not live up to or realize the nature of a play. It is not fully a play. If we follow this thought a bit further, we may get a clue as to why the *Poetics*, which purports at its outset to be a book about poetry in general, is largely taken up with a discussion of tragedy.[2] If the nature of a thing is seen most fully in the perfection of that thing, then the nature of poetry should be seen most fully in the most nearly perfect form of poetry. There is some indication in the *Poetics* that Aristotle regarded tragedy as the most nearly perfect form of poetry. Among the Greeks the two main contenders for the crown of poetry were evidently epic poetry and tragedy. In the final chapter of the *Poetics*, Aristotle argues that the crown should go to tragedy because it contains everything epic poetry contains and more, and, in addition, it realizes the purpose of poetry more fully.[3]

By pursuing this line of thought even further, we see that Aristotle is concerned in the *Poetics* not with any tragedy, but with the best tragedies, those which provide the models and standards for all other tragedies. It is mostly to Sophocles, Euripides, and Shakespeare that Lessing turns when seeking models to demonstrate the truth of Aristotle's canons for tragedy.

However, things are said to be perfect in two ways, as wholes in themselves and as parts of larger wholes.[4] The latter consideration entails reflection on the function of tragedy within the larger whole of political and social life.

II

Although the *Poetics* begins with a discussion of poetry in general that lasts for five chapters, which culminates, at the beginning of chapter six, with the famous definition of tragedy. The book contains twenty-six chapters, and seventeen of these, chapters 6–22, are devoted to tragedy. The definition of tragedy reads as follows: "Tragedy is an imitation of an action that is serious and complete, and of a definite magnitude, with sweetened or pleasing language, each form of which is used separately in the parts of the tragedy. The imitation is done by means of men acting, not through narration, accomplishing through pity and fear the catharsis of such passions." Most of the rest of the book could be regarded as an analysis of that definition. The definition tells us first what tragedy is in general, namely, imitation. Imitation of what?—of a serious action and an action that is complete and of a definite size. What is the medium used to convey the imitation to its audience?—pleasing or embellished language. How or in what manner is the language presented?—through men acting, not through narration.

Up to this point Aristotle builds on his previous discussion, and discusses only the work of art in itself. But with this statement about the effect, end, function, or purpose of tragedy, something new enters in. What should the tragedy do to or for its audience or readers? By means of pity and fear it should effect a purgation or purification of these kinds of emotion.

This answer is by no means as lucid as the others. Why are pity and fear selected as the key passions? What does catharsis mean? We shall take up the last question first. There is, perhaps, no subject which has divided interpreters of the *Poetics* more. This problem is not only a problem of textual interpretation, but is a reflection of a basic difference of opinion about the fundamental purpose of art and the role of the artist. To put it simply: Is it the primary function of the artist to please, move, and entertain his audience, or should he be a moral teacher?[5] We shall examine the catharsis problem with a view to this larger question.

The word catharsis in Greek means both purgation and purification. Purgation is used here primarily as a medical term in homeopathic medicine. The old theory could be characterized roughly as follows. If the body is suffering, say from an excess of acidity, the physician gives the patient, in some form or another, more acid, which, somehow, causes a reaction to acid that purges away or removes the excess. The removal of the disturbing excess and the return of the body to health are accompanied by a feeling of being lightened or relieved, which is pleasant. Let us apply the theory to tragedy. Those of us with an excess of pity and fear in our souls go to the theater. After feeling fear with pity for the hero of the tragedy, our excessive pity and fear are drained off, and we experience pleasure from the relief. The production of this special pleasure is said to be the end of tragedy. There are some difficulties which come to mind immediately. First, it would seem that only those who are somewhat sick, suffering from an excess of pity and fear in their souls, can fully benefit from tragedy. One could reply that the poet first arouses pity and fear before purging them away; that is, he first creates the excess so that he can provide the pleasurable relief from the purgation. Yet, as one considers how most appreciative spectators feel after seeing a great tragedy, this theory becomes more and more implausible. Such spectators are not simply drained of emotion, relieved and contented, but stirred and moved by powerful feelings somewhat different from those they came in with. The purification theory of catharsis is simpler. The artist arouses pity and fear in his audience in order to train them to fear those things which ought to be feared and to pity those things which ought to be pitied. For example, from Sophocles' *Antigone* the spectator might learn to feel that dishonor is more to be feared than death. Purification here means moral purification. As Euripides says, in Aristophanes' *Frogs*, speaking for the poets: "We make men better. . . ." Those who hold strictly to the purgation theory tend to regard the *Poetics* more as technical treatise.[6] They would tend to argue that Aristotle, the scientist, concentrating on differences in subject matters, freed Western man's understanding of art from the preoccupation with morality which limited the vision of his predecessors, especially Plato. Those who hold to the purification theory say that in fundamentals Aristotle agreed with Plato and held a moral theory of art.[7]

It should be clear that both theories require art to be pleasant, but the status of that pleasure is what is in question.

According to what we are calling the pure purgation theory, the great artist has no other aim, as artist, than making a work of art that produces that pleasure in his audience. According to the purification theory, the pleasure is subordinate to, and in the service of, moral improvement. These distinctions correspond to what has been called the difference between pure or autonomous art and didactic art. The other places in Aristotle's writings where the word catharsis occurs are not especially illuminating. In the *Politics*, in the section on music in education, catharsis is discussed in what seems to be the medical sense of purgation.[8] The word occurs only once more in the *Poetics*, and there it clearly means purification, a religious purification from sin.[9] Perhaps the best way out of the difficulty is to try to analyze the whole problem from the beginning.

The more fundamental problem we have in mind is, to repeat, What is the function and purpose of tragedy? By means of pity and fear to accomplish the catharsis of such emotions, Aristotle tells us in chapter six; and in chapter fourteen we are informed that tragedy has its own special kind of pleasure, the pleasure from pity and fear through imitation. Aristotle was not the first man to single out pity and fear as key passions in poetry. In the *Ion*, among other places, Plato touches on the subject.[10] Ion, a man who made his living by reciting epic poems, is being questioned by Socrates about how he most amazes his spectators. Socrates mentions five instances of moving passages in Homer. The first is the scene just as Odysseus is about to kill all of the panic-stricken suitors. The next is Achilles chasing Hector around the wall. Hector, the hero of Troy, is, we know, about to be killed. Our fear for his life is mixed with pity. The next three examples concern Andromache, Hector's wife; Hecuba, his mother; and Priam, his father. Each is more pitiful than the preceding. In Ion's answering speech, where he describes how moved he is himself when he moves others, the only passion mentioned are pity, terror, and fear. Fortunately, Aristotle has analyzed these passions in his *Rhetoric*; a large part of our discussion will be based on that analysis.

I believe that the order of Socrates' examples was not accidental: fear first, changing to pity. Fear and pity go together, and this is the usual order. As the revelations about Oedipus begin to unfold, we begin to fear that we will learn that he is the murderer, the cursed one. As the evidence comes in and the evil and suffering are upon him, our fear changes to pity. When King Lear strips himself of all his power and puts it in the hands of his unworthy daughters, along with Kent, we fear for the evil approaching him and the country. And when that evil has arrived, the fear has transformed itself into pity for his suffering. Fear, Aristotle says, is a kind of pain or trouble from the imagination of an imminent evil, a deadly or painful evil. Fear is different from grief. We grieve when some very painful evil has already happened. A sense of urgency goes along with fear; while we still fear there is hope of escape. Perhaps the old shepherd will assure Oedipus that Laius was killed by a band of robbers, not one man and not Oedipus himself. Perhaps Lear will pay heed to Kent's warning or his Fool's prodding. Pity, according to Aristotle, is a kind of pain which comes from the occurrence of a manifest evil to someone else who does not deserve it. Or, to use the shortened formula of the *Poetics*, we feel pity for someone who suffers undeserved misfortune. As hope dies out and we see suffering coming on, our initial fear, the fear for what is about to happen to the tragic hero, transforms itself for the most part into pity.

Pity and fear are connected in another way. Fear is felt primarily for ourselves or those who are very close to us and then for those who are like ourselves. And all of those things which men fear will happen to themselves they can pity when they happen to others. This suggests that there is no pity without fear[11] though there can be fear without pity. Thus, the fear allied with pity, a more generalized fear stemming from the entire course of action imitated by the plot, can be distinguished from the initial fear of the specific disaster approaching the tragic hero. And so we move from this initial fear to a fear of the causes of such events. Pity, here, is to be distinguished from what Aristotle calls humaneness or fellow-feeling, which is not necessarily painful and does not involve a sense of justice.[12]

What Aristotle says in the *Poetics* about fear being aroused by terrible things happening to one who is like ourselves seems to correspond to what in modern psychological terms would be called identification. The tragic hero must be sufficiently like ourselves to enable us somehow to conceive of ourselves undergoing his or a similar fate. Otherwise, we will not be able to fear the impending disaster, enjoy the suspense, and receive the full effect of the tragedy. What is implied is that in order fully to experience a great tragedy, an act of imagination is required. The spectator must be able, in a sense, to imagine himself in the tragic situation. The presentation of a drama on the stage can be more moving than the reading of the drama, for since the evil and the suffering are brought right before our eyes less imagination is required. But according to Aristotle, spectacle, though it is able to lead on the soul, is hardly a concern for the poet. The pity and fear should be built into the incidents of the plot, so that they are felt also by readers, who, with the poet's help, are able to rely on their own imaginations. In chapter twenty-six of the *Poetics,* Aristotle indicates that the great poet places a higher value on his reading audience than on his seeing audience.

The conditions of pity and fear, then, play a large role in determining the character of the tragic hero. He must not be so good that it is impossible to imagine what it would be like to be in his position nor so bad as to forfeit our active pity. He does terrible things, but not out of baseness, because we would not pity the suffering he undergoes for his errors if they stemmed from baseness. On the other hand, if he did and suffered terrible things simply from bad luck or by chance, it would be sad, but not very frightening. It becomes really frightening when the terrible things he does and suffers result from some natural cause, some flaw in his nature, a flaw that is likely to be found in all natures like his—which means in our natures too, insofar as we are like him, or would like to be like him. His flaw prevents him from foreseeing the evil consequences that will result from his actions. Or, it betrays him into becoming an instrument for evil men. That he does not intend or foresee evil is shown by the misery and remorse he undergoes when the evil is recognized by him. His sense of guilt and repentance is our sign that he was not fundamentally malicious and thus entitles him to our pity.[13] Yet his suffering is not meaningless. He is partly responsible for being the kind of man he is. It is both just and frightening that his lack of self-knowledge can be atoned for only through suffering. The tragic hero is generally a man in a very high position, not only because every fall must be from some height, and the higher the height the harder the fall, but because the fates and fortunes of many more people are involved with the errors of men in great positions; hence, the disasters they bring about are more frightening, and their sufferings and sense of guilt are usually greater.[14] The life of every Theban is affected by Oedipus' and Antigone's doings. All England is plunged into war as a result of Lear's mistakes. Also, what happens to our betters is more frightening because, as Aristotle notes in the *Rhetoric*, those who are able to harm our betters are more able to harm us.[15]

One reason the great tragedians have concentrated on the passions of pity and fear, Aristotle's analysis suggests, is that they are aware that these two passions were better adapted for safeguarding and improving morality and religion than any others. What passion moves most men more readily than fear? What or who are those most fearful beings which, because they are able to harm and humble our betters, are more able to harm us? To speak in the vein of Greek tragedy and King Lear, the answer would be the gods. The gods are the guarantors of public morality. The epic and tragic poets, by showing how even the most lofty can be brought down by the gods, help to instill in people a proper fear of those gods. Pity tends to instill in us a sensitivity to the sufferings of others, and thus renders us less apt to harm others.

The best tragic plots, Aristotle tells us, are those wherein the sufferings are inflicted by and occur among loved ones and the hero discovers what he has done only after it is too late to remedy it. As a result of a flaw[16] natural to his kind, the tragic hero harms and destroys those he loves most. It is those very qualities for which he is admired and honored that cause him to wreak great evils. Furthermore, the more noble the character of the tragic hero, the more dreadful is his suffering when he realizes what he has done. All of this leads to the impression that in some frightful and pitiable way human excellence and mankind's noblest aspirations are inextricably linked with evil. As this impression makes itself felt both in the tragic hero and in his audience, a certain sense of guilt naturally arises, a sense of guilt that comes close to being a sense of original sin. Tragic pity and fear might be thought of as the human roots of the sense of sin.

The connection of pity and fear in tragedy is important in still another way: the two passions tend to purify each other.[17] Terror, Aristotle tells us, casts out pity. It tends to fill us with a selfish and narrow concern for our own safety. The tragedy, by linking our fear with pity for the tragic sufferer, tends to prevent our fear from degenerating into narrow selfishness. On the other hand, the characteristic vice of pity is to degenerate into a loose or morbid sentimentality. By linking pity with things which are truly frightening as well, and by inviting us to play at sitting in judgment upon his characters, the poet teaches us to pity things truly worth pitying. Tragic pity is the basis of true charity.

John Milton may have had these things in mind when he recommended the study of Aristotle's *Poetics*: "This would make them [students] soon perceive what despicable creature our common-rhymers and play-writers be; and show them what religious, what glorious and magnificent use might be made of poetry, both in divine and human things."[18] The purification and purgation interpretations of catharsis do not necessarily contradict each other. In the light of the foregoing analysis, catharsis would be fundamentally purification. But, by arousing pity and fear and by leading them toward objects worthy of them, the poet purges these passions of their unhealthy elements. Pity and fear are purified into a kind of humane reverence or awe.

Seen in this light, the *Poetics* could be regarded as the primary source for the Aristotelian analysis of piety and religion. Since religion, for Aristotle as well as Plato, is a political matter, the *Poetics* would have to be regarded as, in a sense, a political book.[19] The perfection of a tragedy then is also to be determined by how well it functions in taming the pride of the powerful and, in general, elevating the moral sense—the sense of justice—of the political community.

Although purification may be the poet's chief aim, the largest part of his audience comes mainly to be pleased or entertained. Unless the poet pleases, he will have little opportunity to purify. We still face the problem of understanding tragic pleasure. The pleasure proper to tragedy, Aristotle tells us, is the pleasure from pity and fear through imitation. But pity and fear are forms of pain. If it is not contradictory, it certainly is paradoxical to speak of a pleasure from pain. What this indicates is that the pleasure appropriate to tragedy is a very complicated phenomenon. We shall try to distinguish some five constituents of that pleasure.

A Hobbesian might argue that the pleasure comes from a somewhat malicious satisfaction at being free from the miseries we see engulfing others. But this is not sufficient; it hardly does justice to the feeling of elevation that seems to be a part of the pleasure from tragedy.

Aristotle, however, speaks of pleasure from pity and fear through imitation. Imitation is the most natural thing in the world for men. All men as children first learn how to get on in the world through imitation. There is no one who is not familiar with the pleasure from a successful imitation. We learn from imitation, and though study may be hard, the actual learning itself is naturally pleasant. Learning is most pleasant for all men according to Aristotle. In the *Poetics* and the *Rhetoric*, he says we get pleasure from something that has been well imitated, even if that which has been imitated is itself not pleasant, for it is the reasoning, the inferences connecting the imitation with the object imitated, the learning, that is pleasant.[20] Art which cannot communicate, which cannot represent or imitate, also cannot teach and cannot appeal to those things in our nature which gave rise to art in the first place.

But does not the character of the things imitated also contribute something to the pleasure? We learn through suffering, say the poets. But through the tragedies, safe in our seats, or at our desks, we learn about things which could otherwise be learned only through suffering them. By playing at suffering we learn and are, so to speak, rescued from the suffering that would normally accompany such learning. Also, is not the pleasure from tragedy more intimately involved with the great sufferers themselves? Perhaps the fact that the suffering and sufferers are great may account for the feeling of exaltation mentioned earlier. The characters, Aristotle says, should be better and usually more illustrious than we are. We experience a sense of exaltation from being admitted into a kind of intimacy with the great, and perhaps even beyond that, a feeling that we have somehow been brought nearer to the greatest powers of all, the powers controlling all human destiny, all nature.

Also, if the function of the poet is, as Aristophanes' Euripides says, to make men better, to purify and educate their passions, the pleasure from learning through playing at great suffering would also contain a certain satisfaction based on the sense of having been made better.

The last constituent of the pleasure from tragedy we should

like to mention is rooted in wonder. Tragic heroes are generally better than we are. They are usually men from whom we expect exemplary conduct—consider Othello, Coriolanus, Lear, Macbeth, Oedipus. They are, in a sense, exemplary and noble, and yet they come to do terrible things. "How all too riddling and unclear is everything you say," Oedipus says to Tiresias. "Are you not best at finding out riddles?" Tiresias answers. "Yes taunt me in those things where you will find me great," is the reply. "Indeed this very luck has destroyed you," Tiresias answers. The very things which make the tragic hero great cause him to wreak great evils and in the end destroy him. This is something not only to be feared and pitied, but also something to be wondered at. The best plots, full of suspense, arouse our wonder, and, Aristotle explains, "to wonder is pleasant for the most part, for in wondering is the desire to learn." The best plots, wondrous, though tragic, are also pleasant, because they offer a promise of and invitation to further learning.

III

Earlier we spoke of poetic imitation as imitation of nature, and mentioned that the phrase "imitation of nature" occurs nowhere in the *Poetics*. It does occur in other writings of Aristotle, but chiefly in reference to the useful arts. However, it is clearly implied, almost clearly stated, in what Aristotle says about a good plot or myth. The plot is the controlling element, as it were, the soul of the tragedy. The plot, he says, following Plato's *Phaedrus,* should be an organic whole. The composition or synthesis of the incidents should end up in the formation of one overall action. The plot is the direct imitation of such an action. There ought to be nothing superfluous, nothing whose absence or displacement would not change the unity of the whole. What is a whole? Aristotle's answer seems absurdly simple: that which has a beginning, a middle, and an end. It is not so simple. The beginning need not be connected with any other events by necessity; it may come about by chance. But it must be followed by events which develop *naturally* out of it. The middle comes after such events. And from the middle, events follow naturally either by necessity or for the most part, leading up to the end or completion. What we have here is a three-fold classification of events which also occurs elsewhere in the works of Aristotle. Things come about either always in the same way, by necessity; or they come about usually in the same way, so that we say it will probably be or it is likely to be this way. We cannot say that events in the latter class always come about in the same way, because sometimes in this class things happen in an unusual way, contrary to what is likely. These unusual and unexpected events are chance events. The three kinds of events, then, are (1) those which occur by necessity, (2) those which are probable or occur for the most part, or usually, and (3) those which occur by chance.

According to Aristotle, chance events, as chance events, are essentially unintelligible or irrational. We can know in general why there are such things as chance events, but the chance element in the events themselves is essentially unintelligible.[21] We can have genuine knowledge only of those things which are or come to be by necessity and for the most part and those things are identified in the *Poetics* with what comes about naturally. What comes about naturally is susceptible to rational explanation. (We can make valid universal statements about what exists or comes into being by necessity, and valid general statements about what comes into being for the most part.) Chance is ruled out of the best plots, according to Aristotle. The great poet conquers chance, intellectually and imaginatively. There should be an intelligible reason for everything which happens from beginning to end. The length of the story cannot be any chance length, but one appropriate to the action. And it is necessary, Aristotle says, for the characters, as for the connection of incidents in the plot, to act in accordance with necessity or likelihood. From this we can understand Aristotle's strange remark that poetry is more philosophical than history. It is strange because Aristotle, a philosopher, is naturally concerned with the truth, and history aims at the truth, while poetry is manifestly fiction and Homer is praised for knowing how to tell lies well. Poetry is more philosophical than history because history, which deals with what actually happened, must also include what happened by chance, what happened for no intelligible reason. Poetry, by excluding chance, is more rational, more meaningful, than history. For the same reason, it is more meaningful than real life. Plots based on chance events are not convincing, they are episodic; we do not learn from them and are consequently less pleased by them.

Lessing has made a distinction between the poetic genius and the great poetic wit. Genius, he says, loves simplicity, wit complication. "Genius is only busied with events that are rooted in one another, that form a chain of cause and effect." Wit, he says, is concerned with events that just happen at the same time; it thrives on invention and shock, on throwing us so rapidly from one surprise to another, that we do not have time to consider the improbability of the whole action. But with every step taken by the personages invented by a poetic genius,

> we must acknowledge that we should have taken it ourselves under the same circumstances and the same degree of passion, and hence nothing will repel us but the imperceptible approach to a goal from which our imagination shrinks, and where we suddenly find ourselves filled with a profound pity for those whom a fatal stream has carried so far, and full of terror at the consciousness that a similar stream might also thus have borne ourselves away to do deeds which in cold blood we should have regarded as far from us.[22]

The irrational, then, should be excluded as much as possible from a plot, Aristotle says. However, irrationalities, which include stories about the gods and supernatural contrivances, must be introduced, sometimes out of deference to what most men assert and find convincing and sometimes in order to arouse the sense of wonder.[23] But even irrationalities or things which happen by chance will be more wondrous if they seem to be in accordance with natural human desires, if they appear to fit into some rational and providential design, like the statue of Mitys which fell upon and killed the man who was the cause of Mitys' death.

But the best way to arouse the sense of wonder is to have the events inspiring pity and fear come into being in a way that runs counter to accepted opinion and expectation, and yet in such a way that the events come about on account of one another. As Samuel Butcher put it, it is the combination of the unexpected with the inevitable.[24] In this passage, near the end of chapter nine of the *Poetics*, we can see how closely the understanding of the great poet approaches that of the philosopher. Philosophy, both Plato and Aristotle say, begins in wonder and begins with common opinion and awareness of its inadequacy. The great poet arouses our wonder by presenting events which run counter to common opinion and expectation. He who is willing to part company with common opinion, to look deeper and harder at those wondrous events, will be rewarded by the discovery of a marvelously lucid, though hidden, chain of natural causes.[25] It must have been such an understanding of poetry that led Plutarch to speak of poetry as a kindly and intimate friend leading young men into the presence of philosophy.[26] Tragedy exists not only as a part of political life, a part of the political whole. Its perfection is also to be determined by how it functions in relating the life of man to the larger all-comprehensive whole, to nature.[27]

Epilogue

It is through the turn-about or reversal of the protagonist's fortune and his recognition or discovery of who has brought on the tragedy that the fear, surprise, pity, and wonder arise, Aristotle says. The tragic effect is attained most successfully when the actions undertaken by the protagonist, which bring about his downfall and remorse, destroy or ruin those closest to him, his loved ones, his immediate family. But who can be closer to a man than himself? Oedipus has not only destroyed his father and his wife and mother, he has destroyed himself as a political man. Lear has not only brought on the destruction of his daughters, he has destroyed himself as a political man.

In the best plots—like that of *Oedipus*, as Aristotle says, and like that of *King Lear*, as we suggest—the reversal and recognition are conceived so as to develop out of the incidents of the plot at the same time in an organic unity. That is to say, the recognition should take place at the most poignant time, when the tragedy is seen to be inevitable, when that hope on which the suspense is based is decisively frustrated and the initial fear is relieved, transforming itself into pity. Oedipus' most important discovery is the discovery about himself. Lear finally learns who does and does not love him. But in order to learn that he is loved for what he is, not for what he has, he has had to strip himself of all worldly and nonworldly powers and protections. Cordelia's experience prefigured Lear's: it was only after she had been stripped of all wealth and power that the difference between the false love of Burgundy and the noble love of France could be discovered. "Gods, Gods!" France says about Cordelia "'tis strange that from their coldest neglect my love should kindle to inflamed respect." What Aristotle says about the conjunction of reversal and discovery in the best plots points, we suggest, to what may be the highest theme of tragedy, namely, what sacrifices men must make for the sake of self-knowledge.

It could be argued that *King Lear* is not a very good illustration of Aristotelian poetic principles, for unity of plot is the central consideration for Aristotle, and in *Lear* we have the unfolding of two related but not unified lines of action:

the story of the house of Lear and the story of the house of Gloucester. The unity of the two lines of action can be seen, we suggest, in the unity of the philosophic theme underlying them. As Harry Jaffa has pointed out,[28] the Lear story illustrates the natural limits of political and legal authority. The natural force of noble love cannot be commanded or controlled by any political or conventional authority. The Gloucester story and perhaps the stories of Goneril and Regan as well illustrate exactly the other side of the coin: how the natural force of ordinary, or physical, love needs to be bounded by the law, by political authority. Edmund was conceived in adultery. Because he is illegitimate he is banished from the family circle. He is devoid of family-feeling. He is an "unnatural" son. Gloucester pays dearly for his transgression of the law.[29] The Lear story points to the tension or opposition between nature and convention; the Gloucester story points to the need for cooperation between nature and convention, how human nature has to be completed by the legislative art.

There are grounds for thinking that Sophocles himself adhered to a conception of tragedy not far from that of Aristotle.[30] Sophocles, it seems, has always been regarded as the master craftsman of plot and character formation. Yet the plot of his *Ajax* seems strangely out of joint.[31] The story builds up with great dramatic intensity to a climax with the suicide of Ajax. If considerations of dramatic effect alone were to prevail, one would expect the play to end there, but it continues for roughly one-third of the play's entire length with a large part of that time devoted to rather mean wrangling between Teucer, Ajax's brother, and Agamemnon and Menelaus about whether Ajax' corpse is to have an honorable or dishonorable burial. Odysseus, Ajax' chief enemy, persuades Agamemnon and Menelaus to allow Ajax an honorable burial. Odysseus, because of his powers of reflection, his power to generalize from the fate of Ajax, and his power to apply his generalizations successfully, rises above the hate, enmity, and pride gripping all the other characters in the play. In the first part of the play, he seems to show his superiority to the goddess Pallas Athene, the conqueror of the hero, Ajax. In the last undramatic one-third of the play, he shows his superiority to all the other human characters. The last undramatic one-third of the play would appear to indicate that Odysseus' superiority, fundamentally an intellectual superiority, is essentially untragic, essentially undramatic.[32]

CHAPTER THREE

Gratitude, Nature, and Piety in *King Lear*

> And they go to trial on a charge on account of which men hate each other most, but go to trial about least, that is, ingratitude. And him whom they know to be able to return a favor, but does not return it, they also punish severely. For they think that the ungrateful would also be most neglectful about gods, about parents, about country, and about friends; and what seems to follow upon ingratitude most of all is shamelessness, and it is this indeed which seems to be the greatest leader towards every baseness.
>
> —Xenophon, *Cyropaedeia* 1.2.7

I

In the fourth act of *King Lear* the cruelly blinded Duke of Gloucester is saved and guided by a man disguised as a mad beggar. The strangeness of beggar guiding duke is compounded by the fact that Gloucester's unknown guide is his son Edgar, who had assumed this wretched disguise to escape the sentence wrongfully laid upon him by his gullible father. Edgar serves not only as his father's eyes, he becomes his provider, the nurse of his broken spirit, his teacher, and the savior of his life. He saves him from Oswald's murderous attack and from a more formidable foe, despair. He concocts what for Gloucester is a divine miracle, to arouse within him the strength to live; and he preaches the lessons that enable Gloucester to avail himself of that strength. Edgar fulfills parental offices, and more, for his father. The once masterful father, helpless as a babe, is, as it were, fathered, sustained, and educated by his own son. This unsettling reversal of normal stations is pitiful and thought-provoking.[1]

Small debts of gratitude can be paid without much difficulty. But what recompense can be made to those who are the very sources of one's being? Does not every recompense fall short, is not every recompense simply disproportionate to what is owed? Since one is always in their debt, the command "Honor thy father and thy mother" can be invoked almost without any reservations.[2] Although this debt of gratitude is normally impossible to discharge, Edgar either did discharge it or came as close to doing so as any man could. The story of Edgar and his father seems to have been designed to show what would be required for such a debt to be paid in full.

The mercantile aspect of the language of gratitude—debts, payments, owing—is vaguely offensive, but apparently unavoidable. Lear, raging in the storm, calls out:

> . . . Spit, fire! spout, rain!
> Nor rain, wind, thunder, fire, are my daughters:
> I tax you not, you elements, with unkindness;
> I never gave you kingdom, call'd you children,
> You owe me no subscription: . . . (III.ii.14–18)

The hunted Edgar, consoling himself with the thought that "The lowest and most dejected thing of Fortune, / Stands still in esperance," goes on to say:

> . . . Welcome, then,
> Thou unsubstantial air that I embrace:
> The wretch that thou hast blown unto the worst
> Owes nothing to thy blasts. (IV.i.3–9)

Nothing good received, nothing owed.[3] But what if just being itself is good?

Although we prosecute and punish those who buy or borrow and do not pay, such offenses do not evoke the gravest condemnations. But "sharper than a serpent's tooth it is to have a thankless child." And ingratitude is a "marble-hearted fiend, more hideous when thou showest thee in a child than the sea-monster." The seriousness of the wrong can also be reckoned roughly by its effect. Kent speaks of "how unnatural and bemadding a sorrow" is the filial ingratitude that Lear suffers. When that sorrow has nearly done its work, Gloucester addresses Lear as "O ruin'd piece of nature."

Gratitude is akin to grace and graciousness, as their etymologies indicate.[4] Capacities or incapacities for gratitude seem to be direct reflections of character; the obligation when regarded as genuine is self-incurred. It becomes suspect when external compulsion is in the background, when it does not "come from the heart." To pay one's bills grudgingly is not gracious but does not violate the spirit of commerce. Can gratitude be paid grudgingly? Coming from within, it seems to be a natural movement in the sense of the Aristotelian distinction.[5] In this way it is akin to love.

Gratitude might be thought of as being between justice and love. Like commutative justice, which seeks arithmetical equality in exchanges of goods and services, gratitude involves an element of calculation.[6] Gratitude should be proportionate to benefits or favors bestowed.[7] But unlike the demands of commutative justice, these obligations are unenforceable, at least by any human court. Unlike commercial and contractual obligations, here there is no explicit promise to return an equal value for what has been received.[8] What occurs depends entirely upon the grace of the benefactor. The beneficiary cannot be forced to pay this kind of debt, which is also a debt that he was in no way responsible for incurring. Whether he pays or not depends upon the kind of man he is. Is he to be held responsible for the kind of man he is? Gratitude then, in so far as its payment is unenforceable, in so far as it must be rendered willingly, and in so far as it reflects the character of those engaged in it, is like love.

Where benefits causing gratitude and where love depend essentially on the personal merits of the benefactor or the beloved, distributive justice, which concerns itself with the proportionality of rewards to personal merit, comes into consideration.[9] Despite their connections or parallelism, gratitude and love, at least noble love, may be distinguished. Lear's failure to appreciate this difference seems to have been an important part of what led to his downfall.[10]

II

Lear introduces what has been called his love test with the following words:

> Tell me, my daughters,
> (Since now we will divest us both of rule,
> Interest of territory, cares of state)
> Which of you shall we say doth love us most?
> That we our largest bounty may extend
> Where nature doth with merit challenge.[11] (I.i.48–53)

He will give most, he says, to that daughter that loves him most, and the implication is, each daughter will receive a share of bounty proportionate to her love for her father. If Lear intended to test or to measure the amounts of his daughters' loves by their speeches, he would have waited till each daughter had spoken and each speech could have been compared with the others before making his distribution. But after each speech, before hearing those remaining, he disposes of a share in accordance with what appears to be and is once explicitly referred to by him as a prearranged plan (I.i.37–38). Moreover, the plan, which had been discussed with, or at least presented to, his advisors and council, seems to have been a sagacious one.[12] The love test then may first have been thought of by Lear as a mere formality, staged for the sake of a public ratification of a well-thought-out succession scheme. The question as to why this form was used still remains. It is through Cordelia's actions that the love test becomes decisive for Lear and for the play as a whole: For Cordelia's love and being sure of her love were, more than he knew, overwhelmingly important for Lear. Cordelia's experience in scene 1, in important respects, prefigures Lear's.

The Duke of Burgundy and the King of France are in Lear's court to sue for the hand of Cordelia, Lear's favorite daughter. When Lear strips Cordelia of all her inheritance, of her dowry, and of his paternal favor, the difference between Burgundy's and France's loves becomes plain. Burgundy will take Cordelia only with the portion first proposed by Lear. Lear says:

> . . . Sir, there she stands:
> If aught within that little-seeming substance,
> Or all of it, with our displeasure piec'd,
> And nothing more, may fitly like your Grace,
> She's there, and she is yours.

Burgundy replies, "I know no answer." Lear intensifies his condemnation and urges France not even to consider his former suit. France wonders what Cordelia's offense could have been. She replies; and he addresses himself to Burgundy:

> . . . My Lord of Burgundy,
> What say you to the lady? Love's not love
> When it is mingled with regards that stand
> Aloof from th' entire point. Will you have her?
> She is herself a dowry.

After Burgundy applies to Lear again for her dowry, is rejected, and withdraws his suit, Cordelia says:

> Peace be with Burgundy!
> Since that respect and fortunes are his love,
> I shall not be his wife. (I.i.247–49)

France speaks again:

> Fairest Cordelia, that art most rich, being poor;
> Most choice, forsaken; and most lov'd, despis'd!
> Thee and thy virtues here I seize upon:
> Be it lawful, I take up what's cast away.
> Gods, gods! 'tis strange that from their cold'st neglect
> My love should kindle to inflam'd respect. (I.i.250–55)

"Inflam'd respect" might well serve to characterize noble love.[13]

After being stripped of the accoutrements of power, wealth, and favor, Cordelia does learn who loves her for herself, for herself and her virtues, as France puts it, and who loves her for what she possesses, whose love "is mingled with regards that stand / Aloof from th' entire point." The dismantling of "so many folds of favor," including the favor of gods and fortune, not only reveals the qualities of her suitors' loves, but, more importantly, reveals what she is herself, reveals her lovability. France, as Kent conjectures (III.i.28–29), may have some political reasons for wanting to marry Cordelia: these, however, need not be incompatible with those manifest reasons that lead him to love her for her own sake. To believe that she could have deserved the condemnation she received from Lear, France says, "Must be a faith that reason without miracle / Should never plant in me." Positively put, reason without miracle confirms Cordelia's virtue and her lovability. France's love then could be described as a kind of rational faith based on what he has learned about her character.

It is not easy for a king, a princess, or anyone with large and evident powers to bestow benefits and ills, to learn what people truly think of them. Lear finally learns who loves him and what those about him think of him, but like Cordelia, he must be stripped and must strip himself of the trappings of majesty first.[14]

III

Private and public interfere with each other for Lear: The very proposing of a love test evidences a certain confusion about the properly public and the properly private. To command public declarations or testimony in the execution of one's office is certainly appropriate for a judge, magistrate, or king; but Lear seems to have tried, as it were, to absorb the private into the public, to have confused what can be demanded and enforced by right of law and majesty with what can only arise naturally, what is beyond all external command or control.[15]

However one conceives of the Lear of the love test,[16] his vulnerability with respect to Cordelia is crucial. Lear deserved gratitude from his daughters, perhaps especially from Cordelia. And gratitude, or thankfulness, should be proportionate to how much one has to be thankful for. But Lear demands professions of love. He fails to appreciate how demeaning it would be for Cordelia to allow her love to seem to be proportionate to the magnitude of the fortune he bestows on her. The preciousness of her love is tied necessarily to its proud independence from mercenary influences or threats. It cannot be bought, not with fortune, power, sensual pleasure, protection, or anything else less than virtue. Cordelia's refusal to participate in Lear's ceremony, her disobedience (and Kent's also), is correctly diagnosed by Lear as rooted in pride.[17] Lear, however, fails to see how that pride, with its occasionally offensive honesty, necessarily goes along with the love for which he craves. In its critical pride such a love reflects the lover's estimate of the intrinsic merits of the beloved.[18] If Lear had succeeded in humbling Cordelia, he might have destroyed what he loved most.

Lear never accuses Cordelia, as he does his other daughters, of ingratitude. Her love, or certain evidence of her love, is what he wants. He loved her most, he says, as if this gave him the right to command her to love him most. But even if love, or noble love, could be deserved, it cannot be commanded. There does not seem to be any court competent to grant compensation for the "pangs of dispriz'd love."[19] Lear, it seems, needs Cordelia's love because it would be evidence for himself (and for others) of his own excellence. If he were a wise man or a philosopher, he would "know himself" and perhaps not need such confirmation.[20] But Lear is not a philosopher. Regan is not the best witness, but she is not entirely wrong when she says of Lear, "He hath ever but slenderly known himself" (I.i.294, cf. I.iv.238 and 260). In commanding, or expecting love where he could only rightly expect gratitude, in thinking that he could simply disclaim "Propinquity and property of blood," in expecting full honors of kingship, after having relinquished power and responsibility, Lear presumes upon an intrinsic authority and self-sufficiency that he does not, and perhaps no man could, possess.[21]

IV

"In none of the fifty or sixty versions of the Lear story in existence before Shakespeare's play does the old king go mad."[22] Gloucester and Lear suffer most in this play. Reflecting on the madness of the king, Gloucester says to himself:

> Better I were distract:
> So should my thoughts be sever'd from my griefs,
> And woes by wrong imaginations lose
> The knowledge of themselves.

And yet the contrast between the two shows rather how much more pathetic Lear's suffering in the mind is:[23] The loss of eyes—the way-finders for physical movement, the conditions for independent action—is not so pathetic as losing the light of reason, the intellectual guide that lets us grasp the general meanings of things.[24]

There is a connection, it has been observed, between pride and madness.[25] Proud men do not like to justify and explain themselves. Their rectitude, they feel, should be taken for granted. They balk at the inferiority, or equality, implicit in being required to explain themselves, for example, Lear before Albany, Kent before Cornwall, Gloucester and Regan, and Cordelia before the court (I.iv.248 ff., II.ii.61 ff., and I.i.87 ff.). The proud see or feel themselves to be within a definite hierarchical order. They prize their place within the order and, accordingly, the order itself. They are most sensitive to insult and most prone to the passion most consequent upon insult, anger. Anger, unlike grief, contains within itself a desire to strike back. And, most importantly for our argument, the desire to strike back for most men, if not for all men, exists even when there is nothing to strike back against. Men derive relief from cursing the table or bench they have knocked against. When loved ones suffer some grave and irremediable illness or misfortune, men can speak, not of misfortune, but of "affliction," thus, as it were, striking back in speech against the causes of the suffering. All the affections of what is poetically called the "heart"[26] may tend to personify, and thus obscure, the difference between the living and the dead, but anger seems peculiarly prone to personification. Something similar often happens in love. It seems that men desire what they love, or what they think they love, to love them in return, whether such love is capable of being returned or not. Hope rises from desire. Hope and desire find fulfillment in fact or in fantasy.

In some of its extreme forms this personification is what is called madness. Lear insists that it must have been the unkindness of Poor Tom's nonexistent daughters that brought him to such lowness (III.iv.48 ff.). He will take a joint-stool for his daughter and Poor Tom and the Fool for Justices, if that is the only way he has to bring his daughters before the bar of justice (III.vi.20 ff.). Lear's pride, his self-respect, his sense of where he belongs in the hierarchical order of things, is, so to speak, the point of origin for his orientation in the world. As his self-respect is assailed, he finds it increasingly difficult to be objective, as Edgar says to Gloucester, to "Bear free and patient thoughts," that is, thoughts free from the presumption that everything that happens in the world has been personally directed with a view to its effect upon himself. His pride and his love of justice lead him to refuse to accept the existence of the world where his worth is denied. He will try to see the world as it is only if the world makes place for his pride. And yet one of the measures of his worth is the intensity with which he struggles to save his sanity. If his pride did not have some basis in truth, even his own love of truth and justice, his madness could not be as significant as it is.

V

In the early acts of the play Lear swears by those specific divinities, the sun, the night, Hecate, Apollo, and Jupiter; he also calls on the heavens and calls nature goddess. He seems to see himself and his kingdom as part of one grand natural and divine order, a just hierarchical order, with the heavenly powers, the gods, especially Jupiter, at the summit of the cosmic hierarchy and himself correspondingly at the summit of that subordinate order, his kingdom. When his daughters, his fool, and his shame, the correlate of his pride, destroy his self-respect, "abuse," "subdue," "oppress," "ruin," and "bemad" his nature, what is bemadding is that at the same time they are destroying the basis of his orientation in the world, driving his soul into a storm of questions, doubts, and partial insights too heavy for his patience and judgment to bear.[27]

The disorder in the moral and political world is associated in Act 3 with tumult in the cosmic order, the rage in Lear's soul with the raging of the heavens. The gentleman who meets Kent speaks of how the "impetuous blasts with *eyeless* rage" catch Lear's white hair in their fury. But for Lear lightnings are "thought-executing fires," and the elements are addressed as seeing and thinking beings. At first he bids them, "Let fall your horrible pleasure." They owe him no subscription. However, that soon changes:

> But yet I call you servile ministers,
> That will with two pernicious daughters join
> Your high-engender'd battles 'gainst a head
> So old and white as this. O, ho! 'tis foul.

His outrage seems to turn toward the gods themselves. But his faith is not yet entirely destroyed. He realizes that patience is what he needs. Perhaps his suffering is some divine affliction, later to be redeemed? He calls out as if the storm were herald to a day of judgment when justice and honesty will prevail and he will be revealed as a man more sinned against than sinning.

> Let the great Gods,
> That keep this dreadful pudder o'er our heads,
> Find out their enemies now. Tremble, thou wretch,
> That hast within thee undivulged crimes,
> Unwhipp'd of Justice; hide thee, thou bloody hand,
> Thou perjur'd, and thou simular of virtue
> That art incestuous; caitiff, to pieces shake,
> That under covert and convenient seeming
> Has practis'd on man's life; close pent-up guilts,
> Rive your concealing continents, and cry
> These dreadful summoners grace. I am a man
> More sinn'd against than sinning.[28] (III.ii.49–59)

Later, after he has agreed to enter a nearby hovel, he says, "I'll pray and then I'll sleep." But he does not pray, if praying means addressing divinities.[29] He directs his words not to the high, to the gods, but to the poor, the wretched and the low:

> Poor naked wretches, whereso'er you are,
> That bide the pelting of this pitiless storm,
> How shall your houseless heads and unfed sides,
> Your loop'd and window'd raggedness, defend you
> From seasons such as these? O! I have ta'en
> Too little care of this. Take physic, Pomp;
> Expose thyself to feel what wretches feel,
> That thou mayst shake the superflux to them,
> And show the Heavens more just. (III.iv.27–36)

Like thoughts are expressed later by Gloucester, as he gives a purse to the man he believes to be Poor Tom:

> Here, take this purse, thou whom the heav'ns' plagues
> Have humbled to all strokes: that I am wretched
> Makes thee the happier: Heavens, deal so still!
> Let the superfluous and lust-dieted man,
> That slaves your ordinance, that will not see
> Because he does not feel, feel your power quickly;
> So distribution should undo excess,
> And each man have enough. (IV.i.64–71)

Lear's statement goes further: The very justice of the heavens is called into question.[30]

The decisive point in this process is reached when Lear strips off his royal garments, after he has encountered Poor Tom, the exemplar of human wretchedness in the extreme.[31] Gratitude, its bonds, its cosmic and divine implications, have proved snares and delusions for Lear. Here, with Poor Tom as his model, undeceived by a groundless reliance on gratitude and the flattery of pomp and majesty, he thinks that he can see the truly fundamental situation of man.

> Is man no more than this? Consider him well. Thou ow'st the worm no silk, the beast no hide, the sheep no wool, the cat no perfume. . . . Thou art the thing itself; unaccommodated man is no more but such a poor, bare, forked animal as thou art. Off, off you lendings! Come; unbutton here. (III.iv.105–12)[32]

Tom owes the worm no silk because he has no silk, the sheep no wool because he has no wool. Lear takes Tom, the unaccommodated man, as the "natural man." But does Tom have nothing? He has his life and he has his misery; and as gratitude is one of the chief roots of natural piety, so fear and wretchedness can theologize and moralize as well. Tom has his catechism:

> Take heed o' th' foul fiend. Obey thy parents; keep thy word's justice; swear not; commit not with man's sworn spouse; set not thy sweet heart on proud array. (III.iv.80–83)

Each of these six commandments corresponds to one of the Bible's Ten Commandments: the last most tenuously to the Bible's Tenth, Tom's fifth to the Bible's Seventh, his fourth to the Bible's Third, his third to the Bible's Ninth, and his second to the Bible's Fifth.[33] Lear has proclaimed twice in this play that "nothing can be made out of nothing."[34] If nothing comes from nothing, everything that does come to be must come from something, something which itself does not come to be, that is, is unchanging. It is not altogether unreasonable for Poor Tom and anyone who would take him as the man himself to regard what most men call God, the ultimate source of his misery, as a foul fiend. Tom's first commandment corresponds to the Bible's First Commandment: "Thou shalt have no other gods before me."[35] The question about filial gratitude, about what children owe to their parents, to the sources of their being, is here extended to the limit: What is owed, or due, to the guiding principle, or principles, of life as a whole, to the sources, or source, of all being?

When Lear strips himself of his royal garments, those "lendings," he tries to strip himself of every vestige of royalty. When Kent asks him, "How fares your Grace?" he does not even acknowledge that the term could be meaningful and replies, "What's he?" His divestment of his royal garments is the outer sign of his soul's divestment of its former protections and supports, of those beliefs and convictions that heretofore had sustained and guided his activity in the world. He thinks that now he is in a position to come to know man, to know himself, to philosophize (I.iv.238 and 259). But the conditions required to make him want to philosophize are those that he declared earlier would make a truly human life impossible. "O! reason not the need," he replies to his daughters' questioning his need for attendants of his own:

> our basest beggars
> Are in the poorest thing superfluous:
> Allow not nature more than nature needs,
> Man's life is cheap as beast's. Thou art a lady;
> If only to go warm were gorgeous,
> Why, nature needs not what thou gorgeous wear'st,
> Which scarcely keeps thee warm. But, for true need,—
> You Heavens, give me that patience, patience I need!—[36]
> (II.iv.266–73)

Not only does Poor Tom become the representative of humanity for Lear, but because he of all men is least likely to have been blinded by gratitude or flattery, he becomes after Lear's divestment the philosopher for Lear. "First," before accepting fire, food, and shelter, "let me talk with this philosopher," he says. His first question is: "What is the cause of thunder?" Shortly before divesting, he apparently had no doubts about the cause of thunder, that is, Jupiter.

> I do not bid the thunder-bearer shoot,
> Nor tell tales of thee to high-judging Jove. (II.iv.229–30)

But now such questions have become open. He never addresses a god by a personal name again. During all the time of his madness he speaks of the divinities ("Gods," IV.vi.128) only once. Lear seems now to be in a position to see deeper into the nature of things than he ever was before.

The word nature and words with nature as their root are used fifty times in what has come to be the generally accepted text of *King Lear.* The word unnatural occurs seven times, more than twice as often as it occurs in any other play of Shakespeare. Lear uses words with nature as root more than twice as often as any other character in the play.[37] These usages could be classified under five, not always clearly distinguishable, headings. Nature sometimes means (1) the general order of the social, political, and cosmic whole within which the activity of any one person or group can only be a part; (2) the constitution, or character, of an individual as a whole, that is, the unity arising from both endowment and habit; (3) the original endowment of an individual with the powers directed, though not necessarily compelled, toward definite ends, or purposes. This is the meaning expressed most often by Lear. Nature also means (4) the original endowment of an individual with powers supplied to be used howsoever their possessor wills. This is the meaning expressed most powerfully by Edmund. (5) Nature is twice personified as goddess: once by Lear conflating meanings 1 and 3, and once by Edmund conflating meanings 1 and 4. The play has often been understood as presenting the world as a great arena where the principles of ethical and unethical nature contest for dominion over the whole.[38] The disagreements of the commentators are just one more reflection of the fact that Shakespeare has been far more explicit about raising the question of nature, raising the question about the relation between nature and morality, than he has been about presenting any definite solution.

There is more clarity, however, about who is wrong: The transgressions of Edmund, Goneril, Regan, and Cornwall lead ultimately to their own destruction. Nature repels simple viciousness. And about the meeting of Lear and Gloucester in Act IV, scene vi: "What could better point the transcendent issues Shakespeare has developed . . . than this encounter of the sensual man robbed of his eyes, with the wilful man, the light of his mind put out."[39] Royal Lear's understanding of how morality is effected within nature is certainly not adequate. He conceives of the relation between morality and nature as being more organic than it is (III.iv.14–16); he overestimates the power of law; he is insufficiently attentive to the limits set by nature to what authority and law can command. He relies overmuch on divine enforcement of nature's directives, and consequently is unaware of the extent to which the accomplishment of nature's purposes is left to chance and, on the basis of the conditions provided by nature and chance, to human prudence. In other words, the substitution of divine intervention for chance leads to an underestimation of the possibilities for evil and an insufficient awareness of the need for prudence. Lear's faith in the rightness of the divine and natural order is shattered by his suffering. But what does his shattering experience open him to?

VI

In his madness Lear becomes estranged, not only from the divinities he swore by before, but from nature as a whole, especially from nature as the source of generation.[40] From the outset in Lear's mind the themes of generation, gratitude, and justice are intertwined. In his first great storm scene he bids the thunder, as if it were a divinity with authority and power over nature, to:

> Strike flat the thick rotundity o' th' world!
> Crack Nature's moulds, all germens spill at once
> That makes ingrateful man! (III.ii.7–9)

Destroy the world's pregnancy, he cries: Destroy nature's means for producing man, who shows by his failure to appreciate rightly the sources of his being how undeserving he is of the gift of life. What Edmund can speak of as "the lusty stealth of nature" is, for Lear, associated with:

> hell . . . darkness,
> . . . the sulphurous pit—burning, scalding,
> Stench, consumption; fie, fie, fie! pah, pah!
> Give me an ounce of civet, good apothecary,
> To sweeten my imagination. (IV.vi.129–33)

Mad Lear comes to a view of nature somewhat similar to Edmund's, nature as the primitive, undeveloped beginnings of things. But his anguish and revulsion indicate how much more he originally expected from nature: He feels and suffers the absence of what he can no longer believe in.

Like Jesus he speaks against the Old Testament sentence for adultery.[41] He goes to extremes and, as if all possibility of redemption were lost, declares: "Let copulation thrive." Jesus was more sober: After delivering the adulteress from condemnation, his last words to her were "go and sin no more" (John 8:1–11). Lear, however, condemns women generally, confounding sex with Biblical, mostly New Testament, images of hell.

In his condemnation of the world's justice, Lear cries:

> Thou rascal beadle, hold thy bloody hand!
> Why dost thou lash that whore? Strip thine own back;
> Thou hotly lusts to use her in that kind
> For which thou whipp'st her. The usurer hangs the cozener.
> (IV.vi.162–65)

Again we are reminded of the New Testament: "But I say unto you, That whosoever looketh on a woman to lust after her hath committed adultery with her already in his heart" (Matthew 5:27–28) and "He that is without sin among you, let him first cast a stone at her" (John 8:7).

Yet universal sainthood failing, decency requires that offenses be punished whether the intentions of the punishers be pure or not. Should thoughts and actions be equally punishable? Do men have as much control over their thoughts and desires as they do over their actions? Are others harmed by thoughts directed against themselves when those thoughts are neither divulged nor acted upon? If in the New Testament, as some would claim, these are deliberate rhetorical exaggerations, Lear seems to have lost the capacity to make the required qualifications.

In a farmer's dog chasing a beggar, Lear says:

> There thou might'st behold
> The great image of Authority
> A dog's obey'd in office.
> . . .
> Through tatter'd clothes small vices do appear;
> Robes and furred gowns hide all. Plate sin with gold,
> And the strong lance of justice hurtless breaks;
> Arm it in rags, a pygmy's straw does pierce it.
> None does offend, none, I say, none; . . .

If none does offend, and consequently none can rightly accuse, at least none who are not themselves spotless, perhaps none could ever rightly accuse: "Judge not, that ye be not judged."[42] Edgar's commentary on this speech is: "O! matter and impertinency mix'd; / Reason in madness." An attempt should be made to separate some of the reason from the madness. The farmer's dog does often chase away the thief, but the dog cannot, unfortunately, distinguish between villainous and innocent, not to speak of undeserved, lowness.

Authority and law are usually more rigorous with the poor and weak, partly because they are less capable of protecting themselves, and partly for less simple reasons. Wealth, power, and authority usually go together. And just as the unsuccessful can exaggerate the part played by chance and accident in human affairs, so the successful can flatter themselves by exaggerating the extent to which their good fortune is owed to their merits. By reasoning obversely about the misfortunes of others, they can allow themselves to become obtuse and callous to the miseries of the unfortunate, smothering charity in self-complacent rigor.[43] Such is the man "that will not see / Because he does not feel . . ." When Gloucester in the fourth act asks the disguised Edgar who he is, Edgar replies:

> A most poor man made tame to Fortune's blows;
> Who, by the art of known and feeling sorrows,
> Am pregnant to good pity.

The sufferings of Lear, Gloucester, and Edgar would seem to be the remedy for this, the occupational disease of greatness.[44] Yet if suffering of such magnitude is required, the price of sufficiently educating authority in mercy or equity is hopelessly high. Few can do as much, perhaps, as the educator Shakespeare, who by his art, his presentations of feigned experiences, has made it possible for some to feel, without fully suffering, what they might need to feel in order to see.

Lear's suffering, however, and the perspective he has come to adopt, have not prepared him for governing more responsibly, but rather for a renunciation of the "world." His suffering has completely destroyed him as a political man. Perhaps the most poignant expression of Lear's death as a political man is his reception of Kent in the last scene. Kent's affection for Lear is never severed from a political context. He always approaches Lear, even in defiance and in death, as servant to master, never simply as man to man.[45] At the end, although other explanations are possible, Lear's cold reception of Kent indicates that Kent and what he stands for have faded into almost complete insignificance for Lear. Yet his renunciation of the world is not complete. The desire for vengeance remains: "And when I have stol'n upon these son-in-laws, / Then, kill, kill, kill, kill, kill, kill!" (IV.vi.188–89).

VII

When Lear awakes after his long sleep, "Our foster-nurse of Nature" (IV.iv.12), "the great rage," the doctor reports, ". . . is kill'd in him" (IV.vii.78–79). Clad in new garments, the images Lear uses are resurrection from the grave and entry into a new life, a life characterized by the interchange of blessing (from Lear) and forgiveness (from Cordelia) and mutual love.[46] After the battle and their capture, Lear is given over almost entirely to love, the love of Cordelia.

> Come, let's away to prison;
> We two alone will sing like birds i' th' cage:
> When thou dost ask me blessing, I'll kneel down,
> And ask of thee forgiveness: so we'll live,
> And pray, and sing, and tell old tales, and laugh
> At gilded butterflies, and hear poor rogues
> Talk of court news; and we'll talk with them too,
> Who loses and who wins; who's in, who's out;
> And take upon 's the mystery of things,
> As if we were Gods' spies: and we'll wear out,
> In a wall'd prison, pacts and sects of great ones
> That ebb and flow by th' moon.
> . . .
> Upon such sacrifices, my Cordelia,
> The Gods themselves throw incense. Have I caught thee?
> He that parts us shall bring a brand from heaven,
> And fire us hence like foxes. (V.iii.8–23)

Lear seems to be perfectly fulfilled. He has no lingering regrets. The worth of being reconciled in love with Cordelia is beyond price: It cannot be measured by any of the measures Lear used in the first scene. No sacrifice, be it rule, extent of territory, honor, even freedom itself, seems too great, or even comparable with what Lear has gained. And with his love and the prospect of love's joy that he holds before himself has come patience. His patience and his love go together with his renunciation of the world. His desire for revenge is as dead as his pride. When Cordelia proudly says:

> For thee, oppressed King, I am cast down;
> Myself could else out-frown false Fortune's frown.
> Shall we not see these daughters and these sisters?

Lear answers, "No, no, no, no! Come, let's away to prison." And at the moment of his death, with the dead Cordelia before him, it is clear that Lear can live no longer in the world where even these last hopes are dashed. He dies in a vision of reunion with Cordelia living once again.

There has been extensive debate about whether these scenes are to be understood in a Christian sense or not.[47] Was Lear's moment of joy at his death "based on an illusion"?[48] Or, was it the triumphal culmination of his purgatorial, his redemptive suffering, a loving glimpse into that better world to come where all righteous hopes will be fulfilled?

What we have been describing is the development of attitudes and a perspective that Shakespeare has presented in terms that are recognizably Christian.[49]

This development in *King Lear,* however, is presented as a natural development. What was Shakespeare's perspective, as distinct from Lear's? The dramatic poet does not speak in his own name. His perspective can be inferred only from the play as a whole. "Hard were it for me, as if I were a god, to tell of all these things," says Homer.[50] The poet stands as a god over the world of his play, but a god limited to what nature leaves to possibility and to chance: For nature, or the poet's understanding of nature, provides the framework. "Is there any cause in nature," Lear asks, "that makes these hard hearts?" (III.vi.78–79). Shakespeare seems to have asked: "Is there any cause in nature that makes these Christian hearts?" Nature, or the problem of nature, as articulated by classical philosophy, we suggest, provides the framework for *King Lear.*[51]

The major classical philosophers, Plato and Aristotle, of course, never elaborated an answer to what we suppose was Shakespeare's question. This could be due to historical accident. The serious question is: Are the principles and the framework they first articulated adequate to comprehend such an account? Must not the rise and triumph of Christianity be explained? Can the decision about the best way of life be compelling unless all fundamental alternatives have been examined? It is incumbent upon classical philosophy to try to see whether the revealed religions and the souls formed by them can be rendered intelligible to natural reason. Shakespeare seems to have been exploring this possibility, especially in *King Lear.*

Yet, it could be argued, nature has its place also within the Christian cosmos. Could not Shakespeare have been showing rather how God's invisible law might, "from the creation of the world," have been written by nature in men's hearts? Might he not have been showing what would have to be endured by a "natural man," that is, a man with no knowledge of Jesus Christ and the Bible, for that law to begin to become visible to him?[52]

If the issue were to be put in terms of the primacy of compassionate love as compared with the primacy of insight, Shakespeare may have provided a clue to his own opinion in Act IV of *King Lear.* An unnamed gentleman describes Cordelia's tears while she reads of her father's sufferings as "pearls from diamonds dropped." "Tears of compassion are pearls; eyes are diamonds . . .": Tears of compassion are compared to rare and precious stones, but eyes, that is, insight, are more precious still.[53]

"Hath not God," wrote the Apostle Paul, "made foolish the wisdom of this world?"[54] For Paul the "foolish" of faith possess a wisdom far deeper than anything accessible to natural reason. Is this what Shakespeare suggests by echoing this language about wisdom and folly in his articulation of the problem of morality and justice in *King Lear*? The Fool tells Kent:

> That sir which serves and seeks for gain,
> And follows but for form,
> Will pack when it begins to rain,
> And leave thee in the storm.
> But I will tarry; the Fool will stay,
> And let the wise man fly:
> The knave turns Fool that runs away;
> The Fool no knave, perdy. (II.iv.78–85)

In this play the word fool moves through a range of meanings.

The official Fool in motley is "foolish," funny, and privileged because he seems, or is licensed to pretend, not to know the most ordinary conventions.

In general, a fool is a man who does not know what every man is expected to know. Somewhat less generally, assuming that in everything a man chooses to do, some benefit to himself is intended, a fool is a man who does things that harm himself, who lacks judgment about what benefits himself. This is the elementary meaning of the word in the play that is presupposed by the four meanings following.

The honest fools, best exemplified by Gloucester and by Edgar of the early scenes, are overtrusting and, as in Gloucester's case, overcredulous about heavenly influences on human actions. They fail to understand people unlike themselves, to understand vice and malice. They are easily gulled by those clever and unscrupulous enough to exploit and betray their trust.

The loyal and dutiful are "moral fools." So Albany is regarded by Goneril and Kent spoken of by the Fool. The same could be said of the servant who mortally wounds Cornwall and is killed by Regan. Lear in acting on the expectation that his elder daughters would be bound by filial gratitude and duty is another kind of "moral fool." The moral fools tend to act as if moral laws were as inviolable as natural laws, as if moral laws were natural laws. They are regarded as fools by the "worldly wise" for not appreciating sufficiently the arbitrary and conventional factors in morality, the bestial elements in human nature, and for not appreciating sufficiently how self-seeking usually masks itself in moral guises. For the worldly wise self-seeking is the only kind of seeking sanctioned by nature. What the moral fool senses or sees and the worldly wise are blind to is the extent to which the humanity of any one man's life is a function of the larger moral, social, and political orders of which that individual life can only be a part.

Examples of what we might call the "noble fool" are France, the Fool, Edgar, Cordelia, and Lear: those capable of being touched and moved by noble love, by "inflam'd respect."[55] By their willingness to risk themselves and everything that could be subject to calculations of worldly success, they exhibit their own conviction, and rouse admiration and hopes, in those capable of appreciating them, that mankind is capable of attaining states of being that are simply good in themselves. The worldly wise are blind to this possibility.

In the light of what the moral fool and the noble fool see, the knavery of the worldly wise reveals itself as the final folly. By their blindness to what raises man above the beasts, the "wise" knaves finally bring themselves down with those whose justice they violate. By their blindness to what directs men toward the divine, to what is good in itself, they are deprived of nature's graces, the love and friendship of the noble.

But do the love and insight that Lear and Gloucester attain fully redeem what they have suffered? What is to be inferred from the disproportion between their sins and their terrible suffering?

"We glory in tribulations," wrote the Apostle Paul,

> knowing that tribulation worketh patience; and patience experience; and experience, hope. And hope maketh not ashamed; because the love of God is shed abroad in our hearts by the Holy Ghost which is given unto us. (Romans 5:3–5)

And from the Apostle James:

> Be patient therefore brethren, unto the coming of the Lord. Behold the husbandman waiteth for the precious fruit of the earth, and hath long patience for it, until he receive the earlier and the latter rain. Be ye also patient; stablish your hearts: for the coming of the Lord draweth nigh.

It is Cordelia, her love, "The holy water from her heavenly eyes" (IV.iii.31), that near the end sustain Lear's patience. The gentleman describes how she read Kent's letters recounting Lear's ordeal:

> Ay, sir; she took them, read them in my presence;
> And now and then an ample tear trill'd down
> Her delicate cheek; it seem'd she was a queen
> Over her passion; who, most rebel-like,
> Sought to be king o'er her.

"O! then it mov'd her?" Kent asks.

> Not to a rage; patience and sorrow strove
> Who should express her goodliest. You have seen
> Sunshine and rain at once; her smile and tears
> Were like, a better way; those happy smilets
> That play'd on her ripe lip seem'd not to know
> What guests were in her eyes; which parted thence,
> As pearls from diamonds dropp'd. In brief,
> Sorrow would be a rarity most belov'd,
> If all could so become it. (IV.iii.12–24).

Later Cordelia prays:

> All bless'd secrets,
> All you unpublish'd virtues of the earth,

> Spring with my tears! be aidant and remediate
> In the good man's distress! (IV.iv.15–18)

In the reconciliation scene, Lear asks, "Be your tears wet?" He answers himself, "Yes, faith." These scenes too are often taken as argument that "King Lear is a Christian play about a Pagan world . . ."[56]

Sunshine and rain, however, suggest natural growth, that Cordelia's smiles and tears were nature's means for curing Lear's abused heart. It does seem, however, to be a most Christianlike use of nature. But, unlike Lear, Cordelia, whose patience is so movingly described, is proud to the end. She never asks for forgiveness. She is prepared to "outfrown false Fortune's frown." Is she prepared to live out her life "in a walled prison"? She has not renounced political life: She calls Lear king and queenlike puts down her rebel passions. She is ready to confront her sisters: "Shall we not see these daughters and these sisters?" Yet what is perhaps most significant, though obvious, for the question of Christianity in *King Lear* is that there is no promise or expectation "for the coming of the Lord."

The word patience is ambiguous. In the Christian sense it seems to mean bearing tribulations in the loving faith that their promised miraculous reversals will surely come to pass. In the classical, or stoic, sense of the word it seems to mean endurance: endurance that does not anticipate miraculous change, that accepts evil in the world as a necessity, that bases itself only on rational hopes and the conviction that what is itself good deserves loyalty whether that loyalty receives any other reward or not. The unforeseen mischances of the world that bring down the just and innocent too often with the guilty, in the classical view, engender the wish for particular providence at the same time that they constitute evidence for its absence. It is not incompatible with the love of truth to respect the love of justice that is the father to that wish.

VIII

Who is the paradigm of virtue in this play? The gentleman says, addressing himself to absent Lear:

> Thou hast one daughter,
> Who redeems nature from the general curse
> Which twain have brought her to.[57]

Why then was Cordelia killed? Cordelia's honesty, her proud refusal to join her sisters in their demeaning hypocrisy, precipitated the catastrophe of this play. Her death raises the question about what the moral limits of proud honesty in an imperfect world might be.[58] Pisanio and Cornelius in *Cymbeline* avert tragedy by, as they put it, being false (to the bad) in order to be true (to the good) (I.v.43–44 and IV.iii.42). In Sonnet 94 those "who rightly do inherit heaven's graces / And husband nature's riches from expense" are also those "that have pow'r to hurt and will do none, / That do not do the thing they most do show." This last line could never apply to Cordelia.

Edgar is the character in King Lear who most of all does not do the thing he most does show. He successfully assumes six different guises in the play. During the play, he develops from

> a brother noble,
> Whose nature is so far from doing harms
> That he suspects none; on whose foolish honesty

the practices of a confirmed villain ride easily, into a model of virtue armed and resourceful.

Edgar seems to be a mean between his father and his bastard brother. Their opinions about heavenly influences over human affairs are at opposite extremes. The father is overcredulous, Edmund undercredulous. Both are perhaps equally at fault intellectually, but the moral fault is clearly more the son's.[59] In Shakespeare's world he who scorns all idea of heavenly influence on human affairs rarely comes to much good. Edgar's speech to his dying brother gives the last word of the play on the adultery theme and constitutes an answer as well to Gloucester's "As flies to wanton boys, are we to th' Gods; / They kill us for their sport."

> The Gods are just, and of our pleasant vices
> Make instruments to plague us;
> The dark and vicious place where thee he got
> Cost him his eyes. (V.iii.170–73)

Edmund replies, "Th' hast spoken right, 'tis true. / The wheel is come full circle; I am here." Edgar spoke of the gods, but Edmund speaks of fortune's wheel. Lear preaches to Gloucester, drawing lessons from man's beginnings:

> Thou must be patient; we came crying hither:
> Thou know'st the first time that we smell the air
> We wawl and cry. . . .
> . . .
> When we are born, we cry that we are come
> To this great stage of fools.[60] (IV.vi.180–85)

Edgar preaches to his suicidal father on the same theme:

> Men must endure
> Their going hence, even as their coming hither:
> Ripeness is all. (V.ii.9–11)

This sermon is more adequate because it is more comprehensive. It considers not only the beginnings but the middle and the end as well.[61] Man's chief concern, the image suggests, should be not with what happens when the fruit falls and dies, nor especially the beginnings, but rather with coming to fullest maturity in the world.

IX

King Lear is based on two stories, the Lear story and the Gloucester story. Critics have long been concerned by the apparent lack of complete unity between them.[62] The unity of *King Lear* comes to sight on the level of reflection, reflection on the one philosophic theme underlying both stories, of which both stories are necessary and complementary parts: namely, that nature, while constituting the ground and limits of convention and law, requires in man the cooperation of law and convention for its fulfillment.

Lear in trying to command love and gratitude fails to see that the natural growths of noble love and gratitude are beyond the control of law and political authority. The Lear story illustrates the natural limits of legal and political authority and the tensions that arise between nature and law when those limits are not rightly observed.[63] The Gloucester story, the adultery theme, and the stories of Lear's elder daughters illustrate the other side of the same coin: how certain natural passions and powers, most manifestly the power of procreation, need to be controlled by conventions, laws, and authority.[64] Ordinary love and passion, not to speak of base love and passion, need to be controlled by law and authority. Being conceived outside the "order of law" (I.i.19), Edmund was banished from the family circle. He is, not altogether "unnaturally," devoid of family feeling. As the bodies of Goneril and Regan are brought in, the dying Edmund exclaims, "Yet Edmund was belov'd: / The one the other poison'd for my sake, / And after slew herself." Goneril and Regan as well as Lear seem to have died for "love."

How would nature and convention, or law, be related when cooperating harmoniously? Nature provides the materials, the human materials and powers, and ordains, or manifests to natural reason, what purposes and ends would perfect the materials and fulfill the powers. But the accomplishment of nature's purposes is left to chance and to men: On the basis of the conditions provided by nature and chance, the responsibility for forming the materials and developing the powers so as to function in accordance with those ends is left to men themselves through custom, habituation, training, law, art, and education.[65] Human nature is so constituted as to require the formation of conventions and laws for its fulfillment.

Edgar does represent the natural man in this play, not as the poor, bare, forked animal Lear saw, but as he is in himself, the man of many disguises, the educable man, whose heart does not enslave his mind and whose mind does not silence his heart,[66] whose heart and mind remain sound no matter how his outward trappings change. He is the natural man, not in that sense of nature that means only primitive beginnings, but where "nature" includes fulfillment, "ripeness."[67]

The same consummate irony that led him, correctly, but for the wrong reasons, to be called "the thing itself," that is, the natural man, by Lear may be at work also in his being called "philosopher."[68] Edgar, though not the most tragic, nor the most pathetic, character in the play, is the true hero of patience in *King Lear.*

CHAPTER FOUR

Francis Bacon and the Conquest of Nature

> The whole prospect and outlook of mankind grew immeasurably larger, and the multitude of ideas also proceeded at an incredible rate. This vast expansion was unhappily not accompanied by any noticeable advance in the stature of man, either in his mental faculties or in his moral character, but it buzzed the more. The scale of events around him assumed gigantic proportions while he remained about the same size.
>
> By comparison therefore he actually became much smaller. We no longer had great men directing manageable affairs. Our need was to discipline an array of gigantic and turbulent facts.
>
> To this task we have so far proved unequal. Science bestowed immense new powers on man and at the same time created conditions which were largely beyond his control. While he nursed the illusion of growing mastery and exulted in his new trappings, he became the sport and presently the victim of tides and currents of whirlpools and tornadoes amid which he was far more helpless than he had been for a long time.
>
> —Winston S. Churchill[1]

The so-called conquest of nature by modern science, the science associated with the names of Bacon, Descartes, Galileo, and Newton, has transformed human life almost beyond description. The new dependency of human life upon science, or its product, technology, pervades our thinking as well as our practical lives. It might even seem, from the recent suggestion to replace the term technology with the term "techtronics," that *logos* too had become outdated. Our awareness of the depth of this fundamental dependency should help us to avoid the hypocrisy of indulging in loose anti-scientific talk. Yet the threat of nuclear war, overpopulation, environmental pollution, the imbalance and disappearance of nature in the wild, self-perpetuating nature, and so forth, have all made the problematic character of the great project for the conquest of nature increasingly evident, even to non-philosophic thought.

But dangerous consequences can be dealt with in more than one way. If the conception of nature underlying the conquest of nature by science is sound, the remedies for the ills consequent upon the so-called conquest of nature are to be found not in less, but more science, or in a fuller use of science to solve the problems inherent in the application of science to practice. If, on the other hand, the dangers brought on by modern science are natural consequences of fundamental defects in the understanding of nature presupposed by the project, we are directed not only to the correction or reform of modern science, but to a consideration of the fundamental alternatives to it. In either case the fundamental problem turns out to be not only the problem of dangerous consequences, but rather understanding the truth, or adequacy, of the conception of nature underlying the notion of the conquest of nature.

The modern project, especially with Bacon and Descartes, was worked out in explicit opposition to classical philosophy and science. This is not simply historical accident. The meaning of the conquest of nature cannot be adequately understood without understanding the reasons for rejecting the view of nature it was formed explicitly to oppose, the classical or Platonic-Aristotelian idea of nature.[2] The idea of the conquest of nature cannot itself be adequately understood apart from an understanding of the fundamental alternatives to it.

I

The first word of the first aphorism of Bacon's *Novum Organum* is "Man," the second "nature": *"Homo, naturae minister et interpres, . . ."*: "Man, the servant and interpreter of nature, does just so much and understands just so much of the order of nature as he has observed in the thing or in the mind: he neither knows nor is able to know more." Man is the servant of nature in so far as he can do or make nothing except by obeying the hidden chain of causes. Man is the interpreter of nature in so far as he does not accept what he receives as if it were self-evident, but rather as being results and signs only of the hidden chain of causes. Signs must be interpreted. Man should distrust both his natural faculties for judgment and the signs which nature on her own provides him.

It is in the third aphorism that we find the decisive phrase: "For nature is not conquered, except by being obeyed."[3] The phrase is on its face absurd, or self-contradictory: the same thing cannot be both conquered and obeyed. Bacon too solicits interpretation. The word "nature" here is being used in two senses. In his discussions of natural history, Bacon provides us with the distinctions which resolve the contradiction. Natural history is divided according to the three conditions in which nature is found. There is (1) nature in its ordinary course, free and left to itself, as it presents itself to the ordinary understanding in the normal movements of heavenly and terrestrial bodies, the normal generations of plants and animals; then (2) there is nature wandering, or in error, when prodigies and monstrosities are produced; and finally (3) nature constrained and vexed, forced out of her "natural" state, pressed and molded by the art and hand of man. It is from this third kind of history that Bacon expects most. "For just as in civil affairs a man's disposition and the secret sense of his mind and affections are better discovered when he is troubled than at other times, so likewise the secrets of nature bring themselves forward through the vexations of art more than when they go their own way."[4] The nature to be conquered is nature in its ordinary course. The conquest is to be accomplished through the discovery of and obedience to the secret chain of causes hidden within and operative throughout nature, which are to be revealed by experimental history and true interpretation.

What is given to human cognition in its ordinary course, by nature in its ordinary course, does not provide the clue to the discovery of nature's fundamental structures and laws. We cannot assume, as the ancients did, that there is a natural harmony between the mind of man and the world, that science and philosophy are the refinement and perfection of the natural understanding working on what is given to human cognition by nature. On the contrary, what is given by nature to ordinary cognition obscures and obfuscates man's way to the discovery of the fundamental course of nature, to nature's fundamental laws. The first part, then, of the way to the conquest of nature is the "refutation of the natural human understanding." This culminates in the refutation of those philosophies that have been based upon this understanding. These are, most notably, the philosophies of Plato and Aristotle, which take as their fundamental task thinking through the presuppositions and implications of the orientation of the natural human understanding.[5]

The refutation of the natural human understanding is set forward most fully by Bacon in his discussion of the Idols of the Mind in aphorisms 38 to 67.[6] The idols are first mentioned in aphorism 23 as "certain empty dogmas" in contrast to "the ideas of the divine mind" which are "the true signatures and impressions made on creatures, as they are discovered." What Bacon intends by "ideas of the divine mind" is not at first altogether clear. The next aphorism, as if in answer to the question, How is one to know what kind of principles to seek?, remarks that principles constituted by arguments are not to be relied upon, since the subtlety of nature is greater many times over than the subtlety of argument. Rather, principles that lead to the discovery of new works, new particulars, that render the sciences active, are to be sought. In the search for these true signatures and impressions of the divine mind one is to look not for the divine ideas themselves, as ideas, but as forces and laws, as it were, impressed in and shaping and governing creatures. This is not because Bacon was more interested in practice, power, or useful inventions than he was in theoretical truth, but because he thought that the active principles governing nature are to be discovered primarily by determining what, how, and under what conditions things can be *done*, or produced. A theory is not confirmed as true simply because it leads to the production of new works, but new works are signs or pledges that one is at least on the track of truth. Bacon's emphasis is on light-bearing over fruit-bearing experiments, that is, on discovering causes rather than on immediate usefulness. He was fond of recalling "the divine procedure, which in its first day's work created light only and assigned to it one entire day, on which it produced no material work."[7] Those who confine themselves too closely to practical utility, he argues, defeat their own purposes in the long run; for from the right kind of light-bearing experiments and theories, not just occasional and isolated inventions will result, but whole "troops" of inventions. The right kind of theory and inventions, or works, go together.[8]

Human reason as ordinarily used in the study of nature is called by Bacon "Anticipations of Nature (as a thing rash and premature)." Anticipations of nature are contrasted with what he calls Interpretations of Nature, human reason rightly used. For gaining assent, that is, for rhetorical purposes, anticipations and the "sciences" and dialectic,[9] or logic, based upon them are far more powerful than Bacon's art of interpretation. They are more powerful as rhetoric precisely because they base themselves on and merely refine those universally shared delusions, or radical errors, inherent in the primary experiences and notions of the native human understanding. The analogies by which new things are related to old in philosophies based on anticipations, like the philosophies of Plato and Aristotle, lie in every man's common experience; the way of interpretation, on the other hand, must at first sight seem forbidding and uncongenial. It requires an initial suspension of belief about common experience itself, and its expositors must supply their own similitudes and comparisons in order to gain passage to men's minds. What they must rely on most, however, is leading men to particular things, or facts, themselves, or to those new experiences based on experiment which the understanding left to its natural inclinations would never come to.

The first class of idols, or false notions, which are rooted in the common nature of the human mind itself, Bacon calls Idols of the Tribe, that is, the tribe or race of men. The human intellect is prone to suppose that there is more order and regularity in things than it finds there. It is more moved and excited by whatever agrees with and affirms opinions already adopted than by what negates them. It is permeated by infusions from the will and affections, and especially those wants that foster superstition. Without warrant, it restlessly presses on beyond all ends or limits, on to the unconditioned, as Kant would say. "But by far the greatest impediment and aberration of the human intellect," Bacon says in aphorism 50, "proceeds from the dullness, incompetency and deception of the senses." In his less popular natural history, *Sylva Sylvarum,* (paragraph 98), there is an interesting discussion of the subject of this aphorism, given as "touching the secret processes of nature."

> The knowledge of man hath hitherto been determined by the view or sight; so that whatsoever is invisible, either in respect of the fineness of the body itself, or the smallness of its parts, or of the subtilty of the motion, is little inquired. And yet these be the things that govern nature principally; and with-

> out which you cannot make any true analysis and indication of the proceedings of nature. The spirits or pneumaticals, that are in all tangible bodies, are scarce known. Sometimes they take them for *vacuum*; whereas they are the most active of bodies. Sometimes they take them for air; from which they differ exceedingly, as much as wine from water; and as wood from earth. Sometimes they will have them to be natural heat, or a portion of the element of fire; whereas some of them are crude and cold. And sometimes they will have them to be the *virtues* and *qualities* of the tangible parts which they see; whereas they are things by themselves. And then, when they come to plants and living creatures, they call them souls. And such superficial speculations they have; like prospectives, that shew things inward, when they are but paintings. Neither is this a question of words, but infinitely material in nature. For spirits are nothing else but a natural body, rarified to a proportion, and included in the tangible parts of bodies, as in an integument. And they be no less differing one from the other, than the dense or tangible parts; and they are in all tangible bodies whatsoever, more or less; and they are never almost at rest: and from them, and their motions, principally proceed arefaction, colliquation, concoction, maturation, putrefaction, vivification, and most of the effects of nature. . . .

Aphorism 50 in the *Novum Organum* goes on:

> For the sense by itself is a thing infirm and erring; neither can instruments for enlarging or sharpening the sense do much; but all the truer kind of interpretation of nature is effected by instances and by experiments fit and apposite wherein the sense judges the experiment only, and the experiment nature and the thing itself.

Distrusting ordinary sense experience, one must by careful thinking and planning subject the things of nature to conditions of all kinds: pressures, forces, mixtures, and so on, which would never be found in the ordinary course of nature, in order that nature's normally secret operations "which are too subtle for the sense" are forced to produce "some effect comprehensible by the sense."[10] Given nature is contorted and transformed under the guidance of the notions the experiment is devised to confirm, disconfirm, or illuminate, in order to produce the kind of experience the experiment aims at. And it is still the senses, but the senses lawfully married to the rational faculty, that are our sources for evidence about the nature of things. Bacon's refutation of the natural human reason is not meant simply to disparage the intellect. The controlled experiment is to judge "nature and the thing itself." And the controlled experiment is the product of mind, duly warned and chastened, but also instructed and even inspired. "A complete separation and solution, therefore, of nature must be made; not by fire indeed, but by the mind, as if by a divine fire."[11] In his preface to the second edition of the *Critique of Pure Reason* Kant speaks of this "intellectual revolution" in natural science partly discovered by and partly inspired by Bacon and carried on by men like Galileo, Torricelli, and Stahl.

> They learned that reason has insight only into that which it produces according to a project of its own, and that it must not allow itself to be kept, as it were, in nature's leading-strings, but must itself show the way . . . constraining nature to give answers to questions of reason's own determining . . . [like] an appointed judge who compels the witnesses to answer questions which he himself has formulated.

Bacon takes the name of the next class of idols, Idols of the Cave, from what he once speaks of as Plato's exquisitely subtle allegory. But he speaks of our spirits being confined within "the caves of our bodies" and restricts these idols to those innate tendencies to error rising from the special nature of individuals, and their special habits, education, and accidental circumstances. Plato's image of the cave, on the other hand, could be thought of as encompassing the subject matter of all of Bacon's first three classes of idols, idols of the tribe, of the cave, and of the forum.

The idols of the forum, or market-place, being partly innate and partly acquired from without, are placed between idols that are innate (those of the tribe and the cave) and those which are not innate (the idols of the theater). The idols of the forum are most troublesome of all, for they stem from the way words and names are formed. Words, being for the most part framed according to the capacity of the vulgar, draw the intellect along the lines and divisions that seem most evident to vulgar intellects. More acute and diligent observers find words standing in the way of communication of what they have seen in nature. The prudence of the mathematicians in beginning with carefully framed definitions is good, but cannot cure the evil in dealing with natural and material things. What is required there are methodical and orderly arrangements of individual instances. Men form names for things which do not exist, like Fortune or Prime Mover; and they form confused names on the basis of hasty and unskillful abstractions from things.[12]

The last of the four classes of idols, the idols of the theater, are from the dogmas, or fables, or plays of philosophy. They are not themselves innate, that is, they depend upon the acquisition or acceptance of some philosophy; yet like everything else they have a natural basis. The peculiarities of the different idols of the theater are to be traced back to different special combinations of effects derived from the workings of the innate idols of the tribe and cave. The idols of the forum affect all the philosophies.

Bacon speaks of three prominent types among the idols of the theater. The first is the sophistical, which, to ensnare the assent of the greater number, bases itself upon common experience and common notions. The most conspicuous example is Aristotle, who led by the idol of the cave mentioned in aphorism 44 corrupted his natural philosophy and his metaphysics with his favorite study, dialectic, or what Bacon also calls the vulgar, or common, logic, the logic of the "Old" Organon. Aristotle fashioned the world out of categories, he tried to account for sensible differences and substances with words like "entelechy" and "act," which are words describing certain kinds of thoughts rather than things. Even when he did resort to experiment in his more specialized physical and biological works Aristotle framed his questions in such a way that his resort to experience was bound to confirm the positions he had decided upon in advance, a procedure warned against in aphorism 49 of the idols of the tribe.

The second class of idols of the theater is the empirical school of philosophy, those who on a narrow basis of certain experiments and experience fly or leap up to universal principles and try to explain everything else on the basis of the principles observed in their experiments. With great foresight Bacon warns that if his admonitions are heeded and men begin to leave sophistical philosophy, by which he means Aristotelianism, to devote themselves seriously to experiments, this kind of idol could become a much greater hindrance to sound inquiry.

The third class of idols of the theater, superstitious philosophy, the corruption of philosophy by admixture of theology and superstition, is far more widespread, in his times, at any rate, Bacon claims. While contentious Aristotelian, sophistic philosophy ensnares the intellect, this more poetical, more fanciful philosophy misleads it by flattery. The natural ambition of the intellect to fly beyond all limits, warned against in aphorism 48, and the susceptibility of the intellect to influences from the affections and imagination, warned against in aphorism 49, are catered to and flattered by this kind of philosophy. All idols are not of equal rank, and, Bacon explains, this kind of idol is keyed to the natural dispositions of more noble and lofty spirits. The most important example here is

"Plato and his school";[13] but this "apotheosis of error" shows itself in scholastic Aristotelianism as well, in the introduction of abstract forms, final causes, and first causes. This unwholesome mixture of religion and philosophy must be stopped, Bacon said, not only because it makes for fantastic philosophy, but also because it leads to heretical religion. Effecting this separation seems to be one of the most incontrovertibly successful parts of Bacon's project.

The great failure of ancient philosophy, however, a failing even of the Atomists whom Bacon praises as superior to Plato and Aristotle in natural philosophy, is that they investigated the quiescent principles of things *out of which* they are produced rather than the moving principles *through which* they are produced. The six received Aristotelian, or vulgar, distinctions of motion are merely popular and make no penetration into nature. Bacon gives fifteen and, later, nineteen different motions in his own published accounts of the simple motions.[14]

The ultimate or natural causes of these failures are dealt with in the last of the particular idols of the tribe in aphorism 51: "The human intellect is carried to abstractions according to its own nature; and things which are in flux it feigns to be constant." The fault of abstractions is that they feign things in flux to be constant. In aphorism 52 Bacon provides a further clue to his meaning where he speaks of this idol arising from "the mode of the impression." What he seems to have in mind is that the moving thing makes an impression or impressions which remain constant in what is impressed, that is, in the sense, memory and intellect, thereby suggesting that what caused it in the thing itself is also fixed, whereas it is really in motion. The aphorism continues: "But it is better to dissect nature than to abstract; as the school of Democritus did, which penetrated into nature more than the rest. Matter ought rather to be considered both in its schematisms and meta-schematisms, and pure act, and law of action or motion:

for forms are figments of the human spirit, unless you are willing to call those laws of action, forms."

Bacon uses the word form to describe the ultimate objects of science because that word had become so venerable for so many of those he wanted to lead down the path of his new science; what he means are laws of motion.[15] The intellect in dealing with things in flux moves toward the constant, but "in nature nothing truly exists besides individual bodies producing pure individual acts according to law."[16] The given compounded bodies of nature are to be dissected down to the latent schematisms of more fundamental bodies constituting them, the schematisms, or meta-schematisms of the more fundamental simple natures constituting them are to be studied especially with a view to the laws of action inseparable from their existence. The natural appetite of the intellect for constancy is to be satisfied by fixed modes, orders, or laws of change.

Beginning with natural history and the naturally given forms of the ordinary course of nature, like lions, oaks, men and water, physics studies their material and efficient causes, that is, their latent schematisms and latent processes, with a view to discovering the truly simple natures and motions out of which they are compounded. What simple natures are is not yet determinable, says Bacon, but he speaks of them as being more abstract and general natures like heat and spontaneous rotation, attraction, and magnetism.[17] The suggestion may be that in the simple natures material configuration and simple motion coalesce as two inherently connected factors of what we might call unitary ordered material dynamisms.[18] However that may be, the simple natures constitute the "alphabet of nature." Metaphysics, in the literal sense of "meta," after-physics, begins with the alphabet and studies its "grammar," that is, how the simple natures are collected, compounded and combined to form the bodies and to produce the operations of the ordinary course of nature. Metaphysics studies formal causes, that is the laws of actions of the simple natures, the laws which order and constitute any simple nature in any subject matter susceptible of that nature. The operative part of metaphysics Bacon calls "magic" suggesting by the term that on the basis of the new natural science men will be able to generate things never before seen in nature and of such a character as to rival in power, fineness and durability the things produced by nature in its regular course. The term also suggests that such things being alien to the ordinary course of nature could seem to be of supernatural origin. Bacon's use of the term metaphysics, like his use of the term form, cannot be understood apart from considerations of his philosophical rhetoric, for it seems to have been designed first to appeal to those who might still be attracted by the traditional name, but only in order to lead them toward a very different notion of the thing. "All physics," Bacon wrote, "lies in a mean between natural history and metaphysics." Metaphysics is "itself a part of physics or of the doctrine concerning nature."[19] That is, physics, in the broad sense of the word, begins with natural history and ends in metaphysics, with the laws of action of the simple natures. Bacon knew that there would be little left of traditional metaphysics, if his way were followed. A private letter of 1622, to a Father Baranzano in Italy, reveals his intention in part: "Be not troubled about Metaphysics. When the true Physics have been discovered there will be no Metaphysics. Beyond true Physics is Divinity only." "The human intellect," he wrote in the *Novum Organum*, "must not be supplied with wings, but rather with lead and weights."[20]

Are Bacon's "forms," his laws of motion, forerunners of the mathematical formulas of Newtonian physics? It is difficult to be certain. He did say that physics should end in mathematics. He did not seem to appreciate what might be accomplished by framing one's initial hypotheses in terms that are representable by mathematical symbols.[21] One might say that he foresaw what the goals of mathematical physics were to be, without being clear about the mathematical means to those goals.[22]

"Inquiries into nature have the best result when they begin with physics and end in mathematics." The nearer one approaches simple natures, he said, the easier and plainer everything becomes, as one moves from the incommensurable to the commensurable, from surds to rational quantities. Again, "everything relating both to bodies and virtues in nature [should] be set forth (as far as possible) numbered, weighed, measured, and determined. For we pursue works not speculations, and physics and mathematics well mixed generate practice." And most interestingly, we must "measure virtues, [forces], according to the quantity of the bodies in which they subsist and show how far the mode of the virtue depends upon the quantity of the body . . . we must proceed to inquire what proportion the quantity of a body bears to the mode of its virtue."[23]

However, the technique of representing physical entities by mathematical symbols, so as to allow what one already knows from mathematics to suggest undiscovered relationships between the represented physical entities, was evidently not known to him. Mathematics, he said, "should terminate natural philosophy, not generate or give it birth."[24] He does not seem to have been very well informed about the history of mathematics or mathematical advances being made during his own times.[25] Yet the Baconian experiment seems to lend itself to combination with the approach of symbolic mathematical physics. Both methods approach nature with a view to discovering the extent to which nature is subject to laws devised in advance by human reason. Both the Baconian experimenter and the mathematical physicist, in the Kantian phrase, "prescribe to nature its laws." Baconian influence can, of course, be seen in other approaches to physics, and also in other sciences, like chemistry and biology. However this may be, we now turn our attention to an area where the extent of Bacon's influence is less questionable: the new relation which was to be established between science and society.

II

The "Great Instauration," great renewal, of the sciences called for a radical change in the way science and philosophy were to carry on their affairs.

> And then let them consider what may be expected (after the way has been thus indicated) from men abounding in leisure, and from association of labors, and from succession of ages . . . in which the labors and industries of men (especially as regards the collecting of experience) may with the best effect be first distributed and then combined.[26]

Bacon's way was "not a way over which only one man can pass at a time (as is the case with reasoning)." His way required a vast new institutionalized science, coordinating the efforts of many men in a complex, hierarchical organization that was meant to outlast any of the individuals who were parts of it; that is, as we say, it was to become "historical" and progressive. This vast enterprise would require far greater support from society at large than science and philosophy had ever received before. There would come a time, Bacon hoped and expected, when society's dependence on science would be extensive and obvious; but before that time came about, and if that time were to come about, the powers that be, "who are but in very few cases even moderately learned,"[27] would have to be won over to the new cause. He devoted a considerable amount of thought and writing to this, his rhetorical task.

To the extent that his project has succeeded, the need for, and the understanding of, his rhetoric has diminished. Yet without some understanding of that philosophical rhetoric, what Bacon accomplished, both theoretically and practically, cannot be appreciated. He regretted that it was necessary for him, the architect of the new edifice of science, to become herald, recruiter, and even ordinary workman as well.

We have already seen some of the consequences of his need to recruit new men of science in an atmosphere dominated by Aristotelian, Platonic, and Scholastic learning in his use of the terms "form" and "metaphysics." In one of his interesting unpublished writings, which are often more open and less colored by classical terminology, he speaks about how his plans must be communicated and transmitted:

> inveterate errors like deliriums of the insane must be subdued by art and by wit, and are aggravated by violence and opposition. We must, therefore, use prudence and humor them (as far as we can with simplicity and candor), that contradictions may be extinguished before they are inflamed.[28]

Jonathan Swift in his *Full and True Account of the Battel Fought Last Friday, Between the Antient and the Modern Books in Saint James's Library* pays a certain tribute to Bacon in this regard: "Then Aristotle, observing Bacon advance with a furious Mien, drew his Bow to the head, and let fly his Arrow, which mist the valiant *Modern* and went hizzing over his Head; but Des Cartes it hit. . . ."[29]

Evidently Bacon ducked.

In addition to those whom he called "true sons of science," to whom "the lamp" is to be handed on, a new army of assistants, managers, and administrators had to be recruited. Appeals had to be made to men who never before would have been connected with science, to induce them to forsake their green fields, humble workshops, and profitable businesses to become partners in the hitherto too fastidious, or too exalted, quest for truth. Bacon encouraged them with the partial truth that "our way of discovering sciences almost levels men's wits and leaves but little to individual excellence," just as a man with a compass can draw a more perfect circle than anyone else, no matter how excellent, who uses his hand and eye alone. There will be a vast array of new technical and mechanical activities that will leave little to special intellectual excellence; but Bacon was more aware of the difference between ordinary men and men of talent and genius than are those who criticize him for ignoring it. Some four pages after his statements about leveling in the *Novum Organum,* he remarks that what he is attempting "cannot be brought down to the apprehension of the vulgar except by effects and works only."[30] This should be considered also in connection with the question about the relative importance of fruit, works, or power, on the one hand, and light and truth, on the other, for the Baconian philosophy.

The new institutionalized science of the future, Bacon saw, required a new relation between science and political life. Throughout his long and eminent political career he tried to gain official support for his projects. He was much more successful after his death, as Abraham Cowley's ode "To the Royal Society" of science, written in the middle 1600s, indicates.

> From these and all long Errors of the Way
> In which our wandring Predecessors went,
> And like th' old *Hebrews* many Years did stray,
> In Desarts but of small Extent,
> *Bacon,* like *Moses,* led us forth at last,
> The barren Wilderness he past,
> Did on the very Border stand,
> Of the bless'd promis'd Land
> And from the Mountains Top of his exalted Wit,
> Saw it himself, and shew'd us it.[31]

Bacon's success (and its having been taken for granted) has made it more difficult for us to see the problem as he saw it. The relation between political society and science and philosophy is always a delicate one: for, he wrote, there is no form of polity or society that does not have "some point of contrariety towards human knowledge." And conversely, the arts and sciences are always somewhat suspect from the point of view of civil society:

> For surely there is a great distinction between civil affairs and the arts: for the danger from new motion and new light is not the same. In civil affairs, truly, even a change for the better is suspected as likely to bring on disturbances; for civil affairs rest on authority, consensus, fame and opinion, not demonstration. But in the arts and sciences, like metal mines, there should be a clamor of new operations and further progress.[32]

Although Bacon wrote extensively on political subjects and working one's way through the labyrinth of his political thought can be a fascinating enterprise,[33] we must confine ourselves here to his specifically scientific politics. A most important part of his treatment of that subject is found in one small book, the fable, or scientific utopia, called the *New Atlantis*. But there too Bacon's ideas are not simply exposed to view, but become accessible only to a certain art of interpretation. For as he says in the *Advancement of Learning* beginning his treatment of government: "it is a part of knowledge secret and retired, in both those respects in which things are deemed secret: for some things are secret because they are hard to know, and some because they are not fit to utter." And in the expanded Latin version of this book he begins his discussion of civil or political science by telling an old story:

> that many philosophers being met together in the presence of the ambassador of a foreign prince, each endeavoring to give a sample of his wisdom, that the ambassador might be able to make a report of the wonderful wisdom of Greece; one of them remained silent . . . the ambassador turning to him, said, "What have you to say for me to report?" To whom he answered, "Tell your king that you have found a man in Greece who knew how to hold his tongue."

Bacon goes on to speak of an "art," even an "eloquence in silence" on these matters. There is also a simpler reason for the indirectness of the political discussion in the *New Atlantis*. If it is the case that the scientists control politics in the New Atlantis, Bacon is in effect asking the great political men of his own times to contribute to the founding and support of institutions which were intended eventually to deprive them, or men like them, of any real political power. Bacon had surely read, but did not need, the advice tendered by Machiavelli, that if you intend to kill a man and you want his weapons, you should not say, "Give me your weapons, I want to kill you." It is sufficient to say, "Give me your weapons."[34]

Bacon's *New Atlantis* is written in explicit correction of Plato's *Critias*; both works are formally incomplete.[35] The old Atlantis in the *Critias*, a luxurious, technological, or mathematically organized, society, was destroyed by earthquakes; the New Atlantis goes back as far, but thanks to its science does not fall prey to cycles of natural catastrophe as do all societies in Plato's account. The *Critias* ends just as Zeus is about to speak; what formally corresponds to Zeus's speech is the completed speech of the Father from Salomon's House, the great new scientific institute of the future, "the noblest foundation . . . that ever was upon the earth; and the lanthorn [or as elsewhere, 'the very eye'] of this kingdom." The speech is a description of Salomon's House, or as they also call it, the College of the Six Days Works. The society of Bensalem, for so it is called[36] in the language of the natives, enjoys prosperity, all kinds of health-producing fruits and foods, good health and medicines surpassing anything in Europe; and most natural, most chaste, and most pious customs. Salomon's House, it seems, is the source of all their greatest blessings. Science is devoted to the twin aims of finding out the true nature of things, to the greater glory of God, and the relief and prospering of man's estate. The island is Christian, having received both Old and New Testaments through a special revelation, which was confirmed by a witnessing Father from Salomon's House as a true miracle. But Jews, Persians, Arabs, Chaldeans, and Indians also live there and are left to their own religions, and they too love and respect the ways of the nation of Bensalem.[37]

It is a Jew with the interesting name of Joabin who arranges the meeting of Bacon's narrator with the Father from Salomon's House. Salomon's House itself was founded by Solamona, the great lawgiver of Bensalem, who reigned about 300 B.C. Although the founding of Salomon's House depends upon the political act of a great king, and Bensalem is called a kingdom still, by the time Salomon's House has come into its own the power of the king is scarcely visible. Orders are given to the visitors not in the name of the king, but in the name of the "state." When the Father from Salomon's House makes his procession into the city, the first such visit in twelve years, his chariot, described in detail, reminds one of the Ark of the Covenant in the Old Testament. He, as Jesus is often characterized, "had an aspect as if he pitied men." Fifty attendants of his own precede his chariot, and two others directly preceding bear, one a cross, the other a pastoral staff like a sheephook. All political and other officials walk behind his chariot. "He held up his hand as he went, as blessing the people, but in silence." In some of the factories of Salomon's House, the Father reports in a private meeting with the narrator, they have all kinds of ordnance and instruments of war, flying machines of a sort and submarines. There are thirty-six Fellows of the College; under them are novices and apprentices and "a great number of servants and attendants, men and women." The Fellows decide which of their inventions and experiences should be published and which not. They "take an oath of secrecy, for the concealing of those which we think fit to keep secret: though some of these we do reveal sometimes to the state, and some not."

What all this indicates is that the ultimate rule both of

the state and religion, ("which has most power over men's minds"[38]), is in the hands of the Fellows of Salomon's House, the philosopher-scientists.

Bacon envisaged a vast expansion of human power as a consequence of science's conquest of nature. He evidently thought that these powers, powers for evil as well as for good, were not to be put into the hands of mere statesmen; control was to be kept in the hands of those who would be expected to comprehend them, the most powerful and highly trained philosophic and scientific minds. While the arrangement of a marriage between science and society clearly forecasts a new era of mutual interest and concern between the parties, rule by the wise was regarded as the condition for success. The leaders of science apparently were also meant to become masters of statecraft, of human philosophy, to guarantee that the newly discovered powers would fall into hands fit to use them well. In aphorisms 127 and 80 of Book One of the *Novum Organum* Bacon makes clear that he is speaking about perfecting not only natural philosophy in the narrow sense, but the sciences of logic, ethics, and politics as well; they were all to be nourished by, and brought to perfection along with, natural philosophy. The new science, in its inception, was meant to be a universal science.[39]

The failure to develop the expected human philosophy would seem to be the most conspicuous failure of Baconian philosophy. Can any philosophy or science which does not take the orientation of prescientific and prephilosophic cognition seriously ever be adequate for understanding human things?[40]

However this may be, Baconian science wins the support of society and the people at large by catering to their fears and desires, as they understand those desires, that is, by providing them with protection against injury from man and especially from nature, with prosperity, with comforts and new pleasures, and especially with stronger and healthier bodies. The latent, and not always latent, antagonism between science and philosophy, on the one hand, and society, on the other, is not to be bridged by mere words, by the flimsy art of the *Gorgias*, by the consolations of philosophy, by exhortations to virtue, but rather by the tangible comforts of Baconian charity. Consolation for and bowing to the ravages of fortune are not as good as conquering fortune; for in truth, Bacon says, fortune is a name for something which does not exist, just as the theoretical presupposition of the notion of fortune, variable and unstable matter, does not exist. The Ancients produced theoretical excuses, blaming their failure to radically improve the estate of man on the nature of things, rather than on their own ignorance, especially their ignorance of the forms, or fixed laws governing all matter.[41]

The depreciation of nature, at least of given nature, or nature in its ordinary course, implicit in the idea of conquest of nature, is a, or the, common theme of modern philosophy. In Kant and Hegel it culminates in a thorough disqualification of nature for the provision of ethical and political standards. Or, in other words, Kant and Hegel found the nature uncovered by modern science, the nature which Bacon said is to be obeyed, altogether incapable of supplying man with ethical and political standards. As a consequence, for Kant and Hegel moral and political standards must be traced to some other, non-natural sources: freedom, pure practical reason, spirit, and history. Something that anticipates, or corresponds to, the later development occurs also in Bacon, as can be seen by considering the following difficulty. Men, like lions and oaks, are not fundamental, but rather compounded forms of nature in its ordinary course. But one of these ordinary, compounded forms is to become the conqueror and master of all the forms of nature in its ordinary course. There must be something special, or fundamental about this one of all the non-fundamental forms, man. Bacon's division of all philosophy (apart from natural theology) into natural and human is a kind of tacit acknowledgment, insufficient though it may be, of the new special status of man in his philosophy. Yet, unlike

Kant and Hegel, Bacon still looked to nature and its fundamental laws in order to discern the principles of morality.[42]

Sometimes he claimed to share the ethical goals of the ancient philosophers, adding only the teaching they neglected about how to attain those goals; but that position is not long maintained. The discourses of the ancients on morals and politics, he said, are beautiful and lofty, like "the stars, which give little light because they are so high."[43] Bacon, following Machiavelli (*The Prince* ch. 15), lowered his goals in order to guarantee actualization. This is one way to understand the so-called conquest of fortune. A Baconian may reply that goals which can almost never be put into practice cannot be regarded as serious practical goals. In his widely read *Advancement of Learning,* Bacon divides the "Platform of the Good" into two basic divisions, Individual or Self Good, which concerns itself with virtue, and the Good of Communion, or Social Good, which concerns itself with duty. Individual Good is subdivided into Passive Good and Active Good, and Passive Good is subdivided finally into Conservative Good and Perfective Good. The first division is explained as an appetite imprinted in everything toward a twofold nature of good, the one as everything is a totality in itself, the other as it is a part of another body: Iron moves toward the lodestone in individual sympathy, but if it exceeds a certain quantity, like a good patriot, it moves to the earth, the country of its connaturals. The conservation of the more general form, the good of communion, controls all the lesser inclinations, as is emphasized by the Christian faith, which more than any other sect or philosophy exalted the good of communion and depressed the private or particular good. "All other excellences . . . are subject to excess; only charity admitteth no excess." This also decides the question concerning whether the contemplative or the active life is to be preferred, against Aristotle. For all the reasons he brings forth in favor of the contemplative life are private. As far as the private pleasure and dignity of a man's self are concerned, Aristotle is right.

"But men must know that in this theater of man's life it is reserved only for God and angels to be lookers on . . . for contemplation which should be finished in itself, without casting beams upon society, assuredly divinity knoweth it not." In his much less reserved and unpublished, but privately circulated, *Valerius Terminus*, these same divisions of good are discussed with no admixture of Christian theology or classical terminology, as appetites, desires, and motions operating throughout material nature. Bacon begins this discussion with the remark, that "if the moral philosophers that have spent such an infinite quantity of debate touching Good, and the highest good, had cast their eye abroad upon nature," to see the "quaternion of good" which he presents as laws of motion, then they might have "saved and abridged much of their long and wandering discourses of pleasure, virtue, duty and religion." (See Figure 1.) In the expanded version of *Advancement of Learning*, the *De Augmentis Scientiarum*, the section on physics, in the discussion of simple or elementary motions, these same motions with still different names and no obvious connection to morality show up in the central places. Morality, it seems, is to be reduced to physics. It is in Bacon's thought rather than Hobbes' that these two great powers of modern thought, Machiavellian political morality and modern natural science, are first brought together. The Machiavellian principles, however modified, are found by Bacon to be operative not only in human nature, but throughout nature as a whole.

But let us try to understand how this works out in human terms by trying to see what the best, or highest, way of life would be for Bacon. The Active Good of extending and multiplying oneself, in conformity with the Social or Communal Good, takes precedence over the Perfective Good and the Preservative Good, that is, pleasure. Internal perfection, contrary to Plato and Aristotle, is secondary to acting upon and relating to others in and for society. Foreign policy, as it were, takes precedence over domestic policy. In his most popular

FIGURE 1
Platform or Exemplar of the Good*

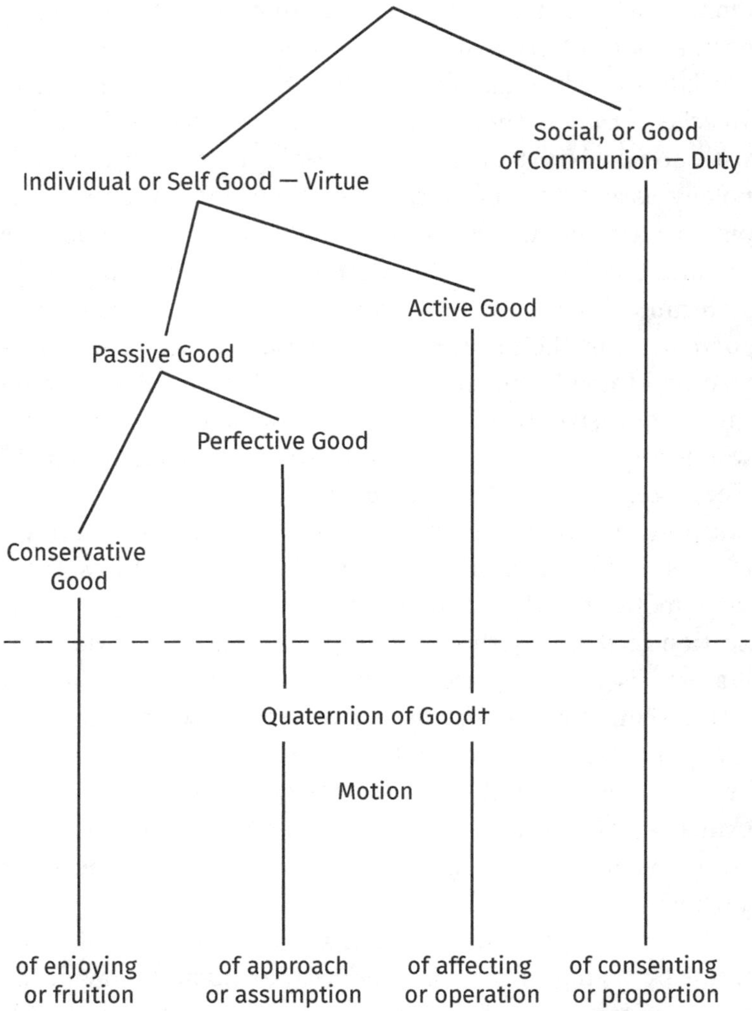

*From *Advancement of Learning*, 1605, and *De Augmentis Scientiorum*, 1623.

†From *Valarius Terminus*, estimated 1603.

book, the *Essays* (No. 55), Bacon assigns the highest place of honor to founders of empires, states, and commonwealths, like Romulus, Cyrus, Caesar, Ottoman, and Ismael. In the *Novum Organum*, however, in distinguishing three grades of ambition, the highest political ambition is assigned the second place. The first place goes to him who would "endeavor to instaurate and extend the power and empire of the human race itself over the universe of things" through the sciences and the arts. "And yet, to speak the whole truth," Bacon says later in the same aphorism, ". . . the very beholding of the light is itself a more excellent and fairer thing than its many uses: so surely the very contemplation of things as they are without superstition or imposture, error or confusion, is in itself more worthy than all the fruits of inventions." And at the end of the First Book of the *Advancement of Learning*:

> We see then how far the monuments of wit and learning are more durable than the monuments of power, or of the hands . . . the images of men's wits and knowledges remain in books, exempted from the wrong of time and capable of perpetual renovation. Neither are they fitly to be called images, because they generate still and cast their seeds in the minds of others, provoking and causing infinite actions and opinions in succeeding ages. . . . letters . . . as ships pass through the vast seas of time, and make ages so distant to participate of the wisdom, illuminations, and inventions, the one of the other. . . .

Apparently Bacon did conceive of contemplation as the highest perfection of man, but a kind of politic contemplation, contemplation of the most far-seeing practice, or action, the theory which discloses knowledge of "all possible operations," the theory productive of the most long-range practice. He evidently envisaged a complete coincidence of private and social good on the highest level. Ambition in the highest sense, the ambition of the founder of the empire of man over nature, who is that founder *because he is the first discoverer of the cosmological truth,* becomes at the same time the performance of the highest of duties. The ambition of the founder of the greatest of all empires is the highest form of the active or extensive good; it is realized by means of the highest perfective good, contemplation. Since it is aimed at securing the maximum of relief, comfort, and power for mankind as a whole, it also constitutes the highest of duties, as Bacon defined duty, the action of an individual with regard to the well-being of society. In the very last entry of his natural history it is difficult not to think that Bacon had himself in mind:

> The delight which men have in popularity, fame, honour, submission, and subjection of other men's minds, wills, or affections (although these things may be desired for other ends), seemeth to be a thing in itself, without contemplation of consequence, grateful and agreeable to the nature of man. This thing (surely) is not without some signification, as if all spirits and souls of man came forth out of one divine limbus; else why should men be so much affected with that which others think or say? The best temper of minds desireth good name and true honour: the lighter, popularity and applause: the more depraved, subjection and tyranny; as is seen in great conquerors and troublers of the world; and yet more in archheretics; for the introducing of new doctrines is likewise an affection of tyranny over the understandings and beliefs of men.

As this quote indicates, the lowest of Bacon's classes of good, the conservative good, or good of enjoyment, will also be fulfilled for the founder of the empire of man over nature, through the pure delight men have in fame, honor, and the subjection of other men's minds.

The Father from Salomon's House "had an aspect as if he pitied men." As Bacon says elsewhere:

> There is implanted in man by nature itself a noble and excellent spirit of compassion, that extends itself even to the brutes which by the divine ordinance are subject to his command. This compassion, therefore, has a certain analogy with that of a prince towards his subjects. Moreover it is most true, that the more worthy a soul is, the more objects of compassion it has.[44]

The true temper of Baconian charity, of the Baconian scientist, evidently must combine the spirit of compassion with the spirit of domination. A synthesis of these qualities along with Herculean, Promethean courage[45] would seem to constitute something like the grand passion of generosity discussed by Descartes in his *Passions of the Soul.*

Both Bacon and Descartes believed that the vast expansion of powers to be wrought by the new science would have to be matched by correspondingly great resources of courage in the souls of those men who were to release and administer those powers. But moderation, the ancients tell us, is the core of almost all the virtues. And courage without moderation is rashness. The beneficence of the project for the conquest of nature seems increasingly to be matched, or perhaps even more than matched, by its rashness. An open-minded reconsideration of the principles underlying the project and the alternatives to it would seem to be called for.[46]

CHAPTER FIVE

Thomas Hobbes

A FOUNDING FATHER OF MODERN SOCIAL SCIENCE

Hobbes presented his political philosophy thematically in three books, *The Elements of Law* (1640), *De Cive* (*The Citizen*, 1642), and *Leviathan* (1651). The most manifest differences among the books concern the development and elaboration of theological doctrine in the later books.

Hobbes's intention can be seen as twofold: (1) to put moral and political philosophy, for the first time, on a scientific basis; (2) to contribute to the establishment of civic peace and amity and to the disposing of mankind toward fulfilling their civic duties. These two intentions, theoretical and practical, were in Hobbes's mind closely connected. This latter intention, the civic or civilizing intention, identified Hobbes with the tradition of political philosophy that he associated with the names of Socrates, Plato, Aristotle, Plutarch, and Cicero. The entire tradition, according to Hobbes, had failed, however, both in its quest for truth and in its inability to lead men toward peace. Hobbes's emphatic break with the tradition was decisively prepared by Machiavelli and, following Machiavelli, Bacon. The classics failed, according to Machiavelli, because they aimed too high. Because they based their political doctrines on considerations of man's highest aspirations, the life of virtue and the society dedicated to the promotion of virtue, they render themselves ineffective; as Bacon said, they made "imaginary laws for imaginary commonwealths." Machiavelli's "realism" consists in a conscious lowering of the standards of political life, taking as goals of political life not the perfection of man but those lower goals actually pursued by most men and most societies most of the time. Political schemes framed in accordance with men's lower but more powerful motives are much more likely to be realized than the utopias of the classics. However, unlike Machiavelli, Hobbes elaborated a code of moral or natural law, natural law as a morally binding law, determining the purposes of civil society. But, following Machiavelli's "realism," he separated his doctrine of natural law from the idea of the perfection of man.[1] He attempted to deduce the natural law from what is most powerful in most men most of the time: not reason, but passion. Because of what he regarded as his discovery of the true roots of human behavior, his knowledge of human nature, and his scientific way of proceeding, Hobbes believed that he had succeeded where all others had failed, that he was the first true political philosopher. In accordance with these convictions he recommended that his books be established in the universities as authoritative and continually attacked the doctrines of Aristotle, "whose opinions are at this day and in these parts of greater authority than any other human writings," as both subversive and false.[2]

For Hobbes, scientific knowledge meant mathematical knowledge, or geometrical knowledge. Hitherto, he wrote, geometry has been the only science that has attained indisputable conclusions. The term geometry was sometimes used by Hobbes to refer to all the mathematical sciences, the study of motion and force, mathematical physics, as well as the study of geometrical figures. Philosophy, or science, proceeds in either of two ways: (1) with the compositive method, or "synthetically," by reasoning from the first and generating causes of all things to their apparent effects, or (2) with the resolutive method, or "analytically," by reasoning from the apparent effects, or facts, to possible causes of their generation. The first principles of all things are defined by Hobbes as body, or matter, and motion, or change of place: "every part of the Universe, is Body; and that which is not Body, is no part of the Universe: and because the Universe is All, that which is no part of it is Nothing. . . ." In accordance with the synthetic or geometrical mode of proceeding one would begin with the laws of physics in general, from them deduce the passions, the causes of the behavior of individual men, and from the passions deduce the laws of social and political life. However, it is by means of the analytic method, the analysis of sense experience, that one arrives at adequate definitions of the first principles themselves.

The analytic method is especially important for political philosophy. For Hobbes expected the moral and civil science which he elaborated to be able to be convincing not only to natural philosophers, but also to any man "that pretends but reason enough to govern his private family." This expectation is reasonable because the facts upon which his analysis is based are known to all normal men by experience. Hobbes invites his reader to test the truth of what he wrote by looking into himself and considering whether what Hobbes says about the passions, thoughts, and natural inclinations of mankind apply to him; then by learning to "read" and know himself, through the similitude of passions and situations he will be able to read the passions and thoughts of all other men. Although his conception of scientific method influenced Hobbes's formulations, presentation, and analysis of human experience, he indicates that it is not to his conception of science but to his understanding of common prescientific experience that we are to look in order to determine the truth and importance of his political philosophy. He suggests that the adequacy and correctness of his judgments of, or insights into, what are the fundamental human experiences can be considered and understood independently of his physics.[3]

Human behavior, according to Hobbes, is to be understood primarily in terms of a mechanistic psychology of the passions,[4] those forces in man, which, so to speak, push him from behind; it is not to be understood in terms of those things which could be thought of as attracting man from in front, the ends of man, or what for Hobbes would be the objects of the passions. The objects of the passions, Hobbes says, vary with each man's constitution and education and are too easy to disguise. Furthermore, good and evil, the words with which men characterize the objects of their desires and aversions, are strictly relative to the man using the words, "there being nothing simply and absolutely so; nor any common Rule of Good and Evil, to be taken from the nature of the objects themselves. . . ." What men really mean when they say something is good is that it pleases them. Yet it is true that as the passions issue in actions, men are guided by their imaginations and their opinions of what is good and evil; but the thoughts do not control the passions; on the contrary, "for the Thoughts are to the Desires, as Scouts, and Spies, to range abroad, and find the way to the Things Desired."[5]

Hobbes was in agreement with the tradition, stemming from Socrates and including Thomas Aquinas, that the goals and character of moral and political life should be determined by reference to nature, especially human nature. However, he determined the way in which nature sets the standards for politics very differently than did the tradition, namely, through the construction of a theory of "the state of nature." The theory of the state of nature, deduced, Hobbes says, from the passions of man, is one way of dealing with the old psychological problem, a problem of decisive importance for political philosophy: Is man by nature social and political? Hobbes denies that man is naturally social and political.[6] The grounds of this denial are made evident by the theory of the state of nature, that prepolitical condition in which men live without civil government, or without a common power over them to keep them in fear.

If man is not by nature social and political, then all civil societies must have grown out of presocial and prepolitical states of nature, that is, the state of nature must have existed among the progenitors of all men now living in civil society. Hobbes did not believe that there ever was such a state all over the world, but, he said, in many places of America "at this day," during civil wars, and between independent sovereigns such a state actually exists. The historical question, however, is not very important for Hobbes. The state of nature is deduced from the passions of man; it is meant to reveal and clarify what it is about man's natural inclinations that we must know in order to form the right kind of political order. It serves primarily to determine the reasons, the purposes, or the ends for the sake of which men form political societies. These ends being known, the political problem becomes one of how to organize man and society in order to realize the ends most effectively.

What would the condition of mankind be if there were no civil society? How would men be related to each other? First of all, Hobbes argues, men are much more equal in faculties of both body and mind than has hitherto been recognized. The most important equality is the equal ability all men have to kill each other. This is the most important because the most important concern of men is their own self-preservation. Self-preservation, in turn, is most important because fear, the fear of violent death, is the most powerful passion. Equality of ability leads to equality of hopes and to competition among men, among all who desire the same things. This natural enmity is intensified by the diffidence, or distrust, men without government have for each other as they anticipate how each would like to deprive all others of whatever goods (including life) they have, so that each is led to think of subjugating all the rest until there is no power left capable of threatening his security. Contrary to what is said "in the Books of the old Moral Philosophers," Hobbes says, happiness, or felicity, consists in a continual progress of the desire from one object to another. Since this is so, what men seek constantly is some means of securing the way to their future desires. Men seek not only to procure, but also to be ensured of a contented life for themselves "So that," Hobbes says, "in the first place, I put for a general inclination of all mankind, a perpetual and restless desire of power after power, that ceaseth only in death."[7]

The problem of civil life is further complicated by the presence in our nature of the love of glory, or pride, or vanity. All pleasures which are not bodily, or sensual, pleasures Hobbes calls pleasures of the mind. All pleasures of the mind are directly or indirectly derived from "glorying." Glorying is based upon the good opinions a man receives or has of himself or of his power. The opinions are always based upon comparisons with others. Every man desires to have others value him as he values himself, and consequently, upon signs of contempt and undervaluing, he becomes quite ready to destroy those who slight him. Even when men gather for pleasure and recreation they seek it mostly through those things which stir laughter. And laughter, Hobbes says, is caused by sudden glory, being pleased by some sudden act of one's own, "or by the apprehension of some deformed thing in another, by comparison whereof they suddenly applaud themselves." This bleak picture is not relieved by any reference to a sense of honor or nobility. Honor and dishonor, properly understood, according to Hobbes, have nothing to do with justice or injustice. Honor is nothing else than an acknowledgement or opinion of someone's power, that is, superiority, especially one's power to help or harm ourselves. Even reverence is defined by Hobbes as the conception we have of another being who, having the power to do good or hurt to ourselves, does not have the will to do us hurt. The emphasis is not upon admiration or love, but fear.

These three great natural causes of quarrels among men—competition, distrust, and glory—make the state of nature really a state of war, "and such a war, as is of every man, against every man." In such a state,

> men live without other security, than what their own strength, and their own invention shall furnish them withal. In such

> condition there is no place for industry; because the fruit thereof is uncertain: and consequently no culture of the earth, no navigation, nor use of the commodities that may be imported by sea; no commodious building; no instruments of moving and removing such things as require much force; no knowledge of the face of the earth; no account of time; no arts; no letters; no society; and which is worst of all, continual fear, and danger of violent death; and the life of man solitary, poor, nasty, brutish, and short.[8]

Furthermore, there is no appeal to justice in the state of nature; nothing there can be unjust, for justice and injustice are such only in terms of some preceding law and there is no law outside of civil society. In short, man is not by nature social; on the contrary, nature dissociates man. The state of civil society, then, is radically conventional. This does not mean that there are not present in men certain natural impulses or forces that drive them toward civil life. It does mean that the antisocial forces are as natural as, and, when unmitigated by convention, even more powerful than, the forces promoting civil life. Instead of serving as direct guide to human goodness, nature indicates what man has to run away from. The only redeeming thing about the state of nature is the possibility of getting out of it. With Hobbes we are already in an atmosphere congenial to the idea of the conquest of nature.

Fear of death, desire for comfort, and hope of obtaining it through their industry incline men to peace. Reason, working along with these passions of fear, desire, and hope, suggests rules for peaceful living together. By comparing these passions with the three great natural causes of human enmity, we see that fear of death and desire for comfort are present both among the inclinations toward peace and among the causes of enmity; vanity, or the desire for glory, is absent from the former group.[9] The task of reason then is to devise means of redirecting and intensifying the fear of death and the desire for comfort, so as to overpower and cancel out the destructive effects of the desire for glory, or pride. By understanding human nature mechanistically, we become capable of manipulating and finally, Hobbes seems to hope, conquering it. Hobbes calls these rules of reason Laws of Nature, the Moral Law, and sometimes the dictates of reason. In using these names he admits he is bowing to traditional usage; for him the rules are merely conclusions or theorems concerning what conduces to self-preservation. Properly speaking, only commands of the civil sovereign are laws. These rules, however, in so far as they are commanded by God in the Scriptures, may be called laws.

All the laws of nature and all social and political duties or obligations are derived from and subordinate to the right of nature, the individual's right to self-preservation. To the extent that modern liberalism teaches that all social and political obligations are derived from and are in service of the individual rights of man, Hobbes may be regarded as the founder of modern liberalism. Social, moral, and political rules and institutions in the service of individual rights can be expected to be much more effective than the utopian schemes of Plato and Aristotle. For the individual rights themselves are derived from the most powerful selfish passions and desires of men, the desire for comfortable living and, most powerful of all, because it is the fear of what is worst of all, the fear of violent death, the passion underlying the right to self-preservation. Because the rights are backed up by the passions, they can be, in a sense, self-enforcing. As the foundations of the traditional doctrines of moral restraint and contempt for selfishness become discredited, the way is opened for a new legitimation or sanctification of human selfishness.

The right of nature is the blameless liberty to do or refrain from doing whatever one can to preserve one's life.[10] The right to an end also implies a right to the means to that end. Because men differ in intelligence and prudence, some understand the requirements of preservation better than others.

Yet these intellectual differences are not decisive for Hobbes. Regardless of his intelligence, no man, Hobbes argues, is sufficiently interested in the preservation of others; hence in the state of nature, each man must be the sole judge of the means necessary to his own preservation. Therefore, each man has a natural right to whatever means he judges conduce to his preservation. In the universal enmity of the state of nature, anything not under a man's own power can be regarded as a danger to his preservation, and therefore there is nothing which cannot be regarded as a means to his preservation. Hence, in this state "every man has a right to everything." No man is secure in such a state. The laws of nature, as distinguished from the rights of nature, are precepts of reason which instruct men as to what they ought to do to avoid the perils to their own self-preservation that follow equally from their natural rights and from their irrational desires.

For the securing of their own self-preservation, the first and fundamental law of nature enjoins men to seek peace and to defend themselves against those from whom peace cannot be obtained. All the rest of the moral law, the laws of nature, is directed toward establishing the conditions of peace. The first law of nature derived from the fundamental law is that each man ought to be willing to divest himself of his right to all things when others are also willing, and ought to be satisfied with just as much liberty against other men as he allows other men against himself. This mutual laying down of rights is accomplished by what has come to be known as the social contract. Civil society is constituted by the social contract, wherein each one of a multitude of men obliges himself, by contract with each of the rest, not to resist the commands of that man or council that they have recognized as their sovereign. Each man contracts only with a view to what is good for himself, and above all with a view to the security and preservation of his life. Therefore it cannot be presumed that any man has contracted away those rights whose loss would defeat the purpose of all contracts. No one, for instance, can be regarded as having laid down his right to resist anyone who attempts to deprive him of his life.

When a man has by contract or covenant given away or renounced any right, he is obliged or bound not to hinder those to whom he granted or abandoned that right from enjoying the benefit of it. In other words, according to the next law of nature, men should perform their covenants. If this principle did not hold, society itself would dissolve. This principle, fidelity to contracts, according to Hobbes, is the basis of all justice and injustice; for where no covenant has preceded, no rights have been relinquished or transferred, and each man has a right to everything. Thus injustice, or injury, is nothing other than the nonperformance of covenants, exercising a right that one has already legally relinquished. All genuine legislation then becomes a form of self-legislation, and injury is like a self-contradiction, willing to do that which one has already willed not to do.[11] All duties and obligations to others derive from covenants. But covenants, contracts where one or both of the parties promise to perform in the future, depend upon trust. There is no trust and no valid covenant where there is a reasonable fear of nonperformance on either side. There is then no trust in the state of nature. Therefore, before it is correct to use the terms just or unjust, there must be some coercive power, the sovereign, which can compel all contractors equally to perform their covenants. The sovereign must see to it that the terror of punishment is a greater force than the lure of any benefit which could be expected from a breach of covenant. No moral force is appealed to in order to establish conditions of trust; once again fear is the passion to be relied upon. According to Hobbes, intelligent calculation of self-interest is all that is required to make a man just. The fact that he acts under compulsion does not make him less just, for self-interest is the only basis of morality. One consequence of this kind of reasoning is a broadening of the traditional notion of a just war. For Hobbes, as for Bacon, the intention to rectify a previous injury is not necessary to justify war; the subjective criterion, fear of a neighboring nation's strength, is sufficient.

Hobbes addressed himself directly to Aristotle's idea of distributive justice. The doctrine that some men by nature are more worthy to command and others more worthy to serve is the foundation of Aristotle's political science, Hobbes wrote. The doctrine is false because in the state of nature all men are equal, the inequality found now among men has been introduced by the civil laws. Furthermore, the doctrine is dangerous because it contributes to pride. Distributive justice properly conceived is the justice of an arbitrator and consists not in distributing to each in proportion to his virtues and vices, but in treating all as equal. For, Hobbes said, if nature made men equal, that equality ought to be acknowledged. Even if nature made them unequal, men will always consider themselves equal and thus will enter into conditions of peace only on equal terms. Therefore, for the sake of peace, such equality ought to be admitted, even if it does not exist. Hence it is a law of nature that all men should acknowledge each other as equal by nature. The natural differences between men are then either nonexistent or politically irrelevant. One purpose dominates Hobbes's discussion of the laws of nature: to make men sociable and peaceable, and accordingly to end or reduce to a minimum the friction, resentment, and hostility generated among men by pride, partiality, and excessive self-love in general. Among the laws of nature are rules for the arbitration of controversies and for the impartial distribution of disputed property. Ingratitude is forbidden. Expressions of hatred, contempt, or disesteem, even by judges for convicted criminals, are not to be allowed. Lest one think that not all men are able to comprehend all these laws of nature, Hobbes asserts that they can all be comprehended, even by those who are too neglectful or too busy to learn them, through the rule: Do not do unto others what you would not have them do unto you.[12] The moral law is not directed toward the perfection of our natures. Aristotle was wrong about virtue and vice. Because his opinions were merely the opinions received during his own times and still received by most unlearned men, Hobbes said, they were not likely to be very accurate.[13] Virtue, if it means anything more than a man's power, is the habit of doing what tends to our own self-preservation, and to its fundamental condition, peace; vice is the contrary.

The essential defect of the laws of nature, the dictates of reason, is that they bind men in their consciences only, and the actions and wills of men are determined not by conscience or reason but by fear of punishment and hope of reward. There is fear of invisible powers, God or gods, in the state of nature, but this fear is not powerful enough.[14] What is needed, according to Hobbes, is the establishment of conditions that really make it safe to obey the laws of nature, otherwise one who obeys such rules only puts himself at the mercy of those who do not obey. In short, civil or political government, visible powers, are required. Security requires first of all the cooperation of many men, a multitude large and powerful enough both to make the breaking of covenants and invasion of each other's rights very dangerous, and to provide defense against foreign enemies. There is no set limit to the size of a civil society. The size should be great enough to deter any enemy from risking war, and therefore depends upon the size of the enemy. These requirements and the antisocial elements in man's nature indicate that the unity achieved through consent, many wills agreeing in one object, one common good, is not sufficient to bind men together. Political society, or the commonwealth, requires a real unity, or union.

This union, like justice and injustice, is defined by Hobbes in legal terms. The commonwealth must be constituted as one legal person by a great multitude of men, each of whom covenants with all the others to regard the will of this legal, civil, or artificial person as his own will. This legal person, the sovereign, "is" the commonwealth. In practical terms this means that every subject should regard all the actions of the sovereign power as actions of his own, all legislation by the sovereign as his own self-legislation. In fact, the sovereign power, the power of representing and commanding the wills of all, can be vested in one man or in a council. Hobbes was the first to define the commonwealth as a "person." He found this necessary for the following reasons. Since the only legitimate obligation is ultimately self-obligation, the freedom of man in the state of nature must survive, in some form, in his subjection to the government; "there being no obligation on any man, which ariseth not from some act of his own; for all men equally, are by nature free."[15] This is accomplished through the legal fictions that the sovereign is a "person" with a will that can represent the wills of all his subjects, and that the sovereign's legislation is self-legislation of the subject. Through such a union the powers and faculties of every subject can be brought to contribute fully to the maintenance of peace and the common defense.

The social contract has two parts: (1) a covenant of each member of the future civil body with each of the others to acknowledge as sovereign whatever man or assembly of men a majority of their number agrees upon; (2) the vote determining who or what is to be the sovereign. All those who are not parties to the contract remain in the state of war and are, therefore, enemies of the rest.

The validity of the covenant is in no way affected by whether it was entered into under duress, fear of death and violence, or not. The body politic, Hobbes says, can be founded "naturally" as well as through institution. All paternal and despotic government arises in the first way, through fear of the sovereign himself, for example, when he is a conqueror in war; all government by institution arises through mutual fear of the individuals. Fear is the motive in both cases. Both foundations are equally legitimate: there is no difference, as far as right is concerned, between foundation by conquest and foundation by institution. In the acquisition of sovereignty by conquest, it makes no difference whether the war was a just war or not. Since no one can really transfer his strength and faculties to another, the social contract in fact obliges all not to resist the will of the sovereign power. That all citizens have not explicitly entered into such a covenant is obvious; but anyone who lives in a commonwealth accepting the protection of the government, the sovereign, is to be regarded as having tacitly entered into the covenant. Apparently, for Hobbes, that exactness in political life which corresponds to mathematical exactness in theoretical matters is legal exactness. And just as controversies are put to rest in mathematics, so evidently he hoped that the political controversies that had always disturbed the peace of the political world could be put to rest by an exact deduction, from the social contract, of the rights and duties of sovereign and subject.

The social contract is binding only when the end for the sake of which it is entered into, security, is realized. Obedience is exchanged for protection. Not that men can ever be made completely safe from injury by others. It is sufficient for each citizen to know that anyone who intends to injure him has more to fear from punishment by the sovereign than he has to gain from his crime.

The first right of the sovereign is the right to punish or the right to wield the police power. This follows from the fundamental renunciation of the right of resistance agreed to by all the citizens. No subject can be freed from his subjection by claiming that the sovereign has committed a breach of covenant, for the sovereign has made no covenant with any subject, the subjects have covenanted only among themselves. Since the sovereign has not covenanted with anyone, he alone retains the right to all things that all men had in the state of nature. Consequently he can neither injure anyone nor commit injustice, since injustice, or injury, in the strict or legal sense is nothing but nonfulfillment of covenant, assuming a right which one has already covenanted away. Furthermore, since the sovereign represents the will of each of the subjects, anyone accusing the sovereign of injury is accusing himself, and to do injustice to oneself is impossible. Hence the sovereign cannot justly be punished in any way by his subjects. The right to make war and peace, which includes the right to levy taxes and to compel citizens to take up arms for their country's defense, is also annexed to the sovereign, for these rights must be in the hands of the same power that can punish those who will not obey.

The legislative power must also in the sovereign's hands for the same reason: men will not obey the commands of those they have no reason to fear. The power of the sword, the punitive power, and the legislative power must be in the same hands. The civil laws of each commonwealth are nothing else than the commands of the civil sovereign. They prescribe what goods a man may enjoy, that is, they define what is and what is not private property. They determine what actions a man may do without being molested by his fellows, that is, they prescribe what is good, evil, just, unjust, honest, and dishonest. They contribute to peace by attempting to determine all controversial questions before controversy arises.

The judicial power, for the same reason as the legislative power, is also committed to the sovereign. Because the sovereign must be able to determine the means of discharging his functions, the executive power, and the power of appointing all counselors, ministers, magistrates, and officers, also is invested in him, Furthermore, because all voluntary actions of men depend upon their wills and their wills upon their opinions of the good and evil, or reward and punishment, they will receive from acting or omitting to act, the sovereign is to be judge of all doctrines and opinions which may be delivered to the citizens. The criterion of censorship is what doctrines are conducive, and what repugnant, to peace. This power of absolute censorship applies to religious opinions as well. As a matter of fact religion is defined with a view to this power by Hobbes. Both religion and superstition are defined as "fear of power invisible." The difference between them is that the former is allowed by the public authority, the latter not allowed. The opinions which, according to Hobbes, have most disturbed the peace of the Christian world, are the opinions that lead citizens to believe that they owe obedience to others besides those to whom the supreme civil authority is committed. We shall take up this subject again in our discussion of Hobbes's teaching regarding Christianity.

It is clear from this list of powers that the power of the sovereign is absolute, that is, no greater power can be conveyed by men to any man. The sovereign is not bound to obey the civil laws, for they are only his commands and he can release himself from them at his pleasure. No one can claim any property rights against him because all property is derived from the laws, that is, his will. Opposing the sovereign's will in any particular case would be opposing the ground of all property and, hence, self-defeating. When citizens are allowed to sue the supreme authority, the question cannot be whether the sovereign or his ministers had a right to do what was done, but rather what it was that the sovereign in fact willed in this matter. That absolute power is really implicit in all governments can be seen through the cases of generals who are granted absolute powers temporarily in wartimes. Only the possessor of absolute power can grant absolute power, even temporarily. And when, for example, a constitutional assembly prescribes limits to the powers of a government, the exercise of the power of limitation is itself an exercise of absolute power. The objection that such an absolute power has never been acknowledged by citizens anywhere is, as arguments from practice generally are, invalid, for practice may be faulty practice. The art of making and maintaining commonwealths consists in following certain definite rules like the rules of arithmetic and geometry. Hobbes believed himself to be the first discoverer of those rules.

There are certain rights of the subject that are unalienable, that is, that cannot be transferred or resigned by covenant. For there is no obligation of man which does not proceed from some act of his own, and every act of his own is presumed to aim at some good to himself; therefore no contract, including the social contract, should be so construed as to deprive a man of the condition of all good for himself, his life, and the means of securing it. Every man may justly disobey any command to kill or wound himself or to abstain from anything that he requires to live. The right to self-preservation remains inviolable. But are not soldiers required to sacrifice their lives in war? And is not the fear of violent death in a sense the basis of all legitimacy, and therefore a sufficient motive to justify civil obedience? Hobbes faced this problem and concluded that to run away from battle out of fear is dishonorable and cowardly but not unjust. It is the sovereign's task to see that the fear of desertion outweighs the fear of battle. To refuse the sovereign's command to fight against an enemy is not unjust if a man finds a suitable substitute. For a condemned man to resist an executioner lawfully doing his duty is just. No man in a criminal trial is bound to testify against himself, for no covenant, including the fundamental covenant, can oblige a man to harm himself. No man is obliged, for example, to execute his own parent, or a benefactor, or to do any act that is so shameful that it would result in his being so miserable and despised that he would grow weary of his own life.[16]

It is clear that these inviolable liberties of the citizens could be extended and construed as providing standards for distinguishing good from bad sovereigns, that is, as providing citizens with standards by which they could legitimately criticize, judge, and thereby weaken the sovereign authority. If given institutional form they could lead to limited sovereignty. Hobbes tried his best to guard against the revolutionary principle inherent in all attempts to set forth the principles of government: he who sets forth principles justifying authority by that very act provides standards for justifying the alteration or abolishment of that authority when it departs from those principles. Despite these exceptions to the obligation of obedience to the sovereign, the sovereign's absolute right remains: he may rightfully punish with death any refusal or resistance, however just. If the sovereign exercises his right contrary to right reason, however, he, like every man in the state of nature, sins against the laws of nature and therefore is answerable to their author, God, for his iniquity. Furthermore, Hobbes admits, there is a certain natural punishment for negligent government, that is, rebellion.

In all matters where the laws are silent, the subject retains the right to do or forbear as he wishes. And sometimes a sovereign may prudently forbear to exercise his right, though that in no way diminishes the right. There is no valid reason for sovereigns to desire to oppress their subjects, for the strength of sovereigns is directly dependent upon the strength and well-being of their subjects. Certainly, Hobbes admitted, such absolute power can be abused, but there is no condition of human life without inconveniences. "The obligation of subjects to the sovereign, is understood to last as long, and no longer, than the power lasteth, by which he is able to protect them."[17] And there is no avoiding the fact that he that has the power to protect all also has the power to oppress all. Following the book of Job, Hobbes compared the sovereign to Leviathan, whom God called "King of the Proud." Only the greatest of earthly powers can govern the pride of man. Hobbes's *Leviathan* is also such a Leviathan in so far as it rules the minds of men and crushes and roots out the seeds of human pride.

There are three kinds of commonwealths, differing as the respective sovereign powers differ. When that power is committed to one man, the government is a monarchy; when committed to an assembly of men where every citizen has a right to vote, it is a democracy; when committed to an assembly where only a part of the citizens have a right to vote, it is an aristocracy. The ancient Greek and Roman writers also distinguished between good and bad governments. They called bad rule by one man tyranny, bad rule by the people, or many, anarchy, and bad rule of the few oligarchy. Good and bad governments were distinguished according to whether the rulers ruled primarily for the sake of the common good or common advantage, or for their own selfish advantages. These moral distinctions, according to Hobbes, are unsound. They indicate only the subjective like or dislike of those who use them. Those who dislike monarchy call it tyranny, likewise anarchy is a name for democracy disliked, oligarchy a name for aristocracy disliked. This rejection of what Hobbes calls Aristotle's distinction between governments which rule for the benefit of the subjects and those which rule for the benefit of the rulers makes the distinction between a tyrant and a legitimate monarch politically meaningless. Both subjects and rulers, Hobbes argues, share equally in the first and greatest benefits of all government, peace and defense. All suffer equally from the greatest misery, civil war and anarchy. Since the ruler's strength and power always depend upon the strength and power of his subjects, both suffer the same disadvantages if the ruler weakens the subjects by depriving them of money and goods.

A deeper ground, perhaps, for the rejection of the distinction was Hobbes's conviction that no ruler or bearer of the sovereignty could be expected not to pursue his private advantage, the advantages of family and friends, as much as and even more than the public advantage. On the basis of Hobbes's reduction of good and evil to pleasure and pain and his doctrine of sovereignty, the age-old political controversies about what form of government is best become much less important. These controversies were necessarily connected with the question about what over-all purposes civil society should serve, for example, liberty, empire, or wealth. Contrary to the misleading doctrines of Aristotle and Cicero and other Greek and Roman writers, who were, according to Hobbes, prejudiced in favor of popular government, the power of the government and the liberty of the citizen in each form of government is the same. The sovereignty is absolute in every commonwealth. The goal, or purpose, of each form of government is the same, peace and security. The decisive political, or practical, questions tend to become technical or administrative questions, such as under what kind of administration of the sovereign powers peace and security are most conveniently produced.[18]

Since those who bear the sovereign authority, being men, will always be most concerned with their private interests, the public interest will be most advanced where it is more closely united with private interests. This occurs under monarchy, which is therefore the best form of government. In democracy, where each man bears some part of the sovereignty, the number of those capable of enriching and serving themselves at the expense of the public interest is at a maximum. In a monarchy there can be only one Nero, in a democracy there can be as many Neros as there are orators flattering the populace. A monarch may promote unworthy persons but often will not. In a democracy the promotion of unworthy persons cannot be avoided. For within democracy there is always keen competition between popular orators, or demagogues, and the power of each demagogue is dependent upon his power to control and dispense patronage. Those who did not endeavor to benefit and attach as many people as possible, worthy and unworthy, to their side, or faction, would soon be overwhelmed by those who did. From this it is easy to understand the chief defect of democracy, the tendency to breed factions and civil wars. An aristocracy in this regard stands somewhere between the other two forms. It becomes better the more it approaches monarchy, worse the more it approaches democracy. As far as the actual exercise of the sovereign powers is concerned, one can doubt whether democracy is really ever anything different from an aristocracy of orators or a temporary monarchy of one orator. Those who complain of a lack of liberty under monarchy do not understand what they really want. For the liberties of a subject, as defined by the doctrine of sovereignty, are the same under all governments, but under a democracy the accusers of monarchy would be rulers as well as subjects. It is not liberty but dominion or power and its attendant honor that they want. The true cause of their disaffection is that monarchy deprives them of the opportunity to show off their wisdom, knowledge, and eloquence in deliberating, or seeming to deliberate, about matters of the greatest importance. The love of liberty, according to Hobbes, turns out to be only a mask for the desire for praise, for vanity.[19] Despite these criticisms and others, like irresolution from divided counsels, the difficulty of proceeding secretly, and so on, democracy has a certain privileged position within the framework based upon the idea of the state of nature and the doctrine of sovereignty. This may be seen as follows.

The institution of monarchy or aristocracy requires a previous official nomination or designation of certain particular persons as sovereign. Democracy, however, can be instituted directly by the separated individuals themselves. Hence the original or first form of all instituted government is democracy. Since all men in the state of nature are equal in rights, and all legitimate obligation is ultimately self-obligation, the first part of the social contract, in order to be binding, must be an agreement of each man with every other man to accept as sovereign that person or persons designated by a majority of all of them. This first agreement of every man with every other man constitutes the multitude of a democratic people; the act nominating the sovereign, each man having one equal vote, is a democratic act. One could say that only a democratic procedure is consistent with the equality of men in the state of nature. In accordance with a principle often enunciated by Hobbes, that whoever has the power to dispose of the sovereignty is the true sovereign, one could say that the people, as a democratic people, are the ultimate sovereign of every instituted commonwealth. Hobbes guarded against this conclusion by addressing himself to a more fundamental argument, namely, as all contracts depend upon the consent of the contractors, they may be dissolved by the same consent. Hence the people by withdrawing their consent may dissolve the government. First of all, Hobbes answers, the original contract obliges each man to all of the others, not to a majority, even an overwhelming majority. So long as one man dissents to the dissolution of the contract, no others have a right to dissolve. It cannot be imagined, Hobbes said, that all the people with no exception would combine against the supreme power. But there is a distinct obligation to the sovereign himself, for every man by agreeing to acknowledge the sovereign's acts as his own has transferred his natural right to use his powers as he sees fit to the sovereign. He cannot take away what now belongs to the supreme power without committing injustice against the sovereign.[20]

The traditional arguments for the mixed regime, or limited government, are rejected by Hobbes as being based upon an insufficient understanding of what a true union is. Where, for example, the sovereignty is supposedly divided between a monarchical executive, an aristocratic judiciary, and a popular body with power of the purse, the liberty of the subject is as much restricted as it can be under any government, so long as the three branches are in agreement. The advantage of such a division of powers would then be seen to exist in the disagreement or mutual checking of the three powers; but that disagreement, according to Hobbes, constitutes civil war and the dissolution of the government. He acknowledged that many governments have lasted a long time thinking wrongly that they were governments of this kind. But in the limited monarchies and temporary dictatorships known to history, the true sovereigns were not the monarchs but the assemblies that limited the monarchs. A genuine body politic, he argues, is constituted not by agreement, or concord, but by union, the uniting of the wills (and thereby the strength and power) of all in the will of one legal person, the sovereign.

A true monarchy, according to Hobbes, is a hereditary monarchy, for the true sovereign of an elective monarchy is the electing body. The chief difficulty for monarchies is the problem of succession, especially the problem of who is to appoint the royal successor. The present possessor of the sovereignty is to determine his successor. Hobbes works out detailed rules about what is to be understood as the will of the monarch in any case where he has not expressly indicated who shall inherit his power. He proceeds, speaking generally, from the presumption that the nearest in kindship is the nearest in affection and thereby should be understood as successor.

Hobbes defines law in terms of will, not reason. Counsel, on the other hand, bases itself on reasons, reasons deduced from the benefit to be gained by the one counseled. Counsel aims, or pretends to aim, at the good of another. But law is command, not counsel, and a command is expected to be obeyed only because it expresses the will of the one commanding. Since the object of every man's will is some good to himself, every command aims at the good of the one commanding. Law is a command addressed to one who has been obliged formerly to obey, a command from one who has already acquired a right to be obeyed. Civil law is such a command issued by the commonwealth, the sovereign. More fully, civil laws are those rules, commanded by the commonwealth to every subject through some sufficient sign of its will, which are to be used by the subjects for distinguishing right from wrong. Hobbes's political teachings, the laws of nature themselves, are merely counsel until commanded by some civil sovereign.

Custom in itself has no power to create law. Customary law derives its authority from the tacit consent of the present sovereign. The common law and the law of equity were said to be guided by the standard of right reason, a standard which, because it is considered to be independent and above all political authority, could be and was used to check and question the unreasonable actions of all civil authorities. Hobbes reinterprets the traditional understanding of the common law in such a way as to make appeals to any authority higher than the civil sovereign impossible. He agrees with the lawyers that the law can never be against reason. But whose reason, he asks? Not the reason of scholars, or wise men, or subordinate judges, but the reason of that artificial person, the commonwealth, he answers. In his discussion of the common law, Hobbes does not distinguish the reason of the commonwealth from its will. In every just decision, the judge refers to the reason which moves the reigning sovereign to make or consent to the law governing the case under consideration; the judge does not recur to the reasons that influenced the sovereign under whom the law in question was first promulgated. Hobbes's approach would seem to lead to the idea of the absolute supremacy of current statute law. The canon of the church, or ecclesiastical law, also is law only in so far as it is constituted by the civil sovereign. All laws, of course, require interpreters, that is, judges, to apply the laws to particular cases. The sovereign is the supreme interpreter of the law and constitutes all subordinate interpreters, or judges, as such.[21]

Nothing which mortals make, says Hobbes, can be immortal. Yet with the help of a very able architect, commonwealths can be so constructed as to prevent their perishing from internal disorders. Hobbes describes those forces in the nature of man which have always tended toward the dissolution of peace and civil order. Yet those forces are not to be counteracted by way of moral reform, by appeals to what had been regarded as the nobler part of man's nature. Hobbes appeals instead to enlightened self-interest and, on the basis of knowledge and manipulation of the mechanism of the passions, relies on the devising of the right kinds of institutions. There was no need for him, as there was for Aristotle, to distinguish the kinds and levels of peoples in order to determine what kind of government is suitable for each. He aimed at devising a scheme of government which was to be right for all times, peoples, and places. By building his edifice upon the lowest common denominator of human motivation, he could expect it to stand firm anywhere and everywhere. For when commonwealths "come to be dissolved, not by external violence, but intestine disorders, the fault is not in men, as they are the Matter; but as they are the Makers, and orderers of them."[22]

One great mistake is often made at the very beginning of a commonwealth when men, in order to gain a kingdom, are content with less power than is necessary for maintaining peace and defense. Then, when the public safety requires the exercise of those renounced powers, their resumption appears as an act of injustice. This, in turn, disposes large numbers of men to rebellion and connivance with foreign powers, which always welcome an opportunity to weaken their neighbors. Thus William the Conqueror's pledge not to infringe the liberty of the Church led to Thomas Beckett's defection and his enlisting the support of the pope against Henry II. And because neither the senate nor the people of Rome claimed the whole power, the seditions of the Gracchi developed, then the wars between senate and people under Marius and Sulla and Caesar and Pompey, and finally popular government itself in Rome was destroyed and the monarchy was instituted. Thus it is a breach of his duty for the sovereign to lay aside any of his rights.

Furthermore, it is a breach of his duty to allow the people to be misinformed or ignorant of the grounds of his rights. The first task in this regard is to purge the commonwealth of "the poisons of seditious doctrines." The first group of seditious doctrines proceeds mainly from the words of unlearned divines, who, misconstruing Scripture, induce men to think that sanctity and natural reason cannot stand together. They teach that every private man is the judge of good and evil actions. This is true in the state of nature, but in civil society the civil law and the sovereign are the measure and the judge of good and evil.

A second doctrine repugnant to civil society states that whatever a man does against his conscience, including those things he is commanded to do by his sovereign, is sin. If the commanded act is sinful, it is the sovereign's sin and he is answerable to God for it. It is not the subject's sin. On the contrary, disobedience to the sovereign is sin. For by disobeying, the subject arrogates to himself the knowledge and judgment of good and evil, conscience and judgment being really one and the same thing. Third in order is the doctrine that faith and sanctity are not to be attained by study and reason but by supernatural inspiration or "infusion." If this doctrine is granted, Hobbes said, he cannot see why every Christian is not a prophet, obliged to take his own inspiration rather than the law of his country for the rule of his action. This doctrine, too, leads men to set themselves up as judges of good and evil. Then there is that group of "eloquent sophistries" penned by Aristotle, Plato, Cicero, Seneca, Plutarch, and the rest of those maintainers of the Greek and Roman anarchies, the "sophistries" taken over by the lawyers to serve their own interests, such as the doctrine that sovereigns are subject to their own laws; that the supreme authority may be divided; that private men have absolute rights over property which exclude interference from the sovereign; and, finally, the doctrine, also held by many divines, that tyrannicide is lawful and even laudable. This last amounts to saying, according to Hobbes, that it is lawful for men to rebel against and to murder their kings so long as they call them tyrants first. Finally, there is that doctrine rooted in the fear of darkness and ghosts, and drawn out of the "darkness of school distinctions," the doctrine of the division of civil, or temporal, power from spiritual, or ghostly, power. That the distinction has no significance and that no man can serve two masters Hobbes attempts to prove by Holy Scripture in his theological discussion.[23]

Rooting out seditious and false opinions is not enough. It is the duty of the sovereign to have the true grounds of his rights taught to the people. This meant, first of all, adopting Hobbes's books as the authoritative texts on morals and politics in the universities. Apparently Hobbes regarded his as a long-range educational project, for, he said, he was not very interested in whether his books would be adopted "at this day." Nevertheless he looked forward to his books being officially recommended by some sovereign for teaching in the universities, "the fountains of civil and moral doctrine." One should begin, he said, with young minds uncorrupted by the doctrines of Athens and Rome. Those who are properly educated, after they leave the universities as preachers, gentry, men of affairs, and lawyers, in the conduct of their everyday affairs will transmit the true grounds of civil right to the people. The difficulties in the way of teaching the people are usually overestimated, Hobbes thought. For, first of all, it is not too hard to learn what appeals to one's own selfish interests and secondly, in a judgment reminiscent of Machiavelli's estimation of the people, Hobbes remarks that the people lack the pride and ambition that obstructs the minds of the rich, the powerful, and those with a reputation for learning. In spite of his exaltation of sovereignty and monarchy, Hobbes evidently expected that some day his doctrines would be popular.[24]

There is not much said in a positive way about the good society which Hobbes looked forward to, once the conditions of peace are established. The emphasis in Hobbes is upon the extreme situations like civil war, where all law and order break down, upon the dangers to peace resulting from attempts to question and restrict the sovereign authority, upon negative standards rather than positive standards. Yet evidently he looked forward to a much milder regime than his total arming of the sovereign power would suggest. In the first place he looked forward to a nonimperialist society. This, however, is inconsistent with his doctrine that independent sovereigns and nations are necessarily in a state of nature with respect to each other and, hence, naturally obliged to do all they can to subdue or weaken their neighbors. The policies are inconsistent so long as there is no world state. However this may be, he also looked forward to a state with laws encouraging husbandry and fishing, laws against idleness and inordinate expense and consumption, and laws to encourage and honor industry, navigation, mechanics, and the mathematical sciences. Public burdens are to be distributed equally. Men are to be taxed according to what they spend or consume: frugality is to be rewarded, luxurious waste discouraged, and each man is to pay the commonwealth in proportion to the benefit he derives from its protection. There is to be equality before the law, strict penalties against corrupt judges, and easy access to courts of appeal. The safety of the people is to be the supreme law, and safety is to be understood as including all the contentments and delights of life a man can earn lawfully without hurting the commonwealth.[25]

The peace of civil society depends upon the sovereign's having the power of life and death over his subjects. If men believe that there are other powers capable of granting greater rewards than life and inflicting greater punishments than death, they will obey such powers and the authority of the sovereign will be destroyed. Eternal life and eternal torment or "eternal death" are greater goods and evils than natural life and natural death. Because, or so long as, men believe in the power of other men, acting as ministers of powers invisible, to grant them eternal bliss or eternal torment, theology, according to Hobbes, cannot be separated from political philosophy.[26] We must confine ourselves to a rough sketch of Hobbes's Christian theology, omitting the numerous passages from Holy Scripture that he cites as authorities.

Although from the Creation God has ruled over all men through the power of nature, the kingdom of God, in most places of Scripture, contrary to the interpretation of most divines, signifies a political kingdom with definite subjects, the Jews. Adam and all those living up to the Flood and Noah and his family after the Flood were commanded by God directly through His voice. The first in the kingdom of God by covenant was Abraham with whom God made a contract, offering Abraham the land of Canaan as an everlasting possession in return for his obedience and the obedience of his posterity. Thus God was instituted as the civil sovereign of the Jews. God needed to speak only to Abraham, the father, lord, and civil sovereign of his family, for the wills of all his family and seed were involved in his will. As the family and seed of Abraham received the positive commands of God from their earthly sovereign, Abraham, so in every commonwealth those with no supernatural revelation to the contrary ought to obey the laws of their own sovereign in all the external acts and professions of religion. Every sovereign, as did Abraham, has the right to punish anyone who pretends to a private revelation in order to oppose the laws. As was Abraham in his family, so only the sovereign in a Christian commonwealth can be the authoritative interpreter of the Word of God. God's contract was renewed with Isaac and Jacob, but was suspended while the Jews were under the sovereignty of Egypt.

The contract was renewed again by Moses at Mount Sinai. Since Moses could not inherit Abraham's authority, his authority was grounded in the consent of the people and their promise to obey him. Again, only Moses, as civil sovereign under God, was called up to God, not Aaron, the chief priest, nor any other priest, nor the aristocracy of seventy elders, nor the people. By Moses' throwing over the calf made by Aaron, and by Moses' control of those who prophesied in the camp, it was shown that all priests and prophets in a Christian commonwealth derive their authority from the approval and authority of the sovereign. The kingdom was a sacerdotal kingdom: Moses ruled as God's high priest and viceregent on earth. The kingdom was inherited by Aaron and then by his son Eleazar. After the deaths of Joshua and Eleazar it was said that there was no king in Israel. This was true only as far as the exercise of the sovereign power was concerned. The right to govern, the sovereign power, was still lodged in the high priest. The powers of the judges were extraordinary or temporary emergency powers. By deposing Samuel, the high priest, the people deposed the peculiar kingdom of

God and instituted a monarchy of the usual type. Solomon's treatment of Abiathar, his dedication of the temple, and the whole of biblical history show that from the first institution of the kingdom of God until the captivity, the supreme religious authority was in the same hands as the civil sovereignty. And after the election of Saul, the priest's office was ministerial with respect to the sovereign, not magisterial. During their captivity the Jews had no commonwealth, and after their return everything was so confused and corrupted that nothing of value for state or religion can be learned from those times.

The "office of our Blessed Savior," the Messiah, wrote Hobbes, is threefold: Redeemer, Teacher, and King. Christ on earth was Redeemer and Teacher, not King. He never did anything to call into question the civil laws of the Jews or Caesar, nor gave anyone else warrant to do the same. He is to be King only after the general resurrection; the kingdom he claimed is to be in another world. He never actually commanded anyone. As Redeemer he was sacrificed to ransom men's sins, and as Teacher he counseled men about the path to salvation, that is, eternal life. The meaning of the Trinity is that the one person of God was represented at three different times and on three different occasions. Moses represented God the Father, Christ God the Son, and the apostles and their successors, by receiving and transmitting the Holy Spirit, represented God the Holy Ghost. So long as there was no Christian commonwealth, no civil sovereign converted to Christianity, the ecclesiastical power was in the hands of the apostles and those they ordained as ministers. They had no power of command, their office was only to instruct and advise men to believe and have faith in Christ. That Jesus is the Christ is the sole article of faith necessary for a Christian. If commanded by an infidel sovereign to profess the contrary with one's tongue, martyrdom is not necessary; confession is but an external thing, a sign of obedience to the law. If commanded by the sovereign to do actions such as worshipping false gods, which, in effect, deny the Lord, the sin is not that of the obedient subject but of the sovereign. It is never just for Christians, or anyone else, to attempt to depose even an infidel or heretical king once he has been established; for that would be a violation of faith and thereby against the law of nature which is the eternal law of God.

The first Christian emperor was Constantine, who was also the supreme bishop of Rome, just as all Christian sovereigns are supreme bishops in their own territories. This office adheres essentially to the sovereignty. Hobbes educes long arguments, especially against the writings of Cardinal Bellarmine, to oppose the claims of the popes of Rome. All priests in a Christian commonwealth are only the sovereign's ministers, deriving their authority from him, the chief priest. Where a foreigner has authority to appoint teachers or priests, he does it only by the authority of the sovereign in whose domains the teaching or ministry takes place. In fact, "church" as the word is used in the Bible means nothing else than a Christian commonwealth. From all this it is clear that the distinction between spiritual and temporal government is false. All government in this life, both of the state and of religion, is temporal and under the command of one civil sovereign.[27]

Hobbes says that the doctrine concerning the Kingdom of God has so much influence on the kingdom of man that it should not be decided by any but those that have the sovereign power. However, since his own country is in a state of civil war, he writes, and the authority is undecided, he will set forth his own novel doctrine tentatively. The Kingdom of God, wherein men shall enjoy eternal life, shall be a kingdom under Christ here on earth and at the time of the general resurrection. Hell is also on earth, and Satan is any earthly enemy of the church. The torments of Hell signify metaphorically that grief of mind, envy, caused by the sight of others enjoying that eternal felicity which the tormented, because of their disbelief and disobedience, have lost. The sinners will also have bodily pains and will die a second death. For everlasting fire and everlasting death do not mean that the tormented will be granted everlasting life, which everlasting torments would require. What is meant is rather that the tormenting fire will burn eternally and the supply of sinners to be tormented and killed will not fail, because the sinners will eat, drink, generate, and die perpetually after the resurrection as before. In fact, under Hobbes's interpretation it becomes difficult to see how the life of sinners is in any way changed by the resurrection. Eternal death then turns out to be not so much, if at all, worse than natural death. The over-all conclusion that Hobbes evidently wanted the readers of his theology to draw was that there was really no essential difference between the Word of God as revealed in the Scriptures and the word of Hobbes set down in his political philosophy.[28]

However, one is forced to raise the question of whether Hobbes believed in the truth of his theology. He does not say about God that "it is manifest we ought to attribute to him, existence: For no man can have the will to honor that which he thinks not to have any being." But the relation between truth and worship or honor is by no means unambiguous. For, he writes, "all words and actions that betoken fear to offend, or desire to please, is worship, whether these words or actions be sincere or feigned: and because they appear as signs of honoring, are ordinarily also called Honor." Because of these and many other statements, Hobbes became notorious as an atheist during his own lifetime.[29]

Perhaps the most charitable conclusion that one can draw from his theology is that in his dauntless zeal to destroy all opinions which he believed to be inimical to a proper understanding of the rights and duties of man, Hobbes showed that, for him, nothing was more sacred than the pursuit and promulgation of the philosophic truth.[30]

CHAPTER SIX

Putting Things Back Together Again in Kant

Any study, including the study of philosophy, usually begins with making distinctions, refining differences. With a comprehensive, precise philosopher, a philosopher with a system, like Kant, it seems as if one could spend a lifetime just trying to work out the distinctions, without ever coming around to bring together the things that have been distinguished, that have been separated in thought. I would like in this talk to try to account for how some of the major factors distinguished by Kant come together and cooperate within the wholes that they constitute. The lecture divides into two basic parts.

Experience and the sciences based on experience, according to Kant, are based on two primary sources, sense intuition and conceptual thought. Concepts without intuitions, he argues, are empty, and intuitions without concepts are blind. How do they come together? The contrast with Aristotle's treatment should be revealing. The fundamental question behind this first part is: How to account for the cognition we do experience, how to account for the partial intelligibility of our world?

The realm of nature, natural science, and experience, according to Kant, is determined strictly by necessary laws of cause and effect. The realm of morality, on the other hand, proceeds in accordance with laws of freedom. Like parallel lines, it would seem, the two realms never meet. Kant speaks of the great gulf that separates these domains, that "completely cuts off the domain of the concept of nature under the one legislation, and the domain of the concept of freedom under the other legislation, from any influence that each . . . might have had on the other" (Kant 1987, 35).

The question then naturally raises itself: How are the realm of nature and the realm of morality related or connected in one and the same world?

In his long and difficult book the *Critique of Judgment,* Kant develops the concept of purposiveness, especially the purposiveness of nature, that in some way is intended to bridge the gap between nature and morality. I am not able at this time to do more than touch on that subject. The purposiveness that Kant talks about is not found in nature but is supplied by the reflective judgment of the investigator whenever the investigator comes across phenomena like those of living organized beings for which the laws of mechanical cause and effect do not seem adequate. A purpose is defined by Kant as an effect that is possible only through the concept of that effect, the concept that is itself the cause of the effect. Like Thomas Aquinas, Kant argues that ends in nature only make sense when they are thought of as intended by some intelligence. The intending intelligence can be either in the being effecting the purpose or not. The innumerable complexes of purposive activities operative throughout nature, especially in animate nature, in beings not intending them, require some other being that does intend them, namely, God (*Summa Theologiae* I-II Q.40 A.3, and Q.1 A.2. Cf. also I Q.2 A.3. *Critique of Judgment,* secs. 75 and 76).

Teleology, Kant argues, finds its consummation in theology. But, unlike Thomas, for Kant this God is not to be assumed to have objective reality. The idea of such a being is produced by us in order to satisfy the subjective needs of our cognitive faculties. These purposive laws are to make sense of the phenomena *as if* some intelligent cause, a God, had made them.

The realm of the reflective judgment also contains Kant's analysis of the aesthetic judgment, the account of the beautiful and the sublime. The pleasure derived from an object judged beautiful comes from reflection on the free and harmonious play of one's own faculties of imagination and understanding in its judging.

The reflective judgment sometimes seems to be a judgment that, possessing an indeterminate particular, is on the search for the universal or universal law under which the particular could be subsumed, which, if found, would transform it into a determinate judgment. Reflection evidently plays a key role in a very important subject not extensively discussed by Kant, concept formation. In his *Logic* he speaks of concept formation as based on three logical operations of the understanding: comparison, reflection, and abstraction,

> the essential general conditions of generating any concept whatsoever. For example, I see a fir, a willow, and a linden. In comparing them with one another I notice they are different from one another in respect to trunk, branches, leaves, and the like; further, however, I reflect only on what they have in common, trunk, branches, and leaves, and [then] I abstract from their size, shape, and so forth; thus I gain a concept of a tree. (*Critique of Judgment,* Introduction [2], sect. 4; and *Logik,* AK IX, 94–95; Kant 1974, 100–101.)[1]

In this context reflection would seem to be the power in the Kantian system that comes closest to the *noēsis,* or intellectual intuition, of Plato and Aristotle.

The gap between nature and morality also raises another question which is both theoretical and practical, namely, How do nature and morality coexist in one and the same human being?

Almost everyone who aspires to be generally educated in philosophy reads Kant's the *Foundations* [*Grounding*] *of a Metaphysics of Morals,* usually after reading his *Prolegomena to Any Future Metaphysics* or selections from the *Critique of Pure Reason.* His *Metaphysics of Morals* is much less read. One is almost bound, it seems to me, to get a distorted picture of Kant's moral philosophy from reading the *Foundations* alone. In the *Foundations* Kant clarifies the *ultimate* principle of morality, the categorical imperative, by distinguishing it from what others claim are the sources of moral principle. The source of moral principle, he argues, is not nature, not divine revelation, not moral sense or feeling, not pleasure. The discussion usually takes the form of arguing why those plausible alternatives are to be ruled out as sources of moral worth. Kant's view appears as a noble, but narrow, inflexible formalism: "so act that the maxim of your action can be made into a universal law"—period.

The chief difficulty for those who have read only the *Critiques* and the *Foundations* is to see how Kant applies the categorical imperative. In ethical and political matters the meaning of principles usually does not become clear until one sees how they work out in practice. The *Metaphysics of Morals* is devoted entirely to working out how the categorical imperative is applied within the varying circumstances of human life. Despite the formalism, it reveals Kant to be a deep, wide-ranging student of human nature, who is very much aware of the importance for morality of the sources that he rejects as *ultimate* sources of morality. In the second part of this talk I propose to illustrate how, in the *Metaphysics of Morals,* Kant tries to make sense out of morality, in part by showing how the moral law comes together with some of the alternative principles that were rejected in the *Foundations.*

I

Most discussions of Kant begin with his modifications and deepening of doctrines inherited from Descartes, Spinoza, Leibniz, Locke, Berkeley, Hume, and others whose philosophies can be associated with modern mathematical physics. By emphasizing those modifications, the premises which these thinkers all share, in particular those premises formed in opposition to the classical Platonic-Aristotelian approach, are taken for granted, and as a consequence, are both insufficiently questioned and thereby insufficiently clarified.

If there is genuine knowledge, must not that which the knower knows be in some way the same as that which constitutes the object known? In the *Meno* (72c) Socrates speaks of the form (*eidos*) as that through which things are what they are and that towards which one looks in order to give an account of what they are. Aristotle speaks of how in sense perception the sense is receptive of the forms of sensible things without their material, just as the wax receives the mark of the signet ring without the iron or the gold. (*De Anima* 424a17–21. Aristotle joins Plato's Socrates' "second sailing," taking "refuge in speeches [*eis tous logous*] to look in them for the truth about the beings" [*Phaedo* 99c–100a], by coming around to concentrate on the form [*eidos*] "according to speech" [*kata ton logon*]. See *Physics* 193a31 and *Posterior Analytics*,100a1–3, and the whole of 2.19.) As Joe Sachs put it, "the same form that is at work holding together the perceived thing is also at work on the soul of the perceiver" (Aristotle 1999, liii–liv).

On the basis of what evidently lies in both prephilosophic and philosophic experience, and on the supposition that genuine knowledge is possible for human beings, Plato and Aristotle and their followers argue that human beings are endowed by nature with two interconnected kinds of intuition or insight, sense intuition and intellectual intuition (*nous*), which open themselves correspondingly to two kinds of forms, sensible and intelligible forms, the forms implicit in human speech as well as the forms of sense experience. According to the analyses of Plato and Aristotle, the intelligible forms are understood to be primarily responsible for the way the world and things are as they are. And accordingly they become objects of the highest kind of inquiry, the study which came to be called metaphysics.

The great early modern opponents of the classical tradition and its medieval offshoots seemed to regard this presupposition of harmony between the mind and discourse of human beings and the nature of things as a naive, if not gullible, optimism. Nature is not a kind mother, she deceives us: the cognitive equipment she endows us with conceals rather than reveals the true character of things.

Bacon, in book I of his *Novum Organum*, especially in his treatment of the Idols of the Mind, devotes himself to "the refutation of the natural human reason." That refutation includes a refutation and account of those philosophies, especially the philosophies of Plato and Aristotle, that "idolize" or even "idolatrize" natural human reason (see chapter 4, above, 68–82, especially note 5). Kant acknowledges the continuity of his great project with that of Bacon through his choice of a long excerpt from the *Novum Organum* as the epigraph to *The Critique of Pure Reason*.

Thomas Hobbes was unrivaled for the lucidity with which he stated his opposition to classical thought. In his *The Elements of Law (Natural and Politic)* we read "whatsoever accidents or qualities our senses make us think there be in the world, they be not there, but are seeming and apparitions only" (2.10). What we are led to think are the characteristics of things in themselves are rather the effects upon ourselves of causes or things which in themselves are utterly unknown to us. As for intelligibles, universals, Hobbes tells us that there is "nothing in the world Universal but Names; for the things named, are every one of them Individual and Singular" (*Leviathan* ch. 4). He often criticizes Aristotle for mistaking discourse about our thoughts and the ordering of our thoughts for discourse about things in themselves. Traditional metaphysics from this point of view is absorbed by logic, if not by psychology.

Kant continued and developed this critique. We cannot know things in themselves, he argues. Science, the study of nature, is concerned only with what appears to us, with what lies in our experience and, as far as we can know, lies only in our experience. We are led by nature to think that what is present in our experience is of, or refers to, things that exist independently of our experience. And when we speak about our experience, especially in our use of common nouns, we speak as if we possessed a power to intuit intellectually the intelligible natures of things in themselves. But, Kant asserts, sense intuition is the only intuition available to us; there is no such thing as intellectual intuition for human beings. To emphasize both the denial and the temptation at the same time, he defines the word noumenon (which he and his readers knew in Greek means object of nous, object of intellectual intuition) negatively, as a word to refer to that which we can in no way know, an unknowable *x*, the unknowable thing in itself.

Kant seems to have never given an explicit and direct refutation of the intellectual intuition he so emphatically rejects. Years ago I was puzzling about this with the distinguished Kant scholar Lewis Beck, and Beck finally said that he guessed Kant must have thought that he has given us everything valid that intellectual intuition was thought to have supplied and with more adequate explanations of its grounds. Beck was referring in part to the fact that although, according to Kant, we cannot go beyond phenomena to things in themselves, we can have objective, universal, and necessary judgments about them, that is, about the phenomena that constitute our experience. We can accept Hume's critique and starting point without the burden of his skepticism. In fact, Kant argues, objectively valid natural science, mathematics, and moral law, now, on his basis, can be more adequately grounded than they have ever been before. Kant's categories, the pure a priori concepts that ground experience, his substitutes for Platonic and Aristotelian ideas or forms, have no special purely intellectual objects of their own; they are valid and meaningful only in application to human experience, meaning sense experience. Reason, the ultimate source of understanding, and its concepts, is not intuitive, for Kant, but legislative: it provides rules for the meaningful organization of sense experience, these rules we call concepts.

Despite these fundamental oppositions, there is a deep stratum of concurrence in Kant's approach and the Platonic-Aristotelian approach: both find the meaningfulness of ordinary sense experience fundamentally dependent on what is primarily at home in thought, even in logic. Kant might be thought of as, in his own way, joining Socrates' taking refuge in the *logoi*. (See the reference to Plato's *Phaedo*, above, and the *Critique of Pure Reason*, B 105 or A 79, B 107, and B 370.) The same function of the mind that in discourse determines a certain kind of judgment, as a category provides the necessary conditions of meaningfulness that determine particular objects, as objects of sense experience.

Thus, Kant can say paradoxically that "Reason prescribes to nature its laws." He must also have been thinking about how Newton in his *Principia* presents mathematical reason prescribing its laws to nature: that is, after working out different general mathematical force laws for bodies traveling in different kinds of geometric orbits (in book I), some two hundred or so pages later (in book III) he determines the astronomical "System of the World" in a few pages by simply setting down the observational data, the phenomena, and seeing to which of those force laws they conform. (As every history of these matters makes clear, the actual discoveries of the mathematical laws were made very much in interaction with observations of the things governed by them.)

But Kant spoke of his critical philosophy and Newton's procedure as part of the more general Copernican intellectual revolution of modern science. Let us take the most important example: we see the sun rise, move across the heavens, and set each day. The Copernican hypothesis accounts for the apparent daily movement of the sun by the rotation of the earth, or more generally, by the activity and movement of the observer. Kant accounts for the meaningfulness of sense experience in terms of its conformity to the rules set by our own conceptual activity. Hitherto, he argues, it has been assumed that all our knowledge must conform to objects, but he reverses the priority by asking whether it is not rather that we attain knowledge of objects when those objects, sense objects, conform to the conditions that our concepts and understanding set for all objects of experience. Experimental science too is seen as part of this intellectual revolution: in the experiment reason approaches nature with fixed laws in mind, and then creates conditions that would never occur in nature's own ordinary course in order to force nature to answer reason's own questions about which laws prevail.

I spoke earlier of how Kant cut off intellectual intuition as one route from experience to things experienced as things in themselves; but what about gaining access to the things themselves that are sensed through sense intuition, the one kind of intuition that Kant asserts we do possess? That avenue is cut off by Kant's notion of what it is that we receive through our senses. Following Hume, Kant agrees that what our senses present to us are impressions, or as later writers who follow this approach say, sense data; not sense objects, but sensations, mere matter for sense objects. (To what extent does this depend on Kant's "Boscovichian" reduction of material "solids" to tensions of forces, especially repulsive and attractive forces? See his *Metaphysische Anfangsgründe der Naturwissenschaften* [*Metaphysical Foundations of Natural Science*], especially chapter two on dynamics, "Metaphysische Anfangsgründe der Dynamik," AK IV, 496–535.) Sensation for Kant is not yet sense *intuition*. For sense intuition of sense objects to occur, the matter must be ordered or formed into appearances and experiences. The formative or ordering power does not come from the object formed, but lies in the mind a priori, that is, independently of all sensation or experience. "[T]he form of all appearance must altogether lie ready for the sensations a priori in the mind; and hence that form must be capable of being examined apart from all sensation" (*Critique of Pure Reason*, B 34). The form of outer objects of experience is Space, the form of inner objects of experience is Time. Space presents no properties or relations of things in themselves; "it is the subjective condition of sensibility under which alone outer intuition is possible for us" (*Critique of Pure Reason*, B 42). Kant's "outer sense" might better be called

> the sense of externality. "Outer" here has less to do with going outside the subject than with the form of space itself. Space, as extended, is quintessentially that each of whose parts is outside of all the others. (Brann 1991, 92–93)

As the a priori form of inner sense, Time is the condition of possibility for any intuition or experience of simultaneity or succession. If, as we shall shortly see, all experience itself depends upon synthesizing activities of the subjects of experience, taking place in time, then time is the subjective condition of possibility for all intuition, for all experience, and for all cognition. "Time is the formal condition a priori for all appearances in general" (*Critique of Pure Reason*, B 46, 49–50).

How, according to Kant, are intuition and concept brought together to produce experience and knowledge? The crucial link is the imagination. The pure imagination, Kant tells us, is

> a basic power of the human soul *which underlies a priori all cognition*. By means of pure imagination we link the manifold of intuition, on the one hand, with the . . . necessary unity of pure apperception [the source of the categories], on the other hand. By means of this transcendental function of the imagination the two extreme ends, namely sensibility and understanding, must necessarily cohere; for otherwise sensibility would indeed yield appearances, but would yield no objects of an empirical cognition, and hence no experience. Actual experience consists in [1] apprehension of appearances, [2] their association (reproduction), and thirdly their recognition; in this third [element] (which is the highest of these merely empirical elements of experience), such experience contains concepts, which make possible the formal unity of experience and with it all objective validity (truth) of empirical cognition. Now these bases of the recognition of the man-

> ifold, insofar as they concern *merely the form of an experience as such,* are the *categories.* (*Critique of Pure Reason,* A 124–25, trans. Kant 1996a. Emphasis supplied)

Kant also spoke about the difference between the "two extreme ends," sensibility and thought, as the difference between receptivity, the receptivity of blind sense impressions, and spontaneity, the source of all thinking (transcendental apperception). The two are defined in opposition to one another. Understanding, the ability to *think* an object of sensible intuition, is our spontaneity of cognition, that is, the ability opposite to receptivity, the ability to produce mental presentations by ourselves, to go through, take up, and combine mental presentations in acts of synthesis. "By synthesis, in the most general sense of the term," he says, "I mean the act of putting various presentations with one another and of comprising their manifoldness in one cognition." Spontaneity, he asserts, is the basis of the threefold synthesis that brings sense intuition and conceptual thought together. The three syntheses are called (1) the synthesis of apprehension in intuition, (2) the synthesis of reproduction in imagination, and (3) the synthesis of recognition in the concept.

The first two syntheses are, if I understand them, under the aegis of what Kant calls the productive imagination. (*Critique of Pure Reason,* A 118. It can be argued that the second synthesis, as its name suggests, is not under the productive but only the reproductive imagination. Imagination, in general, is defined in the *Critique of Pure Reason,* B 151, as "the power of presenting an object in intuition even *without the object's being present.*" In the B edition the synthesis of apprehension is called the figurative synthesis.)

What the first synthesis, of apprehension, accomplishes is the taking together of the received impressions as existing in one ("my") consciousness in time. The individual becomes conscious of a unity of intuition in him or her self, as existing "in me." It is only when the received appearances are apprehended and combined within a definite consciousness that Kant will call them perceptions.

The next stage, the synthesis of reproductive imagination, depends upon an association of perceptions brought together so as to produce an image of an object. This depends on a power of the mind "to call over" (*herüberzurufen*) a preceding perception to a subsequent perception to form a series of perceptions. The objective ground of the association, Kant says, is the affinity of appearances in the unity of apperception. A non-Kantian might be tempted to ask, "Is this a surreptitious glance at the outlawed thing in itself?" But, Kant argues, this process depends on the unity of consciousness of original apperception and is an a priori synthesis, thereby traceable to the action of the productive imagination (*Critique of Pure Reason*, A 122 and 123).

The third synthesis, synthesis of recognition in a concept, is more familiar to everyone who has read about the pure concepts of the understanding, the categories. Here there is a recognition that the manifold of former syntheses is a unity of syntheses according to a rule, that is, according to a concept. We have now reached the pole of thought. We now recognize the former syntheses of appearances, associated perceptions, and finally an image as unified according to a rule, a category, under which they are subsumed and validated as conforming to the conditions of possibility of an object of experience.

At the end of this account Kant is satisfied that he can now say:

> Hence the order and regularity in the appearances that we call *nature* are brought into them by ourselves; nor indeed could such order and regularity be found in appearances, had not we, or the nature of our mind, put them into appearances originally. (*Critique of Pure Reason*, A 125)

There are two other important accounts of imagination mediating between sense and understanding that I can only mention briefly. Kant's transcendental deduction of the categories culminates in his discussion of the schematism. A schema is not an image, but a product of the power of imagination, a rule of synthesis for the imagination that governs the production of images that then will be suitable for subsumption under concepts. (Cf. Brann 1991, 89–99, especially 93–95.)

Another most important function of imagination is its provision of a priori intuition, the foundation of mathematical knowledge, according to Kant. Kant, like Newton and Hobbes, defines mathematical objects operationally rather than theoretically as Euclid mostly does. A line is what is generated by the path of a moving point, rather than a breadthless length. The intuition is a priori, because we, through our imagination, supply it; it is not derived from experience. In mathematics concepts are constructed, that is the universals, the concepts, are operative as rules of construction for the a priori images. The universal is found in the particular. (Euclid, *Elements* I.32, the proof that the three angles of any triangle equal two right angles, provides a beautiful example: As soon as you supply the line parallel to one of the sides of the triangle [keeping in mind what you have just learned about equalities between interior, exterior, and alternate angles], the conclusion jumps out at you. See *Critique of Pure Reason*, B 744–45. In B 745 this notion of a priori intuition is shown to embrace also the "symbolic constructions" of algebra. Cf. Jacob Klein: "A new kind of generalization, which may be termed 'symbol-generating abstraction,' leads directly to the establishment of a new universal discipline, namely 'general analytic,' [algebra], which holds a central place in the architectonic of the 'new' science" [Klein 1968, 125. Cf. 117–25, 163–78 and 192–211].) Construction of concepts is defined by Kant as the production and exhibition a priori, that is, in pure imagination, of the intuition which corresponds to the concept. Because in his mind the geometer produces a circle with every radius exactly equal, "he can demonstrate by means of a circle which he draws with his stick in the sand, no matter how irregular it may turn out to be, the attributes of a circle in general, as perfectly as if it had been etched on a copper plate by the greatest artist." The production in pure imagination of the intuition corresponding to the concept Kant calls schematic in contrast to the merely empirical intuition on paper or drawn in the sand. (Allison 1973, 111, especially Kant's note [AK VIII, 191–92]. Kant's way of conceiving the object of mathematics is elaborately contrasted with the classical Greek way in Lachterman 1989. Lachterman develops and builds on Klein 1968; and Klein 1985, 1–34.)

In the middle of Kant's account of the threefold synthesis we have just gone through a curious and revealing footnote appears.

> That the imagination is a necessary ingredient of perception itself has, I suppose, never occurred to any psychologist. This is so partly because this power has been limited by psychologists to reproduction only, and partly because they believed that the senses not only supply us with impressions, but indeed also assemble these impressions and thus bring about images of objects. But this undoubtedly requires something more than our receptivity for impressions, namely, a function for their synthesis. (*Critique of Pure Reason*, A 120, trans. Kant 1996a)

This criticism of what is evidently a premodern notion of perception seems to beg the question by assuming that what the senses supply are atomistic impressions, which then would require some other power to assemble them into representations of sensible things. Sensible things, as Kant knows, are what most people think they are perceiving through their senses. Kant was familiar with Aristotle's logic, but evidently not with *De Anima* (nor with Thomas Aquinas' commentary on *De Anima* and what he wrote on perception and imagination in his own name, cf. *Summa Theologiae* I Q.84 A.6 and especially A.7 and Q.85 A.1).

Aristotle's account of these matters seems to be much simpler; it remains very close to the ordinary and general experience in which they are found. As Joseph Owens put it, he "lets things speak for themselves." Aristotle and Kant, it seems to me, are considering pretty much the same phenomena, however differently they account for them.

In the beginning of his *Metaphysics* Aristotle speaks of how all animals by nature come into being with sensation and how, for some, memory emerges from sensation which makes them more intelligent and able to learn. He assumes that, of course, memory presupposes imagination. An animal remembers by recalling an image of something which has been perceived in the past and is no longer present, Kant's reproductive imagination. And so, Aristotle goes on,

> the other animals live by imaginings and memories, but have little share in experience, but the human race lives also by art and reasoning. Experience arises out of memory for human beings; for many memories of the same thing bring the capacity for one experience to completion. And experience seems to be almost like knowledge, or science, and art; and knowledge and art come about from experience for human beings.

Experience is the link between memory and science and art. Experience, then, arises from memories, when many memories of the same thing are linked together in a unity: for example, this cured Smith, it also cured Jones, and Green and Quinn, therefore it should cure Collins as well. The doctor, thinking about Collins's illness, is led by *something* to call up the images of those former patients and their cures. The intelligible character (*ennoēma*: *Metaphysics* 981a6) of the illness of the patient before him recalls that same intelligible character he had noticed in the illnesses of Jones, Smith, and so on. The intelligible character of the illness is at work both in and through the perceived patient before him and in the doctor's mind, as well as in and through the images recalled of past patients.

Aristotle has a name for the kind of human imagination that works together, that is, cooperates, with thought: he calls it rational (*logistikē*) imagination. It is distinguished from the kind of imagination that human beings share with the other animals, sensible imagination (*De Anima* 433b29–31). Let us recall, however, that experience is cognition of individuals. The intelligible form is working away in the linkage and the unity of experience, but it, so to speak, has not come into its own yet. In science and art when one can say this *kind* of medicine cures this *kind* of illness, the intelligibility of the form that was at work in experience is explicitly and fully recognized in speech as a universal. This culminating contemplation of the form as a universal is described by Aristotle in a way that at first seems strange; he describes it as a coming to rest of the soul out of its normal and natural disorder. But it is not the rest of inertia; it is the very active and untroubled calm of natural fulfillment, the gratifying fulfilling of a potency that was there from the beginning (*Physics* 247b5–18 and *Posterior Analytics* 100a6).

The Kantian account is more technical and impressive. It tells us about all sorts of processes that remained hidden until Kant explicated, or invented, them. The imagination plays a larger role than it does for Aristotle. The sense-data, for Kant, must first be assembled or synthesized by the imagination before we can recognize them as constituents of sense objects. The Kantian account describes a world that in its intelligible essentials is of our own making.

The Aristotelian account sticks much more closely to given experience; the causal factors it invokes almost seem to be extrapolations from the descriptions. (Aristotle does distinguish objects of sense that are proper to a sense, like the visible to sight, the audible to hearing, from incidental sense objects like "the white thing [that] is the son of Diares" [*De Anima* 418a7–26]. *What* that colored thing is, is incidental to its simply being colored. But for human beings primary sense experience usually includes the *what* that is part of what constitutes the object of perception as a sensible *thing.*) It finds intelligibility, perhaps even intelligence, in things and the natural world. We are instructed not so much to grasp or construct it, as to open ourselves to it.

II

Freedom in the sense of autonomy, self-legislation, is the fundamental principle of Kantian morality. Rousseau, whom Kant speaks of as a kind of Newton of the moral world (Cassirer 1963, 18), was perhaps the first to define freedom as self-legislation, but the idea is already implicit in Hobbes's theory of sovereignty and the social contract. We must obey the sovereign, Hobbes argues, because each of us through the social contract has agreed to allow his will to represent each of our wills. He is our representative. His legislation, because of the social contract, is, legally considered, our own self-legislation. Hobbes also formulated the more general principle underlying this conception: "there being no Obligation on any man, which ariseth not from some Act of his own; for all men equally are by Nature Free" (*Leviathan* ch. 21). Obligation seems to be something like a contract with oneself.

This becomes even more explicit in Rousseau's doctrine of the general will. Freedom in society consists in uniting oneself with all the rest under the general will that declares the law, while at the same time remaining free, that is, self-legislating, in so far as one has contributed to the making of that law, either by taking part in the legislative assembly oneself, or taking part in the election of legislators. The process that makes the will general also makes it moral. Being compelled to express one's will in such a form that it can become a general law, so that it can coincide with the wills of all the others, moralizes the will. For example, I don't like to pay taxes. If I generalize my desire into a law that no one ought to pay taxes, I am compelled to see that then the police, public schools, courts, the enforcement of contracts, and so on, would all disappear. The irrationality of my original desire becomes manifest.

This idea is fully developed as a moral principle in Kant's doctrine of the categorical imperative: so act that the maxim of your action can become a universal law. The truly free or moral person, according to Kant, bows only to the moral will or practical reason within him or her self, and not to any standard coming from without.

The standard of autonomy, self-legislation, is opposed by heteronomy, legislation by another. The two most powerful and prominent forms of heteronomy that are to be dethroned are the standard of nature derived from philosophy and the standard of God derived from biblical revelation. Pure practical reason is the only source of moral law. Anything, therefore, empirical or sensual in origin is disqualified as a source or standard of moral worth: that rules out moral sense, moral feeling, and pleasure. It also rules out happiness as a standard, happiness being understood by Kant as a kind of sum of satisfaction of empirical desire, or (as he puts it) of inclination. The rational principle of heteronomy, the concept of perfection, at least does not, as the empirical principles do, undermine morality, but by its emptiness and vagueness is "altogether incapable of serving as its foundation" (*Grundlegung zur Metaphysik der Sitten*, AK IV, 443). With this glance at certain programmatic aspects of the *Grounding [Foundations] of a Metaphysics of Morals*, we can now turn to the *Metaphysics of Morals*.

The book is divided into two parts that correspond to the traditional division between political philosophy and ethics, the doctrine of right and the doctrine of virtue. Duties of right are defined as externally enforceable obligations, the external enforcer being a just, lawful, or right-protecting political order. Duties of virtue, ethical duties, are internal obligations. Duty is a necessitation or constraint of free choice through the law. The constraint in ethical duties, then, is "self-constraint through the representation of the law alone, for only so can that *necessitation* (even if it is external) be united with freedom of choice" (AK VI, 380). Free choice is not indeterminate, free choice is that choice that can be determined by pure reason. (This appears to be an echo, or variant, of Spinoza's conception of freedom. Everything, according to Spinoza, is determined: freedom is the ability of the best human beings to be determined by clear and distinct ideas. [If we are not determined in our actions by clear and distinct ideas, we will be determined solely, or mainly, by natural causes like instincts, emotions, and inclinations.] For Spinoza and German Idealism, as a whole, see Strauss 1965, 15–17.) And just to wrap this up: throughout both parts of the book "obligation" refers to "the necessity of a free action under a categorical imperative of reason" (AK VI, 222).

But before we enter into some of the substance of the book, it is time to clear up one fundamental point. Kant frequently speaks of the unbridgeable gap between the domain of sensible empirical nature and the domain of moral freedom, as our earlier quotation illustrated. Those statements turn out to be only provisional, to help us get clear about where our different principles are coming from. Freedom is a kind of causality. Although the natural causality of the sensible world cannot determine the subject as a moral, supersensible, being,

> yet the reverse is possible (not . . . with regard to our cognition of nature, but . . . with regard to the consequences that the concept of freedom has in nature); . . . this possibility is contained in the very concept of a causality through freedom, whose *effect* is to be brought about in the world. . . .

Those effects manifest themselves as appearances in the world of sense. (*Critique of Judgment*, Kant 1987, 36; AK V, 195, see especially the note on 195–96.)

This causality of freedom is another way of talking about how pure reason becomes practical: This can only happen when reason makes the individuals' maxims (subjective principles of action) fit for becoming universal law. And further, since we human beings are under the sway of nature's causality as well as freedom's, that power of reason can be exercised, Kant says, only by its prescribing the moral law in the form of imperatives that command or prohibit absolutely (AK VI, 213–14; Kant 1996b, 13–14). A divine being, with no countervailing natural tendencies to oppose pure practical reason, acts in accordance with the moral law as a matter of course, with no need for any imperatives, any commands. (Cf. the distinction between the continent man and the temperate man in book 7 of Aristotle's *Nicomachean Ethics.*)

Since my general aim here is to illustrate how Kant's sensible natural realm and supersensible moral realm come together in one and the same world, I will concentrate on the doctrine of virtue, because that is where those sources of morality rejected in the *Foundations* as ultimate principles of morality are done justice to, as important factors in moral life.

An end, Kant explains, is an object of free choice, the object of some action, and is thereby empirical. The traditional, or classical, procedure of clarifying the rank order of one's ends and then setting one's personal maxims of duty in terms of the rank order of those ends, violates the concept of duty according to Kant. Duty with its categorical ought is rooted in pure reason alone, and thereby must be in control of the maxims by which one sets one's ends. The ends to be sought in ethics then are ends that are also duties.

Although both nature and the concept of perfection seem to have been ruled out as fundamental moral standards in the *Foundations,* in section viii of the doctrine of virtue we find the end that is also a duty to cultivate one's own natural perfection. As Kant also says in the *Foundations,* ends that are necessary and objective ends for every rational being, that is, ends in themselves, can serve as moral laws. Rational nature, he declares, is an end in itself. It follows that human beings, being rational natures, are obliged in their own person or in the person of another to always treat humanity as an end, not a means. The end of humanity in our own persons is linked to the duty to make ourselves worthy of humanity by cultivating our natural capacities to realize the ends set forth by our reason. Then Kant goes on, "That is to say, the human being has a duty to cultivate the raw abilities of his nature by which the animal first raises itself into a human being." (Cf. *Muthmasslicher Anfang der Menschengeschichte,* AK VIII, 107–23: Kant 1963, 53–68.)

Happiness, we remember, was also excluded from moral goals, but, Kant declares, the happiness of others is an end that is also a duty. The argument here is rather interesting; it seems to ground itself on universalizing a not very exalted natural and selfish principle. The reason why we have

> a duty to be beneficent is this: since our self-love cannot be separated from our need to be loved (helped in case of need) by others, we therefore make ourselves an end for others; and this maxim can never be binding except through its qualification as a universal law, and hence through our will also to make others our ends. The happiness of others is therefore an end that is also a duty.

Shortly thereafter Kant again puts his prodigious deductive power in the service of his good sense by qualifying this duty. "How far it should extend depends . . . on what each person's true needs are in view of his sensibilities, and it must be left to each to decide this for himself." For to promote the happiness of another at the sacrifice of one's own happiness (one's own true needs) would be in itself a self-conflicting maxim, if one made it into a universal law (AK VI, 391–94; Kant 1996b, 154–56).

In the light of the *Foundations,* section xii of the *Metaphysics of Morals* is especially interesting: outlawed feeling and pleasure come into their own. The subject is those "moral endowments" resting on feeling that are required to prepare the mind to receive concepts of duty and to act on them. There are *duties* to cultivate these right dispositions of feeling.

Moral feeling is "the susceptibility to pleasure or displeasure merely from the consciousness that our action is either in agreement with or is contrary to the law of duty." Shortly thereafter a remarkable statement follows: "for all consciousness of obligation depends on this feeling." It is this feeling that makes us aware of the constraint that lies in the concept of duty. There is no duty to have or acquire it, because every human being (as a moral being) already has it. The obligation can "only be to cultivate it and, through wonder at its inscrutable [*unerforschlichen*—not to be searched into] source, to strengthen it" (AK VI, 399–400). To lack it is to be morally dead. Kant continues, in appropriately passionate language, "and if, (to speak in medical terms) the moral life-force could no longer excite this feeling, then humanity would dissolve (as it were by chemical laws) into mere animality and be mixed irretrievably with the mass of other natural beings" (Kant 1996b, 171).

The other great source of heteronomy, both the *Foundations* and *The Critique of Practical Reason* tell us, is the biblical God of revelation. Kant ends the *Metaphysics of Morals* by speaking of religion as an integral part of the general doctrine of duties, but says that considered as a doctrine of duties to God it lies outside the boundaries of pure moral philosophy. The necessity for religion is stated quite clearly: "we cannot very well make obligation (moral constraint) intuitive [*anschaulich*] for ourselves without thereby thinking of *another's* will, namely God's (of which reason in giving universal laws is only the spokesman)." This duty with regard to God, he goes on, is really a duty to the idea we ourselves make of such a being, it is really a duty of a human being to him or her self, "for the sake of strengthening the moral incentive in our own lawgiving reason" (Kant 1996b, 229–30). Kant hints that if we would really like to follow up this subject, we could consider his book *Religion within the Bounds of Reason Alone,* where the agreements between pure practical reason and the teachings of history and revelation are explored.

That book, like the *Metaphysics of Morals*, is one of those rare places where Kant describes human beings as we know them, whole human beings who are at one and the same time natural and moral beings.

It may be fitting to end this talk with some brief remarks about Kant's discussion of religion. The *Critique of Pure Reason* established, according to Kant, that we have no *knowledge*, positive or negative, concerning the existence of God. Religion, Kant argues, is unambiguously subordinated to morality, to moral reason. "Pure moral legislation, through which the will of God is primordially engraved in our hearts, is not only the unavoidable condition of all true religion whatsoever, but is also that which really constitutes such religion." True religion, he argues, "is a purely rational affair" (*Die Religion innerhalb der Grenzen der blossen Vernunft, Religion within the Limits of Reason Alone,* AK VI, 104; *Der Streit der Fakultäten,* AK VII, 67, Kant 1979, 123). Religion within the limits of reason alone establishes what in the absence of knowledge we are obliged to believe, in order to strengthen our capacities to obey the moral law.

Kant had trouble getting his book on religion printed. Permission to publish was withheld because of opposition from officials of the theological faculties at the universities. Morals and religion, they argued, fell under the jurisdiction of the theological faculty, not the faculty of philosophy to which Kant belonged. (This jurisdictional issue was probably not the deepest ground for their opposition.) Kant had argued as early as *The Critique of Pure Reason* that moral theology in answer to the question, What may I hope?, was an indispensable part of philosophy. After a few years of rejection by some censors and acceptance by others, Kant did get his *Religion* book published. But the practical and theoretical questions connected with the affair evidently led him to write what became a part of his last book, *The Conflict of the Faculties*.

I bring this talk to a close with Kant's comments in that book on the traditional idea that philosophy is the handmaid of theology (AK VII, 28). He grants theology's "proud claim," but raises the question: Is she, however, the handmaid that walks behind bearing her gracious mistress's train, or the torchbearer that walks ahead to light the path?

CHAPTER SEVEN

Radical Historicism and the Attempt to Transcend Philosophy

SOME REFLECTIONS ON STRAUSS, HEIDEGGER, AND HUSSERL

This paper is concerned with some fundamental differences between the thought of Leo Strauss and Martin Heidegger. We conclude with some observations on Strauss's critique of what can be regarded as Husserl's approach to political philosophy. Strauss's explicit criticisms of historicism can be found, among other places, in his chapter "Natural Right and the Historical Approach" in *Natural Right and History*.[1] I am more interested here in the principles bearing on that criticism that are implicit in his thought as a whole.

I

We begin with some elementary agreements and disagreements. Husserl, Heidegger, and Strauss all agree that the understanding of man that is based on methodical or systematic rejection of what is primordially or naturally given to human experience, that is, modern science's understanding of man, is inadequate. They agree with Plato and Aristotle that science and philosophy must begin from prescientific, prephilosophic experience, the world of ordinary experience, in Husserl's language, the "life-world." An accurate description, or articulation, of that world is then one of the first tasks of philosophy.

Plato, Aristotle, Husserl, and Strauss are open to the possibility that science can uncover the true, or intelligible, world underlying the world of ordinary experience.

For Husserl, following Kant, transcendental subjectivity underlies and constitutes both the world of natural experience and the world of "objective" science. Objectivity, from this point of view, is understood as universal subjectivity, or undeniable intersubjective agreement. If the constituting subjectivity is conceived of as decisively determined by the uniqueness of its historical situation, this position becomes historicist. Some characterize the thought of the early Heidegger and the late Husserl in this way. If science is simply part of a world view that is valid only for some limited period of time, the question rises as to what objectivity could mean.

For Heidegger, one might say, the ancients and Husserl are correct in trying to begin from the natural, the given world, the life-world; but in their descriptions they all fail to reach the primordially given, the *pragmata*, the fundamental objects of human concern. This failure, to put it in non-Heideggerian terms, is the failure to articulate the fundamental attitude of religiosity permeating the perspective of the life-world. A Christianized anthropology is used by Heidegger to articulate the structures of human existence: The foundations of morality are discussed in terms of conscience, guilt, and fallenness; history, *Geschichte*, is connected to *Geschick*, what has been sent; objects of thought "at the end of philosophy" are to give themselves or to be given to thinking that opens itself in grateful acceptance.[2] "But what lies obscurely at the basis of everything Heidegger ever said, and induces many to become attentive and listen is something unsaid: The *religious motive*, which has surely separated itself from Christian belief, but just in its dogmatically uncommitted indeterminateness appeals the more to those who are no longer believing Christians, but still would like to be religious."[3] Religious sentiments are presented in more or less respectable academic garb ("existential analytic"), without the academically less respectable theological presuppositions that might ground those sentiments.

That classical philosophy grounded itself in natural prescientific cognition was often emphasized by Strauss. Yet in a sense, he implicitly acknowledged, Heidegger was correct. Classical philosophy in its accounts of prephilosophic experience does not present the concern with the divine as that concern exists normally within the prephilosophic perspective, "because for it [classical philosophy] the concern with the divine has become identical with philosophy." Yet,

> Philosophy is the ascent from what is first for us to what is first by nature. This ascent requires that what is first for us be understood as adequately as possible in the manner in which it comes to sight prior to ascent. . . . the city as it primarily understood itself [is] distinguished from the manner in which it was exhibited by classical political philosophy: the holy city in contradistinction to the natural city. . . . what is "first for us" is not the philosophic understanding of the city but that understanding which is inherent in the city as such, in the prephilosophic city, according to which the city sees itself as subject and subservient to the divine in the ordinary understanding of the divine or looks up to it.[4]

II

Strauss often noted the absence of any thematic treatment of piety in the *Nicomachean Ethics,* and that the most prominent mention of piety in that book occurs just before Aristotle launches into a critique of the Platonic idea of the good. The passage is instructive. The introducers of the ideas are referred to by a verb that reminds one of the original charge accusing Socrates of introducing new divinities. To criticize these men is difficult, he says, because they are our friends, because they are dear to us. But while both the truth and our friends are dear to us, since we are philosophers, it is more pious for us to honor the truth before our friends. Piety comes into view with the conflict between the love of one's own and the love of truth. Classical philosophy was never permitted to ignore piety: The danger of being charged with bringing in new deities was never altogether absent. From the point of view of classical philosophy, one might say, there is little danger of the religious perspective ever being neglected, for philosophy itself will always necessarily coexist with one kind of public religion or another. If the religious impulse is rooted in human nature itself, it is not accidental that the tendency of modern philosophy to incorporate religious notions into itself began with, or shortly after, the philosophic project to dispense with revealed religion through "enlightenment." However this may be, for Strauss and classical philosophy the natural perspective is constituted essentially by a tension between the demands of piety and the demands of what leads to objective science and philosophy. This is exhibited in a classic manner by Strauss's account of the discovery of nature out of theology in *Natural Right and History*.[5] Just before that account, Strauss writes: "To grasp the natural world as a world that is radically prescientific or prephilosophic, one has to go back behind the first emergence of science or philosophy. . . . The information that classical philosophy supplies about its origins suffices, *especially if that information is supplemented by consideration of the elementary premises of the Bible*."[6]

What causes great difficulty for conventional scholarship, with its more or less legalistic canons of evidence, is that from the classical point of view these matters cannot be properly discussed, at least in writing, with full explicitness. I refer to Strauss's rediscovery of exotericism.[7] Human beings, the classics argued, are radically individual and radically social at the same time.[8] Society, in order to reconcile this tension in human nature, is always political society. For society to exist decently with at least a modicum of freedom, the sanctification of norms is required. This sanctification is necessary to provide individuals with sufficient strength to make the sacrifices required for overcoming radical selfishness as well as external enemies. The sanctifications that back up the personal commitments required to keep society decently free have the cognitive status of opinions. Philosophy as the ascent from opinion to knowledge calls into question all opinions, regards all, even the best, opinions as insufficient knowledge. The canons of philosophic and scientific evidence, therefore, tend to dissolve such commitments by calling the cognitive status of their supports into question. In that public speech, then, which is his writing, the philosopher mutes whatever might tend to weaken the sources of human decency and freedom, not only because the improvement of society is good in itself, but also because, generally speaking, no society without a modicum of freedom and decency is likely to tolerate or harbor philosophy within itself.[9] The serious student, then, seeking the unmuted meaning of his philosophic teachers, especially in what concerns the "fundamental structures of human existence," must have recourse to the implications of their philosophic rhetoric. Heidegger approaches these themes of political philosophy in Sections 27 and 35 of *Sein und Zeit*,[10] but does not seem to have thought through how this might have affected and modified the presentation of all premodern philosophy.

III

Classical political philosophy, then, in Strauss's view consisting of ethics and politics, is that branch of philosophy that is devoted to the articulation and understanding of the prephilosophic and prescientific perspective and the negotiations of the tensions constituting it. Does Heidegger by his rejection of, perhaps even contempt for, ethics miss the fundamental sense of the initial *pragmata*? Can one articulate the fundamental concerns of human existence without ever raising the question of justice, not to speak of the questions who, or what kind of men should rule, which way of life is best, what is human excellence, its varieties, their order of rank? Is it accidental that in trying to understand the political implications of Heidegger's thought one must have recourse to his embarrassing public statements of the thirties? Despite many disagreements, Strauss took Heidegger's rejections of ethics as a sign of his greatness: Heidegger, he said, faced the problem of ethics. Heidegger, Hans-Georg Gadamer writes, provided us with the philosophic means for uncovering

> the *illusion* that science—*in whatever style*—could ever be responsible for the decisions of a "universal praxis". . . . we owe to his critique then this, that the way of knowing implied in the Aristotelian critique of Plato's knowledge of the Good, which as *philosophia practica* dominated the tradition till well into the 18th century, *before it lost its legitimacy*, could now be grounded anew.[11]

Heidegger supplies that "grounding" in his sections on conscience in *Sein und Zeit* (Heidegger 1957, 286), where the foundations for "morality in general" are laid down. The distinction between a virtuous act and a virtuous man (*Nicomachean Ethics* 2.4 1105a17 ff.) or, more generally, between a certain kind of act and being a certain kind of man is developed into the distinction between vulgar conscience and existential, or authentic, conscience: a concern with reckoning up one's good and bad deeds in contrast with a serious concern with what one is, with whether one measures up to what one could be.

The threefold of "fundamental existentialia,"[12] (1) Disposition,[13] (2) Understanding, and (3) Discourse, is used to disclose the resoluteness of the man who "wants to have conscience," the man of authentic conscience. This resoluteness is constituted by (1) anxiety; (2) understanding how one is not what one might be, that is, guilt; and (3) the silent discourse, or call, that calls one back from the never totally escapable idle talk of the public, that calls one back to oneself and to one's unfulfilled present and "factical" possibilities. To be resolute is "to be already taking action," and Heidegger anticipates, indeed quite rightly, that resoluteness might be, as he claims, misunderstood as "a special way of behavior of the practical faculty in contrast with one that is theoretical."

Resoluteness, he argues, is the authenticity of care, and care is said to be so primordial as to precede any distinction between theory and practice. The concern with what kind of man one is to be precedes the choice of one kind of life rather than another. The emphasis here seems to be on the efficient causes, the emotional dispositions impelling that concern, rather than the rational consideration of final causes that might shape and guide it toward some state of felicity. If the choice is to be reasonable, or "ontologically adequate," it should be based on a more or less accurate estimate of one's own natural capacities. Fortunately, or providentially, nature usually helps in these matters by making what one is better suited for more pleasant. A fuller discussion of pleasure, love, and desire might be even more instructive than a discussion of radical anxiety. In this context Heidegger speaks continually of one's "ownmost potentiality-for-being" (*Seinkönnen*). He wants to avoid the concession to the theoretical perspective that reference to nature would entail. Can a potentiality be made intelligible without reference to its term or end? One is reminded of the complaint frequently leveled at Kant: Heidegger's account is too formal; the account of the virtues and ways of life that would fill out the discussion of "potentiality-for-being" is missing.

Nature, for classical philosophy, provides the potentialities, but any adequate account of potentialities must include a discussion of the ends, the virtues, for which they are potentialities. "By reason of the law of development embodied in every nature, 'natural' can be predicated of either of these opposites: the initial, the incipient, the primitive, the native, the rudimentary, and the terminal, the final, the accomplished, the perfect."[14] The crucial Aristotelian text, literally translated, is to be found in *Nicomachean Ethics* 2.1 1103a24–

26: "Therefore, neither by nature, nor against nature are the virtues engendered in us, but *by our being natured to receive them and by our being completed (or perfected) by habit.*" Nature provides both the capacities to receive the moral virtues and the ends implicit in them: Men by their habits and laws fulfill or pervert those capacities.

There is, in fact, an ethical stance implicit in Heidegger's substitute for virtue, "authenticity,"[15] his "resoluteness,"[16] and, above all, his descriptions of "falling," of the shallowness and emptiness of *das Man* and his idle talk. In doctrine, however, "we must avoid giving [falling] any ontically negative 'evaluation'." Heidegger's *Eigentlichkeit* is the offspring of the modern notion of freedom as self-legislation, that ethical criterion that was conceived so as to be compatible with a nonteleological science of nature.

IV

The rank order of the virtues and the different ways of life for classical philosophy are connected to a rank order of powers of the soul. For Heidegger, the bounds and framework of the potentiality-for-being referred to are determined by one's historical situation but cannot be set by nature or any scheme of "reification" or "objectification." Despite the doctrinal barriers he has placed in its way, it may nevertheless be useful to interpret Heidegger's account of human existence from the point of view of classical psychology, especially the psychology of Aristotle. In addition to Aristotle's distinction between a virtuous act and a virtuous man, so, too, as Gadamer has mentioned, was his doctrine of *phronēsis* important for Heidegger's account of conscience. The former distinguishes the mere performance of virtuous actions from the being of the kind of man who acts virtuously (1) knowingly, (2) from deliberate choice, and (3) from a fixed and unchanging disposition so to act.[17] The latter, the doctrine of *phronēsis* (a word that in Aristotle has a range of meanings from elementary prudence to practical wisdom) distinguishes "mere" objective, detached knowing from a form of knowing that depends on being a certain kind of man, a knowing, in Gadamer's words, "within the concrete situation of existence." The same facts were looked at by Strauss in another way: He was fond of quoting Thomas Aquinas's observation that the intellectual virtues with the exception of *phronēsis* do not presuppose moral virtue. *Phronēsis,* the intellectual virtue by which one chooses the means conductive to virtue, presupposes a man who is disposed and habituated to want virtuous ends.

The different powers of the soul, since in each case they are the powers of a single person, form some kind of unity. Philosophic psychologists distinguish those "parts" or powers, deal with the relations between the powers, and try to determine which one of the parts should be dominant in determining the unity and the character of the whole. That unity, one may say, is a unity of interpenetrating powers in tension. When Aristotle says in the beginning of the *Metaphysics* that all men by nature desire to know, he knows that most men, while they do desire to know, desire other things more. Most men, he reports at the end of the *Nicomachean Ethics,* live by passion. Men are distinguished, as Plato's *Republic* most dramatically shows, by the powers that dominate their souls. The best men for Plato and Aristotle are those in whom intellect, or understanding, dominates. The moving power in practical action, linked with reason, is appetite, which is further subdivided into three "parts" in an ascending order of closeness to reason: desire (*epithumia*), which seeks pleasure; spiritedness (*thumos*), which is the source of those feelings primarily directed to the care for one's own, especially fear, hope, anger, and love; and wish, or wanting (*boulēsis*), which aims at the apparent good. Many factors conspire to indicate that spiritedness is the dominant power for Heidegger. There is the emphasis on "mineness," "ownness," and anxiety, a radicalized fear. If resoluteness approaches any Aristotelian virtue, it would seem to be courage, the virtue that refines spiritedness.

Furthermore, "the Being of Dasein itself is to be made visible as care" (Heidegger 1957, 57).[18] As Heidegger has anticipated, from an Aristotelian perspective this discussion and his doctrine of *Zuhandenheit* (readiness-to-hand) as a whole lead us to conclude that for Heidegger human existence is primarily practical existence.[19]

The problem of spiritedness has been stated classically by the Athenian Stranger of Plato's *Laws* (731e–732a): "In truth the cause of every sin comes to each person each time through excessive love of oneself. For the one who loves is blinded about the beloved, so that he judges the just and the good and the noble things badly, believing that he is bound always to honor what is his own before the truth." This consequence of our particularity, our *Da*sein, the tendency to sacrifice truth to the love of one's own, points to moderation as an indispensable virtue of practical life, especially of political life. Heidegger, as we have indicated, particularly appreciated the psychological distinctions of the *Nicomachean Ethics*. But, as his immoderate exaltation of spiritedness indicates, he may not have equally appreciated the substantial treatment of the virtues, for example, the beautiful way Aristotle describes the defects of small-souledness, the dispirited state of those whose lack of self-esteem keeps them from enjoying the virtuous deeds they could enjoy, and especially inirascibility (*aorgēsia*), which he deals with in the context of a discussion of gentleness, good temper, or patience.

V

Strauss and classical philosophy, we have argued, understood the natural or prescientific, prephilosophic perspective to be constituted at its core by a tension between the demands of piety and the divination of an impersonal nature that leads to philosophy and science.[20] Political philosophy, as he understood it, articulates that fundamental tension, not only by its study of the straightforward questions of ethics and politics but also by the study of the origins of philosophy, the quarrel between the poets and the philosophers, the question of the possibility of philosophy as a way of life, the principles of revealed religion. In Strauss's view, then, this tension is natural in both senses of the word (158–59, above), which includes the sense, "healthy." From this we can begin to understand Strauss's remark that the mutual irrefutability of biblical revelation and science and philosophy may be the secret of vitality of Western civilization.[21] The negative and critical side of Strauss's argument is his sweeping and meticulous demonstration, especially in *Natural Right and History,* that historicism is rooted not in an open-minded analysis of human existence but in a mode of interpreting human existence ultimately derived from the questionable principles and crises of modern political philosophy.[22]

One important common ground for the paths blazed by Heidegger, on the one hand, and Klein and Strauss, on the other, was the conviction that the attempt to understand human existence on the basis of modern science and its "conquest of nature" was a failure. But they account for the failure differently. For all his profound understanding of the differences, Heidegger stresses the continuity between modern science and classical philosophy. Put roughly, classical philosophy is held responsible for what modern science has wrought. Strauss and Klein emphasize the differences. The failure is traced to modern philosophy's break with classical philosophy.[23]

Both Strauss and Heidegger faced the problem of the difficulty of finding one's way to the "natural cave," the world of prescientific experience, in a technological society where the ordinary workaday world and its discourse are permeated by science. Heidegger's way is the "deconstruction" of the tradition that led to the difficulty, and the alleged uncovering of the primordial ontological or existential ground that underlies all traditions, that is, existential analytic. For Strauss, the way out of our air-conditioned pit (modern thought's alleged progress beyond all earlier thought) beneath the cave requires primarily a recovery of the classical philosophy that the great moderns oppose and reject, and thereby presuppose they understand.[24]

VI

The fundamental tension we have referred to has been discussed in different ways. The most prominent way in the writings of classical philosophy takes the form of the distinction between theory and practice. Strauss approved of Jacob Klein's way of putting it:

> In Greek *episteme* the life of "cognition" and "knowledge" was recognized for the first time as an ultimate human possibility, one which enables men to disregard all the ends they might otherwise pursue, to devote themselves to contemplation in complete freedom and leisure, and to find their happiness in this very activity. This possibility is contrasted with the bondage imposed by the affairs of the day. Here science stands in original and immediate opposition to a nonscientific attitude which yet is its soil and in which it recognizes its own roots. In attempting to raise itself above this nonscientific attitude, science preserves intact these given foundations. It is therefore both possible and necessary to learn to see Greek science from the point of view of this, its "natural" basis. In its sum total Greek science represents the whole complex of those *"natural" cognitions* which are implied in a prescientific activity moving within the realm of opinion and supported by a preconceptual understanding of the world.[25]

The whole of human cognition, however, embraces both theory and practice. If it is a hierarchic whole, as each of the powers contends, then which of the major parts should be authoritative for determining its character? The ranking, it would seem, should be a reflection of the rank order of the parts that constitute the whole of the objects of cognition. What then is the character of the principle that governs the whole of things? This, I believe, is behind the marvelous way Strauss ends *The City and Man,* with "the all-important question which is coeval with philosophy although the philosophers do not frequently pronounce it—the question *quid sit deus.*"

What is God? Is it the loving, caring God of justice, for whom righteous action is the one thing needful, or impersonal intelligence, self-sufficient in its intellection, the model and ground of the human capacity to understand things as they are?

VII

On one level, the lowest level, the political drift of Heidegger's position did not seem, to Strauss, difficult to discern. Resoluteness is exalted without clarification of the ends of resoluteness. All transcendent, that is, transhistorical, ethical and political principles that could support or induce moderation and a critical stand toward the given goals of one's own historical situation are disparaged. It was a spiritual resonance with the National Socialist Revolution that prevented Heidegger, albeit only temporarily, from seeing Hitler's ruthlessness for the degradation and the perversion of heroism it was.

The practical bent of Heidegger's thought, however, enters the political plane on another level, the highest possible level. Appalled by the prospect of an approaching spiritual unity of the planet on the lowest level of humanly empty, calculating, technical thought, wrought by the victory of Western technology, Heidegger tried to prepare the ground, a possible common but deeper ground for the meeting of East and West in dialogue. The ground Heidegger tried to prepare was to make it possible for each side to preserve something of its own noble depths while joining with the other to forge the unified humanity imposed upon us by . . . history? Destiny?

The gods? This seems to be Heidegger's way of responding to Nietzsche's call to his philosopher-poets of the future to prepare themselves for planetary rule.

The fundamental tension we have referred to seems, in Heidegger's thought, to have been resolved. Theory has culminated in the worldwide victory of technology and the end of philosophy. Theory does not seem to be an alternative coeval with human existence. The task of thinking at the end of philosophy is to develop the depths in our Western thought ultimately derivative from the Bible, the East in us, but freed from those dogmatic underpinnings that might prevent them from becoming planetary.[26]

Strauss's criticism of Husserl's approach to political philosophy brings us back more directly to our main theme, the rootedness of science in an opposed "nonscientific attitude which yet is its soil and in which it recognizes its own roots."

Husserl's *Philosophy as Rigorous Science,*[27] published in 1911, begins with the sentence: "From its first beginnings philosophy has raised the claim to be the science that would satisfy the highest theoretical needs and *in regard to ethics and religion render possible a life regulated by pure rational norms.*"[28]

Heidegger seems to dissolve one element of the fundamental tension, Husserl the other. In 1911, Strauss suggests, Husserl failed to think through what the effects of a successful single-minded pursuit of philosophy might be. What is likely to happen if the spirit of science were increasingly to dominate practical life, religion, and politics? Husserl did not consider the possible adverse effects the success of scientism would have on the doctrines most men live by, and then what the effects these reactions would have on philosophy as rigorous science itself. A variety of opposing doctrines and fighting faiths could be called into being. For example, if philosophy as rigorous science appears to have a monopoly on reason and yet is thought (by calling tradition into question) to be harmful to life, a world view might be called into being that would be antirational. It would take the form of illiberal antirationalism, that is, fascism. Or, perhaps, when scientism has sufficiently weakened the tradition, a revolution even in the name of a kind of reason will impose a single world view on all members of society and will no longer tolerate the open-minded inquiries of philosophy as rigorous science, except, of course, in strictly technical fields. Its political form might be called pseudorationalism, that is, communism.[29] Husserl, who so profoundly understood that the scientific understanding is dependent upon the natural understanding, apparently overlooked some essential characteristics of that understanding.

By 1935, Strauss suggests, events moved Husserl to extend these reflections. In his Vienna Lecture he said:

> Those who are conservatively contented with the [religious] tradition and the circle of philosophic human beings will fight one another, and surely the fight will take place in the sphere of political power. Already in the beginning of philosophy persecution sets in. The men who live toward those ideas [of philosophy] are outlawed. And yet: ideas are stronger than all empirical powers.

Strauss comments: "in order to see the relation between philosophy as rigorous science and the alternative to it clearly, one must look at the political conflict between the two antagonists, that is, at the essential character of that conflict."[30] By referring to this conflict as a fundamental tension we indicate our belief that relatively peaceful coexistence on a practical plane is both possible and desirable, especially when the *raison d'être* of both antagonists is under attack from powerful opponents who deny the very possibility of transhistorical goals. It is, then, neither safe nor theoretically rigorous for philosophy and science to become oblivious to the religious and traditional soil in which they find their roots. The most congenial political home for philosophy and science, which we might call rational liberalism, would seem to need to learn to be respectful and even conservative of that soil.

CHAPTER EIGHT

The Relation Between Philosophy and Religion

THREE FUNDAMENTAL ALTERNATIVES

The problem from which these reflections begin can be formulated in a fairly straightforward way: Although philosophy came into the world by separating itself off from religion, in modern times it seems to be incorporating within itself what more properly belongs to religion. The modern philosophy I have in mind is that which takes its relation to the tradition of Western Philosophy as part of its own self-definition. I am thinking primarily of Nietzsche and Heidegger.[1] The incorporation of religious ideas into the thought of Nietzsche and Heidegger, I will argue, fulfills one of the deepest tendencies of modern philosophy as a whole. The aim of this paper is to understand how and, more importantly, why this change has come about it. It will require a general sketch of the history of the relation between philosophy ("Western Philosophy") and religion. The sketch will culminate with Hegel, whose attempted integration of religion within philosophy is, it seems to me, most clear, most explicit, and most thoroughgoing.

The contrast here is not between philosophy and theology: natural theology, discourse about god or gods based on natural reason and naturally acquired evidence, is a part of philosophy. It is traditionally and correctly, I believe, distinguished from the supernaturally revealed theology of religion. The two, however, are not always kept apart, as the famous saying of Heraclitus illustrates: "That which alone is wise is one, it does not wish and it does wish to be called by the name of Zeus" (32B).

An illustration might be useful. The Declaration of Independence of the United States asserts that the laws of nature and of Nature's God entitle all men to certain natural rights, among which are life, liberty, and the pursuit of happiness. What is the basis in nature of these natural rights? The traditional and correct answer, I believe, is the natural superiority of the rational animal, man, to nonrational animals, beasts. But that may be only half the story. We notice that God is referred to in the Declaration at least four times in the following order, once as legislator of the laws of nature, once as Creator,[2] again as Supreme Judge of the World, and finally as the executor of Divine Providence. In the divine Governor of the world, legislative, executive, and judicial powers are united. The Founders of the United States, like intelligent men of all times, disagreed about many things, but if there is anything about which they all seemed to agree, it is the necessity to separate the powers of government. Humanly speaking, the uniting of legislative, executive, and judicial powers in the same hands, they declared, is the very definition of tyranny. Only a divine being with supreme wisdom and goodness, with no truth-obscuring and excessively self-regarding passions, could rightly possess such powers. The natural theology of the Declaration is then an extrapolation from the idea of good government to the idea of perfect government, and the perfect governor. No human being can measure up to such a standard. No human being is sufficiently godlike to be entrusted with such despotic power over other human beings. The natural rights of the Declaration then stem from human superiority with relation to the beasts and human defect with relation to God. All men are equal in that they are neither beasts nor gods. Does such a God exist? That might require faith to believe. But the natural theology of the Declaration, the idea of such a God, clarifies what it is meant to clarify whether one conceives of such a God as existing or not. By its reference to the Creator and His Providence, however, the Declaration brings both traditions together, it combines its natural theology with the revealed theology of the Biblical tradition.[3]

I. The Separation of Ancient Philosophy from Religion—The Incorporation of Religion into Modern Philosophy

Both the lovers of myth and philosophers, Aristotle says, wonder about the first things, the things whose characters and actions govern all the rest. The first philosophers distinguished themselves from the lovers of myth by no longer speaking of the first things as gods, but as nature. Science and philosophy come into the world, Aristotle suggests, with the discovery of nature. They were and still are people who have no distinct idea of nature. The words nature and natural do not occur in the Hebrew Bible or in the Gospels.[4] The prephilosophic equivalents of the word nature seem to be the words "way" or "custom." Before the discovery of nature men spoke about the gods ordering and commanding things to go in their customary ways. The way or custom of fire is to go up and burn, for the earth to bring forth plants, for human beings to speak, for one tribe to bury its dead, for another to burn its dead. At some point a curious and thoughtful person must have noticed that some ways are always the same no matter what anyone does about them, while others vary from time to time, and still others would vary from time to time more if men did not make them happen the same way. Such a person begins to become aware of the distinctions between the necessary and the accidental or contingent, the necessary and the customary, and the necessary and the artificial. The ways that vary from place to place, from city to city, from tribe to tribe, must have been most striking at first because they most contradict "our way." Herodotus tells how horror-struck Greeks and Indians were on learning of each other's diverse burial customs (III.38). These divergencies extend to differences about the nature of the gods themselves.

The suspicion begins to arise that the ways that are everywhere the same are primary, permanent, and fundamental, and those that differ from town to town and from tribe to tribe are secondary, transient, and derivative. The manmade things owe their existence to forethought; the ways which are everywhere the same seem to occur by themselves automatically inside the things characterized by them. Way or custom splits up into nature, on the one hand, and convention or law, on the other.[5] That human beings can speak is natural, that this tribe speaks its particular language, that tribe its particular language, is conventional. Impersonal nature replaces divine ordination. The good life is no longer determined by the divine law but by the quest for what is right by nature. In Plato's *Republic* the torch race in honor of the goddess, which all the interlocutors were supposed to watch, is forgotten in favor of the discussion in quest of the life that is good according to nature. Philosophy and science come into the world by separating themselves from religion.

To see the other pole of our initial problem, the incorporation of religion into philosophy, we turn to Heidegger. For Heidegger, philosophy, or what he would rather call Thinking, cannot be academic or isolated from the spirit of society, from the spirit of one's own times, from history. The deepest sense of what things are, he argues, depends on History, and History, in German *Geschichte,* he connects with the word *Geschick,* that which has been sent. The sender, this mysterious ground of existence, or ground of the relation between being and human thought, of human fate (*Schicksal*), he sometimes calls gods, sometimes god.

The great danger of our time, Heidegger argues, is that we are so overwhelmed by the power of scientific, mathematical, technological thinking that we have begun to think of human beings as just one more product of scientific laws to be serviced, used, and conveniently disposed of. In contrast to the focus on the depersonalized, the dehumanized, the cybernetic, he argues that the deepest truths about the world reveal themselves to thought and to thinkers that are caring, committed, concerned with what they regard as "mine" and ours, with home and homeland. Authenticity, the standard the he erects as a replacement for ethical virtue, emphasizes the personal and particular. The German word *Eigentlichkeit* has no direct English equivalent; its literal meaning is "one's ownness." In his "existential analytic," which allegedly exposes the deeper grounds of any ethics, conscience, anxiety, guilt, and "fallenness" become central.

That your and my being here, our particularity, our individuality, even the fall of a sparrow, should have ultimate significance would make sense, if we and our world are the creations of a loving, caring omnipotent God. Heidegger has incorporated Christian religious ideas and sentiments into his thinking without articulating the theological premises they presuppose.

In fairness to Heidegger, however, it should be said that he emphatically rejects the account of the origin of philosophy out of religion and myth as a Platonic-Aristotelian prejudice. "The fall of thinking into the sciences, on the one hand, and faith, on the other, is the evil, fateful sending of Being."[6] Religious *mythos* and philosophic *logos* "became separated and opposed only there where neither mythos nor logos could maintain their original essential presence. This happened already with Plato." He denies that logos could destroy mythos. "Nothing religious is ever destroyed by logic; it is destroyed only by the god's withdrawing himself."[7]

II. The Distinctions Between Ancient, Medieval, and Modern Philosophy

For our purposes, a sketch of the history of the relation between philosophy and religion, the usual distinctions ancient, medieval, and modern seem adequate. They are distinguished here not according to the times of their origin and predominance, but in terms of what each takes to be the ultimate source of meaningfulness in the world: ancient philosophy as nature-centered (physiocentric); medieval philosophy as God-centered (theocentric), and modern philosophy as man (human)-centered (anthropocentric). Although the later positions presuppose the existence of the earlier, they are not considered here as time bound. They are presented as much as possible in their own terms as permanent alternatives.

The way representatives of each position account for the appearance of purposiveness or end-directed activity in nature can serve to illustrate the differences.

The primary prescientific or prephilosophic meaning of the Greek word for nature, *physis*, is growth, which includes that into which a thing grows, the end or term of growth, the state in which the thing is most capable of doing the work, or, as we say, the function, characteristic of that thing. End-directed activity is most characteristic of living things. The acorn becomes intelligible as a possible oak. The structure of the eye becomes intelligible with a view to its function of seeing. Aristotle speaks of such an end as a cause, the cause "for the sake of which," in its Latinate form, final cause. (We concentrate here on the most influential part of ancient philosophy, Platonic-Aristotelian Philosophy.) Aristotle defines nature as a principle or cause of motion and rest in that to which it belongs primarily and not by accident. The end of natural growth is a potentiality inherent in the living thing from the beginning, in its constitution, so to speak, in its very matter. He frequently compares natural, end-directed activity to the end-directed activity of human making. The crucial differences are that in artifacts the final form of the work of art exists primarily in the mind of the artisan; both the end and the formative action have their source in the artisan, external to the thing produced (*Nicomachean Ethics* 1140a1–23;

Metaphysics 1032a12 ff.). The unapprehended ends of natural activities like respiration, metabolism, animal instinct, etc., do not require an external mind intending them as purposes. They are simply inherent in natural things as potentialities.

For Thomas Aquinas, as representative of the theocentric view, there is no end or final cause that is not intended as such by some intelligence, as the artist intends the completed work of art. If the being in which the end is being actualized does not have the intelligence to apprehend it, it is apprehended by the intelligence of another, namely the intelligence of God. We quote from his discussion of natural instinct:

> the sensitive appetite of dumb animals, and likewise the natural appetite of insensible things, result from the apprehension of an intellect, just as the appetite of the intellectual nature . . . called the will. But there is a difference, in that the will is moved by an apprehension of the intellect in the same subject; whereas the movement of the natural appetite results from the apprehension of the separate Intellect, Who is the Author of Nature; as does also the sensitive appetite of dumb animals, who act from a certain natural instinct. . . . [I]n the actions of irrational animals and of other natural things, we observe a procedure which is similar to . . . the actions of art.[8]

According to Immanuel Kant, as representative of the modern anthropocentric view, the necessary and universal laws which constitute objective knowledge of nature are not found in the things themselves, but are prescribed to nature by the human understanding. When we come across phenomena like the phenomena of living organized beings for which the laws of mechanical cause and effect do not seem adequate, the reflective judgment of the investigator should supply the phenomena with purposive laws that make sense of them *as if* some intelligent cause, a God, had produced them. Like

Thomas, Kant argues that ends in nature only make sense when they are thought of as intended by some intelligence, namely God. Teleology, he argues, finds its consummation in theology. But this God cannot be assumed to have objective reality. We produce and supply the idea of such a being to ourselves in order to satisfy the subjective needs of our cognitive faculties (*Kritik der Urteilskraft*, Einleitung and sections 75 and 76).

The ultimate source of the appearance of end-directed activity in irrational nature for the ancients is the inherent nature of things in themselves, for the medievals the mind of God, for the moderns the human understanding itself.

III. Ancient Philosophy and Religion

The Platonic-Aristotelian, or Socratic, way of seeking the primary, permanent, and fundamental things that are nature (among other things, by thinking through the implications of human speech) culminates in a doctrine that the truly fundamental is the intelligible. For Plato it seems to be the eternal ideas, or forms, or species; for Aristotle the thinking, or active intellection, that is the life or energy constitutive of those forms or ideas, or as he sometimes calls them, the universals. If there is to be genuine knowledge, or even true opinion, of things in themselves, these intelligibles must be able to exist at one and the same time both in the things they characterize and in the mind knowing them, in the things as enmattered, in the mind as thought (Plato, *Meno* 72c6–d1). Corresponding to the intelligibility in things, then, is the power in all rational beings to apprehend it, the power called *nous*, intellectual intuition.

There is another way to put this: for the classical philosophers the intelligible is the divine, and the concern for the truly divine is philosophy. The self-sufficiency of the intelligible is the standard for both theoretical and practical life;

in this respect there is a harmony between theory and practice. But the intelligible is manifested in universal or general principles, or, as we often say, in general laws, and every practical action is a particular action, an action of one's own. It is true that every human action is more or less permeated by the intelligible, by understanding, but it is always a particular action mixed with the accidental and the contingent, the inherently unintelligible (Aristotle, *Metaphysics* 1072a14, 1036a9). According to this philosophy then, it is impossible for any particular or contingent event to be absolutely sacred. There seems to be a tension in our souls between the love of the good recognized by intelligence and the love of one's own that guides our spirited part. It is the natural favoritism of parents for their own children and its conflict with pure justice that leads to the unnatural family arrangements of Plato's *Republic*.

Since both, the love of one's own stemming from our particularity and the love of the good stemming from our intelligence, are rooted in human nature, the tension between them can assume tragic proportions. We have no choice about the genetic makeup with which we are endowed, the family and country in which we are born. Yet to be deprived of pride of ancestry is barely supportable for most individuals, families, and societies. Virtue is not virtue, knowledge is not knowledge, until it becomes one's own. The love of own's own and the love of the good are both equally primordial or ineradicable. But to say that both are equally primordial is not to say that both are of equal dignity. As Leo Strauss put it, classical "idealism" held that "the form is higher in dignity than the matter. . . . The practical meaning of this idealism is that the good is of higher dignity than one's own. . . ."[9] On the highest level, according to Socrates in the *Symposium*, the love of one's own and the love of the good are reconciled in the beautiful, the true object of love is "to have the good be one's own forever" (206a).

But for most of us most of the time the words of Plato's Athenian Stranger seem appropriate:

> In truth the cause of every failure comes to each person each time through excessive love of oneself. For the one who loves is blinded about the beloved, so that he judges the just and the good and the noble things badly, believing that he is bound always to honor what is his own before the truth (*Laws* 731e–732a).

This consequence of our particular needs, this tendency to sacrifice the truth to the love of one's own, points to moderation as a key virtue in moral and political life, even the moderation of our highest hopes.

The sublime *Alenu* prayer sung at the close of almost every Jewish religious service calls out:

> We therefore hope in thee, O Lord our God, that we may speedily behold the glory of thy might, when the abominations will be removed from the earth . . . when the world will be perfected under the kingdom of the Almighty, and all the children of flesh will call upon thy name and all the wicked of the earth will be turned to thee.

Compare this with Socrates' reply in the *Theaetetus* to an enthusiastic Theodorus: "But it is not possible for evils to be done away with, Theodorus, for it is necessary that there always be something contrary to the good." The moderate Socrates, however, does not silence the voice of his heart; he goes on to add that of course evils cannot be established among gods, but necessity forces the evils "to haunt mortal nature and this region here." Flight from these evils, he says, partial assimilation to the divine as far as possible in justice, holiness, and intelligence, may be possible for some individuals but not for society as a whole (*Theaetetus* 176a–b).

That moderation is the virtue of the philosopher's action,

but not his thoughts is exhibited by this statement of the tenth-century Arabic philosopher Alfarabi on the relation of classical philosophy to religion.

> There are two ways of making a thing comprehensible: first, by causing its essence to be perceived by the intellect, and second, by causing it to be imagined through the similitude that imitates it. Assent, too, is brought about by one of two methods, either the method of . . . demonstration or the method of persuasion . . . when one acquires knowledge of the beings or receives instruction in them, if he . . . perceives their ideas . . . with his intellect, and his assent . . . is by means of . . . demonstration, then the science that comprises these cognitions is *philosophy*. . . . if they are known by imagining them through similitudes that imitate them, and assent to what is imagined . . . is caused by persuasive methods then the ancients call what comprises these cognitions *religion*. . . . Therefore, according to the ancients, religion is an imitation of philosophy. . . . Religion sets forth their images [of the ultimate principles] by . . . similitudes . . . taken from corporeal principles and imitates them by their likenesses among political offices . . .[10]

Further, to enable us to overcome the passions bred by radical selfishness and the love of one's own, counteracting lawabiding passions must be bred by the sanctification of norms, in order to enable us to live decently in society with a modicum of freedom. Such sanctifications require divinities that can address us passionately, individually and collectively, here and now. Classical philosophy never considered itself able to become a substitute for public religion.

If Aristotle's treatment of religion is to be found anywhere, I believe it is most of all in his *Poetics*,[11] and in scattered remarks in *Ethics*, *Politics*, *Rhetoric*, and *Metaphysics*. For Thomas Aquinas, on the other hand, it is much clearer: religion is classified in the *Summa Theologiae* as a part of the moral virtue of justice, religion is the worship which is properly due and paid to God.

IV. Medieval Philosophy and Religion

Medieval philosophy is characterized by the attempt to reconcile classical philosophy with revealed or scriptural religion, with the religions of the Bible and the Koran. For the most influential medieval philosophers the natural world, as far as natural reason unaided by supernatural revelation could comprehend it, was to be understood through the philosophy of Aristotle. The fundamental presupposition for medieval philosophy is belief in the truth of the revealed word and in the God that is its supernatural source. This assumption entails important modifications of and deviations from Aristotelian doctrine. Aristotle evidently held that the visible universe is eternal, at least, with Plato, that its intelligible underpinnings, the forms, are eternal.

All philosophers seem to have accepted what has been called the principle of causality, namely, that nothing comes into being out of nothing. The positive consequence of the principle is not: Everything comes into being out of something.[12] It is rather that: Everything that comes into being comes into being out of something. Those "somethings out of which" have either themselves come into being or have not come into being, that is, are unchanging. The task for scientific and philosophic knowledge then is to discover the permanent or unchanging somethings, or principles, underlying change.[13] As Thomas Aquinas says, "that the world did not always exist is held by faith alone, and cannot be proved by demonstration."[14]

The Bible tells us that in the beginning God created the heaven and the earth. If the ultimate principles are unchanging or eternal, philosophy tells us, there was no ultimate beginning. To meet the challenge of ancient philosophy, religious or scriptural philosophers declare that Almighty God supernaturally, miraculously, created everything out of nothing. The Platonic and Aristotelian forms are thoughts in the divine mind in accordance with which He creates the laws of nature. Creation is unlike any human making; it is not bound by the limitations of its materials, for all material limits too are grounded in God's will. There is, therefore, no eternal order independent of divine will, no source of principles for human guidance apart from that will. If the God of the Bible is omnipotent, He is also omniscient. Not the least action of the least of his creatures escapes his notice.

In practice He is a caring God, a just and loving God. There is no necessary conflict between the love of one's own and the good, if the love of one's own is sanctified by the ultimate principle of the universe. Particularity is not disparaged: the ultimate principle of the universe reveals itself in personal address to particular men, particular families and nations, on particular occasions. If their souls are immortal, each individual is of everlasting importance. One can be fully at home in the world when the world is one's Father's house (Psalm 139).

On the other hand, one might say that the gulf between man and the God of the Bible is unbridgeable. In the Hebrew Bible the mutuality of the Covenant and the gift of the Law bridge the gulf. In Christianity the gulf itself, one is tempted to say, is overcome by the mystery of God's becoming a particular man, by the very notion that full divinity can exist in a particular man. The pain of the mortal gulf between man and God is relieved by Jesus' assumption of the world's sin, for all those who are justified by believing in that sacrifice.

Morality for the Bible as a whole takes on heightened importance when error and perversion become sin, an ungrateful personal affront to the loving all-powerful source of all goodness. In explaining why divine law was needed in addition to natural and human law Thomas Aquinas says that because "of the uncertainty of human judgement . . . on contingent and particular matters . . . that man may know without doubt what he ought to do and what he ought to avoid, it was necessary for man to be directed . . . by a law given by God, for . . . such a law cannot err" (*Summa Theologiae* I-II Q.91 A.4). This, however, is moderated by the arguments of philosophers like Thomas that the great bulk of morality is given to men through the natural law, the law of reason. Virtues are habits that perfect natural powers in a world so designed as to allow reason to discover ends implicit in nature. Something like classical moderation, the moderating of unreasonable expectations, is also preserved in the medieval distinction between this world and the kingdom of heaven, the world to come, the "other" world.

How can classical and medieval philosophy deal with each other's fundamental assumptions? Thomas' harmonizing formula is that revelation goes beyond, but cannot contradict, reason. Because revelation is superior, philosophy is the handmaid of theology. That is not acceptable to Alfarabi's ancient philosopher: religion is an imitation of and therefore subordinate to philosophy. The possibility of Creation, Revelation, and miracles seems to rest on the assumption that God is omnipotent and his will is unfathomable. Can reason refute that assumption? Is it self-contradictory? Can revelation refute reason? Can they both even agree about what would constitute a refutation, what would constitute evidence? A rational proof demands suspension of belief, or doubt, until all the evidence is in. Revelation claims that its truth requires faith in the revealed and revealing God in order to be accepted and to be understood. From the point of view of rational philosophy, faith or belief is simply insufficient knowledge. Each can refute the other only by begging the question in dispute, presupposing its own canons for understanding. They appear to be mutually irrefutable.

Faith, Thomas Aquinas tells us, is an act of the intellect wherein the intellect is moved to assent, not by the clarity and evidence of the intellect's proper object, but by the command of the will, the practical faculty.[15] This subordination of the theoretical to the practical faculty is another fundamental difference between ancient and medieval philosophy.

V. Modern Philosophy

The mutual irrefutability of philosophy and revelation, Leo Strauss has suggested, has created a tension that is perhaps the secret of the vitality of Western Civilization, a civilization that will not allow the mind to silence the voice of the heart, nor the heart to drown out the voice of the mind. This tension must trouble philosophy more than faith. If faith in the omnipotent God of Creation, Revelation, and miracles cannot be refuted, does philosophy itself rest on indemonstrable premises, just a different kind of faith, or at best, disputable opinion?[16]

To free itself from this unresolvable tension and uncertainty, Strauss suggests, a new kind of philosophy, modern philosophy, comes into the world, rejecting both the idea of nature of classical philosophy and the omnipotent God of medieval philosophy—a new philosophy with a new basis, that is, man: the ultimate source of meaning for humanity's understanding of the world is the human understanding itself.

> If one wished to refute Orthodoxy, no other way remained than to attempt to demonstrate that the world and life are fully understandable without the assumption of an unfathomable God. That means that the refutation of Orthodoxy depended on the success of a system. Man had to prove himself theoretically and practically the lord of the world and the lord of his life. The world he created had to make the world that was merely "given" to him disappear. Then Orthodoxy was more than refuted, it was "outlived."[17]

The medievals in their very effort to harmonize classical philosophy with revealed religion face and articulate the essential tension between them. Modern philosophy incorporates the religious motive, but "supersedes" that essential tension by rationalizing and secularizing revealed religion's sanctification of individuality. This, I believe, is behind Leo Strauss's remark at the end of *Natural Right and History*: "The quarrel between the ancients and the moderns concerns eventually, and perhaps even from the beginning, the status of individuality." If this is what Strauss meant, the sources of modern philosophy would be the idea of philosophy and science first articulated by classical philosophy and, negatively, the Guarantor of the significance of individuality, the omnipotent God of revealed religion. The source then would be the wish to supersede the tension arising from their mutual irrefutability. In the introduction to his *Logic*, Kant says that the basic questions determining the basic divisions of philosophy, What can I know? (Nature), What ought I to do? (Morality), What may I hope? (Religion), can all be referred to the single question, What is man?

The classical understanding of nature is opposed by the modern idea of the conquest of nature and its practical goal, in Descartes' words, of making men "the masters and possessors of nature." The classical and medieval standard for morality, virtue, seen as natural fulfillment of natural powers, is replaced by freedom, or, more precisely, autonomy. And last in our sketch of modern thought, the idea of history as a determinate process rather than a certain kind of study, becomes a secular substitute for Divine Providence.

A.

Nature, Bacon declares, cannot be conquered except by being obeyed.[18] The nature to be conquered must be different from the nature to be obeyed. The nature to be conquered is nature as it presents itself to ordinary prescientific experience, with its apparent purposivity and unpredictability due to chance. The nature to be obeyed, through which the conquest is to take place, is the nature to be discovered by methodical experimentation keyed to (following Galileo and Descartes) mathematical laws. Final causes are to be excluded from physics. To prepare the way for the new science, the classical reliance on, or "idolization" of, natural experience and natural speech is to be refuted by a critique or refutation of the natural human understanding. This critique culminates in Kant's assumption that there is no intellectual intuition that permits us to gain access to the nature of things in themselves. There is no natural harmony between the natural human understanding and the natural world. Nature is not a kind mother, she must be tortured by methodical experimentation and forced to reveal her secrets. Furthermore, the ideas of chance or fortune and the subordination of art to nature must be rejected as breeding a "premature despair in human enterprises" (*De Augmentis Scientiarum* II.2). The Aristotelian notion of unstable matter, pure potency, underlying the notion of fortune is altogether to be rejected. Matter is to be understood as acting in accordance with fixed and unwavering laws. Above all, Bacon insisted in opposition to medieval philosophy, physics must be separated from theology in order to avoid fabulous philosophy and heretical religion. With Bacon clearing the way, Descartes' "I think" becomes the exemplar of finding a beginning for thought that in no way depends upon anything outside of man.

B.

The new philosophy was obliged to find a new moral standard that would be compatible with a nonteleological physics. That standard, again, is freedom, autonomy, self-legislation.[19] Just as the "intelligible world" is "our" world, a world we have construed, that is, constructed,[20] so part of the reverence or respect we feel for the moral law of autonomy, Kant suggests, is a love for what we have produced ourselves (*Grundlegung zur Metaphysik der Sitten*, footnote to IV, 401). Rousseau was the first to define freedom as self-legislation, but it is already implicit in Hobbes's theory of sovereignty and the social contract. According to Hobbes, we must obey the sovereign because each of us through the social contract has agreed to allow his will to represent each of our wills. His legislation, because of the social contract, is, legally considered, our own self-legislation. He is our representative. Hobbes also formulated the more fundamental principle underlying this conception: there is "no Obligation on any man, which ariseth not from some Act of his own" (*Leviathan* ch. 21).

This is all made even more explicit in Rousseau's doctrine of the general will. Freedom in society consists in uniting oneself with all the rest under the general will that declares the law, while at the same time remaining free in so far as one has contributed to the making of that law. The process that makes the will general also makes it moral. Being compelled to express one's will in such form that it can become a general law, so that it can coincide with the wills of all the others, moralizes the will. If I generalize my desire not to pay taxes in a law that no one ought to pay taxes, I am compelled to see that then the police, public schools, courts, and so on, would disappear, the irrationality of my original desire becomes manifest.

The idea is fully developed as a moral principle in Kant's doctrine of the categorical imperative: so act that the maxim of your action can become a universal law. The truly free or moral person, according to Kant, bows only to the moral will or practical reason within him or her self, and not to any standard imposed from without, either by nature or by God.

Hegel extends the notion of freedom as self-legislation beyond politics and morality to make it a logical and metaphysical principle. The life of the concept, the life of that Spirit or Mind that forms and informs the human mind, human History, and the objects of human knowledge—the mind of God—proceeds in accordance with the principle of freedom, self-legislation. Hegel begins his "Doctrine of the Concept" with these words: "The Concept is the principle of freedom, the power of substance self-realized." And later:

> . . . the concept is the genuine first; and things are what they are through the action of the concept dwelling in them and revealing itself in them. In our religious consciousness this comes forth in such a way that we say God created the world out of nothing, or, in other words, the world and finite things have issued from the fullness of the divine thoughts and divine decrees. Thus religion recognizes thought, more exactly the concept, to be the infinite form, or the free creative activity which can realize itself without the help of a matter that exists outside it.[21]

At the same time modern ethical and especially political thought is said to be characterized by a certain Realism associated with the name of Machiavelli. Classical and medieval political thought, the moderns argue, failed because they aimed too high. Because they based their political doctrines on exalted notions of virtue and societies devoted to the formation of virtue, they made themselves ineffective. As Bacon put it, their discourses are beautiful like the stars, which give little light because they are so high. Effectiveness can be secured by lowering one's goals, by accepting and exploiting those lower motives that move most men most of the time: pleasure, comfort, acquisitiveness, and especially that all powerful negative motive fear, fear for the loss of one's life and fear for the possible loss of what one already possesses.[22]

C.

History, the meeting place of modern morality with modern realism, seems to have been conceived as the secular substitute for divine providence. One of the first signposts on the way to the idea was Machiavelli's observation that the conflicts between nobles and plebeians in Rome, the vicious civil strife universally deplored by the philosophers, actually led to the greater good of Rome as a whole. Adam Smith extends the notion of private vice, public benefit, to the economic sphere.

Merchants intending only their own gain increase the annual income and well-being of society as a whole; led by an invisible hand they promote beneficial ends which are no part of their intentions.

Kant calls for a history that will show how the antagonism of men in society, their ambition, lust for power, and greed, cause them to develop their talents and, consequently, their moral discrimination so as to prepare them for citizenship in the perfectly free and moral societies of the future (*Idee zu einer allgemeinen Geschichte in weltbürgerlicher Absicht, Idea of a Universal History with Cosmopolitan Intent*). Hegel, as it were, takes up Kant's call, finding Kantian freedom and reason, linked up with this own doctrine of logical opposites, operative everywhere in History, making Smith's invisible hand visible as the self-unfolding of the human spirit and Spirit in general. This self-unfolding culminates in the self-consciousness that all spiritual goods are produced not by any external source, but by Spirit itself. The idea of History and the modern idea of freedom seem to be inextricably linked, history allegedly showing that man's freedom is basically limited only by the ideas of those limits that human consciousness has imposed on itself; man's freedom is limited by his earlier use of that inchoate freedom, and not by his nature or by the whole order of nature and creation.[23]

VI. Philosophy of Religion

Modern philosophy's world of natural science and its moral world of autonomy have been spoken of here as peculiarly "ours" because in some decisive sense we make them. If it is permitted to interpret this development as, in part, rooted in a desire to be fully at home in *the* world, and to want to be fully at home in the world is a religious motive, perfectly appropriate for a world governed by an omnipotent, beneficent, and loving God, then perhaps we can speak of a religious motive permeating modern philosophy from its beginning, even in its antitheological stances. If this is correct, one can say that this motive begins to become explicit with the formal acceptance of philosophy of religion as an accepted branch of philosophy.

The modern scientific conception of nature, according to Kant, is incapable of supplying ethical and political standards. Morality is traced to a source independent of nature, namely, practical reason. The realm of nature and the realm of freedom or morality, according to Kant, do not contradict one another, but like parallel lines simply do not meet. This thoroughgoing separation becomes a special problem for Kantian philosophy. How can natural man and moral man coexist in one and the same man? How can the two realms be brought together in systematic unity?

Kant experimented with a philosophy of history, but finally settled on a philosophy of religion. *The Critique of Pure Reason* established, according to Kant, that we have no *knowledge*, positive or negative, concerning the existence of God. Religion within the limits of reason alone establishes what in the absence of knowledge we are obliged to believe in order to strengthen our capacities to obey the moral law. Religion is unambiguously subordinated to morality, moral reason: "pure moral legislation, through which the will of God is primordially engraved in our hearts, is not only the unavoidable condition of all true religion whatsoever, but is also that which really constitutes such religion." True religion, he argues, "is a purely rational affair."[24]

His position is brought out dramatically by his interpretation of what he calls the myth of Abraham's sacrifice: Abraham should have replied to this supposedly divine voice that even if your voice rings down from heaven, if you order to kill my good son, contrary to the moral law, you cannot be the voice of God.[25] Some might regard this as superficially rational; but would the story of Abraham's sacrifice have had the influence it has had if he had indeed sacrificed Isaac?

Hegel's thought aims to absolute comprehensiveness. It aims not only at comprehending and superseding all previous philosophies and theories, but also the truth not only *about* but also *within* practical life and reality as a whole. Its all-comprehensiveness will allow it to supersede all finite standpoints. One most important part of that reality is religious life and religious thought.[26] The incorporation of religion into philosophy reaches its culmination in Hegel. "Culture has," he declares:

> raised this latest era so far above the ancient antithesis of reason and faith, of philosophy and positive religion, that this opposition of faith and knowledge has acquired quite a different sense and has now been transferred into the field of philosophy itself. In earlier times philosophy was said to be the handmaid of faith. Ideas and expressions of this sort have vanished and philosophy has irresistibly affirmed its absolute autonomy.[27]

Kant, too, he argues, tried to accomplish this synthesis, but his notion of reason was too narrow. Alongside the narrowly intellectual and rational, "religion has its sublime aspect as feeling, the love filled with eternal longing . . . it yearns for eternal beauty and bliss . . . it seeks . . . the Absolute and the eternal" (Hegel 1970, 290–91 [German]; Hegel 1970, 58 [English]). Hegel's philosophy must encompass the full range of religious experience. For Kant, Jesus was a representation of "the Idea of Humanity in its full moral perfection." For Hegel, Jesus was the epoch-making revelation that the universal divine Spirit, God, that permeates and enlivens the universe dwells in and comes to full self-consciousness in man, in the *human* spirit. This consciousness goes through stages, the highest of which is the conceptual. "Every philosophy sets forth nothing else but the construction of highest bliss as Idea." "The sins of him who lies against the Holy Spirit cannot be forgiven, and the lie against the Spirit is that he is not a universal. . . ."[28]

But this sanctification of the universal must be combined with the sanctification of the individual subject for Hegel. He rephrases the Platonic statement that evils will not cease for humans until "state power" and philosophy come together by arguing that not only state power and philosophy, but "state power, *religion*, and the principles of philosophy" must come together. "Plato, he [Hegel] asserts, did not know the idea of freedom, an outgrowth of the Christian doctrine that 'the individual *as such* has an infinite value'; according to Plato man is free only in so far as he is a philosopher."[29] Plato, in opposition to the religion of his time, found the ground of righteousness in the Idea, but the Idea in its most general and abstract form; he did not do justice to the subjective side of the Idea, its being for itself, its life in concrete individual subjectivity, in feeling, intuition, and pictorial representation. In religion (Protestant religion) only is the holiness of subjective individuality adequately expressed. And consequently, in the modern constitutional order only, where the spirit of the state is permeated by the spirit of such religion, will there come to be adequate recognition of and protection for subjective freedom, for individual liberty (*Enzyklopädie*, 482 and 552).

The expected transformation of human life, Hegel's rational kingdom of heaven on earth, is long overdue, according to his schedule. Kierkegaard, revolted by Hegelian rationalism, turned to revelation as intrinsically irrational. Nietzsche continued the modern project of finding the source of meaning in, rather than outside of, man, no longer as reason, however, but as will. Heidegger urges us to be resolute without clarifying what the ends of that resolution are to be. The classical and medieval dependence of morality on nature and natural law is replaced by an exaltation of human "creativity" coupled with despair of finding a rational source of ends to guide that creativity.

However, even if modern thought should have proved an inadequate candidate for articulating the meaning of human life, there is one area in which its success seems indubitable. I refer to the natural sciences. The question for those who lean toward the classical or medieval alternatives is: Can modern natural science be integrated into those allegedly more comprehensive frameworks? One indication, certainly no proof, of this possibility is Werner Heisenberg's turning to Aristotle's concept of potency and Plato's *Timaeus* when he tries to make philosophic sense out of quantum theory.[30]

The unanswered questions raised by this broad survey might seem overwhelming, but it does seem to be clear that we are faced by three fundamental alternatives, and that the attempt to dispense with or transcend the ancient and medieval alternatives is highly questionable. If, as Heidegger says, to question is the piety of thought, such piety requires of both philosophy and religion that each remain open to the claims and questions of the other.

CHAPTER NINE

Spiritedness in Ethics and Politics

A STUDY IN ARISTOTELIAN PSYCHOLOGY

> . . . the light of reason, from which all the clarity and beauty of virtue is derived.
>
> —*Summa Theologiae* II-II Q.142 A. 4

I

Admirers of Aristotle's writings on ethics and politics have often hailed these works for their "sublime good sense," their common and their uncommon sense. We modern scholars are both amazed and puzzled by the concentration, comprehensiveness, and uncommon theoretical seriousness with which the master of the scientific syllogism articulates and analyzes the positions of common sense. Serious thought, we have come to expect, splits apart *the* world of common sense, separating the "real" from the "ideal," or, with Plato and modern science, the knowable from the merely opinable, or with Kant, the realm of nature from the realm of morality. Aristotle's procedures seem, in contrast, to vindicate good common sense. Ethics and tough-minded realism are found together in organic unity. Every goal has its natural basis, every natural power its inherent goal.

Despite this admiration, the depth and competence of Aristotle's greatest detractors command our serious attention. The Machiavellian critique of Aristotle and classical political philosophy was, perhaps, never put more elegantly than by Francis Bacon: "As for philosophers, they make imaginary laws for imaginary commonwealths; *and their discourses are as the stars, which give little light because they are so high.*"[1] Classical political philosophy is beautiful, but too "high" to be truly useful, seems to be the verdict.

Bacon's criticism might seem to be borne out by Book One of the *Politics,* where Aristotle draws the fundamental distinction between ruler by nature and ruled by nature. The distinction is fundamental if the fundamental political question is who, or what kind of man, ought to govern the political community. Among associations or pairings, the pairing of ruler and ruled by nature ranks next in unreflective natural primacy to the first pairing, the pairing of male and female. As male and female pair together for life and procreation, so ruler by nature and ruled by nature pair together for preservation. "For that which is capable of looking ahead through intelligence [by thinking things through] is a ruler by nature and a master by nature, and that which is capable [only] of doing those things [which the former has thought through] with his body is ruled and by nature a [servant or] slave."[2] The political man in this account is defined primarily by his intellectuality, his thoughtfulness, as if only intellectual differences mattered. It requires only a modicum of experience with human affairs, not to speak of the reading of history, to know that something essential seems to be missing from this account. Hobbes's gibing comment seems plausible:

> Aristotle in the first booke of his Politiques, for a foundation of his doctrine, maketh men by nature, some more worthy to Command, meaning the wiser sort (such as he thought himself to be for his Philosophy;) others to serve, (meaning those that had strong bodies, but were not Philosophers, as he;) as if Master and Servant were . . . introduced by . . . difference of Wit: which is not only against reason; but also against experience.[3]

Hegel, the least commonsensical of philosophers, begins his account of political life with a speculative mythology entitled "Lordship and Bondage," which corresponds to Aristotle's distinguishing between ruler and ruled by nature.[4] If we discount the form and concentrate on the content, how much more down to earth is Hegel's account! Driven by the desire for recognition, the Lord is willing to risk his life in a battle for domination. Subordinating his desire for recognition to his desire for self-preservation, the Servant yields and submits himself to the domination of the Lord. It is, in non-Hegelian language, superior spiritedness that most characterizes the political man, the natural ruler.

Aristotle, as is clear to every reader of his *Ethics, Rhetoric,* and *Politics,* knew about and reflected on the importance of spiritedness, *thumos,* in the makeup of the political man. In *Politics* 7.7, he says "For all men, both ruling and freedom derive from this power: for spirit is something inclined to rule [or command] and unbeatable." In the same chapter, Aristotle goes on to describe what the natural qualities of the political multitude of the best regime ought to be: spiritedness and intelligence are the qualities focused upon. The tribes of the cold places in Europe are full of spirit, but lack intelligence. They are free but politically unstructured and unable to rule their neighbors: they have political freedom without civilization. In the empires of Asia the people are intelligent and artful, but lack spirit. Slavish and enslaved they have civilization without political freedom. In Greece, one finds both spiritedness and intelligence; its cities can combine civilization with political freedom.

The human material for the best regime should be, as are the Greeks, not only intelligent, like the natural ruler of Book One, but also spirited. Why was spiritedness left out of discussion in Book One? One possible answer is that in Book One Aristotle is seeking that which can *justify* the rule of one man over another.[5] Spiritedness may be a natural presupposition of that rule, but it cannot justify it: superiority in capacity to discern what conduces to their common good can justify it. Why does spiritedness not justify rule, and more generally, how does Aristotle understand the relation between spiritedness and virtue?

II

Before addressing these questions, some prefatory remarks are in order. The efficient cause of practical action is called forechoice, or pre-election, *proairesis*, by Aristotle.[6] It is usually mistranslated as choice. (Children and animals, Aristotle says, lack forechoice; they do not, as his translators have him say, lack choice.) The full definition of forechoice is deliberative appetite of those things in our power. At one point Aristotle remarks that forechoice is either appetitive intellect or intelligent appetite,[7] thus raising the question as to how appetite and intellect are related in practical action.[8] The efficient cause of forechoice itself then is appetite and reason, reason which is directed to some end. But the distinction between appetite and reason is not altogether clear. Appetite (*orexis*) consists of desire (*epithumia*), spirit (*thumos*), and wish or wanting (*boulēsis*);[9] but wish, Aristotle says, is in the rational part of the soul, while spirit and desire are in the irrational part, though spirit seems somehow closer to reason than desire.[10] This and other evidence indicate that Aristotle did not have high expectations for an unambiguous division of the soul into parts. This in no way prevented him from analyzing and describing its powers and their relations with as much precision as the subject allows.

There are three factors in movement, he argues: the mover, that by which it moves, and the moved. There are two kinds of movers: movers that cause others to move without moving themselves, and movers that are themselves also moved. Forechoice, we recall, is the mover of practical action, and the distinction between unmoved and moved mover reveals the relation between the two parts of the term: "fore" indicates deliberation or reason as unmoved mover, "choice," appetite as moved mover. This matter, however, admits of a more detailed treatment.

The ultimate unmoved mover of practical action is the object of appetite (*orekton*). In the soul, however, the immediate unmoved mover is the object of appetite as presented by the imagination, or fancy (*phantasia*), the power that presents the appearances of things. Irrational animals are moved by the sensitive imagination, keyed primarily to pleasure and pain, while rational animals are moved by what Aristotle calls the deliberative or calculative imagination, the imagination brought under the influence of, or into accord with, what the reason has found to be, in general, good. For rational animals the object of appetite, the unmoved mover, is presented by the imagination as the apparent (*phainomenon*) *good*. Thus, the higher appetite, the part of appetite directed primarily to ends or goals, wish or wanting, is formed.[11] The moved mover is appetite itself, or lower appetite, the affections and passions of the desiring and spirited elements, moved—shaped and prepared—by the imagination. With experience and through habituation this shaping goes on for a long time, if not for a lifetime. In the *Movement of Animals* Aristotle speaks of how the imagination through sensation or intellection fittingly prepares the appetite, the appetite fittingly prepares the passions or affections, and the passions prepare the organic parts. That which is moved, without itself moving another, is the animal itself.[12]

In the beginning of *Politics,* after arguing that the polis develops naturally out of the family household and the village, Aristotle writes,

> And that man is a political animal more than any bee or herding animal is clear. For nature, as we affirm, makes nothing in vain, and man alone among the animals has *logos,* rational speech or reason. Now then voice is a sign of the painful

> and the pleasant, therefore it also belongs to the other animals; for their nature has gone as far as this, to have sensation of painful and pleasant and to signify these things to one another. But *logos*, rational speech or reason, is for making the advantageous and the harmful clear, and so also the just and the unjust. For this in relation to the other animals is special to men, to have alone sensation of good and bad and just and unjust and the rest. And the community of these things makes a household and a *polis*.[13]

Animals possess a great variety of characteristics analogous to human virtues, and many of them have memory and various capacities for learning.[14] Yet governed by sensual or sensitive imagination and passion, they are confined in their mutual signaling to the signification of the pleasures and pains they are feeling at the present moment; they are unable to communicate information about the nature of the causes of their feelings, apart from what is revealed through the effects on their feelings.

Human thought, however, through intellection has access to the intelligible natures, the universals, implicit in what men sense and do. In matters of practice the universals, when fully explicit, issue in a true *logos* about a certain kind of action being good for a certain kind of being, such as a man or a community; the true practical *logos* expresses what right appetite pursues. But, as Aristotle notes, in practice men with experience are usually more successful than those who can discourse in universal terms, but lack experience. In practice there does not seem to be much difference between experience and science or art, for both experience and practice are concerned with individuals, with particulars. Experience (*empeiria*), for Aristotle, is the link between memory and science or art. Experience rises from memory, when many memories of the same thing are linked together in a unity: this was good for Smith, it was also good for Jones, for Green, and for Quinn, therefore it should also be good for Wilson.[15]

Although experience is cognition of individuals, universals (a certain *kind* of good thing or action, a certain *kind* of situation) would seem to be operative in the linkage and the unity, even though not fully and explicitly recognized. When they are fully and explicitly recognized we have knowledge, or science and art. With art and science one knows not only that something is so, but also why it is so.[16]

The advantageous is the good for some individual or some particular group or what conduces to it.[17] The good or the bad in practice, since practice is always the practice of individuals, always takes the form of the advantageous or the harmful. Sound practice in the service of the truly advantageous cannot be carried out by men of experience without some awareness, although not full knowledge, of the goods making that practice sound. *Logos*—rational speech, which is essentially thoughtful, and only accidentally though necessarily audible[18]—makes it possible for men to share and to compare one another's thoughts and experiences, including their thoughts about the advantageous and the harmful. Such thoughtful sharing leads naturally to consideration of how advantages and disadvantages are to be shared, apportioned, and distributed, especially those that accrue from joint or interrelated actions. The right or correct distribution of advantages and harms among men who live together, distributive justice, is their mutual or common advantage, their common good. "Justice is the political good, and this is the common advantage."[19] Some shared awareness of how advantages and disadvantages are to be distributed is operative in every political community. This shared awareness of good and bad and the common advantage, justice, makes the household and the *polis*.

But why does Aristotle say that man is *more* political than any bee or herding animal? In the *History of Animals* he distinguishes between herding, or gregarious, animals and solitary (*monadikoi*—"loners") animals. The distinctions apply to footed, winged, and swimming animals alike. Some animals, he adds, are both herding and solitary: man is one of these.[20] These animals are divided further into the political and the scattered. Examples of political animals are man, bees, wasps, ants, and cranes. "Political animals are all those from which some one and common work comes into being, which is not the sort of thing all herding or gregarious animals effect."[21] Man, then, would be more political than the other gregarious political animals because the result of human association can be a work which is more one and common than that resulting from any other animal association.

Our discussion of man's distinction through the possession of *logos* thus far has focused especially on the capacity to generalize and the capacity for sharing thoughts and experiences.[22] These considerations come together in the argument just presented. The basis of any human community is the "one and common work," the notion of distributive justice that is in fact operative in that community. This notion, the notion of what is most generally held to be the right distribution of advantages and harms in the community, can be more one and common, and hence more political, because human thoughts through intellection are the most sharable beings in the world. Human thoughts, according to Aristotle, can be truly the same in different minds, because the human mind is capable of receiving the very sensible and intelligible forms of things themselves.[23] This is reflected in the literature of both domestic tragedy and comedy, in their reliance on the fact that the deepest intimacy comes only through mutual understanding.

III

The virtue most closely associated with the spiritedness that kept the northern Europeans and the Greeks free is, of course, courage. "For those who are not capable of facing danger courageously are slaves of those who go against them."[24] Our examination of spiritedness and virtue will begin with the treatment of courage in the third book of the *Nicomachean Ethics.*

Again, some prefatory remarks seem to be called for. Serious students of Aristotle have always been interested in how he proceeds as well as what he says. We are struck by how we have been obliged to pull together strands scattered far apart in Aristotle's writings; Aristotle did not seem to make this kind of psychological investigation the central theme of any of his books. Differences between addressees are clearly important, and may be connected with even more important differences.

A heightened sense of prudence accounts for some of the difference of approach. By spelling out the truth implicit in sound practice, political philosophy tacitly or openly exposes the cognitive insufficiency of experience. Aristotle evidently took care, as far as possible, to prevent the natural enemies of sound practice—sophistry, fanaticism, and simple villainy—from taking advantage of such exposures. There is, however, another reason for the difference of approach. Aristotle the philosopher, especially in his writings on human things, where the modes of human understanding become essential parts of what is to be understood, was not content only to talk *about* a particular subject, but seemed rather to try to present his subject matter in its own inner, or natural, articulation.[25] The perspectives within which the subject matter manifests itself are presented as they exist in their prescientific, prephilosophic form. The adequacy of the subsequent analysis and refinement of views depends on the adequacy of the presentation of the initial phenomena.[26] The analysis and criticism is itself presented not as a break with the opinions and perspectives with which it begins, but as a normal and natural development, a fulfillment and refinement of those views.[27] For instance, early in Book 1 of the *Nicomachean Ethics* we are told that it is the mark of an educated man to seek that degree of precision that the nature of the subject matter permits. Aristotle says that ethical virtue, the subject of

Books One through Five, does not permit a high degree of precision. But the articulation of ethical virtue and the problems inherent in it point naturally to the need for greater clarity about the intellectual virtues, the subject of Book Six. At the point where precision constitutes part of his subject matter, intellectual virtue, Aristotle notes that precise speech is now required.[28]

With the thematic treatment of the intellectual virtues a new perspective is opened up. What was seen before as necessary for the sake of ethical virtue is now worthy of itself. Old subject matters are viewed in new ways. For example, the greatest of external goods in Book Four is said to be honor, while in Book Nine it is said to be friendship. The contradiction is to be understood dialectically. The great-souled man at first sees honor as the greatest of external goods, but within that very chapter, as Aristotle presents the inner development of the great-souled man's perspective, the doubts about that position are developed. Honor is as valuable as the cognitive capacities of its bestowers: it only makes sense when it is bestowed for genuine virtue. In Book Nine, after the intellectual virtues have been discussed, it becomes clear that the most perfect form of esteem from other human beings is the mutual love, or friendship, of the virtuous. The friendship is based on understanding, understanding virtue and understanding one another.[29] The following discussion will attend, then, to the mode of presentation as well as to what is said about courage.

Courage, in general, had been defined in Book Two as a mean with respect to feelings of fear and feelings of daring. The thematic discussion of courage in Book Three raises the question of which fears courage is particularly concerned with, since it is not concerned with all (for example, it is not courageous, but base, not to fear disgrace). The presentation takes on the character of a dialogue. "What kinds of fearful things then is the courageous man concerned with? The greatest, I should think; . . . and the most frightening thing is death. . . . What kind of death? The noblest, I should think, and that is death in battle, for that is where the greatest and most noble danger lies. The honors bestowed by cities and monarchies are also in agreement with this. In an authoritative way, then, it might be said that the courageous man is he who is not afraid of a noble death, even when the dangers that bring it on are close at hand; and such are, most of all, the dangers of war." Courage in III.6 comes to sight in its elementary and most conspicuous form, in the perspective of the citizen soldier.

The next chapter begins by noting that the same things are not frightening to all people, but there are some things beyond human endurance. And this sort of thing "is fearful for everyone, at any rate, for anyone who has sense (. . . *tōi ge noun echonti*)." This word, which in its colloquial usage can be translated "sense," is also the technical term for intellect, *nous*. With the almost parenthetical mention of the one who has sense-intellect, a new unannounced perspective emerges, the perspective of the man who endures fears and is bold towards those things which he ought, for the sake of what he ought, as he ought, and when he ought. He both feels and acts as reason dictates, for the sake of the noble, that is, for the sake of what is choiceworthy in itself. The courageous man is a mean, or median, between the altogether fearless man who is either mad or insensitive to pain, and the coward. Rash men, Aristotle says, breaking from the general scheme, seem to be a mixture of both extremes: they pretend to fearlessness and courage before danger is at hand, but hang back and disappear with the cowards when it is to be faced.[30]

Chapter eight speaks of five states that are also said to be courage, but are properly likenesses of courage. The first, and most like true courage, is political, or civic, courage, the courage of the citizen soldier.[31] The hero of the introductory dialogue on courage now has first place among the likenesses. The rhetorical emphasis here is not on political courage's falling short of true courage, but on the excellence that entitles it to first place among the likenesses, "because it arises on account of virtue, for it arises on account of shame, and on account of an appetite for nobility, (that is, for honor), and avoidance of reproach, which is a disgrace."[32] Aristotle here concedes to the common opinion that speaks of shame-respect as a virtue, because it is praiseworthy and good and operates preventively against vice. Both before and after this passage, (in IV.9), Aristotle asserts that, strictly speaking, shame is not a virtue, but a passion.[33] Virtue is not a passion, but a fixed habitual disposition toward passions and actions, determined by reason as the prudent man would determine it. Virtue is the completion, or perfection, of a fixed disposition. The discussion of shame in Book Four anticipates the distinction between continence and temperance of Book Seven. The continent man is and should be commonly praised for virtue; but the base desires that he has and fears, although he does master and "contain" them, keep him from qualifying for virtue in the strict sense of the word. In the general definition of ethical, or moral, virtue, which occurs early in the sections on ethical virtue, the possession of an intellectual virtue is an essential requirement.[34] Not all passions are equal, and those soldiers who are compelled into battle by their commanders are inferior, as the fear of bodily pains is inferior to the fear of disgrace.[35]

The third and central likeness to courage is spiritedness.[36] "Men moved by spirit seem to be courageous, like beasts rushing on one who has wounded them; *because the courageous also are spirited,* and spirit is most ready to encounter dangers."[37] Beasts and spirit itself move from passion. The courageous seek the noble, but spirit works along with them. "The 'courage' due to spirit seems to be most natural, and when forechoice and purpose have been added to it, it is courage."[38] Spiritedness, then, is the natural and passionate basis of courage. It becomes courage when it is formed by forechoice and wish, through habit, into a fixed disposition to act in accordance with the noble.

To summarize briefly: courage comes to sight first in the dialogue form of chapter six as the character of the citizen soldier, who is not afraid of a noble death when it is close at hand. In chapter seven the perspective shifts to that of the man of good sense or intellect, and courage is defined primarily in terms of the reasonable and the noble. In chapter eight the likenesses of courage are presented in descending order of distance from true courage. The citizen soldier, moved by shame-respect and the love of honor, who at first appeared as the exemplar of courage, is now not the exemplar, but the nearest and noblest likeness of the courageous man, the man of good sense-intellect. Spiritedness is shown to be the irrational natural basis of courage, the material of courage, to be shaped and guided by reason. With the ranking of the likenesses the description is completed. It ranges from (1) the mad or anaesthetic fearless man, (2) the coward, (3) the rash man, (4) courageous man, (5) the honor-loving citizen soldier, (6) the experienced professional soldier, (7) the spirted, pugnacious man, (8) the optimist, to (9) the man ignorant of dangers. The final chapter deals with the problem of the intrinsic pleasantness of virtue, where the virtue itself is primarily concerned with enduring pains. There is the briefest indication that true courage cannot be possessed in isolation from the other virtues. "The more a man possesses virtue in its entirety (*tēn aretēn pasan*), the more happy he is, and the more will he be pained by death; for life is most worth living for such a man." The end returns to and qualifies the theme of the beginning. The truly courageous men might not always make the best soldiers.

IV

Unfortunately, in the works of Aristotle left to us there does not seem to be any full and thematic analysis of spiritedness.[39] The word is very common in Greek literature, especially in Homer. Aristotle was, of course, well acquainted with the extended discussions of spiritedness in Plato, and up to a point seems to agree with them.[40]

Spiritedness manifests itself most conspicuously in anger and courage.[41] It is the power of the soul that is activated whenever something threatens or opposes what the soul seeks or cherishes as desirable or good; spirit rises to overcome the difficulty. Fear, "a painful disturbance caused by the apprehension of an impending destructive or painful evil," and hope seem to be the primary passions of spiritedness. Daring, fear's opposite, rises with the strength of the hope of overcoming the fearful evils. The sense of urgency that is part of fear, and distinguishes fear from grief and despair, indicates that fear is never without some hope of escape. A frightened coward deficient in spiritedness could not, then, be altogether devoid of hope; what he lacks is the power to set himself against the impending evil.

Not only is spiritedness the temperamental condition of political freedom, but in social and political life it is the indispensable temperamental basis for the fight against injustice. It is indispensable as well for the individual's fight against the vices within himself. The classical equivalent of conscience would seem to be a certain compound of spiritedness and shame. Shame seems to bridge the spirited and the rational parts of appetite. As fear of disgrace, shame attests to the presence of some moral danger, but the very recognition of the danger points to the simultaneous presence of some standard of goodness, even if it should only be a wish for the good opinion of those before whom one would be ashamed. Some kind of rational estimation, or comparison of the behavior with the standard, seems to be implied.[42] Lacking the standard of comparison, the shameless man fails to see his vices as disgraceful. *Aidōs*, shame-respect, is the natural predisposition for the virtue of moderation, as spiritedness is for courage; although, as we have suggested, the element of self-reproach and sense of danger in shame indicates the presence of spiritedness there too.[43] Yet, if spiritedness is material for virtuous enmity, it is also material for the opposed perversions, for vicious enmity—spitefulness, insolence, self-righteousness, hatred, and cruelty. Much, if not everything, depends upon how spiritedness is guided and trained by its leading powers. "Spiritedness too [as well as desire] perverts rulers, even those who are the best men."[44]

Spiritedness as the soul's fighting element is not difficult to recognize, but in this same small chapter of the politics (7.7), Aristotle informs us, in a reference to the Republic (375e), that "it is the spirit that produces the ability for affection (*to philētikon*); for this is the power of the soul by which we love (*philoumen*)." This is not as easy to understand.

As a sign of the two-fold character of spiritedness, Aristotle refers to spiritedness as rising more powerfully against intimates and friends, when it believes itself to be slighted, than it does against those it does not know. That the intensity of the anger matches the intensity of the affection suggests a common source. Among other lines of poetry, he quotes, "Surely those who loved beyond bounds also hate beyond bounds." "Not without reason, it seems," he says in another place, "did the first teller of myths yoke Ares together with Aphrodite."[45]

There is a feeling or attitude, a substratum as it were, common to both friendship and enmity—care.[46] One shows that one cares by making the cause of one's care one's own. "There are two things which most of all make men care and love (*philein*), one's own and the cherishable (*agapēteon*)."[47] *Thumos,* or spiritedness, would then be the source of those feelings directed primarily to the care for one's own, such as concern for self, parental love, patriotism, perhaps even a feeling for the cosmos itself, seen as an object or product of personal care.[48]

While Plato more than does justice to the political utility of spiritedness, his emphasis is on the tension between the love of one's own and the love of the good, the tension between spiritedness and philosophy.[49] Decent men naturally feel the need to strengthen and encourage the sources of human decency; they are led naturally to exaggerate the strength and significance of the cosmic supports for decency. Indecent men too are led, by some strain of decency in themselves, to justify their own indecency by exaggerating its cosmic supports.[50] Our spiritedness vies with our honesty. This tension can take a great variety of forms, even the self-defeating form of a perverted zeal for honesty that refuses to recognize the very possibility of cosmic support for decency.

The love of wisdom, of course, implies hatred of dishonesty. The philosophic man strives to be good without being dishonest with himself. In Plato's *Symposium*, the dialogue on love, the tension between the love of one's own and the love of the good is resolved. The two come together in the teaching about Eros. The object of love, *erōs*, is to have "the good be one's own forever."[51] However, the tension between spiritedness and philosophy is never resolved. Where love is celebrated as the main theme, its highest human form being philosophy, spiritedness simply disappears unmentioned.[52]

The love of one's own and its spiritedness, for Aristotle, reach fulfillment when together they are shaped and disposed by reason as material for virtue. One's own and the cherishable come together, according to Aristotle, in the friendship of the virtuous. All the appetitive parts of the good man's soul seek the same thing: his desire seeking it as pleasure, his spirit caring for it as his own, and his faculty of wishing wanting it as good.[53] He seeks what is at the same time good for himself and good simply, and that is the good of the dominant part of himself, the part which is most of all himself, the intellect. Since he is by nature political and framed to live with others, living with others like himself will enhance his happiness. The good man extends his relationship to himself to his friend, his other self. The virtuous friends' mutual conversation and their contemplation of their own and each other's goodness is pleasant in itself. Their friendship is itself a celebration of existence: for "to be is itself desirable through one's perception of oneself as being good, and such perception is pleasant in itself."[54]

Something of this difference between Plato and Aristotle seems to have been caught by Raphael in his painting, *The School of Athens*. Plato, with a somewhat troubled expression, is pointing his index finger upwards. The heels of his unshod feet are up, raising him from the ground. Aristotle, a more tranquil expression on his face, makes a calming gesture, holding the palm of his hand down. His well-sandaled feet are planted solidly on the ground.

CHAPTER TEN

Aristotle and the Moderns on Freedom and Equality

I

The modern notion of freedom as self-legislation was first expressly formulated as such by Rosseau.[1] But it is implicit at least in Hobbes's scheme of representation. Why should one obey the sovereign, according to Hobbes? Because through the social contract each of us has covenanted to allow his will to represent each of our wills, to take his will for our wills. He is our representative; his legislation through the social contract is, legally considered, our own self-legislation. In obeying him we are, legally speaking, obeying ourselves. The more fundamental principle necessitating this construction is expressed in the *Leviathan* as follows: "there being no Obligation on any man, which ariseth not from some Act of his own; for all men equally are by Nature free."[2] Rousseau and especially Kant are anticipated also in Hobbes' noticing that, according to this principle, injury and injustice are like self-contradiction, willing to do that which one has already willed through contract not to do.[3]

What does "equally" mean in the statement "all men equally are by Nature free"? It does not mean that all men are equal in natural abilities. In his discussion of the ninth "Law of Nature,"[4] which declares that every man is to acknowledge every other man as his equal by nature if there is to be peace, Hobbes leaves it open as to whether nature has, in fact, made all men equal or not. One decisive equality in the state of nature is the nearly equal ability of all men to kill one another: Even the strongest man may be killed by the weakest when he is asleep. But this is not the equality being discussed here. Locke states very clearly what I take to be Hobbes's meaning: "Though I have said . . . *that all men are by Nature equal,* I cannot be supposed to understand all sorts of *Equality*: Age or Virtue may give Men a just Precedency: *Excellence of Parts and Merit* may place others above the Common Level . . . and yet all this consists with the equality all men are in, in respect of Jurisdiction of Dominion one over another, which was the *Equality* I there spoke of . . . being that *equal Right* that every Man hath, to his *Natural Freedom,* without being subjected to the Will or Authority of any other Man."[5] As Jefferson once put it in the context of a discussion of natural talents: "Whatever be their degree of talent it is no measure of their rights. Because Sir Isaac Newton was superior to others in understanding, he was not therefore lord of the person or property of others."[6] This equality appears to be the negative condition for the positive ethical standard of freedom as self-legislation and the political standard that governments derive their just powers from the consent of the governed.

The development of the notion of freedom as self-legislation was inextricably connected with Rousseau's doctrine of the general will. As he put it in *The Social Contract*: "'The problem is to find a form of association which will defend and protect with the whole common force the person and goods of each associate, and in which each, while uniting himself with all, may still obey himself alone, and remain as free as before.' This is the fundamental problem for which the social contract provides the solution."[7] The solution is a society in which all are subject to the general will that determines the law and at the same time each, as a constituent part of that will, contributes to the making of the law to which he is subject. All are subject to laws that each has in part imposed on himself.[8] For Rosseau and for Kant the process that makes the will general is also what makes it moral. Being compelled to express one's will in such a form that it can be made to coincide with the will of all others moralizes the will; that is, it frees it from the irrationality and immorality of selfish desire.[9] For example: I decide that I do not want to pay my taxes. In a republican manner I transform my wish into the form of a law. The form of law requires me to generalize my selfish desire: No one ought to pay taxes. But then I am compelled to consider that the police, the public schools, the courts, and so on would disappear, and I become aware of the irrationality of my original inclination. The form of general or universal law, then, not only guarantees the freedom of the subject but also keeps the will rational and moral. The idea is fully developed as a moral principle in Kant's doctrine of the categorical imperative, the one fundamental imperative laid down by the moral law: So act that you can will that the maxim of your action can become a universal law. For example, Kant states, a man is hard pressed. He asks himself: May I make a promise with the intention of not keeping it? The categorical imperative impels him to ask again: Would I want the maxim of my action, to get out of a difficulty by making a false promise, to become a universal law? Should everyone make false promises when they can extricate themselves from difficulties in no other way? I then come to see, Kant says, that indeed I can will to lie, but I can in no way will a universal law of lying. By such a law there could be no promises at all. No one would trust in any promise, and my maxim, as soon as it is universalized, would contradict and annul itself.[10]

In Kant the principle of freedom or autonomy (Greek *auto-nomia*, self-legislation) is no longer primarily a political principle, but has explicitly become a moral principle. I will say little here about Hegel, except that for Hegel freedom as self-legislation is extended through and beyond politics and morality to become a logical and metaphysical principle. The life of the concept, the life of that Spirit or Mind that forms and informs the human mind, human History, and the objects of human knowledge—if you will, the mind of

God—proceeds in accordance with the principle of freedom, self-legislation.

When seen in contrast to the naturalistic ethics and politics of Plato and Aristotle, the legalism, egalitarianism, formalism, and emphasis on will common to the moral and political doctrines of Hobbes, Rousseau, Kant, and Hegel can be understood as rooted in their common depreciation or rejection of purposive nature as the ultimate source of political and ethical standards. The watchword of classical ethics is virtue, not freedom. Freedom itself becomes meaningful as the path to virtue. The classical notion implies that we can discern a natural hierarchy of human desires, culminating in the desire for the highest happiness. This, in turn, presupposes a natural hierarchy of human faculties or powers. The soul is the natural ruler of the body and the intellect or mind is by nature the ruling part of the soul. As Leo Strauss noted, it is on this basis that thoughtful men are said to be the natural rulers of the less thoughtful.[11] The modern notion, with one eye to nonteleological mathematical physics,[12] presupposes no such order of ends, an order that might allow for one man who understands it to decide what was better for another who does not understand it.

The depreciation of nature is, of course, implicit in the idea of the conquest of nature.[13] In Hobbes the goals and character of moral and political life are still determined by reference to nature, especially human nature, but in a way very different from the way of the classical tradition. The "condition of nature" is miserable; its only redeeming feature is the possibility of exit and, by means of the social contract, entering into its opposite, the state of civil society. Instead of serving as a positive guide to human goodness, the condition or state of nature clarifies the *summum malum,* what in nature is to be overcome or avoided. Nature is a source of negative standards. Hobbes's emphasis on negative standards is continued and refined by Locke in his making "uneasiness" because of the possible loss or absence of what we desire, the chief spur to human activity.[14] In chapter five of the *Essay on Civil Government*, the subject is treated playfully by his making the part that nature (compared with that which labor) contributes to the value of things shift from 1/10th, to 1/100th, to 1/1000th, to the "almost worthless materials." Less dramatically than the notion of the conquest of nature, this labor theory of value points beyond depreciation to the negation of nature. Natural defect, refined fear and pain, not merit or virtue, become the point of departure for the guidance of human activity. The negating activity of labor, "the pain which removes pain," replaces the classical notion of the art that completes, imitates, and perfects nature.[15]

The depreciation of nature culminates in Kant and Hegel by its complete disqualification as a source of ethical and political standards. For Kant, the student of Newton, nature must be understood as a mechanism. If morality is to be saved, it is to be traced to a source or sources altogether independent of nature, namely, practical reason. Only as a moral being, acting in accord with practical reason and knowing himself to be the cause of what he does, can man see himself (and therefore other men) as a noumenon, as a thing in itself, as outside the chain of mechanical causation, as free. Kant claims to have proved that moral reason and theoretical reason, which sees everything, including man, under the aegis of mechanical cause and effect, do not contradict one another; like Euclidian parallels, they simply do not meet. This thoroughgoing separation of the realm of nature from the realm of freedom then becomes a special problem for Kantian philosophy. How can natural man and moral man coexist in one and the same man? How are the realm of nature and the realm of freedom related in one and the same world? Kant wavered between two solutions to the problem of the unification of nature and freedom, a philosophy of religion or a philosophy of history. The philosophy of religion was his more fully elaborated solution. But in his reflections on history he might be said to have been the Kepler for Hegel's Newton.[16] The way two of his essays on history, *Conjectural Beginning of Human History* and *The End of All Things*, are keyed to the book of *Genesis* on the one hand and *Revelations* on the other, points to how the theory of history was intended to become a secular substitute for Biblical faith.[17] While for Kant philosophy of religion comprehends philosophy of history, for Hegel philosophy of history comprehends philosophy of religion. For Hegel nature is mere externality, the "not real"; morality moves on a lower plane than History, and all morality and History, in fact all meaningfulness in things and in minds, is ultimately traced to the free self-legislating movements of Spirit.

The essential connection between the philosophy of freedom and the philosophy of history was discussed by Leo Strauss as follows: "The so-called discovery of history consists in the realization, or in the alleged realization, that man's freedom is radically limited by his earlier use of his freedom, and not by his nature or by the whole order of nature or creation."[18] That men are limited, even in their freedom, in myriad ways is obvious to any perceptive observer. Limits that appear to a scientific or philosophic observer as rooted in human nature and circumstance, or to a religious observer as following from the will or providence of God, according to the philosophy of freedom, must be interpreted nonheteronomously, that is, in a way not inconsistent with human autonomy.[19] Moral man, in his freedom, is understood to be essentially dependent neither on nature nor on God, but on History or historical conditions, which are themselves understood as the products of human freedom. Speaking loosely, freedom is shown to be ultimately dependent only upon itself.

To sum up, the nature uncovered by modern science, which in Bacon, Descartes, Hobbes, Spinoza, Locke, and ambiguously in Rousseau is still to be obeyed, in Kant and Hegel is found altogether incapable of supplying man with ethical and political principles.[20] The classical dependence of morality on nature and of practice on theory is replaced ultimately by an exaltation of human "creativity," coupled with despair of finding a rational source of ends to guide that creativity. The most impressive recent philosophic expression of that coupling is Heidegger's coupling of authenticity with *Angst*.

II

The supposition, that is, the reason for being, of the democratic polity is freedom, says Aristotle.[21] One sign of such freedom is political equality (that is, a system of ruling and being ruled in turn), an equality that is in accord with number, treating each man as one unit and apportioning political authority according to number, not merit. Majority rule then is considered to be just rule. In effect it means rule by the poor, because they always happen to be in the majority. The other great sign of freedom is living as one likes. Living as one likes turns out to be not merely a sign of freedom but also the function or end of freedom. The slave must live as another likes; the freeman can live as he himself likes. What are the relations between freedom, equality, poverty, and living as one likes? Which is more fundamental, freedom or equality? Leo Strauss, whose interpretations of these passages I am following, argued that claims to rule are made in terms of freedom, a distinguishing mark, a superiority, not in terms of a merely shared quality, like equality, and certainly not in terms of an acknowledged defect, like poverty. If living as one likes is the end, how can politics conduce to that end? By providing the conditions for, or removing the impediments from, each to pursue as much as possible what he likes without interfering with the like pursuits of others. Those conditions of uninterferability point in the direction of what comes to be called individual rights.

But is living as one likes a reasonable end? In the *Metaphysics* (1075a19 ff.), where the order of the household is presented as an analogy for the clarification of the order of the cosmos, Aristotle says, "in a household it is the free for whom it is least of all permitted to do what they please but everything or most things are ordered, while slaves and beasts who contribute little to the common good for the most part act at random."[22] Those democrats evidently do not know what true freedom is. In Book VIII of the *Politics*, free or liberal works and deeds are distinguished from the unfree, illiberal, or vulgar: "and that task as well as that art and study ought to be deemed vulgar which renders the body or the soul or the intelligence of free men useless for the practices of virtue." Freedom is neither license nor indetermination.[23] Freedom gets its character from the end it serves, that is, virtue.

The political implications of this view are spelled out in *Politics* III.9, which could be viewed as an anticipation of Hobbes and Locke. What is the end for the sake of which the political association is constituted? What makes a society a political society? It is not an alliance for protections against criminals and foreign invaders simply for the sake of self-preservation. It is not for the sake of exchange, trade, and commerce, the guaranteeing of contracts. It is not constituted to serve negative standards, what must be prevented, minimum guarantees of what each is entitled to, or rights instead of duties. Nor is it for the sake of intermarriage, social pastimes, and religious communion, living together, or the practices of friendship. All these things are necessary if there is to be political community, but they are not sufficient. The end of the political association is virtuous living, the sharing of a good life, a communion of mutual concern for one another's well-being, which means primarily a concern for one another's qualities, one another's character. The purpose of the *polis* is the formation of virtue in the citizens. Care or friendship that does not reach to a concern for what kind of human being one's fellow citizens are is not yet political care or political friendship. Having said all this, however, it is useful to remind ourselves that Aristotle is here speaking of what he calls "political virtue," and political virtue is not complete virtue or virtue unqualified.

What is the practical sense of this emphasis on ethics? Aristotle tells us sadly that very few regimes actually do devote themselves primarily to fostering a certain state of character in the citizens, and when they do, as Sparta and Crete did, it is usually training for war. But since war is for the sake of peace and practical action ultimately for the sake of those activities that are ends in themselves, that is, leisure (*scholē*), explicit political formation of virtue usually misses the mark.[24] On the other hand, the very notion of regime, or polity, implies that every political order has ethical consequences for those that live within it.

No political society exists without some way of distributing the rewards and punishments entailed in living together, without some ranking of the relative values of goods to be exchanged. Implicit in these distributions and exchanges is a ranking of the activities and the men that received the distributions and produced the goods exchanged. Some notion of distributive justice, no matter how defective, is operative in every political community.[25] The most important distributions for setting the style or tone of society, according to Aristotle, are the distributions of political offices, especially the highest offices.[26] The ways of those who receive the highest honors are the ways most likely to be followed in society. Political society forms character whether it purposely aims at it or not. Since the most common regimes are defective regimes, it would seem that for Aristotle political formation of character is often malformation. Aristotle's policy is, on the one hand, to raise our political and ethical sights as high as they can reasonably go and, on the other, to make it perfectly clear how limited are the possibilities for actualizing our goals.

III

The founders of the American polity in their philosophic thinking were in large part followers in the tradition of the "new science of politics" of Hobbes and Locke. To what extent, and how, might their political thinking be reconcilable with the ethical approach to politics of Aristotle? If we assume that philosophers cannot live with inconsistencies, or at best cannot be untroubled by inconsistencies, then the founding fathers were not all philosophers, although they were a remarkably philosophic group of men.

As Strauss put it in connection with *The Federalist*: "These writings reveal their connection with the classics simply enough by presenting themselves as the work of one Publius."[27] It has been argued that when Publius says, "The aim of every political constitution is, or ought to be, first to obtain for rulers men who possess most wisdom to discern, and most virtue to pursue, the common good of the society," he only appears to be espousing classical principles, because he concludes the sentence by indicating that the "virtue" he speaks of is only instrumental not classical virtue: "and in the next place, to take the most effectual precautions for keeping them virtuous."[28] But Aristotle and Plato, too, use the word "virtue" to describe ordinary, or political, virtue as well as virtue in the full sense of the word, the steady habit of acting well, knowingly and with pleasure.[29] In his discussion of the best form of democracy, a judicious mixture of democracy, oligarchy, and aristocracy, where an agricultural populace elects and audits the performance of their officials, and where the highest offices are held by large land holders or those most fit for them,[30] Aristotle says:

> Necessarily those governed in this way are governed well: for the ruling offices will always be held by the best men with the consent of the people and without their being envious of the good men.

The arrangement is satisfactory also to the latter, for they will not be ruled by inferiors,

> and they will rule justly because others are authoritative over calling officials to account. For to be dependent and not to

> have license to do everything that one decides to do is advantageous: for the license to do whatever one wants is not capable of guarding against the base in every human being.[31]

Arrangements "in defect of better motives" (*The Federalist* No. 51) did not have to wait for modern times to be discovered.

There are even intimations of Publius' genuinely new argument, the argument for enlarging the orbit of the representative republic with a view to making "factious combinations less to be dreaded" (*The Federalist* No. 10).

> Wherever the middle class is large factions and dissensions arise least. Large *poleis* too are more without faction for the same reason, because the middle class is large. In small *poleis* it is easy to divide everyone into two groups, so as to leave no middle, and almost everyone is either poor or rich. Democracies too are more safe than oligarchies and last for a longer time through the men of the middle class . . . they partake more of offices in the democracies than they do in oligarchies . . . without the men of the middle the multitude of the poor fare badly and are destroyed.[32]

The men of the middle class are more likely to listen to reason, Aristotle argues, more likely to avoid the domineering arrogance of the very well-to-do and the servile envy of the poor.

The most impressive attempt known to me to combine classical thought with the principles of the American polity is to be found in the work of Harry V. Jaffa. I will for the most part confine myself here to his discussion of the Declaration of Independence in the essay, "What is Equality? The Declaration of Independence Revisited."[33] Jaffa builds on George Anastaplo's observation that the references to God in the Declaration of Independence portray him in terms of the three powers of constitutional government.[34] "All men are created equal" is interpreted by Jaffa in an Aristotelian mode placing man between beasts and God. The respects in which men are equal or the same is understood "as much by understanding what he is *not*, as by understanding what he *is* . . . man is not either beast or God." The three powers of government are properly united in God, but never in human hands; that is, they are properly united in a being that is the perfection of reason, justice, and mercy. It is the very definition of tyranny to unite them in fallible creatures like men, whose partial perfections are subject to corruption by passionate self-love and other such influences. "The equality of mankind is an equality of defect, as well as an equality of rights." The qualitative distinction between animals that possess reason and beasts that do not is more fundamental than any distinction of quantity or intensity of possession between the possessors of reason. Just government presupposes sufficient enlightenment among human beings to recognize that no rational animal is the proper subject of despotic rule, and no man is sufficiently godlike to be entrusted with despotic rule. Reciprocal with these equalities of superiority and defect is the notion that consent is the only just basis of government. Jaffa anticipates the objection that consent is not an adequate replacement for wisdom as the ground upon which rule can be legitimated. The claims of wisdom have dubious political value because of "the fact that it is not the wise who advance under the banners of wisdom but rather pretenders to wisdom." Strauss's account of the classical position in a way admits this last point. The classics favored the rule of gentlemen, that element of society that through its wealth and leisure had the greatest opportunities to acquire a liberal education, which means an education that among other things fosters civic responsibility. This points to the ultimate justification of the rule of the gentlemen: The rule of gentlemen is the political reflection of, for almost all political purposes, the impossible rule of the philosophers, the rule of "the men best by nature and best by education."[35] Jaffa is aware of the impoverishment that would attend the removal of such political reflections.

An interesting contrast to the classicism of Harry Jaffa is to be found in the classicism of George Anastaplo. While Jaffa emphasizes the natural equalities of superiority and defect upon which the moral principles governing the American polity are based, the central consideration for Anastaplo's "Constitutionalist" are the blessings of liberty. He reviews Jaffa's *Equality and Liberty* in an article entitled "Liberty and Equality."[36] Civil liberties, in contrast to civil rights, make for popular influence over, as well as protection against, government. But most importantly during "a time of effective popular rule," they provide for the protection of minorities from the encroachments of majorities, for the protection within democratic government for natural aristocracy.[37] While Jaffa's rhetoric emphasizes the transformation of self-evident truth into "living faith," the sacramental character of our moral and political principles,[38] Anastaplo recurs to the distinctions between human being and citizen, politician and scholar, thoughtful man and partisan, and nature and circumstance.[39] The inevitable partiality and relativity of any effective political statement point to prudence and moderation as indispensable political virtues—even in the pursuit of justice.[40]

The most useful way of beginning to account for these differences may well be in terms of different judgments about the needs of our situation, about "the crisis of liberal democracy," about the political conditions for philosophizing, on the one hand, and the reliability of nature, on the other.

The moral fervor of the political savior is not usually associated with the cool deliberation of the man of prudence. And yet both Jaffa and Anastaplo find their paradigms in Abraham Lincoln. After a careful line-by-line analysis of the Emancipation Proclamation, "recreating" the complex of problems Lincoln had to deal with, Anastaplo reflects on prudence in general:

> We see, of course, what prudence can mean in a particular situation—and hence what prudence itself means. One must

> adjust to one's materials, including the prejudices and limitations of one's community. Such adjustment often includes settling for less than the best. But the most useful adjustment is not possible unless one *does* know what the very best would be . . . how important chance is in human affairs—and hence how limited we often are in what we can do, even when we know what should be done. We should . . . guard against that fashionable opinion which dismisses what is reasonable and deliberate as cold-blooded and calculating. It is also important, however, if one is to be most effective as a reasonable, deliberate and deliberating human being, to seem to be other than cold-blooded and calculating . . . it is important to be a good politician. . . . we are reminded of the importance in political things of appearances, of a healthy respect for the opinions (and hence the errors as well as the sound intuition) of mankind.
>
> Certainly self-righteousness should always be held in check, but not always a show of indignation. Still, indignation even in a good cause should be carefully watched. Consider, for example, the famous Abolitionist William Lloyd Garrison's 1831 promise, "I *will* be as harsh as truth, and as uncompromising as justice. On this subject I do not wish to think, or to speak, or write, with moderation." Such passion may be useful, even necessary, if great evils are to be corrected, but only if a Lincoln should become available to supervise what finally happens and to deal prudently with others (zealous friends and sincere enemies alike) with a remarkable, even godlike, magnanimity.[41]

Last but not least, the classical emphasis on the ethical implications of all political arrangements reminds us conversely that every political arrangement presupposes certain qualities in the populace that is to live under that arrangement. Free government based on enlightened consent is not going to survive if its citizens are regarded as unworthy of such government and if they are incapable of making it work.

The cultivation of excellence, or, more euphemistically, liberal education for leadership, may be indispensable for the survival of such government. If it should be that capacities for liberal education are not created equal in all men, religious education for all the people must supplement liberal education. Did the Founding Fathers rely on the virtues of a religiously trained populace without taking provision for the continuance of that training?[42] However that may be, although they did concentrate more on the structures of government, they did not forget the character of the people. "As there is a degree of depravity in mankind which requires a certain degree of circumspection and distrust, so there are other qualities in human nature which justify a certain portion of esteem and confidence. Republican government presupposes the existence of these qualities in a higher degree than any other form."[43] Classical and American thought seem to come together most in their reliance on "moral principles grounded in thoughtfulness," political prudence, that is, the avoidance of unreasonable expectations, and the concern for enlightenment, for liberal education.

Summary and Conclusion

The modern notions of nature and freedom, I have argued, replacing the classical dependence of morality on purposive nature have led finally to the "exaltation of human 'creativity' coupled with despair of finding a rational source of ends to guide that 'creativity.'" This I understand to be what Leo Strauss spoke of as "the deepest reason for the crisis of liberal democracy." "The theoretical crisis," Strauss goes on, "does not necessarily lead to a practical crisis, for the superiority of liberal democracy to" its currently practical alternatives "is obvious enough. And, above all, liberal democracy, in contradistinction to communism and fascism, derives powerful support from a way of thinking which cannot be called modern at all: the premodern thought of our western tradition."[44]

In my brief discussion of Aristotle I focused on what might be thought to provide some of that "powerful support" directly and as a corrective.

The third section deals with two thinkers who have, with the aid of Leo Strauss and others, liberated themselves from the powerful dogma that a return to classical thought is impossible and devoted themselves to studies in depth of American thought and institutions. In interesting and complementary ways the principles, problems, and virtues of the modern American polity have been shown to require for their clarification not only modern philosophy but also the "premodern thought of our western tradition." We note that when Strauss speaks of our western *tradition*, he refers not only to classical philosophy but also to the Bible. The side of the tradition is more conspicuous in the work of Jaffa, but it is not ignored by Anastaplo.

It may not be amiss here to sketch out some of the intervening steps between the philosophy of freedom and history and the coupling of creativity with despair as it bears on the crisis of liberal democracy. History, that limit and product of human freedom, was conceived by Hegel as a rational process. The rationality of the process in the post-Hegelian development is either transformed as in Marxism or denied as by Nietzsche.

The Marxist-Leninist position looks forward to a transformation of man's moral and political being such as to make moral discipline and the compulsory side of political life dispensable. Liberal democracy, at least in its original American version, which denies that the recalcitrance in nonangelic human nature that requires government will ever disappear, is to be replaced by the dictatorship of the self-chosen representatives of the proletariat, the Communist Party. The required transformation of humanity and the universalization of Communist rule do not seem to be coming closer; the supposedly temporary dictatorship turns stale and takes on many of the odors of traditional despotism. To the extent that measures are adopted that go against the grain of "traditional" human nature, such as the collectivization of agriculture and industry, the despotic powers of government are correspondingly extended and intensified. Unreasonable hopes and expectations produce their opposites. The practical superiority of liberal democracy over communism does seem to be obvious. Yet questions of justice in connection with market conditions and the extent of private property rights under modern liberal democracy deserve notice. A Xenophontic, that is, elementary and nonideological, approach might prove useful.

From the point of view of the ordinary concerns of most men it might be said without too much oversimplification that the most prevalent and persistent forms of injustice are bullying and cheating. Cheating, it has been argued, cannot be eliminated from free market systems. The liberal democracies through the rule of law seem to have concentrated most on preventing men from bullying one another. Like our Communist rivals we are also greatly concerned with preventing cheating, but have taken the precaution of dealing with this problem in such as way to avoid concentrating too much power in the hands of our governmental protectors, so as to avoid putting our protectors in a position to bully us. A prudent decision has been made to accept slippage with one evil in order to prevent more suffering from a greater evil. The reasoning behind this choice seems to be that, although the two are often connected, injury to dignity is usually worse than injury to material well-being. Furthermore, he who is in a position to bully is usually also in a position to cheat, whereas the converse is not true.[45]

The rationality of the historical process is denied by Nietzsche, yet he remains a historicist; that is, he believes that human thought becomes meaningful only as an expression of the psyche of an individual thinker in the context of the given historical conditions of his existence. He rejected all teleology in favor of a doctrine that was to lead to a nobility beyond all past nobilities. He rejected all metaphysics as nothing but personal expressions of the will to power of its "makers," and expanded the doctrine of the will to power to cover the whole of existence, that is, into a metaphysical doctrine. We admire Nietzsche for his intrepid carrying through of the deepest tendencies of modern philosophy: its repudiation of teleology; its critique of reason; its religious devotion to finding a home for man of his own making in the world. We appreciate as well his refusal to give up the riches modern thought has repudiated. We are amazed by the ingenuity of the fantastic notion through which he proposes to hold on to what he has repudiated: the willing of the eternal return of the same. We wonder about what he might have had to endure in making that desperate notion credible to himself.

Arguments for the rule of living reason were called "aristocratic" by Aristotle and Plato. The politically practical counterpart to the rule of living reason is the rule of the liberally educated, of the men of higher education. The liberally educated man in the Aristotelian "polity," or "mixed regime," moderates between oligarchic and democratic extremes. His awareness of natural limitations, the powers of the passions, the obstacles to knowledge, the moral disguises of selfish ambition make him cautious and moderate, a center of opposition to demagoguery, extremism, and fanaticism.

The large middle class that dominates public opinion in the United States and increasingly in liberal democracies throughout the world has so far proved a great anchor of political stability.[46] It can be thought of as consisting of three combinable elements, distinguished in terms of their political objectives: a democratic element aiming at freedom and equality, based on the notion of equal rights, especially the right of each to be free from personal subjection to the will or authority of any other man; an oligarchic element aiming at wealth (the acquisition of property or "the maximization of income"), based on the notion of equality of opportunity; and an aristocratic element aiming at virtue, or excellence, or "improving the quality of life."[47] Freedom from subjection is easily interpreted as living as one likes, and the pursuit of wealth aims, it seems, at living as one likes on a larger scale. In the polity or mixed regime of the United States the political or social function of the aristocratic element might be said to educate people to like what they ought to like. The aristocrats may be defined by the primacy of learning and teaching and self-improvement for their lives. In concrete terms we are speaking of educators, artists, writers, clergy, operatives of the mass media, the "communications industry," and government officials in their educative capacities.

Because of unprecedented educational opportunities in the modern industrial world, technological society's need for a technically educated work force, and the increased accessibility of television and radio, the power and influence of what we have been calling the "aristocratic element" increases exponentially. At this point the theoretical crisis does become a practical crisis. Moral, spiritual, and intellectual autonomy, "authenticity," the reigning standard among modern intellectuals, whose potential nobility might be appreciated by those few willing and able to work for it, seeps into the mass consciousness as the *right* to live as one likes. "License plucks liberty by the nose." Can free institutions survive if the aristocratic element abandons its traditional vocation? Who is to educate the educators? This is now a pressing political, but not only political, question. The future of liberal democracy may indeed depend on our ability to avail ourselves of the resources of the premodern thought of our Western tradition.

CHAPTER ELEVEN

Aristotle and Adam Smith on Justice

COOPERATION BETWEEN ANCIENTS AND MODERNS?

I. Sympathy in Smith

The most wide-spread, but ill-informed, opinion about Adam Smith, based on his reputation as the founder of modern economics, makes him out to be a Social Darwinist for whom the most important form of human interaction is competition. In fact, the most important principle in Smith's moral psychology is what he calls sympathy, broadly understood as fellow feeling: the imaginative placing of ourselves in the situation of another, representing to ourselves what we would sense, think, and feel were we in his or her situation. We not only conceive some idea of what the other is experiencing, but in a weaker degree also feel something like it; for to conceive or imagine that we are feeling something "excites some degree of the same emotion, in proportion to the vivacity or dullness of the conception."[1] Mutual sympathy, a sense of a "correspondence of the sentiments of others with our own," seems to provide a distinct pleasure of its own: grief can be alleviated and mirth and joy enlivened by being sympathetically shared. Teaching, for example, would lose much of its relish, if one could not enter into and enjoy the feelings good students have in being introduced to important and exciting ideas—ideas that may no longer be that exciting in themselves for their teacher. Sympathy then, the key notion in *The Theory of Moral Sentiments*, provides the foundation for Smith's understanding of natural sociality: society, or association, proves to be an association in morality.

The Wealth of Nations, which for the most part considers human behavior insofar as it is governed by "the desire of bettering our condition" and "the propensity to truck, barter and exchange one thing for another," was first published in 1776.[2] The first edition of the more comprehensive *The Theory of Moral Sentiments* was published in 1759, when Smith was the professor of moral philosophy at the University of Glasgow. The last years of his life were spent preparing the sixth edition, which was published in 1790 some weeks before his death.

The chief motive for the pursuit of riches and place, according to *The Theory or Moral Sentiments*, is the honor and attention that they naturally draw to their possessors; the chief gratification of those possessors lies in their sense of how others sympathetically think and feel about the joys and exultations naturally connected with their situation. The other side of this coin is the depression felt by the visibly poor and unfortunate as they sense the effect of the presence of their miseries on others. "It is because mankind are disposed to sympathize more entirely with our joy than with our sorrow, that we make parade of our riches, and conceal our poverty" (1.3.2). While recognizing this disposition to admire, almost worship, the rich and powerful, and to despise or neglect their opposites, as a natural and necessary psychological engine of social order, at least for any relatively civilized or prosperous society, Smith faces the difficulty that it "is, at the same time, the great and the most universal cause of the corruption of our moral sentiments" (1.3.3, 4.1.8–10).

II. Fellow-feeling in Aristotle

Near the beginning of his treatment of friendship in the *Nicomachean Ethics* Aristotle speaks of *philanthrōpia*, literally affection for humanity, as the human manifestation of a natural affection for members of their own species running through almost all animals (1155a12–29; cf. 1161b3–8). The *Rhetoric* provides a more general argument.

> Since what is according to nature is pleasant [cf. 1369b33–1370a25], and things that are akin are natural to each other, all things that are akin and alike are for the most part pleasant, as human to human, horse to horse, youth to youth. . . . And since everything like and akin to oneself is pleasant, and each self feels this most of all in relation to himself, all men are fond [or lovers] of themselves more or less, because all such relations [that is, likeness and kinship] belong most of all to oneself. And since all are lovers of self, also what is one's own [literally, the things of themselves] is necessarily pleasant for all, for example, one's own deeds and words. Therefore men are also, for the most part, fond of flatterers, of lovers, of honor, and of offspring, for children too are works of one's own. And to complete things that are deficient is pleasant, for then they become work of our own. (1371b12–26)[3]

Smith's "sympathy," like Aristotle's *to philanthrōpon,* seems to be a certain imaginative extension of what Aristotle could call an interest in one's own. Hume, from whose notion of sympathy Smith seems to have developed his notion, says that it is "evident that the idea, or rather impression of ourselves is always intimately present with us."[4] He then recurs to "the great resemblance among all human creatures." Smith insists, on the first page of his *Theory of Moral Sentiments,* that "as we have no immediate experience of what other men feel, we can form no idea of the manner in which they are affected, but by conceiving what we ourselves should feel in the like situation." It follows from this that "sympathy . . . does not arise so much from the view of the passion, as from that of the situation which excites it" (1.1.1.10).

The closeness of Smith's "sympathy" to Aristotle's *to philanthrōpon* can, however, probably best be seen through a passage from the *Poetics* (1452b32–1453a7). He is explaining how the finest tragedies should be composed so as to imitate actions that arouse fear and pity. Fear is a kind of pain or trouble from the imagination of some imminent deadly or painful evil. It is felt for ourselves, or those very close to ourselves, or those like ourselves. Pity is a kind of pain from an undeserved evil or misfortune suffered by another. The qualification "undeserved" implies that a sense of justice is involved in what Aristotle defines as pity. In his chapter on pity in the *Rhetoric* (2.8 1385b12) he notes that all those things that people fear in regard to themselves, they can pity when they happen to others. The suggestion is that some possible fear is always associated with pity, that is, that this is happening to someone who, in some sense, is like oneself. The tragic hero then should be sufficiently like ourselves to enable us to feel that we could undergo a similar fate. In his discussion of the composition of tragic plots Aristotle uses the combinations of two kinds of protagonists, good and bad, with two kinds of outcomes, good fortune or bad. The fall of a very wicked man from good fortune to bad, Aristotle says, would have *to philanthrōpon*, that is, would, as Else translates, "arouse sympathy," but not pity or fear. Not pity, because the misfortune would not be undeserved; not fear, because his wickedness makes him too unlike ourselves. Yet he is sufficiently like ourselves in kind, that is in humanity, to arouse the fellow-feeling Aristotle calls *philanthrōpia*. Smith's sympathy then is very close to or the same as something Aristotle never elaborated, but did note and speak of as *to philanthrōpon*.

In what was meant to be a provocative subtitle, I spoke of the possible cooperation between ancients and moderns. Smith was not an Aristotelian.[5] His chief mentor, I believe, was his good friend Hume. I do not mean that he *intended* to cooperate with Aristotle. I will attempt to show, however, that Smith gave impressively plausible psychological accounts of things, especially the sentimental side of ethics, that Aristotle observed, noted, and alluded to, but did not elaborate. In this sense he could be thought of as "working together" with Aristotle, working together to make the same things more understandable. The fact, if it is a fact, that from very different philosophic stances different philosophers see very much the same, or very similar, things could suggest that the things have an intelligible articulation of their own. Despite their differences, Aristotle, Hume, and Smith all share a certain empiricism, that is, they all begin from what aims at being a most careful description of original experience.[6] Their adherence to what Hume calls "the experimental method of reasoning" seems to have been part of what made fidelity to experience so important to Smith and Hume that they became able to see again with Aristotle what earlier moderns on principle had looked away from.

III. Virtues and Vices

Virtues and vices are divided into two basic classes in Smith's system: (1) propriety and impropriety, and (2) merit and demerit, which includes justice and injustice.

> The sentiment or affection of the heart from which any action proceeds and upon which its whole virtue or vice must ultimately depend, may be considered under two different aspects, or in two different relations: first, in relation to the cause which excites it, or the motive which gives occasion to it; and secondly, in relation to the end which it proposes, or the effect which it tends to produce.
>
> In the suitableness or unsuitableness, in the proportion or disproportion which the affection seems to bear to the cause or object which excites it, consists the propriety or impropriety, the decency or ungracefulness of the consequent action.
>
> In the beneficial or hurtful nature of the effects which the affection aims at, or tends to produce, consists the merit or demerit of the action, the qualities by which it is entitled to reward, or is deserving of punishment. (1.1.3.5–7)

This, it seems to me, corresponds roughly to the distinction between passions and actions made by Aristotle in his discussion of how the mean of virtue falls between vices of excess and defect in passions and actions (1107a5).[7] The judgment of the propriety or impropriety of another's sentiments, according to Smith, is made basically by their correspondence or disagreement with our own. This definition does not prevent him from talking about the admiring approbation one can feel for the extraordinary acuteness of those whose sentiments "not only coincide with our own, but lead and direct our own" (1.1.4.3). In matters that do not touch us personally, for example, matters of taste or science, Smith observes, that correspondence of sentiments and the sympathizing it entails are not sought with special intensity. We can easily overlook disagreements about paintings, poems, even systems of philosophy; but if you have no proportionate fellow-feeling for griefs that preoccupy me, no indignation for grave injustices I suffer under, we will not be able to tolerate each other's company very long. You will disapprove of the violence of my passion, and I will resent your cold insensibility. Yet a spectator of someone else's misfortune, even though naturally sympathetic, cannot be expected to work up that degree of passion animating the person principally concerned. The thought of their own safety and that they are not really the sufferers will soon follow the imaginary change of situation their sympathy is based upon, reducing the intensity of their sympathy with the person principally concerned. At such a juncture a most important complication enters the natural development of sympathy. The person principally concerned, while desirous of the most complete sympathy, puts him or herself imaginatively in the place of the spectator and recognizes that he or she can obtain the consolations of sympathy only "by lowering his passion to that pitch, in which the spectators are capable of going along" (1.1.4.7). As spectators are led to imagine what they would feel if they were sufferers, so sufferers are led to imagine what they would feel if they were spectators; thus naturally desirous of sympathy, they endeavor to bring their own passions down to that pitch which the company they find themselves in can be expected to go along with. Smith observes that this is not merely the control of appearances; that the presence of a mere acquaintance is more likely to get us to compose ourselves than the presence of a friend, and an assembly of strangers more than an acquaintance, as our expectations for sympathetic indulgence diminish. This effort to bring one's emotions down to what spectators can go along with is the foundation, Smith says, of all the great virtues of self-denial, self-command, and self-government. It seems to me that Smith is describing here a large part of how most human beings go about moderating their feelings, how most human beings go about finding and constituting the mean described in Aristotle's great definition of virtue.

> Virtue then is a settled disposition for [or habit of] deliberately choosing, which exists in a mean, a mean relative to us, determined by reason [*logōi*] and as the prudent man would determine it. And it is a mean between two vices, one of excess and one of defect. And, further, it is a mean by some of the vices falling short and other vices exceeding what is appropriate in both passions and actions, while virtue both discovers and chooses the mean. (II.6 1106b36–1107a6)

As Thomas Aquinas indicates, the activity discussed here is an art.[8] It would be easy to criticize this definition; it is rather obviously circular. Prudence is the intellectual virtue that enables one correctly to choose what conduces to virtue. It's almost as if Aristotle had said virtue is behaving like a virtuous man, which may be good advice, but hardly qualifies as a philosophical definition. When a man who at the least was one of the greatest logicians that ever lived makes what could be taken for a beginner's logical slip, it might be prudent to take another look at the text, and ask, What might he be getting at? (The use of sympathetic imagination evidently also plays an important part in what has been called "careful reading."[9]) The circularity, defining the standard of virtue in terms of a certain kind of man, points, I believe, to a very important consideration: for moral *action* general rules are insufficient; given the variability of circumstances, there is no substitute for the good judgment of a man or a woman on the spot. Aristotle seems to suggest that when we exercise ourselves in steering clear of vices, something like the image of the perfectly prudent man should be guiding our judgment. Or as he says in his chapter (3.4) on wishing, or wanting (*boulēsis*), the good man judges correctly; what seems noble and pleasant to him is noble and pleasant: "he is himself, as it were, a standard and measure of these things" (1113a29–33, 1176a16–23). In progress from continence to full moderation, if that is possible, the suggestion seems to be that the image of that perfectly prudent spectator "within the breast," whose approval one aims at, might begin to look more like oneself, like one's better self. This may also help to understand the remark Aristotle makes about virtuous friends, and only virtuous friends: "a friend is another self." Smith, too, it should now be said, also has an imagined standard, also defined in terms of a certain kind of person, a standard that permits one to rise above the sentiments of one's immediately present company; he calls it the man within, the impartial spectator. The presence and power of the well-informed and impartial spectator works at changing the desire for praise into the desire to be praiseworthy.

At this point Smith also refers to a mean, his term for what translates the Greek *meson* is mediocrity. It has none of the disparaging connotations of the present-day use of the word.

> The propriety of every passion excited by objects peculiarly related to ourselves, the pitch which the spectator can go along with, must lie, it is evident, in a certain mediocrity. If the passion is too high, or . . . too low, he cannot enter into

> it. Grief and resentment for private misfortunes and injuries may easily, for example, be too high, and in the greater part of mankind they are so. They may likewise, though this more rarely happens, be too low. We denominate the excess, weakness and fury: and we call the defect stupidity, insensibility, and want of spirit.
>
> This mediocrity . . . in which the point of propriety consists, is different in different passions . . . high in some, and low in others. (1.2. introduction 1 and 2)[10]

The last part of *The Theory of Moral Sentiments* is a survey of "Systems of Moral Philosophy." In his very short, but accurate, summary of Aristotle's views he recurs to our definition:

> Virtue, according to Aristotle, consists in the habit of mediocrity according to right reason. . . . It is unnecessary to observe that this account of virtue corresponds . . . pretty exactly with what has been said above [by Smith in his own name] concerning the propriety and impropriety of conduct. (7.2.1.12)

This correspondence of views extends beyond formal considerations to matters of moral taste. But first, a preliminary remark. The difference between spectators entering into the sentiments of actors or sufferers, or persons principally concerned, and actors or sufferers toning down their emotions to what spectators can go along with, is said to be the foundation of two different kinds of virtue. The first are the amiable, kind, indulgent, humane virtues, those virtues people usually cherish in others in relation to themselves. The second are the more austere, respectable, dignified, awesome virtues of self-denial and self-government, the virtues which more often go along with authority, which people more often admire and prefer for themselves. The ancient systems, he observes, "seem chiefly to recommend the great, the awful, and the respectable virtues . . . of fortitude, magnanimity, independency . . . [of] fortune, . . . contempt of . . . accidents, of pain, poverty, exile and death." The soft, amiable, gentle virtues of "indulgent humanity" are little insisted on and often regarded as mere weaknesses (7.2.4.2). Aristotle, however, is exempted from the criticism of excessive austerity; he even adds "jocularity and good-humour" to his list of virtues, "qualities which that indulgent philosopher has thought worthy of a place in the catalogue of virtues" even though the lightness of the approval usually given them does not seem "to entitle them to so venerable a name" (7.4.5). Smith notes the importance of habit for Aristotle's ethical teaching, and how it rests on the difference between the quality of an action and the quality of a person. One burst of generosity does not make someone a generous person. That requires a more fixed regularity of character, the habit, or custom, of generosity. In II.4 1105a30–35 Aristotle speaks of how the just and temperate—the virtuous—person, acts from a certain habitual state of being: he or she acts (1) knowingly, (2) deliberately choosing virtuous acts for their own sake (this also means they find them pleasant [1099a7–30]), and (3) from a firm and unchanging disposition. Smith's emphasis throughout his book is on the sentiments from which actions proceed, but in his survey of the moral sense school he makes in his own language what seems to me to be Aristotle's point. Correct moral sentiments, he argues, lead to the greatest accuracy of judgment, especially of the moral or immoral behavior of others. However,

> We cannot indeed be always sure that the *conduct* of such a person would be in any respect correspondent to the precision and accuracy of his judgments concerning the conduct of others. Virtue requires habit and resolution of mind as well as delicacy of sentiment; and unfortunately the former qualities are sometimes wanting, where the latter is in the greatest perfection. (7.3.3.10)[11]

Smith's "accuracy of judgments," it seems to me, corresponds to Aristotle's "knowingly," his "correct moral sentiments" to Aristotle's choosing virtue deliberately for its own sake, and his "habit and resolution of mind" to Aristotle's "firm and unchanging disposition." While arguing that correct moral sentiment "is the happiest foundation upon which the superstructure of perfect virtue can be built" (7.3.3.10), he too explains why it cannot be the whole story. Nevertheless, he concludes, "There are many men who mean very well, and seriously purpose to do what they think their duty, who notwithstanding are disagreeable on account of the coarseness of their moral sentiments." In other words, good intentions and general rules are not enough; even the most well-tempered moral sentiments without good habits are not enough. From certain points of view Smith (and Hume) could be accused of confusing moral judgments with judgments of beauty, taste, or aesthetics. The main reason that Aristotle is not so frequently subjected to that charge is that one and the same word *kalon,* whose basic meaning is beautiful, in ethical contexts is almost always translated differently, translated as noble.

IV. Justice and Reciprocity in Aristotle

Aristotle begins his discussion of justice in book 5 in his usual way, arguing dialectically and critically from generally accepted opinion.

> We see indeed, that in speaking of justice everyone means that sort of settled disposition [or habit] from which people are apt to do just things and from which they act justly and want just things: the same way with injustice, [a disposition] from which they act unjustly and want unjust things. (1129a7–11)

The first four chapters articulate the rational targets of the disposition for justice: general justice, which Aristotle connects with lawfulness, the practice of all the virtues, but considered in relation to other people, is discussed first. It is distinguished from fairness, that is, particular justice, aiming at different kinds of equality, which is then divided into distributive and commutative, or rectifying, justice.

This notion of distributive justice pertains to all the divisible assets of a society, honors and offices as well as material assets. It implies that no political society exists without some way of distributing the advantages and disadvantages, rewards and punishments, entailed in living together. It comprehends what we usually separate into social, political, and economic spheres. In every society some ranking of the values of goods exchanged or distributed is worked out or works itself out. Implicit in these rankings are rankings of the activities productive of the goods and, most importantly, rankings of the men and women who receive the distributions and produce the goods. These rankings point to, or reflect, the goals or ends that predominate in the different societies: freedom in democracies, wealth in oligarchies, and virtue in aristocracies. (In mixed regimes like ours with electoral systems the debate between contending principles is, as it were, institutionalized.) In every political community some such order of distributive justice is operative, even where there might be no explicit expression given to the general idea of justice. Indeed, Aristotle suggests, the political community is constituted by the order of distributive justice it shares (*Politics* 1253a14–18). The polity, the regime, the "constitution," the "soul" of every community is the order of distributive justice operative in that community. It carries into practice the notions of what is appropriate and fitting that dominate society and are reflected in its laws. The secondary order of commutative, or rectifying, justice, the civil and criminal law, then, is derivative from the more fundamental order of distributive justice. That is, laws are laid down in accordance with the operative principles of distributive justice. Civil and criminal laws promote those principles and rectify their violations.

The mean of justice then must be distinguished from the mean of the other moral virtues, which is a mean between two vices, one of excess and one of defect, which steers between contrary states of character and passions, internal goods and evils. The mean of justice, however, concerns itself with persons, things, and external actions; it is to be found in correct relations of equality, proportional and arithmetic, between persons and their merits and external things, especially those external goods and evils that are distributable within the political community and exchangeable between members of the community.[12]

In the fifth chapter Aristotle turns to that justice in exchanges that holds together the political community, that is, proportional reciprocity. The word translated as reciprocity, *antipeponthos,* means literally to have suffered or undergone and be suffering and undergoing in return. It is a technical term in mathematics and physics, meaning inverse or reciprocal proportion, for example, the famous law of the lever in Archimedes's *Equilibrium of Planes* (Propositions 6 and 7): weights in equilibrium are said to be in reciprocal, or inverse, proportion to the lengths of their lever arms. That is, a big weight is to a little weight as the little weight's lever arm is to the big weight's lever arm (bw/lw = lwla/bwla). In equilibrium, it is as if the little weight gets reciprocity for its littleness by the bigness of its lever arm and vice versa for the big weight.

Reciprocity is like commutative or rectifying justice because it is primarily giving a thing for a thing, but it partakes of and reflects the principle of distributive justice, proportional distribution based on a hierarchy of personal qualities. Aristotle illustrates his fundamental principle of exchanges, proportional equality, by explaining that as a housebuilder is to a shoemaker, so is a house to shoes. In other words the values of commodities are set primarily by the values of the work and of the producers of the commodities. Some way must be found to equalize products of different worth, so that one can say *n* shoes equals 1 house: money is invented to provide a conventional commensurability based on need or "demand" for the exchange of intrinsically incommensurable goods. It is clear that this notion of reciprocity includes the entire commercial life of society. Commercial life is, however, only part of the story. What holds civil society together must concern itself with what moves most human beings most of the time: at the end of the *Nicomachean Ethics* Aristotle makes clear that that is passion. "Reasonable speeches . . . can urge on and strengthen generous youths of good character . . . but they are powerless to move most men . . . living as they do, by passion" (1179b4–16). In the chapter on reciprocity he explains how by acting in accord with proportional reciprocity civil society holds and remains together.

> For people seek to reciprocate either evil, or good. If they cannot reciprocate evil, they feel like they are being held in slavery. If they cannot reciprocate good, mutual giving and exchange does not take place; but it is by mutual giving and exchange that they remain together. This is why they set up a temple to Gratitude and the Graces, to promote recompense. For it is characteristic of grace and gratitude that one who has been graced should grace in return, and at another time take the initiative in gracing. (1132b34–1133a5).

In IV.5, discussing gentleness, the mean with regard to temper or anger—a mean between irascibility, bad temper, and inirascibility, lack of temper—Aristotle observes that

> those who do not get angry at those things which they ought, and in the manner in which they ought, at the time and with whom they ought, are held to be fools: for they seem to be without feeling and without a sense of pain, and since he doesn't get angry he is incapable of defending himself; and to put up with being insulted and merely to look around while one's friends are insulted is slavish. (1126a5–9, cf. 6.3.16)[13]

Aristotle points here to gratitude and anger as key passions for reciprocity. Smith's treatment of merit and demerit, justice and injustice, gives us a psychological account that fills out what Aristotle pointed to about reciprocity, but never elaborated.

V. Merit and Demerit, Justice and Injustice in Smith

Merit and demerit are defined by Smith as the qualities of deserving reward, on the one hand, and deserving punishment, on the other. Sentiments which tend to produce beneficial results are meritorious, and prompt us to reward; those which tend to produce harmful results prompt us to punish, or inflict evil upon another. Gratitude is the sentiment which "most immediately and directly prompts us to reward," and resentment is "that which most immediately and directly prompts us to punish" (2.1.1.2–3). Actions, therefore, which appear to be proper and approved objects of gratitude, appear to deserve reward; actions which appear to be proper and approved objects of resentment appear to deserve punishment.

> To reward is to recompense, to remunerate, to return good for good received. To punish, too, is to recompense, to remunerate, though in a different manner; it is to return evil for evil that has been done. (2.1.1.4)

Retaliation, Smith declares, "seems to be the great law . . . dictated to us by Nature" (2.2.1.10).

The senses of merit and demerit, however, are complicated, or, more precisely, compounded. We could not sympathize thoroughly with the gratitude of the beneficiary of an action if we did not directly approve of the affections and motives of his or her benefactor. Similarly, we could not thoroughly sympathize with the resentment of a victim, if we did not have a lack of sympathy, or an antipathy, towards the affections and motives of him or her who did the damage. The senses of merit and demerit then are compound, made up of direct sympathies or antipathies with agents, and indirect sympathies with the gratitude or resentment of recipients of actions.[14]

Beneficence and the gratitude corresponding to it, Smith observes, are free; that is, they cannot be forced. So that ingratitude, while hateful, also cannot properly be punished; for that would amount to enforcing gratitude, and would transform it into something else. There is no court of human law to enforce payments of debts of gratitude. The opposite is, of course, true of violations of justice: the violation of justice is injury, real hurt to particular persons from motives naturally disapproved of. "It is, therefore, the proper object of resentment, and of punishment, . . . the natural consequence of resentment" (2.2.1.5). A society without mutual affection and gratitude would be very poor, but could exist, say among merchants, merely from a sense of mutual utility.

> Society, however, cannot subsist among those who are at all times ready to hurt and injure one another. . . . If there is any society among robbers and murderers, they must, at least, . . . abstain from robbing and murdering one another. *Beneficence, therefore, is less essential to the existence of society than justice.* (2.2.3.3)[15]

We are led by natural principles to form the sentiments and pursue the actions that make society possible. It is a mistake to attribute the operation of those principles to a refined and enlightened human reason, and not to the wisdom of God, the wise Author of nature, who has incorporated them into our being with forces far more reliable than reason.

> Resentment seems to have been given us by nature for defense, and for defense only. It is the safeguard of justice and the security of innocence. It (1) prompts us to beat off the mischief which is attempted to be done to us, and (2) to retaliate that which is already done; that (3) the offender may be led to repent of his injustice, and (4) that others, through fear

> of the like punishment, may be terrified from being guilty of the like offense. (2.2.1.4)

Another one of these great principles is remorse. The persistent violator of the laws of justice, to the extent that he sympathizes with the hate and abhorrence other men feel for him and what he has done, becomes in some measure the object of his own hate and abhorrence. Remorse

> is made up (1) of shame from the sense of the impropriety of past conduct; (2) of grief for the effects of it; (3) of pity for those who suffer by it; and (4) of the dread and terror of punishment from the consciousness of the justly provoked resentment of all rational creatures. (2.2.2.3)

(Is it altogether accidental that Aristotle's book on justice is directly preceded by a chapter on shame?)

Smith observes that the opposite behavior naturally inspires a sentiment opposite to remorse. When someone (1) from proper motives has performed a generous action, and thinks of those he has benefited, (2) he feels himself to be the natural object of their affection and gratitude, and (3) "by sympathy with them, of the esteem and approbation of all mankind." Further, when he looks at his motive from the point of view of the indifferent spectator, he (4) "applauds himself by sympathy with the approbation of this supposed impartial judge." He enjoys the composure, serenity, and cheerfulness of deserving reward, the consciousness of merit. Smith concludes: "It is thus that man, who can subsist only in society, was fitted by nature to that situation for which he was made" (2.2.3.1). Through the mechanism of sympathy the all-wise Author of nature has taught us to respect the sentiments and judgments of our fellows, and

> has made man . . . the immediate judge of mankind; and has . . . created him after his own image, and appointed him his vicegerent upon earth, to superintend the behaviour of

> his brethren. They are taught by nature, to acknowledge that power and jurisdiction. (3.2.31)[16]

This natural jurisdiction of our fellows, however, extends only to the first instance; appeal from their sentence can be made to a much higher tribunal, the tribunal of conscience presided over by the man within the breast, that demigod, the supposed impartial and well-informed spectator; and when and if the forces of unjust accusation appear so powerful as to overwhelm and confound any, even the wisest, human judgment, appeal can be made "to a still higher tribunal, to that of the all-seeing Judge of the world, whose eye can never be deceived, and whose judgments can never be perverted." Thus nature also, Smith suggests, teaches us to hope, fear, and expect that "there is a world to come, where [under the all-seeing Judge] exact justice will be done" (2.2.3.12; 3.2.31–3).[17]

There is an interesting peculiarity that attends the operations of what Plato and Aristotle would call spiritedness, *thumos,* the source of Smith's generosity and resentment: these sentiments seem to observe something like a psychological law of retaliation or recompense of their own. A hot-tempered man curses the table or rock he has bumped into and been hurt by. We conceive something of a grateful affection and respect, as if for an old friend, for a house, tree, even a box, whose service we have long enjoyed. Both gratitude and resentment want their proper objects to be aware of and sensible to what they are receiving, to be not only aware of what but also from whom.[18] We want them to be aware of us, whether that is possible or not. Lear will take a joint-stool for his daughter Goneril, if that is the only way he can bring her before the bar of justice (*King Lear* IV.vi.20). In this context Smith speaks of ancient superstitions, dryads and lares, spirits of trees and houses (2.3.1).

There are other interesting correspondences between Aristotle and Smith, but perhaps at this point something should be said about differences.

VI. The Status of Reason

Aristotle and Smith differ in a significant way about the status of reason. Reason, Smith says, is the source of the general rules of morality and the moral judgments formed on their basis. General rules are a poor substitute for a delicate and accurate sense of propriety; but they and the sense of duty attendant upon them are of major importance for "the bulk of mankind" in the directing of their actions. The first perceptions and experiences on which general rules are founded, however, are not derived from reason, but rather from immediate sense and feeling. Pleasure and pain, the great objects of desire and aversion are derived not from reason, but, again, from immediate sense and feeling. "If virtue, therefore, in every particular instance, necessarily pleases for its own sake, and if vice as certainly displeases the mind, it cannot be reason, but immediate sense and feeling which . . . reconciles us to the one, and alienates us from the other" (7.3.2.7). Reason can be instrumental, but not authoritative in moral matters; it can show that one thing can be a means to something else that is morally satisfying, but cannot itself establish anything as morally satisfying.

As we have seen, Aristotle by contrast believes that human virtue consists in observing a mean determined by reason. Animals move themselves, according to Aristotle, in so far as they are appetitive; and appetite presupposes *phantasia* (usually translated as imagination), the presentation of appearance in the soul. In other words, the object of appetite causes movement by being imagined, or by appearing in the soul. Everyone judges or reasons on the basis of what appears in their souls. The appearances may be illusions, they may be images, or likenesses, or, Aristotle suggests, if the soul is well-constituted and rightly ordered, they may be true. In this case the things that appear would *be* as they appear. There are, Aristotle says, two kinds of *phantasia*, or imagination, sensitive imagination, which all animals possess, and rational, or calculative (*logistikē*), imagination. This difference is beautifully described by Thomas Aquinas. The power of apprehension in animals that operates on sensible particulars, the estimative power, operates by natural instinct, as, for example, when an antelope flees a lion, or a bird takes a piece of straw for nest building. In human beings, however, he calls this a cogitative power, because, although it is a power of sensitivity, it is joined to universal intellect.[19] The cogitative power

> apprehends the individual thing as existing in a common nature, and this because it is united to intellect in one and the same subject. Hence it is aware of a man as this *man*, and a tree as this *tree*; whereas instinct is not aware of an individual thing as in a common nature, but only in so far as this individual thing is the term or principle of some action or passion.[20]

The antelope knows the lion not as *this* lion but as something to flee; the bird knows the straw not as *this* straw but as something to put in the nest. This uniting of intellect and sensation in the human imagination allows the object of sense to be sensed as an object of a certain kind. In practical affairs this rational imagination is also called deliberative imagination by Aristotle. This difference between Aristotle and Smith, it seems to me, is based on the rejection by Smith, following his mentor Hume, and almost all modern philosophers, of the possibility of intellectual intuition, the rejection of *nous*.[21]

The human meaning of this difference may be seen in the different way each man views the perfection of human virtue. For Aristotle, the highest happiness is found in the highest of virtuous activities, which is the activity of the highest power we possess. That power is the intellect; that activity is contemplation, or theory; and that virtue is philosophic wisdom. The wise are the most self-sufficient of human beings. The fact that they require other human beings least of all, less than the just, the moderate, and the brave, for the actualization of their highest power, is cited by Aristotle as a mark of their superiority. Philosophic wisdom is the closest human approximation to what is simply highest, the divine source of cosmic intelligibility (X.7–8 1177a12–1178a24).

Smith's notion is much closer to what most people find preferable.

> The man of the most perfect virtue, the man whom we naturally love and revere the most, is he who joins, to the most perfect command of his own original and selfish feelings, the most exquisite sensibility both to the original and sympathetic feelings of others. The man who, to all the soft, the amiable, and the gentle virtues, joins all the great, the awful, and the respectable, must surely be the natural and proper object of our highest love and admiration. (3.3.35)

Smith knows of the Aristotelian alternative, and in another place observes that "the most sublime speculation of the contemplative philosopher can scarce compensate the neglect of the smallest active duty" (6.2.3.6).

In practice, however, perhaps they are not so far apart: when Smith found the one man who more than any other approached his standard of perfect virtue, it turned out to be the philosopher David Hume.

> The extreme gentleness of his nature never weakened either the firmness of his mind or the steadiness of his resolutions. His constant pleasantry was the genuine effusion of good nature and good humour, tempered with delicacy and modesty, and without even the slightest tincture of malignity, so frequently the disagreeable source of what is called wit in other men. . . . That gayety of temper . . . so often accompanied with frivolous and superficial qualities, was in him certainly attended with the most severe application, the most extensive learning, the greatest depth of thought, and a capacity in every respect the most comprehensive. Upon the

whole, I have always considered him, both in his lifetime and since his death, as approaching as nearly to the idea of a perfectly wise and virtuous man as perhaps the nature of human frailty will permit.[22]

CHAPTER TWELVE

Classical Prudence and the Declaration's Right to Revolution

TWO OLD CONSERVATIVES DISCUSS THE ANASTAPLO CASE (A DIALOGUE)

> "Pericles," [Alcibiades said,] "Can you teach me what law is?" ". . . You desire no very difficult matter, Alcibiades," Pericles said. "For all those things are laws which the majority, after coming together and approving, prescribes, declaring what should be done and what not." "Whether they direct good to be done, or bad?" "Good, by Zeus," he said, "my boy, but not bad. . . . Everything which the controlling power of the city prescribes, after deliberating about what must be done, is called law." "And if a tyrant controlling the city should prescribe what the citizens must do, is this also law?" . . . "Now, Alcibiades, when we were your age we also were terribly clever at . . . and debated about this sort of thing . . ." And Alcibiades said, "Would then, Pericles, I had conversed with you then, when you were most terribly clever about these things."
>
> —Xenophon, *Memorabilia of Socrates*[1]

Lawyers and judges concern themselves, in great part, with settling the problems of those who are not reasonable or self-controlled enough to settle their affairs for themselves. Occasionally, however, a case arises where it seems as if a man has run afoul of the law not because of his insufficiencies but, on the contrary, because of some superiority. Such cases raise troublesome questions. Are we not enlightened enough to lay down rules for controlling and dealing with substandard behavior without at the same time abridging the liberties men of special excellence require for the development of their talents? On the other hand, should not superior men be expected to be reasonable and prudent enough not to try to force the law to so refine itself as to be ineffective, not to force it to decide matters lying outside the province where it is capable of deciding well?[2]

The Anastaplo Case continues to arouse discussion.[3] The issues it raises are fundamental and will continue to be discussed so long as we possess an alert citizenry and a learned Bar.

The majority opinion in the Supreme Court of the United States has been described as follows:

> To what extent, consistently within the protection afforded by [the first amendment], and without forfeiture of the privilege sought, applicants for admission to the bar may withhold information concerning their political affiliations and beliefs has presented another problem which the [Supreme Court of the United States] has not resolved uniformly.
>
> . . . [In the *Anastaplo Case*,] where there was an absence of independent evidence that the petitioner ever had been a member of the Communist Party, or of any organization which might cast doubt on his loyalty, Illinois authorities were upheld as having been warranted in admonishing petitioner that, according to their established rules, a refusal to answer, albeit on First Amendment grounds, questions pertaining to such membership, would be deemed obstruction of their function of cross-examining him with a view to ascertaining his fitness to practice law, and the basis for denial of his application for admission. These officials acknowledged that they drew no inference of disloyalty or subversion from

> the applicant's refusal, but maintained that public interest in the character of an attorney overrides the applicant's desire to keep his views and associations to himself.[4]

The opinion of the Court, written by Justice Harlan, has been criticized by the dissenting justices and by Anastaplo for its refusal to acknowledge the extent to which Anastaplo had been penalized because of his opinions on the Declaration of Independence's principle of rightful rebellion. Indeed, Anastaplo has characterized the opinion of the Court as presenting a brand new case against him, a case never argued in a court of law.[5]

The following conversation took place several years after the Supreme Court of the United States had ruled on the case. The discussants, who shall be referred to as A and B, had been talking about a recent Supreme Court decision on a First Amendment case. B brought up Anastaplo's interpretation of the first amendment.[6] When B defended that interpretation by referring to the events in the Anastaplo Case itself, the following argument began:

A. What I deplore is the substitution of liberal dogmatism for constitutional doctrine, the insistence that the rights of individuals, selfish rights, even a right to selfishness, come before anything else, and that our duties as citizens count for so little. Anastaplo's efforts, his case as a whole, seem to me to further that trend.

B. But his interpretation of the Declaration of Independence's right to revolution stresses that there are *principles* in terms of which an individual can oppose himself to public opinion, that—

A. That is precisely what we do not need, examples of individuals setting themselves, as being of ultimate importance, against society, as if there were some right to be idiosyncratic, no matter what the cost.

B. Being idiosyncratic is not the point. I deplore that shallow substitute for heroism as much as you do. Perhaps Anastaplo does too. The point I was making is that there are rational principles, moral principles, in virtue of which a man can oppose an irrational public opinion, or an intellectual fashion or a tyrannical government.

A. It seems to me that the last things we need now are public demonstrations of the unnatural grounds of our conventions.

B. What we need are public reminders of the natural, or rational, grounds of our conventions, reminders that our conventions are not mere conventions, guided and determined solely by selfish interest or the convenience of those living under them, that there are moral principles, principles of justice, that any government, law, or constitution must measure up to. If that task is left neglected the feeling grows, as our liberal doctrinaires teach, that now we know "there are no absolutes," so that the field of principles guiding human behaviour is left to selfish or idiosyncratic principles or to the vagaries of public opinion. It wasn't accidental that this ruling dogma of relativism was invoked by the Supreme Court to open up the way for the suppression of political speech.[7]

A. One doesn't need relativism to prove that learning to hold one's tongue can be salutary.

B. Surely, holding one's tongue at the right time, before the right people, and in the right way, but teaching discretion is a task for teachers, for sages, for poets; it's far too delicate a task for government. The wrong kind of silence is not what we want.

A. Certainly, the regulation of political speech in a republic is a particularly delicate problem, but some control there must be. Self-control is obviously preferable. The need for political control, one might say, varies inversely with the self-restraint of the citizenry, the press, and the leaders of public opinion.

B. And the probability that such a power will be abused varies inversely with the intelligence and self-control of the governors—and they have police powers at their disposal.

A. Of course! We can hope that such a power could be dispensed with, and one can argue that perhaps, with the exception of emergency situations, it should be dispensed with, but then again—there are quite a few people who need the help of the fear of punishment to learn how to control themselves, to acquire even a modicum of discretion. It's hardly higher education, but the educative functions of the penal law are not inconsiderable.

But what has what you were saying before got to do with the Anastaplo Case?

B. There is no more dramatic way to remind people of the principles which should guide and govern political life than a properly—that is, carefully—qualified assertion of the right to rebel, to remind them that no group of men, no government, no work of merely human hands is in itself sacrosanct. The whole case revolved around his stand on the right to revolution. He qualified his arguments very carefully, citing the Declaration of Independence and Thomas Aquinas as authorities, stressing that the possession of a right does not automatically license the possessor to exercise the right, that the circumstances for a prudent and justifiable exercise of that right do not now exist and are not, in his opinion, likely to exist in this country in the foreseeable future—but that the higher principles justifying such a right must not be lost sight of, if our polity is not to lose its soul.

A. Yes, but most men—and that means a lot of men prone to abuse or to misunderstand what they hear—will hear only "right" and "revolution"; they will never grasp, or care about, the careful qualifications. The public are well enough aware of their rights as individuals. They don't need to be reminded of them. What is needed is a reaffirmation of the virtues of orderly discipline, the kind of orderly discipline that will enable us to fulfill our obligations as members of society, to fulfill our civic duties. Certainly, two or three friends sitting together in someone's living room, or some people sitting together in a classroom, can properly discuss the natural and unnatural grounds of our conventions. What else does philosophy mean? But public discussions of such matters is not, especially now, what we need.

B. Those people who voted against him, certainly, did not seem to appreciate the careful qualifications. I think we are closer to agreement at this point.

What seems to have happened is that the majorities on the Character and Fitness Committees and the Supreme Court of Illinois, untutored in or forgetful of their country's political principles, and too susceptible to that demagoguery which so magnified the internal dangers from communist subversion, simply recoiled from the abysses his remarks about the right to revolution opened up before them.

A. Whatever made him think they would act in any other way? But, before you answer that, by "abyss" do you mean the sort of thing that caused Anytus to leave the scene in Plato's *Meno*?

B. Yes, or what leads Socrates in the *Gorgias* to declare himself the only statesman in Greece. Or simply the problem faced by everyone who speculates about the fundamental principles of government: that he who speculates about the fundamental principles justifying all government is in that very act speculating about principles which would justify the alteration or abolition of any government which does not measure up to those principles.

A. It has been argued that such speculations should not be exposed unduly to the view of men unequipped to deal with them reasonably, that they should be confined to the councils of the learned. Why did he expect his examiners to face these arguments with equanimity?

B. I suppose, as your question suggests, because he, as a young man might, esteemed his chosen profession a bit too highly. He insisted upon and expected, or at least hoped, that the legal profession would act as a "learned profession." From the very beginning of the case I argued that he was overestimating the learning, intelligence, and virtue of the lawyers and the courts, that they were not up to appreciating his arguments and should not be expected to be, that he did not realize the extent to which contemporary relativistic social science had undermined the moral foundations of the rule of law in America, that the proper place for what he was trying to do was an educational institution, not the open forum of the courts.

But he maintained that the legal profession in this country was always supposed to be a learned profession, that from the beginning they were regarded as the guardians or custodians of the American system of ordered liberty.

A. Surely, Burke and Tocqueville thought that too, but in their day lawyers who wanted to educate themselves nourished their minds with classical Greek and Latin literature, the Bible, Shakespeare, Plato, Aristotle, Locke, and Montesquieu. Nowadays they don't even read a philosophic lawyer like Blackstone. They are confused by the psychologists, demoralized by the novelists, and shunted away from the older thinkers who could really help them by the historical relativism and naive scientism pouring out of the universities. They're trained to be technicians and are babes in the woods as far as competence in dealing with the principles which should be guiding their techniques is concerned. He's flattering them and fooling himself if he really thinks they are a learned profession.

B. Surely not all, or perhaps even most, lawyers were ever learned in the most serious sense of the term, but I don't think it's altogether unreasonable to expect a learned leadership to be able to exert a controlling influence.

But there's a more important ground for his expectations, one that people like us and our political science friends, he argues, are not sufficiently aware of. Lawyers, he maintains, because of their law school training, because of the techniques they learn to work with in the exercise of their craft, develop a certain sensitivity about fairness and unfairness of procedures, a practical sense of justice, that should make them more aware and more appreciative of principles of justice than members of the other learned professions. Nonlawyers, he argues, including those who write about the law, usually fail to understand how rules of law develop and work in practice. By training and experience, lawyers, he maintains, are more appreciative of the blessings of the rule of law and of the inherent justice built into the system.

A. It's a pity they're so inexplicit about it.

B. That's the problem. When it comes to clarifying and making explicit the principles of their own decency, their own virtues, the virtues of rationality, they don't know where to go.

A. Does Anastaplo still think it was worth it?

B. The record of the case, I think, justifies itself. It's a remarkable collection of documents, something like a report of a ten year long experiment to find the place of moral and intellectual excellence in the American scheme of government. It often reads like a drama, an intellectual drama: it sometimes seems too well planned to be a verbatim record. The Platonic dialogues seem most to have influenced his style, the style of his deeds as well as his words.

At the beginning of the case I think he thought he had little choice. He was too honorable and too intelligent to behave much differently. We were in the middle of the McCarthy episode, before things began to turn against McCarthy. The atmosphere created then made him feel obligated to act as he did. The demagogic use of political power to silence debate, especially intelligent debate, seemed to him to strike at the heart of the American scheme of government. If that hadn't been the case, he might have been able to swallow the foolishness of his first examiners. They had been aroused, you know, by what was almost a word for word quotation from the Declaration of Independence. Acquiescence would have meant to him contributing knowingly to what for others was an unwitting subversion of the animating principles of constitutional government in this country. To derive personal profit from what he thought was a disservice both to his country and to his principles must have been utterly repugnant to him.

He admits he might be wrong about his high expectations for lawyers. But if so, is that the profession to which he ought to belong? As one gets into that record, which he so largely shaped, one begins to wonder whether the real issue was his fitness to become a member of the Bar, or the Bar's fitness to be associated with men like him. Although he has done, and continues to do his best to encourage, if not goad, the profession to return to what he regards as its better self, the case, especially near its end, begins to look like the story of one rather uncommon man's search to find out where he rightly belongs.

He certainly has been able to educate himself in a way that he might never have been able to do as a practicing lawyer.

A. It's a funny way to get an education.

CHAPTER THIRTEEN

Xenophon's Alcibiades and Pericles on the Question of Law, with Applications to the Polity of the United States

I.

The Supreme Court of the United States, George Anastaplo argues, has improperly abandoned one of the most important functions implicit in the "judicial power of the United States"[1]—namely, exercising its own independent judgment ("with due deference to the rulings of superior courts") in determining and supervising the common law for the nation as a whole.[2] Underlying this distortion, Anastaplo suggests, is a conversion of more sophisticated jurists

> to a jurisprudential doctrine that explains common-law rulings not *as the products of reasoning with a view to justice, but rather as merely the exercise of sovereign power,* and the States could be looked to as sufficient repositories of such power. (Anastaplo 1989, 131; emphasis added)
>
> The common law is a way of applying, case-by-case, the enduring standards of the community, and in such a way as to bring the community along, even as reforms are being made. . . . judges discover the law; they do not simply make it. Reason looks to nature (instead of will looking to desire) in declaring the rule that is to be followed. (Anastaplo 1989, 138)

Readers acquainted with the history of political philosophy are reminded of those two most important competing definitions of law, Thomas Aquinas's "Law is an ordinance of reason . . ." and Thomas Hobbes's "[Law] is the will of the Sovereign. . . ."[3]

One is tempted to say that Aquinas one-sidedly brings out the rational side of law, Hobbes brings out its coercive side, and both sides are essential; but, concerning Aquinas this would be incorrect, concerning Hobbes insufficient. The full definition of law, according to Aquinas, is "an ordinance of reason for the common good made by him who has care of the community and promulgated." Included in the "care of the community" is the authority to inflict penalties for violations of the law. Human nature being what it is, coercive power (*vis*) or coercive virtue (*virtus*) is an indispensable means for the end of law—namely, to become an effective inducement to virtue.[4] Law *has* coercive force, but it *is* an ordinance of reason for the common good.[5] What gives law its character is its formative principle, reason, and its end, not the necessary condition of its efficacy.

II.

In Xenophon's *Memorabilia* [of Socrates] there is only one Socratic conversation in which Socrates himself does not participate, the conversation between the young Alcibiades and the great Pericles about law. Our discussion will focus on the issues raised by the comparison between Aquinas and Hobbes.

> But I would assert that there is no possibility of education for anyone from one who does not satisfy him. And Critias and Alcibiades did not associate with Socrates for that time in which they did associate with him as one who satisfied them, but from the very beginning they had set out to stand at the head of the city. For while they still were associating with Socrates they did not try to converse with any others more than with those who were most active in political affairs. For it is

said of Alcibiades, before he was twenty years old, that he had a conversation with Pericles, who was his guardian and who stood at the head of the city, of the following sort about laws.

"Tell me, Pericles," he said, "would you be able to teach me what law is?" "By all means, surely," said Pericles. "Then do teach, by the gods," Alcibiades said. "For when I hear certain men being praised because they are law-abiding men I consider that this praise would not justly befall one who did not know what law is."

"Well, it is no very difficult matter you desire, Alcibiades," Pericles said, "in wanting to know what law is. For all those things are laws which the multitude, after coming together and approving, prescribes, declaring what should be done and what not." "If they hold [establish by law] that the good things be done or the bad?" "The good, by Zeus," he said, "my boy, but not the bad."

"And, if not the multitude, but just as where there is an oligarchy, a few [*oligoi*] after coming together will prescribe whatever must be done, what is this?" "Everything," he said, "which the controlling power of the city prescribes, after deliberating about what must be done, is called law."

"And if, then, a tyrant controlling the city should prescribe what citizens must do, is this also law?" "Also all those things which a tyrant ruling," he said, "prescribes, this also is called law."

"But what is coercion and lawlessness, Pericles?" he said. "Is it not whenever the stronger, not after persuading the weaker but after coercing him, compels [necessitates] him to do whatever seems [right] to him?" "So it seems to me," Pericles said. "And all those things then which a tyrant by prescribing but not after persuading compels [necessitates] the citizens to do are lawlessness?" "It seems so to me," said Pericles, "for I take back what I said about those things which the tyrant prescribes without having persuaded being law."

"And all those things which the few prescribe, not having persuaded the many but being in control of them, are we to

> say or are we to deny that this is coercion?" "Everything, it seems to me," Pericles said, "which anyone without having persuaded compels [necessitates] anyone to do, whether he prescribes it or not, is coercion rather than law."
>
> "And therefore all those things which the entire multitude, controlling those who have money, prescribe without having persuaded would have to be coercion rather than law?" "You know, Alcibiades," Pericles said, "we too, when we were your age, were terribly clever about such things; for we also practiced and played the sophist about such things, the very sort of things which you also now seem to me to practice." And Alcibiades said, "Would then, Pericles, that I had been with you then when you were most terribly clever." (1.2.39–46)

Xenophon introduces the story as an illustration of Alcibiades's estrangement from Socrates, of how he preferred to converse with political men rather than with Socrates. By his dialectical skill, his raising the distinctively Socratic What is . . . ? question, his adaptation of the premise that no one could justly be praised as law-abiding who does not know what law is, Alcibiades illustrates by deed his closeness to Socrates.

Pericles does not seem to think that the basic question, What is law? (or a law) is very difficult. He answers without accepting or even acknowledging Alcibiades's premise that praise for law-abidingness is justly bestowed only on those who know what law is. Is someone law-abiding (in the strict sense of the word) who abides by something called law not because he knows it is law but, say, because he knows he will be punished if he does not? Is that not rather fear-abiding? What if he or she abides by some rule because society as a whole is benefited thereby, or simply because they think it is right so to act? They would be good citizens and good people, but if they do not know that such action is required by law are they, strictly speaking, law-abiding? On the other hand, if the answer to the question is not available, or not settled (the question is never answered in this exchange), does it mean that until it is settled and known no one ought to be called law-abiding? Is not the generally understood meaning of law-abidingness subverted for those who take the question seriously?

Pericles has too much good sense to be daunted by considerations such as these. The great proponent of Athenian democracy answers the general question with a democratic definition: those things which the multitude, or majority, after meeting and deciding, set down as what ought to be done and what ought not to be done are laws.[6] Alcibiades's response—Whether they direct good to be done or evil?—leads to a qualification of the multitude's sovereignty, its subordination to rational principle. Pericles agrees, "The good, by Zeus, my boy, but not the bad." It is not enough that the laws have been set down by those authorized to set them down, they must also be reasonable, they must aim at serving the common good. This does not mean that a bad law is not a law, that mistakes can never be permitted. It is not reasonable to expect perfect reasonability from human legislators. The law is to be reasonable in that it is deliberate, in that it intends to promote the common good. It is striking that the political good, the common good, justice, is never mentioned in the exchange.[7] It seems to be implied in the agreement about "good." On a superficial level there would seem to be no problem in Xenophon about the relation between the just and the legal;[8] "the just and the legal are the same."[9] If that is so, in defining law one is also thereby defining justice.

The identification of the just and the legal is affirmed especially in *Memorabilia* 4.4 in an exchange between the famous sophist Hippias and Socrates. This identification holds, Socrates argues, for the unwritten divine laws as well as for human laws. (Pericles too, we recall, linked his agreement about the goodness of law to the divine by his oath to Zeus.) Divine laws are those which are observed in every country (not *polis*) the same way, that is, they are universal and trans-political, and not clearly distinguished from the natural. Hippias at first apparently wanted to accept as divine only such laws as could never be transgressed, laws that are everywhere necessary. He acquiesces, however, in Socrates's distinction between human laws, where punishment for transgression can sometimes be escaped by concealment or the exercise of violence, and divine laws, where although they can be transgressed, the laws of themselves provide their own punishments. Four examples are given of divine laws: first, gods are to be worshipped; second, parents are to be honored; the third prohibits incest between offspring and parents; the fourth prohibits ingratitude. The automatic punishments are discussed only for the third and fourth. Parental incest produces bad children because the disparity of ages means that one or both partners are not in their prime when the bodily seed is best suited for reproduction. The ungrateful become destitute of good friends and are compelled, because their benefactors hate their ingratitude, to pursue those (benefactors) who hate them. In both cases the punishments are the usual, but by no means universal, natural consequences of the transgressions.

The disparity between the thesis mutually asserted by Socrates and Hippias and the evidence presented to substantiate it is alluded to in Hippias's final speech. He submissively replies to Socrates's question that of course the gods do not legislate things other than the just things, "for scarcely would any other legislate the just things, if not a god." The implied argument seems to be that the legal and the just would be the same if the laws automatically brought about appropriate punishments for their transgressions (and rewards for their fulfillment; 4.4.17) as the unwritten divine laws are alleged to do. (The student of Thomas Aquinas's *Treatise on Law* is reminded of his discussion of the Eternal Law.) Or, more generally, the legal and the just would be the same if the laws automatically brought about the appropriate and correct distribution of goods and evils in society and, even more generally, in the world as a whole.

The other great account of justice in Xenophon—the big boy small coat, small boy big coat story in *The Education of Cyrus*—points even less obliquely to the problem of the connection of law with justice. Cyrus, the young prince of Persia, was asked to decide the following case: if a big boy with a small coat meeting a small boy with a big coat takes the big coat for himself and gives the small boy the small coat, and the case is disputed, how should the judge decide? Cyrus decided each should have what fitted him and was promptly spanked by his teacher for judging wrongly. He was asked to judge, not what was fitting, the teacher explained, but what was just, and "the legal [or law-abiding] is just," and the law prohibits the forceful taking away from anyone what one has made or bought for oneself. Again we have a forceful assertion of the identification of the legal and the just with an account that invites one to think about what could make law just.[10]

Pericles and Alcibiades's agreement that law must aim at what is good, not bad, points to the order of distributive justice that underlies, justifies, or, as we say, legitimates each legal code—that is, such justice accounts or could account for why it is good.

Alcibiades's next question points to a correction of the narrowness or partisan character of Pericles's democratic answer by asking about where there is no political multitude but an oligarchy that meets and prescribes laws. Pericles tries to correct that narrowness with a general definition: law is whatever the controlling power of the city, after deliberating, enacts about what must be done. (His "Hobbesianism" is qualified only by the reference to deliberation.) His shaken confidence, or his democratic conscience, or both, lead him to distance himself from his new definition: he claims not to describe what law is, but only what it is called. Alcibiades questions whether, and Pericles affirms that, the new definition includes tyrannical law. Deliberation drops out. Pericles's attempt to broaden his account leads him to name the indispensable condition of law's efficacy, controlling power in the city, as the defining characteristic of law.

As soon as force and coercion are acknowledged Alcibiades shifts the ground again. Coercion [*bia*] is identified with lawlessness. Persuasion becomes the defining element: whatever the stronger compels or necessitates the citizens to do without persuading them is lawlessness. Pericles accepts this rhetorical, or intellectual, or sophistic definition and retracts his hard-boiled statement about tyrants. With consent of the governed an implied standard, his conscience permits him to return from what law is called to what it is. Alcibiades applies the new definition of coercion and lawlessness first to an oligarchy and then to the whole multitude. Pericles welcomes the application of lawlessness to the oligarchy and again generalizes, which makes it easier for Alcibiades to apply the definition to the democracy's treatment of the wealthy. Pericles balks at this, ends the dialectic, and attempts to reinstate his personal ascendancy with a statement belittling the conversation and Alcibiades's sophistication. But Alcibiades tops him once again, ending the section.[11]

Alcibiades's shifting of the arguments from multitude, to few, to tyrant, from actions by different ruling powers in the cities, points to the general principle that what constitutes law differs according to the regime. Law is relative to the regime. The regime is, or receives its character from, the specific order of distributive justice operative in that society. No political society exists without some way of distributing the advantages and disadvantages, rewards and punishments entailed in living together. This notion of distributive justice, what general and authoritative opinion regards as "right" (*dikaion*, "just"), comprehends what we usually separate into economic, social, and political spheres: it pertains to all the divisible assets of a society, its honors and offices as well as its material assets. In every society some ranking of the values of goods and evils exchanged or distributed is worked out or works itself out. Implicit in these rankings are rankings of the activities productive of the goods and evils, and most importantly, rankings of the men and women who receive the distributions and produce the goods and evils. Some such notion of distributive justice operates in every political community, even where there might be no explicit expression or thought given to the general idea of justice. This does not exclude competing and changing notions of distributive justice (i.e., mixed regimes), but at any one time some such more or less complicated order is operative. The rankings of the human beings point to the goals or ends that the most authoritative members of society aim at and which thereby predominate in society. In democracies freedom is said to be prized most; in oligarchies, wealth; in timocracies, honor; in aristocracies, virtue or excellence. Societies then characterize themselves by the orders of distributive justice operative in them and the goals or ends that predominate in them. Law is relative to the regime because legislators are by that very fact authoritative members of society and lay down the laws so as to protect and support the fundamental beliefs, the order of right (*dikaion*), of fairness, of fitness (cf. the big boy small coat story), of distributive justice, that constitutes their society.[12] Civil and criminal laws are designed both to rectify and to prevent violations of the more fundamental order of distributive justice.[13] To say that political justice, the justice that informs the laws, is always either democratically understood justice, oligarchically understood justice, aristocratically understood justice, and so on, is not to say all justice is relative. All justice is relative in the sense that it is relative to the regime, but there is one regime, on order of distributive justice, that is "according to nature everywhere," that "has the same power everywhere and not by virtue of being accepted [or opined] or not"—that is, the justice of the best regime. The order of distributive justice that constitutes the best regime and informs its laws, even though the conditions for putting it into practice are almost always absent, is the standard by which the excellences and defects of the other notions of justice and their regimes are measured.[14]

If we assume that every part of the Alcibiades-Pericles exchange is meant to contribute to the meaning of the whole, a unified definition of the Thomistic type might prove illuminating. Law, then, would be a persuasive ordinance for the political community that good things be done and bad things not done, made and prescribed, after deliberation, by the controlling power of the city. (No such definition, I repeat, is offered in the text. It ends even more aporetically than it began.)

The problem, or contradiction, presented by the unified definition is that law must be made by those with sufficient coercing power to enforce it, and it must be deliberate and persuasive, that is, it must move the citizens to obedience without coercion.[15] If we radicalize the notion implicit in the only use of the word "justice" in the exchange (the adverb "justly") then justice depends on knowledge, understanding. The law then must be reasonable and those who obey it obey it because it is reasonable. Law must be coercive if it is to regulate the behavior of those who are not decisively rational—that is, non-saints, non-angels, rational *animals*—those who must be moved to do what is right without necessarily knowing that it is right and those who know but whose passions move them against their better judgment. Law must be persuasively right and reasonable, its legislators must be reasonable, and those for whom it is prescribed must be reasonable, since they must be capable of being persuaded by right reason. Coerciveness and reasonability are not easily reconciled. Pericles in his third and fourth responses stresses the former. Alcibiades in his fifth, sixth, seventh, and final questions argues as if one could expect all men to control their actions by right reason. The disparity between what law wants and what law gets points to the disparity in human nature itself, the disparity between the animality and the rationality of the rational animal.

III

The question about law leads to the order of distributive justice protected and fostered by the law, to the polity or regime. How should the regime protected and fostered by the United States Constitution of 1787 be characterized? Paul Eidelberg, in an illuminating and careful argument based primarily on *The Records of the Federal Convention of 1787, The Federalist,* Plato's *Republic,* and Aristotle's *Politics,* maintains that it is and was intended to be a mixed regime.[16] James Wilson, delegate to the Constitutional Convention from Pennsylvania argued, "In its principle, it is purely democractical."[17]

Eidelberg argues that the House of Representatives "exemplifies the democratic principle," because of its short tenure (i.e., the frequency of elections), because it is elected directly by the people, and because it in general represents "the interests of the many." The Senate exemplifies oligarchic and aristocratic principles because of its long tenure (i.e., the infrequency of elections), because of its members being appointed by the state legislatures (under Art. I, sect. 3, before the mode of their selection was modified by the Seventeenth Amendment), not by the people directly, and because it in general represents "the interests of the few." The Supreme Court, by its tenure, mode of appointment, and the goals (wisdom and justice) it is meant to serve, is obviously the most aristocratic branch. The mode of choosing the President as well as his term is roughly a mean between the modes of choosing and the terms of Senators and Representatives. In one of his most valuable chapters, Eidelberg shows how the long and thoughtful deliberation that resulted in the presidential electoral system was intended to constitute an office that would guard against both democratic and oligarchic extremes. The educative functions of the presidency too reveal the intended aristocratic, even monarchic, side of the office.

In general, institutions that *The Federalist* characterizes as deriving their authority "indirectly" from the people are characterized by Eidelberg, because the direct and unqualified mandate of the people is not instituted, as non- or anti-democratic.

As if in answer to Eidelberg, James Wilson addresses himself to the question of how the distinction between mixed and simple "species of government" applies to the proposed constitution. Wilson concludes that the Constitution of 1787 is fundamentally democratic but so contrived as to obtain all the advantages of a mixed regime.

He begins by declaring that there are three simple species of government distinguished by where the supreme power ("from which there is not appeal") resides: monarchy, aristocracy (which includes what Aristotle would classify as oligarchy), and democracy:

> Each of these species of government has its advantages and disadvantages.
>
> The advantages of a *monarchy* are, strength, despatch, secrecy, unity of counsel. Its disadvantages are, tyranny, expense, ignorance of the situation and wants of the people, insecurity, unnecessary wars, evils attending elections of successions.
>
> The advantages of *aristocracy* are, wisdom arising from experience and education. Its disadvantages are, dissensions among themselves, oppression to the lower orders.
>
> The advantages of *democracy* are, liberty, equality, cautious and salutary laws, public spirit, frugality, peace, *opportunities of exciting and producing abilities of the best citizens.* Its disadvantages are, dissensions, the delay and disclosure of public counsels, the imbecility of public measures, retarded by the necessity of a numerous consent.[18]

According to Wilson, a mixed regime, like the British government, "would be an improper government for the United States, because it is inadequate to such an extent of territory, and *because it is suited to an establishment of different orders of men.*"[19]

The Convention proposed a constitution where "all authority is derived from the people," a government that "[i]n its principle is purely democratical. But that principle is applied in different forms, in order to obtain the advantages and exclude the inconveniences of the simple modes of government."[20]

Wilson's remark about "an establishment of different orders of men" indicates that he understood that in a mixed regime (in the traditional sense) each of the competing (and cooperating) orders of men made claims for authority in their own names as democrats, aristocrats, oligarchs, or monarchists. They answered the question, Who ought to rule?, differently in terms of their characteristically different goals. Each argued differently for the claims to supremacy of the possessors of freedom or the possessors of excellence, of wealth, or monarchic status. The political authority of the Monarch and Lords in Great Britain is not derived from the authority of the people, but is inherent in the Monarch as monarch, the Lords as Lords. The United States, on the contrary, is a democratic republic judiciously tempered by aristocratic, oligarchic, and monarchical arrangements, never explicitly acknowledged as such, because all such arrangements are ultimately (directly or indirectly) subordinate to the authority of the people. (Hereditary monarchical and dynastic status, of course, is simply ruled out.)

We recall that Aristotle defined the regime as both (1) the order of offices and authorities in a city, especially with a view to the supreme authority, and (2) the way of life of the city. According to the first, more narrowly political criterion Wilson's argument against Eidelberg is compelling.

Nevertheless, although there is no explicit and legally fixed "establishment of different orders of men," the aristocratic, oligarchic, and monarchical arrangements alluded to by Wilson and carefully analyzed by Eidelberg were meant to and do affect the American way of life.[21] Wilson himself is justly noted for what is perhaps the most exalted statement in the Constitutional Convention on the aims of government: "he [Wilson] could not agree that property was the sole or the primary object of government and society. The cultivation and improvement of the human mind was the most noble object."[22] He evidently gave much thought to the subject of American "national character":

> this character will be adapted to the principles and genius of our system of government. . . . there are not on any part of the globe, finer qualities for forming a national character than those possessed by the children of America. Activity, perseverance, industry, laudable emulation, docility in acquiring information, firmness in adversity, and patience and magnanimity under the greatest hardships. . . . In addition . . . I think there is strong reason to believe that America may take the lead in literary improvements and national importance. This is a subject which, I confess, I have spent much pleasing time in considering. . . . The language of the United States will, in future time, be diffused over a greater extent of country than any other that we know. . . . Besides the freedom of our country, the great improvements she has made, and will make, in the science of government, will induce the patriots and *literati* of every nation to read and understand our writings on that subject. . . . By adopting this system, we shall probably lay a foundation for erecting temples of liberty in every part of the earth. . . . The advantages . . . will not be confined to the United States, but will draw from Europe many worthy characters, who pant for the enjoyment of freedom. It will induce princes, in order to preserve their subjects, to restore to them a portion of that liberty of which they have for many years been deprived. It will be subservient to the great designs of Providence with regard to this globe—the multiplication of mankind, their improvement in knowledge, and their advancement in happiness.[23]

The staunchest supporters of American democracy, of the ultimate sovereignty of the people, have never understood that sovereignty to be an unqualified sovereignty. As Jefferson put it in his First Inaugural Address: "All, too, will bear in mind this sacred principle, that though the will of the majority is in all cases to prevail, that will to be rightful must be reasonable. . . ." Yet as we have noted, it is not reasonable to expect perfect reasonability in human affairs. The more sober Lincoln in his First Inaugural set forward what is to my knowledge the best one-sentence definition of American government: "A majority held in restraint by constitutional checks and limitations, and always changing easily with *deliberate* changes of popular opinion and sentiment is the only true sovereign of a free people."[24] His choice of the word *deliberate* was deliberate. We the people of the United States do ordain and establish our Constitution and laws not simply because we are the people: it is the people as a free, deliberate, and thoughtful people that is entitled to rule.

CHAPTER FOURTEEN

Madmen and Philosophers

A NOTE ON XENOPHON'S *MEMORABILIA* 1.1.13 AND 14

And he wondered whether it was not evident to them that it is not possible for human beings to discover these things [sc. divine things, *ta daimonia*]. Since even those who thought most of themselves for their speaking about these things do not hold the same opinions with one another, but are disposed towards one another like madmen.

I.

For of the madmen, (1) some do not fear terrible things, (2) others even fear things not frightening; (3) and some do not hold [*dokein*] it shameful [*aischron*] to say or to do anything whatever in a crowd, (4) while others hold that it is not right even to go out [*oud' exitēteon*] among human beings; (5) and some do not honor any holy thing [or temple, *hieron*], or altar, nor any other of the divine things, (6) while others venerate stones, chance wood things, and beasts.

II.

And of those who worry about the nature of all things [*tōn pantōn*] (1) some hold that the being [*to on*] is one only, (2) and others that they are infinite in multitude; (3) and for some everything is always moved, (4) and for others nothing could ever be moved; (5) and for some everything both comes to be and is destroyed, (6) while for others nothing could ever come to be nor be destroyed.

We have two lists with three pairs in each. Within both lists what is said about each subject in a later pair, depends upon what was said about corresponding subjects in earlier pairs. Of the statements about madmen the first pair is concerned with extreme attitudes about fear, the second with extreme judgments about shame, the third with extreme behavior concerning piety. The subject of the third pair, piety, is derived from or dependent upon the first two, fear and shame, as in the second list generation and destruction are dependent upon number and motion. The suggestion seems to be that to be ashamed is to fear disgrace, while piety depends upon a fear of being in disgrace before divinities or divinity: Correspondingly, movement presupposes limited plurality, mover, moved, and that from which and to which the moving thing moves; coming to be and passing away presupposes the movement of a plurality of elementary beings into and out of different combinations.

The parallel structure of both lists invites coordination. Do each of the attitudes, or dispositions, listed under I correspond to, or are they appropriate to, the view of the whole set down under the same number in II? Is there a characteristic disposition, a peculiar kind of madness, corresponding to each of these major non or pre-Socratic positions?

We will begin from what seems most evident, from the end of the lists. For those for whom everything both comes to be and is destroyed (II, 5), nothing is eternal, there are no immortals, nothing worthy of divine honors (I, 5). For those for whom nothing could ever come to be or be destroyed (II, 6) everything is eternal, and any chance thing they happen upon could be thought to be divine (I, 6). For those who hold that the being is one only (II, 1), everything is one with itself, there is no other to harm one; hence they do not even fear terrible things (I, 1). For those for whom the beings are infinite, unlimited (*apeira*) in multitude (II, 2), there are no bounds to possible sources of danger, to what is other from oneself, to possible sources of fear (I, 2). I, 3 and 4 were concerned with the shameful, *to aischron*. Its opposite is the noble, *to kalon* (1.1.16). The fourth correspondence is most difficult: If, we may conjecture, the origins, the "parents," of everything are noble, and therefore everything was once noble, and nothing could ever be moved or changed (*kinēthēnai*) (II, 4), then one is always in danger of being exposed as a shameful violator of the noble (I, 4). For those for whom everything is always changed (II, 3), nothing noble ever remains such, and therefore there is nothing ever to be ashamed of (I, 3).

Socrates, according to Xenophon and Plato, always avoided these extremes of "those claiming to philosophize."[1] He always sought the mean between fearlessness and timidity, between shamelessness and bashfulness, between superstition and impiety. But sobriety, or moderation, *sōphrosunē*, seemed to be a theoretical as well as a moral principle for Socrates: "He did not draw a boundary between wisdom (*sophia*) and moderation . . ." (3.9.4). By exposing the mad-like extremes, Xenophon indicates what, for Socrates, the sober theoretical means are, that is, the beings are limited in multitude, some things change and some do not, and some things come into being and perish and others do not.

If sobriety or moderation is the characteristic of Socratic philosophizing, and if it is the Socratic element that is common to the philosophies of Plato and Aristotle, that characteristic might be traced to the Socratic thinkers' insistence on doing justice to the cognitive significance of common, ordinary experience (which we understand to include what is *said* about the things experienced).[2] A few illustrations may suffice. Socrates, in the *Theaetetus* (180d), ironically adapting the attitude of adherents of universal flux speaks of cobblers "foolishly supposing that some of the beings are at rest and others in motion." The trouble with "the famous men of old," the Stranger from Elea says on the following day (*Sophist* 243a–b1), is that "looking far beyond [*huperidontes*, overlooking or despising] us, the many, they slighted us; for not caring whether we follow along with them when they speak or are left behind, each of them does his own thing to the limit." He comes back to the discussion of motion and rest later, arguing that the philosopher must, as it seems, not accept the sayings that "the all" is at rest or that "the being" is in every way moving, but rather "in accord with the children's prayer about all things motionless and being moved, he must say that the being and the all are both [motionless and being moved] together" (249c–d). The discussion becomes schematized in Aristotle's *Physics* 8.3, 253a22 ff., where (254a1) he concludes that "from these and other such arguments it is impossible for anyone to believe either that all things are in motion or that all things are always at rest."[3]

In 3.9.6 Xenophon's Socrates says that madness is the opposite of wisdom, *sophia*.[4] Ignorance, however, is not madness, "but to be ignorant of oneself and to opine and to suppose that one knows what one does not know, he reckoned to be very close to madness." This would seem to be a more precise characterization of those mad-like thinkers who worry about the nature of all things. If they thought that by the study of the cosmos they would be able to make and control natural phenomena whenever they wanted to, they would be mad. But they are not mad, if "they expect nothing of this sort and it is sufficient for them just to know by what cause each of this sort of thing comes to be" (1.1.15). But Socrates' continual inquiry seemed to lead many to suppose, not unreasonably, that he too was one of those for whom it was satisfactory "just to know" (*gnōnai monon*). He was accused of making his associates "look beyond [or above, to despise, *huperoran*] the established laws" (1.2.9). Xenophon does not directly refute this charge. He counters it by arguing that Socrates never made his followers violent, but trained them in prudence so that they might accomplish their reforms by means of persuasion. The definition cited above, of those who are very close to madness, who are ignorant both about themselves and about what they do not know, applies as readily to the many as to their speculative despisers. Therefore we are not altogether surprised to read at 1.3.4 that Socrates "himself looked beyond [or above, *upereōra*] all human things," but with a crucial addition, "to counsel from the gods."[5]

Xenophon's Socrates' way then might be characterized as a mean between the ways of the mad-like speculators and of the many. Unlike those speculators who subvert the way of life of the many, of the *polis,* and who fail to learn what they might learn from thinking about the talk of the many, Socrates nevertheless joins them in looking beyond all human things to their principles. His looking beyond, however, is based on a prior or contemporaneous looking through the human things in order to understand them and himself. His "looking beyond" is carried out in such a way as to subvert the many's understanding of the just and noble as little as possible. This he accomplishes by looking with the many in the same direction beyond to the gods. For "do you not believe that they care? For they first set man alone among the animals up straight . . . to be able to look before [*prooran*] and to see better the things from above [*ta huperthen*] . . ." (1.4.11)

APPENDIX

Plato's *Meno* and Aristotle's *Nicomachean Ethics*

> The best introduction to the works of Aristotle are the dialogues of Plato; and the best introduction to the dialogues of Plato are the works of Aristotle.
>
> —Philippides

I. Prudence, Courage and Intelligence

In the final chapter of Book Six of the *Nicomachean Ethics*, the book on the intellectual virtues, Aristotle takes up the question of virtue and prudence (*phronēsis*).[1] Socrates, he says, was "mistaken in thinking that all the virtues are forms of prudence, but in saying that they cannot exist without prudence he spoke well." Aristotle is probably referring to the passage in the *Meno* where Socrates says,

> If then virtue is something in the soul and is itself necessarily beneficial, it must be prudence: since indeed all things that pertain to the soul are themselves in themselves neither beneficial nor harmful, but when prudence or thoughtlessness (*aphrosunēs*) is added to them they become harmful or beneficial. According to this argument, indeed, virtue being beneficial, it must be some kind of prudence. (88c–d [388])[2]

Yet Socrates ends this section with a question that puts it almost the same way that Aristotle put it, "Therefore do we affirm that prudence is virtue, either virtue altogether or some part of it?" (89a [396])

In the *Meno* this conclusion had been prepared for by the observation that sometimes things called virtues, like courage, moderation, and readiness to learn, harm their possessors and at other times they benefit them.[3] "For example, courage, if the courage is not prudence, but some sort of boldness—is it not the case that when a human being is bold without intelligence (*nous*) he is harmed and whenever with intelligence he is benefited?" Meno agrees here and also when next Socrates asks about moderation and readiness to learn (*eumathia*). "When they are learned and trained for with intelligence, they are beneficial, but without intelligence harmful?" (88b [382] and [384]) After these brief appearances, *nous* disappears from the argument. It seems to have been absorbed into the more emphasized "prudence." *Nous* makes an even briefer, but no less crucial appearance in Aristotle's fuller treatment of courage in *Nicomachean Ethics* Book Three. (In Book Six *nous* reappears as the ultimate source of the links between virtuous inclinations and the prudent choice of means that issues in "authoritative virtue," or rightness of action.)[4]

In *Nicomachean Ethics* Book Two courage was defined in general as a mean between fear and confidence. The presentation in Book Three takes on the character of a dialogue:

> About what kinds of frightening things is the courageous man concerned? Would it not be about the greatest? . . . and the most frightening thing is death. . . . In what kind of death then? Would it not be in the most noble (*tois kallistois*)? And that is death in battle, for that is where the greatest and most noble danger lies. The honors bestowed by cities and monarchs are also in agreement with this. In an authoritative way then it might be said that the courageous man is he who is not afraid of a noble death even when the dangers that bring it on are close at hand; and such are the dangers of war.[5]

In this chapter courage comes to sight in its elementary and most conspicuous form, in the context of what starts off as something like a conversation between citizens and citizen-soldiers.

The next chapter begins by noting that the same things are not frightening to all people, but that there are some things beyond human endurance. And "this sort of thing is frightening for everyone, at least for anyone who has any sense (*tōi ge noun echonti*)"—"who has any *nous*." This word, which in its colloquial usage can be translated "sense," is the key theoretical term for Plato and Aristotle translated variously as intelligence, intellect, or intellectual intuition. With the almost parenthetical mention of the one who has *nous* a new unannounced perspective enters into Aristotle's discussion, the perspective of the prudently courageous man who endures fears and is bold towards those things which he ought, for the sake of what he ought, as he ought, and when he ought. The word prudence does not occur in this chapter; we are not to be diverted from our consideration of courage. But we are introduced to the effects of prudence, and prudently prepared by anticipation for its thematic presentation later in Book Six.[6]

The final chapter of Book 3's treatment of courage deals with the problem of the intrinsic pleasantness of virtue, where the virtue itself is primarily concerned with enduring pains. There is the briefest indication that true courage cannot be possessed in isolation from the other virtues: "The more a man possesses virtue in its entirety (*tēn aretēn pasan*), the more happy he is, and the more will he be pained by death; for life is most worth living for such a man" (1117b10–12).[7] This reference to virtue "in its entirety" brings us to the problem raised by Socrates throughout the *Meno*, the question he is never able to get Meno to inquire into seriously:[8] What is virtue itself, the one form of virtue, as distinct from the separate virtues, that which ultimately constitutes them as virtues? Plato, we hope to show, had much more success with his student, Aristotle.

II. Virtue Shattered

The chief complaint Socrates has with the accounts of virtue given to him by Meno is that he is being given swarms of many virtues and not that "one and the same form (*eidos*) [1] through which they are virtues, and [2] upon which one would somehow do well to focus one's gaze," in order to answer "him who has asked him to clarify that, namely what does virtue happen to be."[9] Socrates approaches this question in a variety of ways in the *Meno.* It is probably safe to assume that there is something special to be learned from each approach. Here, however, we will focus only on a few approaches.

In 79a [170] Socrates speaks of his asking Meno "not to shatter virtue or to change it into small coin." This remark was prepared for by Meno's adding acquiring gold and silver into a list of good things (78c [153]). Meno does not object when Socrates restates it as Meno having declared that "to provide oneself with gold and silver, then is virtue." And Socrates goes on to ask whether it makes any difference if the words "justly" and "piously" should be added "to this providing," but "if someone should provide himself with these things unjustly, would you still call these doings virtue?" (78d [156]) Meno answers, "Surely not," and agrees that such providing is not virtue, but vice. Socrates then concludes, "It seems likely that one should add justice or moderation or piety, or some other piece of virtue to this providing," if it is to be virtue (78d and e [160]).[10]

In complaining about Meno's "piece" language Socrates speaks of having "begged you to talk about virtue as a whole."[11] What kind of whole is Plato's Socrates urging us to think of? Are justice, moderation, courage, and piety related to virtue as small change is to gold;[12] or as the different kinds of bees are related to their hive; or as circle, square and triangle are related to figure; or as black, red, yellow, blue, and white are related to color; or as two, three, four and five are related to number; or as the different classes of human beings are related to political society as a whole; or as the organs of a living body are related to the whole living body, the organism? There is one passage in the *Meno* that clearly seems to favor the organism model, where Socrates urges Meno to tell him what virtue is, "leaving it whole and healthy" (77a–b [112]).[13] "Healthy," as Aristotle informs us, is an analogous[14] term, the primary meaning of which is healthy animal.

III. Virtue as a Whole

If we can regard Socrates' "exhibition" with the Slave-boy as a model for inquiry, a good inquiry should culminate in a solution or answer to the problem or question with which it began.[15] As we have noted, all the definitions of virtue attempted by Meno in answer to Socrates' question, What is virtue? are shown to be inadequate. Socrates tells Meno and us in the final speech of the dialogue that we will not arrive at clarity about virtue unless "before we seek whatever way virtue comes to human beings" (Meno's opening question), "we . . . undertake to seek what virtue, itself in itself, is." How might the great definition of virtue in Aristotle's *Nicomachean Ethics* (2.6 1106b36–1107a6) measure up to Socrates' standards?

> Virtue then is a steady disposition for (*hexis*) deliberately choosing (*prohairetikē*),[16] which exists in a mean state (*mesotēs*), a state relative to us, determined by reason (*logōi*) and as the prudent man (*phronimos*) would determine it.[17] And it is a mean state between two vices, one of excess and one of defect. And, further, it is a mean by some of the vices falling short and other vices exceeding what is appropriate in both passions and actions, while virtue both discovers and chooses the mean (*meson*).

At first glance, it would be easy to criticize this definition: it seems to be clearly circular. Prudence is the intellectual virtue that enables one correctly to choose what conduces to virtue. It is almost as if Aristotle had said virtue is behaving like a virtuous man. When a man who at the least was one of the greatest logicians that ever lived makes what could be taken for a beginner's logical slip, it might be prudent to take another look at our text and ask, "What might he be getting at?" The circularity, defining virtue in terms of a certain kind of virtuous man, points, I believe, to a most important consideration: for ethical *action* general rules are insufficient; given the variability of circumstances, there is no substitute for the good judgment of the human being on the spot.[18] Aristotle seems to suggest that when we exercise ourselves in steering clear of vices and finding the right mean, or proportion relative to our own particular nature and circumstances, something like the image of the perfectly prudent man should be guiding our judgment. As Aristotle says in his chapter (*Nicomachean Ethics* 3.4) on wishing or wanting (*boulēsis*), the serious ethical man (*spoudaios*) judges correctly; what seems noble[19] and pleasant to him is noble and pleasant: "he is himself, as it were, a standard (*kanōn*) and measure of these things."[20]

Before directly resuming our discussion of how Aristotle's definition meets Socrates' standards, "leaving [virtue] whole and healthy," it might not be inappropriate to indicate why one might assume that Plato's *Meno* was especially important for Aristotle's *Nicomachean Ethics*. Aristotle does seem to refer to the *Meno* a number of times in the *Ethics*, but Aristotle refers to many other dialogues of Plato as well. I propose to explore this assumption by considering the opening questions that give the dialogue its setting, and asking Aristotle, "What do you make of Meno's opening questions and Socrates' response to them?" Meno begins by asking,

> Can you tell me, Socrates, whether virtue is something teachable? Or is it not teachable, but something that comes from practice? Or is it something neither from practice nor

> from learning, but comes to be there (*paragignetai*) for human beings by nature, or in some other way?

Socrates saw at once, I think Aristotle might reply, that Meno's questions shatter virtue; they disjoin, as separated alternatives, what can only be understood as interrelated and interpenetrating powers working together in a unified whole. He knew that as far as human character is concerned nature provides the capacities; that teaching and learning aim at clarifying the ends, or goals, implicit in the natural capacities, preparing the learner, so far as he or she is able, to understand and to attain the goals; and repetitive practice develops the habits that bring about or impede the actualization of those goals.[21] In his own words (*Nicomachean Ethics* 2.1), Aristotle remarks,

> Therefore, neither by nature, nor against nature are the virtues engendered, but [they are engendered] by our having been natured to receive them and by our being completed [or perfected] by habit (*ethos*). Furthermore, concerning those things that come to be there (*paragignetai*) for us by nature, we are first provided with the capacities for them, and later we render the actualities (*energeiai*) [being at work, activity].[22] (1103a24–28) . . . for it is by acting in dealings with people that some of us become just, and others become unjust; and by acting in dangerous situations we also become habituated to be afraid or to be confident, and, for some, habituated to become courageous and, for others, to become cowards; and similarly it holds with regard to our desires and our getting angry. (1103b14–19)

The questions, then, that set the framework for the *Meno*, rightly or Socratically understood, also set the framework for the *Nicomachean Ethics*.

The mean state determined by prudent reason in which virtue lives is a formative state, incompatible with excess or defect, an ordering form of being at work, which balances, limits, and shapes the materials of our feelings (or passions), practical dispositions, and actions.[23] This state is a "state relative to us"; that is, one must consider the distribution of one's own feelings, dispositions, and habits and one's own particular circumstances, as one moves toward and then lives in the rationally determined, appropriately proportioned distribution of those materials that constitute the mean state of being, in which one who most perfectly attains those ratios and proportions, the prudent one, the *phronimos*, lives.[24]

There is one place in the *Meno* where Meno seems to assert the unity of virtue as encompassed by justice: "For justice, Socrates, is virtue." But Socrates quickly convinces him that justice is one particular virtue among other virtues.[25]

In Book 5, chapter 1, of the *Nicomachean Ethics* Aristotle explores the sense in which justice might be said to be all virtue in sum. It is, insofar as justice is keyed to the law, the written and the unwritten laws, which includes religious law,[26] for "the laws pronounce on everything," ordering the virtues and forbidding their opposites. But this justice, he explains, is not justice unqualified, justice "simply," it is justice "in relation to another," it is justice in relation to our treatment of other people. And it does depend on whether the law has been laid down rightly or not (1129b11–34).[27] Law, decently laid down, then, by encouraging certain tendencies and discouraging others, might be said, along with family life,[28] to begin the ordering of feelings, predispositions, and practices that might later be brought into conscious thought, and, for those capable of it, be perfected by right reason and prudence.

Aristotle has discussed the natural and elementary predispositions from which moral and ethical education begins. Spiritedness (*thumos*) that manifests itself most conspicuously in anger and bravery is the elementary source of courage; shame-respect (*aidōs*)[29] the elementary source of temperance or moderation; and righteous indignation (*nemesis*) of justice.[30] Each of these natural predispositions, left to itself, can go wrong. Can any of the virtues be realized in the absence of the others? Can courage subsist without the moderating of fear and love of self that is the proper office of moderation, without the sense of justice that should control the resistance it presents to what it takes to be a danger? Can justice be served without the courage to oppose dangerous malefactors? Can moderation deal with the not always comic problem of human self-importance[31] in others and especially in oneself without something of the playful nimble-witted sense of humor described by Aristotle as the mean between boorishness and buffoonery (1127b33–1128b4)? It would seem that every genuine virtue has some role to play in the constitution of each of the others, each an organic part in the ethical organism of all the virtues, of Virtue.

Aristotle may seem to have presented "a swarm of virtues," Stewart notes, but they are ultimately to be understood as facets of the "symmetry of the whole man."[32] People do differ naturally in their capacities for "the natural virtues," the steady disposition to want or wish for correct ends, Aristotle says, but for someone who is simply good, the possessor of "authoritative virtue," this lack of symmetry, or due proportion, in the possession of the virtues is not possible. "For when the one virtue practical wisdom (*phronēsis*) is present all the other virtues together will be present" (1144b32–1145a3). While for most, if not all men, this state of *phronēsis* remains primarily an object of aspiration, Aristotle here seems to insist that it is an attainable human possibility. The ethical organism of all the virtues is the ethical nature or soul of the *phronimos*, the man or woman of practical wisdom.[33]

IV. Sense Perception and Experience

The usual word for sense perception in Aristotle and Plato is *aisthesis*. But Aristotle also argues that the universals derived from particulars do depend on *aisthesis*, perception; and "intellect (*nous*) is this perception" (1143b4–5). Aristotelian induction (*epagōgē*—leading or bringing to, as the Latin *inductio*) does *not* proceed by way of abstraction[34] and the collecting of instances for the formulation of generalizations or universals, according to the usual modern accounts of induction, but, as Sachs put it, by being "brought face to face with the universals . . . through a contemplative act whereby the same activity that holds a perceptible thing together works directly on our souls."[35] This can happen through any number of examples, or even just one example.

Sensation and appetite presuppose *phantasia,* the presentation of appearances to the soul, which is usually translated imagination. The existence of memory makes clear that imagination can also present appearances when the things that have appeared are no longer present. Objects of appetite cause movement by being imagined, by appearing to the soul. We judge or reason on the basis of what appears in our souls. The appearances may be illusions, they may be images or likenesses, or, Aristotle argues, if the soul is well constituted and rightly ordered, they may be true. In this case the things that appear would *be* as they appear.[36] In *The Movement of Animals,* Aristotle speaks of how "the feelings (*pathē*) fittingly prepare the organic parts [of animals] for movement, the appetite fittingly prepares the feelings, and the imagination the appetite, and this latter [preparation] comes about either through intellection or sense perception. The simultaneity and quickness [of these activities] stem from the active and passive elements being in relation to one another according to nature."[37] There are, Aristotle says, two kinds of imagination, sensory imagination, which all animals share and rational, or calculative (*logistikē*), imagination. This difference is interestingly (if not in an altogether Aristotelian way[38]) described by Thomas Aquinas, who distinguishes two ways of apprehending sensible particulars: in animals an "estimative power," in human beings what he calls a "cogitative power." The cogitative power "apprehends the individual thing as existing in a common nature, and this because it is united to intellect in one and the same subject. Hence it is aware of a man as this *man*, and a tree as this *tree*." The other animals, Thomas argues, are not aware of an individual thing as in a common nature, but apprehend them instinctively as terms of some action or passion. "Thus a sheep knows this particular lamb, not as this lamb, but simply as something to be suckled; and it knows this grass just in so far as this grass is its food."[39]

Many years ago in Chicago, before his commentary on the *Meno* was written, Jacob Klein began a conversation on the *Meno* with, "Plato's *Meno* is all about seeing and hearing." Let this be my introduction to sense perception in the *Meno*.

Aristotle could not have missed the great proliferation of words in the *Meno* inviting Meno to look, to watch, to observe, and to see.[40] The word *eidos*, for the form through which many things of the same kind are what they are and to which one should look in order to answer someone who asks about what they happen to be, is connected to the verb *eidenai* which is usually translated "to know," but *eidenai* and *eidos* are also connected to the sense of sight, for the elementary meaning of *eidenai* is "to have seen" and the elementary meaning of *eidos* is "looks," as it is used once in the dialogue by Meno to describe Socrates' resemblance to the torpedo-fish.[41]

In the model inquiry[42] that Socrates exhibits for Meno with the Slave-boy, hardly any step is taken without reference to diagrams drawn in the sand at which they are looking as they speak. But, despite his ease in following the geometrical argument, Meno seems to have little respect for looking. When (before the Slave-boy scene) Socrates, in practice for the virtue question, defines "shape," in terms of our fundamental experience of shapes, "that which alone of all the things which are which always happens to accompany color,"[43] Meno finds this too "simple-minded." He then argues, what if "someone should declare that he does not know (*eidenai*) color," which in Greek has the collateral meaning, "suppose someone should affirm that he has not seen a visible surface." As Klein puts it, Meno refuses the practice of defining shape in terms of his own experience, the phenomenon, of shape, "he wants to be *told* what *schema* [shape] is" (Klein 1965, 58). Socrates obliges him with the authoritative geometrical definition of figure: "*schema* is the limit of a solid." As Meno rejects *looking*, his untamed spirit plods on with "what about color . . . , Socrates?" Socrates has learned his lesson and "dialectically" accommodates himself to what Meno has been habituated to, a fancy Gorgian and Empedoclean doctrine that applies to all sense perceptions and distinguishes none. He applies it mechanically to color and ends up with this high-flown and deep-sounding ("tragical") definition: "color is an effluence of shapes commensurate with sight and perceptible." Meno praises this "best possible" response. Socrates returns to the question of virtue, but not before suggesting that he still thinks his first account of shape was better. Meno much prefers *hearing* about what shape and color are without considering the *looking* from which our primary experience of them becomes intelligible. He can, however, rest with the abstractions of geometry.

The relation between experience and knowing is explored in many places in the *Meno*, especially where bad habits come into play, but words for experience (*empeiria*) occur rarely.[44] There is one place where that relation is explicitly discussed, but the word used is the word for being "without experience" (*apeiros*). Socrates wonders why Anytus is so down on the Sophists, he wonders if any of them has wronged him. It turns out that Anytus and everyone under his influence "never associated with any of them."

> SOCRATES: Then you are altogether without experience of these men?
>
> ANYTUS: I am and may I remain so.
>
> SOCRATES: How then, my daemonic one, could you know about this business, whether there is anything good or worthless in that of which you are altogether without experience?

> ANYTUS: Easily: I still know what these people are, whether I am without experience of them or not.
>
> SOCRATES: You are perhaps a diviner (*mantis*), Anytus, for how else, I might wonder, do you know about them, from what you yourself say about them. (92a–92c [427–434])

One can hear from others, but one can only see and experience for oneself. Experience, then, would seem to be not the cause, but rather the condition of natural knowledge.[45]

V. Incommensurability and Justice

After Socrates presents the Slave-boy with a square based on a two-foot line, and they have already figured out by observation that the number for the area can be determined by multiplying the numbers for the lines, and the area number for the square based on the two-foot line is, therefore, two times two feet, that is, four feet,[46] Socrates asks whether there could not come to be a square "two times as large as this one." The Boy says, "Yes," and then in response to Socrates' question, about how many feet the new area will be, says, "Eight." Socrates, then, shifting from the language of numerable quantity (*posoi*—how many?) to the language of continuous magnitude (*pēlikē tis*), asks him how *large* each line of that new area will be. After reconsidering the square with the two-foot line and the four-foot area, the Boy responds, naturally enough, "It is clear, Socrates, that the line is two times as large." Socrates goes along with the Boy, trying the only two numerable lines left, the four-foot line and the three-foot line, and seeing by their drawn diagrams that both are too large. At this point the Boy has earned a decisive hint from his teacher, "But from what sort of line [does the eight feet area come to be]? Try to tell us precisely: and if you don't want to count (*arithmein*), show us rather from what sort of line" (83e–84a [274]). "If you don't want to count" has the sense "if you don't want to do it arithmetically."[47] Socrates here hints that the line that would provide the eight feet square might better be discovered by a showing, that is by pointing to some geometrical construction that gives up counting linear units, but does count area units. When the sought-for line is finally constructed by Socrates, it turns out to be incommensurable with any of the numerable lines they have been using. It is the diagonal of the four-foot square.[48]

> Underlying this conversation between Socrates and the Boy is the great discovery of Incommensurability and the fundamental distinction between discrete (numerable) and continuous quantities. Incommensurability refers to the fact that there are definite magnitudes (lines, surfaces and solids) that do not have to one another the ratio of a number to a number. They are said to be "irrational," *alogoi,* to one another, in that their relation cannot be expressed by a ratio between numbers, or in that both cannot be measured exactly by a common measure of their own kind, although they can be distinguished and ordered in terms of the numerable areas of the squares built upon them (in terms of "square roots"). The favorite example of incommensurability has long been that seen in the relation of a diagonal of a square to the side of the same square. . . . See also Plato, *Theaetetus* 147d ff.[49]

There is much to be explored in Socrates' model prelude to inquiry, but for the purposes of this essay we confine ourselves to examining how the underlying theme of the Slave-boy scene, incommensurability, enter into the *Nicomachean Ethics* in two instances, both in connection with justice.

Aristotle begins his treatise on justice in the *Nicomachean Ethics*, Book 5, by arguing dialectically and critically from generally accepted opinion:

> We see indeed that in speaking of justice everyone means that sort of steady disposition from which people are apt to

> do just things and from which they act justly and want just things: the same with injustice, a disposition from which they act unjustly and want unjust things. (1129a7–11)

The first four chapters articulate the rational targets of the disposition for justice: general justice connected with lawfulness (discussed above, section III) comes first. It is distinguished from fairness, that is, particular justice, aiming at different kinds of equality, which is then divided into distributive (*dianemētikon*) and rectifying (*diorthōtikon*) justice, the justice that "sets things straight."[50]

Distributive justice (chapter three) pertains to all the divisible assets of a society, honors and offices as well as material assets. It implies that no political society exists without some way of distributing the advantages and disadvantages, rewards and punishments, entailed in living together. It comprehends what we usually separate into social, political and economic spheres. Some ranking of the values of goods exchanged or distributed works itself out in every society. Implicit in these rankings are rankings of the activities productive of the goods and, most importantly, rankings of the men and women who produce the goods and receive the distributions. These rankings reflect the goals or ends that predominate in the different societies: freedom in democracies, wealth in oligarchies, and virtue in aristocracies. (In mixed regimes like ours with serious electoral systems the debates between contending principles are, as it were, institutionalized.) In every political community some such order of distributive justice is operative, even where there might be no explicit expression given to the general idea of justice. Indeed, Aristotle suggests, the political community is constituted by the order of distributive justice it shares (*Politics* 1253a14–18). The polity, the regime, the "constitution," the "soul" of every community is the order of distributive justice at work in that community. It carries into practice the notions of what is appropriate and fitting that dominate society and are reflected in its laws. The secondary order of rectifying justice (the subject of chapter four), which includes the civil and criminal law, is derived from the more fundamental order of distributive justice: That is, laws are laid down in accordance with the operative principles of distributive justice. Civil and criminal laws promote those principles and rectify their violations.

The mean of distributive justice must be distinguished from the mean of the other ethical virtues, which is a mean between two vices, of excess and of defect, which steers between contrary states of character and passions, and is concerned with internal goods and evils. The mean of distributive justice, however, concerns itself with persons, things, and external actions; it is found in correct relations of equality, proportional and arithmetic, between persons and their merits and external things, especially those external goods and evils that are distributable and exchangeable within the political community.[51]

The argument here takes an interesting mathematical turn (1131a10 ff.). Let capital letters represent persons and their merits and lower-case letters things or shares distributed. Aristotle begins with the just distribution, A:B :: c:d, shares distributed in the same ratio as personal merits (1131b5). He then alternates the ratio to A:c :: B:d, which seems to say that the same reason for A getting c gives d to B. But, as I assume Aristotle knew, these ratios violate the homogeneity (*homogenōn*) requirement for mathematical ratios: the magnitudes in mathematical ratios must be of the same kind (Euclid, *Elements* V, definition 3, see also proposition 16). Aristotle then saying "the whole [A+c] is to the whole [B+d]" composes the ratios, A+c: c :: B+d: d (Euclid, *Elements* V, definition 14 and proposition 18). He then alternates the ratios to A+c: B+d :: c:d, but since c:d :: A:B, this amounts to saying that A+c: B+d :: A:B, A and his share is to B and his share as A is to B, ending up with the original ratio between persons. This, he says, is the just distribution, a mean between what is "contrary to the proportional" which is "unjust." Letting > represent greater ratio and < lesser ratio (Euclid, *Elements* V, definition 7), the just proportion then is a mean between A+c: B+d > A:B, where A gets more than he or she deserves and B less, and A+c: B+d < A:B, where A gets less than he or she deserves, and B more. Why does Aristotle, the supreme analyst of common sense, turn here to a mathematical treatment?[52]

In the fifth chapter Aristotle turns to that justice in exchanges that holds together the political community, that is, proportional reciprocity. The word translated reciprocity, *antipeponthos,* means literally to have suffered or undergone and be suffering or undergoing in return. It is a technical term in mathematics and physics, meaning inverse or reciprocal proportion, for example, the famous law of the lever in Archimedes's *Equilibrium of Planes* (Propositions 6 and 7): weights in equilibrium are said to be in reciprocal, or inverse, proportion to the lengths of their lever arms. That is, a big weight is to a little weight as the little weight's lever arm is to the big weight's lever arm (bw/lw = lwla/bwla). In equilibrium, it is as if the little weight gets reciprocity for its littleness by the bigness of its lever arm and vice versa for the big weight.

Reciprocity is like rectifying justice because it is primarily giving a thing for an equal thing, but it partakes of and reflects the principle of distributive justice, proportional distribution based on a hierarchy of personal qualities. Aristotle illustrates his fundamental principle of exchanges, proportional equality, by explaining that as a housebuilder is to a shoemaker, so is a house to shoes. The values of commodities are set primarily by the values of the works and of the producers of the commodities. Some way must be found to equalize products of different worth, so that one can say *n* shoes equals 1 house: money is invented to provide a conventional commensurability based on need for the exchange of intrinsically incommensurable goods. It is clear that this notion of reciprocity includes (but is not exhausted by)[53] the entire commercial life of society.

Aristotle's own manner of talking about these things, as well as the substance of his argument, is worth noting.

> For it is not out of two doctors that a community arises, but out of a doctor and a farmer, and, generally, between those who are different and not equal: but these must be equalized. Everything, therefore, of which there is exchange must be comparable.[54]
>
> For this purpose money (*nomisma*) has been introduced, and it becomes a measure (*meson*) somehow (*pōs*)[55] because it measures everything, so that exceeding and falling short [in value] also are measured, just how many shoes, then, are equal to a house or to [some amount of] food. Therefore, whatever a builder is in relation to a shoemaker, so must that many shoes be in relation to a house or to [some amount of] food. For if this is not the case, there will be neither exchange nor community. And this will not be unless the things exchanged can be somehow equal. It is necessary, therefore, for everything to be measured by some one thing, as was said before. And this is, in truth, need (*chreia*) which holds everything together. For if people were to want nothing, or not want in similar ways, there would be either no exchange or not the same kind of exchange. And money has by agreement and compact come to be a sort of exchangeable representative of need.[56] Because of this, money has the name *nomisma*, because it is not by nature, but by convention [*nomos*, also translated custom and law], and it is in our power to change it and to make it useless.

The deeper significance of Aristotle's remarks about this apparently mundane subject is often unnoted. J. A. Stewart is an exception: "It is only this or that particular monetary system which is by convention and can be changed and disused; the institution of money itself is by nature, just as speech is by nature; i.e., like speech, it is essential to the realisation of that political community in which man attains his true nature. With a system of barter, as with a system of dumb signs, man could never have become a *politēs* [a citizen, an active member of a political community], but would have remained an isolated savage."[57] Particular combinations of sounds forming particular words vary from place to place and from time to time: they are by convention. The impulse to form such conventions arises naturally whenever human beings come together, fed by the natural purposes of learning from and communicating with one another. The natural sociality implicit in this process manifests itself also in the invention of money, serving a natural human need for mutual exchange and political communion. Human beings, it seems, are convention-making animals by nature. "[In] the case of man *nomos* [convention, law], which expresses itself through the development of *logos* [speech, reason], is as indispensable an end for *physis* [nature] as *physis* is an indispensable ground for *nomos*, . . . *physis* provides the potentialities, *nomos* the actuality of man, and . . . therefore, *nomos* comes to be *the* key to a final understanding of man's *physis*."[58]

Aristotle sums up this argument:

> Money indeed, as a measure making things commensurable, equalizes them. For if there were no exchange, there would be no community, nor would there be exchange if there were no equality, nor equality if there were no commensurability. Now then in truth it is impossible for things differing so much to become commensurable, but with reference to need they may become so sufficiently. There must then be some unit, and this is set down on the basis of a supposition (*ex hypotheseōs*), which is why it is called *nomisma*, for this makes everything commensurable, for everything is measured by money. (1133b16–23)[59]

Aristotle knows that not everything is measured by money. Besides the fundamental incommensurability discussed here, in his books on friendship (*Nicomachean Ethics* 8 and 9) he discusses a number of necessarily unequal exchanges, for example, between parents and children, people of outstanding virtue and those of lesser virtue who benefit from that virtue, and others. In such cases honor is often due, but it is not thought of as being commensurable with that for which it is "paid." Jewish, Christian, and Islamic theologians extend this thought to its limits by arguing for the utter incomparability of love and reverence due to the Creator with that due to any of his creatures.

The word "sufficiently" in the previous quotation seems to mean "for practical purposes." In truth the things evaluated by money do not possess the natural or intrinsic commensurability that perfect justice in distribution would require. The homogeneity required in mathematical ratios, referred to above, which would ground an intrinsic common measure in societal exchanges does not exist. Nevertheless, the *need* for different kinds of goods, although not being unqualifiedly rational and not a measure of the intrinsic worth of the goods, does provide a kind of homogeneity and commensurability reflected in monetary values that is sufficient for most purposes of exchange and for the social life that exchange supports. The conventional monetary units that roughly measure needs make possible that exchange and reciprocity that civil society requires. Aristotle clarifies, but does not emphasize, the theoretical insufficiencies of this conventional commensurability: he emphasizes its practical sufficiency. Both by the substance and the manner of his treatment he exhibits the inseparability of the genuine search for justice from moderation.

VI. Nature, or Some Other Way

Meno does not seem to find Socrates' way of inquiring and conversing particularly congenial. But there are a few places in the dialogue where he does seem to exhibit a more passionate interest in what Socrates is saying. At 81a–e [189–94] Socrates says, "I have heard from both men and women wise about things divine—," when apparently Meno interrupts with "What was the account they gave?" Socrates keeps Meno on the hook with "A true one, it seems to me, and a beautiful one." Meno repeats, "What was it and who are those who say it?" Those who say it are priests and priestesses who are concerned with giving an account of divine things, and what they speak about turns out to be the immortality of the soul and the doctrine of recollection. The prospect of wisdom about things divine does stir Meno's soul.

At 87d [366] Socrates forecasts his turn at the end of the dialogue to divine dispensation (*theia moira*) rather than teaching, knowing, and nature as the source of virtue:

> Then, if there is something good and it is something else separated from knowledge, it may be that virtue would not be some sort of knowledge; but if there is nothing good which knowledge does not encompass, then we would be right in suspecting what we suspected, that it is some sort of knowledge.[60]

The treatment of nature in this dialogue is objectionable; it would seem, intentionally objectionable.[61] In the long discussion with the democratic politician Anytus (93c–94e [440–58]) about how the great Athenian political leaders, Themistocles, Aristides, Pericles, and Thucydides (not the historian) were unable to pass on their political virtues to their sons, Socrates seems to be exhibiting the lack of natural political capacity in these sons. But he uses these descriptions simply to conclude that virtue is not teachable, which prepares the way for disconnecting virtue from knowledge.[62]

At 89a–c [398–402] accepting the separation of nature and teaching in accordance with Meno's opening question, Socrates makes a rather bizarre argument from which he concludes, "then the good become good not by nature." Setting up what is taken for a contrary-to-fact conditional, Socrates argues,

> If the good were to become so by nature, we would, I guess, have people who recognized those among the youth with good natures, whom, after we took them from those who had revealed them, we would guard on the Acropolis, setting our seal on them much more than we do with gold, so that no one could corrupt them, and that when they should come of age, they could become useful to their cities. (89b [400])[63]

Meno agrees, and Socrates draws the above-mentioned conclusion.

The theme of nature and natural endowment also comes up implicitly in Socrates' discussion with Meno of Theognis' poetry (95c–96a [468–74]). He charges Theognis with "saying opposite things about the same things [i.e., the teachability of virtue] to himself." But, as R. S. Bluck notes,[64] "there is no real contradiction, and Plato can hardly have been unaware of this . . . In the first four lines that Plato quotes a satisfactory native endowment (*noos* [intellect]) is assumed to be present," in the other lines quoted "the necessary native endowment [*noēma*, intelligence] is assumed to be either absent or perverted." This discussion began with the question about whether the Sophists are or are not teachers of virtue, and Socrates, Bluck suggests, is here deliberately mimicking the Sophists' usual manner of taking words out of context in interpreting poetry. The evidence for the power of nature is presented, while that evidence is rhetorically undermined to make way for the more popular and, for Meno, more convincing substitute for nature, divine dispensation.

The "other way" of Meno's opening speech, anticipated at 87d [366], by which "virtue comes to be there for those for whom it may come to be there (*paragignētai*)" (100b [564]), is divine dispensation and divine possession. It can be said to be the opposite of the previous arguments, because through it, Socrates says, the divinely inspired set straight many great affairs without intelligence (*nous*) or knowledge of what they do or say (99c–100a [554–62]).[65]

There are echoes of Plato's *Meno* throughout the *Nicomachean Ethics,* but nowhere more than in the book's final chapter, Chapter Nine of Book Ten, the introduction to Aristotle's *Politics*. Aristotle there explains why, after his *Ethics,* "in order that to the best of our power the philosophy of human things may be completed," a book on "legislation" and "polity as a whole," the *Politics,* is required. The argument is straightforward: "If words and arguments (*logoi*) [like those found in the *Nicomachean Ethics*] were sufficient in themselves to make men decent, many and great would be the fees they would justly bear away, as Theognis says." In Theognis, the if-clause of this hypothetical is: "If god granted this to the physicians, to cure vice and blindly ruinous sentiments of men."[66] As Burnet puts it, Aristotle's "quotation is suggested by Plato, *Meno,* 95e,"[67] where Socrates' if-clause is: "If intelligence (*noēma*) could be put into a man." Some rare, noble young people, it seems, can be moved by words and arguments, but most people are moved more by passion, especially by fear of punishment, than by the shame that accompanies respect and operates preventively against vice. Passion, in general, Aristotle argues, is thought to yield not to reason and to argument, but to force.

The echoes from the *Meno,* both from its beginning and its end, are loudest at 1179b20–23:

> Some suppose that people become good by nature, others that it is by habit, and still others that it is by teaching. Now while it is clear that what characterizes nature does not belong to those things that are in our power; but that it does belong to those who are truly fortunate through some divine cause.

Aristotle here disjoins the conjoined just as Meno did, but as he did before in the *Ethics,* he shows in the ensuing discussion how they work together. And here, he also connects nature and divinity, but not as opposites as Socrates did at the end of the *Meno*, but more moderately, as cooperating causes.

Aristotle goes on to say, "And argument and teaching are perhaps not effective with everyone, but what is needed is for the soul of the hearer to have been worked up beforehand by habits just as the soil is in order to nurture the seed, so as both to enjoy and to hate nobly." This working up beforehand is to be accomplished through the impersonal, but necessitous, authority of the laws, making what was originally unpleasant for the young become customary and no longer painful.[68] As a matter of fact, he goes on, this will be needed throughout adult life too: "For most people are moved to obedience by compulsion rather than by argument and by punishments rather than by the noble."

Whether one might acquire virtue and knowledge about virtue from the Sophists, especially from Gorgias or Protagoras, also seems to be a genuine concern for Meno,[69] yet there is nothing in the *Meno* like the extended critiques of the sophists found in Plato's *Protagoras* and *Gorgias*.[70]

Aristotle's themes in this chapter, the insufficiency of *logoi* and the need for laws enforced within a political order, require him to say something about "the Sophists who advertise themselves as teachers of politics, [but] appear to be very far from teaching it." For, if they knew what it was about, they "would never have set it down as the same as, or subordinate to, rhetoric." They lack political skill and political experience; "for those with experience in particular matters rightly judge the works there produced and understand through what and how they are brought to completion, and what kinds of things harmonize with what."[71]

When Aristotle argues that it is impossible, or at least not easy, to carry out noble actions if one is unequipped with external goods like "friends," wealth, or political power,[72] he seems to be making what Socrates ironically disparaged as Meno's special contribution to the discussion of virtue.[73]

Is this to be understood as a departure by Aristotle from the teachings of his teachers, Socrates and Plato? Perhaps, but could not Aristotle respond, "Did not the same Plato who wrote Socrates' speeches also write Meno's?"

The intractability of human nature, not in all people, but most people ("the many"), is presented in the final chapter of the *Nicomachean Ethics* as a fundamental condition calling for compulsory legislation and political life. This account, however, must be supplemented by what is said in Aristotle's books on friendship and in the *Politics* about human beings as social, political and rational animals by nature, prompted by that nature to yearn, moderately, for a community that might do justice to that rationality.[74] Near the beginning of the *Politics*,[75] speaking of the self-sufficient political community, Aristotle remarks that although it *comes into being* for the sake of life, it *is* for the sake of the good life. The fulfillment of a more primitive potency opens the way for an eventually even more fulfilling potency, all according to nature.

Notes

Introduction

1. See 34–37, especially 311 n. 32.
2. See Descartes, *Passions of the Soul* Article 76.
3. See Plato, *Lysis* 211d–212a and Aristotle, *Nicomachean Ethics* 1.6 1096a11–17.
4. The new subtitle is actually the original title.

Chapter One · The Natural Basis of Political Life: Nature and Convention in Human Speech and Politics

1. Cf. *Politics* 1276a34–b13, 1289a13–20, 1295a40–b1; *Nicomachean Ethics* 1131a10–b24, 1132b31–1133b29, esp. 1133a10–12.
2. See below note 16, second paragraph.
3. Cf., for example, Weisheipl 1955; Simon 1970.
4. The last three oppositions presuppose the nature of modern natural science and are connected with the "conquest of nature." That is, nature is conceived of at first as non-teleological and everything of human value is regarded as derivative from nature's opposite, from human making. These last three oppositions then could be regarded as variations on the opposition between Nature and Art.
5. This discussion is based primarily on Strauss 1953, ch. 3.
6. These enumerations are based on Young 1955.
7. Strauss 1953, 90.
8. *Politics* 1252b22–23.
9. A.T. Murray translation revised (Murray 1919).
10. Insolent and wild seems to be balanced against loving strangers, and not just against being god-fearing in thought.
11. Consider Euripides' addition to the story, *Cyclops* 531–43, 582–84.
12. One etymology of the word communication traces it back to roots meaning sharing a wall, *commoenia*, a city wall. The city wall would seem to be an elementary condition for a more advanced sharing in proportionally linked giving and receiving, charge and privilege, that, according to Emile Benveniste, "constitutes the community." See Benveniste 1971, 276–77.

13. *Die deutsche Ideologie* B.I.A.I in Marx 1953, 361, reading *"nach dem"* for *"auch das."*
14. Homer's treatment in the Cyclops story of the theme of shepherd, on the one hand, versus tiller of the soil and man of the city, on the other, should be contrasted with the Biblical account of Cain and Abel. Cf. Genesis 4. Cf. Isaac Abravanel, "Commentary on the Bible," in Lerner and Mahdi 1963, 255–59. Both points of view are to be found in Plato, *Laws* 676a–681d, 781e–783a. On the *Laws* see Strauss 1968, 39–41. Cf. also Homer, *Odyssey* X 302 ff. with Deuteronomy 4:19 and Genesis 18:11–15.
15. Thus broadly conceived, the logical works include the *Rhetoric* and the *Poetics*. Cf. Alfarabi 1962, 92–93. The ascent from and descent back into the Platonic cave are to be made, according to Alfarabi, by means of the *Organon*: the ascent, in order, by means of the *Categories, On Interpretation, Prior Analytics,* to the *Posterior Analytics*; the descent by means of the *Topics, Sophistical Refutations,* and *Rhetoric,* down to the *Poetics*. Cf. Boggess 1970, 86–90. See also Aquinas 1970, Foreword, 1–3.
16. Cf. Oesterle 1962, Book I, Lesson II, 23–29. Cf. Benveniste 1971, ch. 2, 4, 5, and 6. This volume came to my attention after the writing of this essay.

    The word symbol as used here and in Aristotle's text, with its ultimate referent understood as naturally given, should be distinguished from the modern mathematical symbol whose meaning is determined primarily by those rules of method governing the symbol generating intelligence itself and the systematic context of symbols within which any particular symbol occurs. See Klein 1968, esp. ch. 9, 117–25, ch. 11, C, 2; ch. 12, A and B, 163–78, 192–211. For Vieta, "The letter sign designates the intentional object of a 'second intention' . . . , namely of a concept which itself directly intends another *concept* and not a *being*." The referent of the letter sign, of the symbol "in its merely possible determinateness, is accorded a certain independence which permits it to be the subject of 'calculational' operations." These symbolic formulations are treated with the aid of the imagination by the symbol-generating intelligence as directly apprehensible beings "whose merely potential objectivity is understood as an actual objectivity." Klein 1968, 174–75, 207–8. The way is opened for a symbol-generating intelligence which in a sense "prescribes to nature its [possible] laws" in order to discover laws which would never be "given" to the human understanding by nature left to itself.

17. Consider, for example, what constitutes the unity of the *polis* in Plato, *Republic* 414b–415d. We ignore here the distinction between *logos* and *mythos*. See chapter two, below, 28–29 and especially note 19 on 309–10; note 1, above; Montesquieu, *De l'esprit des lois* Book 29, ch. 19; Abraham Lincoln, "Fragment on the Constitution and the Union," 1860 or 1861, in Basler 1953, 4:168–69; Aristotle, *Politics* 1336b2–6 and 12–14; and Plato, *Cratylus* 388d–390d.
18. See Aquinas 1951, 416–19; and Klein 1964, 53–66; and 1965, 112–25.
19. Cf. Aristotle, *Nicomachean Ethics* 1155a20, 1170a26–b14.

Chapter Two · Tragedy and Religion in Aristotle's *Poetics*

1. Cf. *Poetics* 1451a37–38, 1451b5, 1460b34–36.
2. Another book, or section, on comedy is said to be lost.
3. Cf. 1449a5–6.
4. Cf. Thomas Aquinas, *Summa Theologiae* II-II Q.184 A.1 *ad* 2, A.3, A.4.
5. We shall provisionally use the term "purgation theory" to refer to the former position and "purification theory" to refer to the latter.
6. Cf. Telford 1961, 59 ff. However, Telford's interpretation of catharsis differs from those we have sketched out in one crucial respect; see 103–4, and cf. note 12 below.
7. E.g., Jean Racine, *Phèdre*, Préface, the last paragraph.

   Socrates' criticism of the poets in Book Ten of the *Republic*, in our opinion, is not meant to be taken simply at face value. The best city, according to Socrates in the *Republic*, is the city according to nature. Yet in the *Republic* there is a deliberate and systematic depreciation and distortion of everything strictly private, of everything in human nature that does not directly pertain to justice or philosophy. Those distortions, it has been suggested, serve the purpose of alerting the critical reader to those aspects of human nature which will always interfere with the perfection of justice and philosophy. Just as the power and significance of family feelings are minimized in Books Five and Seven, so are those elements in our nature which call for tragedy and comedy minimized in Book Ten. These distortions would seem to compel the critical reader to try to think his way to a more adequate appreciation of what Socrates has deliberately distorted.

   There is in such natures as ours, Socrates suggests to Glaucon, a certain tenderness or gentleness which from the perspective of citizen-virtue alone (*to dokoun alēthes*, 607c end, see also 607a end) has no place. Tragedy, through pity, caters to and nourishes this part of human nature. Unalloyed citizen-virtue requires a certain harshness or toughness that practice in pitying might tend to dissolve. Pity has no place in the soul of guardians and soldiers in the best city.

In going on to speak of the temptations from comedy, Socrates shifts from "we" to "you" (sing.). Glaucon is particularly susceptible to such temptations, Socrates is not. While the passions nourished by comedy are not explicitly singled out as pity is for tragedy, Glaucon's character (357a, 372c2–374b3, 468b end–468c4) and Socrates' remarks (606d) suggest to us that anger and lust are the chief passions here, anger from the natures of men and gods, lust exhibited by the ridiculously bawdy behavior of men and gods. These arguments could be interpreted as providing materials for arguments about the legitimate and proper function of tragedy and comedy within civil society.

There are certain private psychic needs whose satisfaction civil life cannot provide for, and further, which come into conflict with the requirements of civil life. Institutions are required in all states other than Socrates' Republic to gratify and to temper, civilize, or purify those parts of our souls. Tragedy's task is to soothe, civilize, and purify the gentler element, and comedy is to do primarily the same for anger and lust. Shakespeare's Angelo in *Measure for Measure* best exemplifies, insofar as we know, how anger (moral indignation) and lust can work together, feed on and reinforce each other. Comedy then should aim at making characters like Angelo impossible.

8. 1341b33 ff. See also 1339b11–1340b19.
9. 1455b15.
10. 535b, 535c.
11. I.e., that our pity is always associated with a fear that what happened to the one we pity could have happened or could happen to us. Cf. Sophocles, *Ajax* 118–33 and 1355–73.
12. Butcher explains his translation of *to philanthrōpon* (*Poetics* 1453a and 1456a21–23) as "moral sense" (Butcher 1951, 303 n. 2). Our interpretation follows Lessing, *Hambürgische Dramaturgie* nos. 75 and 76, translated as *Dramatic Notes in Lessing's Prose Works* in the Bohn's Standard Library edition. (Reprinted as Lessing 1962.) According to this interpretation, *to philanthrōpon,* literally "love (or friendship) for mankind," is a more elementary or primitive phenomenon (see *Nicomachean Ethics* 1155a16 ff.), akin to the fellow-feeling of birds and beasts for members of their own species. Compare *Virtues and*

Vices, 1251b2–4, where "pretended (*prospoiētos*) *philanthrōpia*" is linked with slander, flattery, malignity, and unscrupulousness as forms of injustice or unrighteousness. The sense of justice presupposed by Aristotle's definition of tragic pity could exist, as tragedy itself, only in a rather highly developed form of political society. Cf. Else 1957, 367–71. Cf. *King Lear* V.iii.230–32.

13. Cf. Else 1957, 378–383, note 54; 373, 438–439.
14. See Shakespeare, *Hamlet* III.iii.22–23.
15. For the problem of the tragic hero and modern life, see Hazlitt 1817a, the chapter on Coriolanus; Hazlitt 1817b, "Why the Arts Are Not Progressive"; and especially Churchill 1932, "Mass Effects in Modern Life."
16. Butcher 1951, 317–21.
17. Cf. Butcher 1951, 265–266, and Lessing 1962, no. 78.
18. Quoted from his essay *On Education*; cf. the prologue to *Samson Agonistes* and *The Reason of Church Government Urged against Prelaty*, Introduction to Book II.
19. This assertion would appear to be contradicted by Aristotle's statement that correctness in politics and correctness in poetry are not the same (1460b14–15). The statement may mean little more than that the kind of man and action that makes for a good ruler is different from the kind of man and action that makes for a good tragic hero. This is implicit clearly in the notion of the tragic flaw, among other things, and in the differences between the ends of the poetic and political arts. What we are suggesting is that in certain decisive respects the understanding that enables one man to portray a tragic hero well is the same as the understanding that enables another man to practice the art of governing well. Also, that two arts serve some ends that are different in no way prevents them from serving other ends that are the same nor from being subordinate to the same overall end. Furthermore, Aristotle, we suggest, used the word politics in more than one sense, a broad and narrow sense. In *Politics* 1322b17, he speaks of the care of religion and of the priesthood as being a kind of office different from political offices like those of the police, judiciary, executive, and the military. Yet, he asserts, the priesthood and religion are necessary for the political community and are common concerns of the entire *polis* (1322b30–32, 1328b2–24, 1329a27–36, 1330a8 and 9). Religion and poetry are not political in the sense of being directly concerned with the everyday administration of governmental affairs. They are political in the more fundamental sense of determining the habits, ideals, and moral sense of the community, the way

of life which determines the pattern of the administration of the laws, and sometimes the pattern of the laws themselves. The poets and writers are teachers of legislators. (See Plutarch's *Parallel Lives,* the lives of Lycurgus, Solon, and Alexander; and Rousseau, *The Social Contract* II.7, the chapter on the legislator, and Aristotle, *Politics* 1335b2–6 and 12–14.) They are in this sense "legislative." The distinction between the political art in the narrow sense and the architectonic legislative art (*nomothetikē*) is drawn in *Nicomachean Ethics* 1141b23 ff. Cf. also *Poetics* 1450b4–8. Politics and poetics differ also in that poetics deals with those things in our nature which are both beneath and beyond politics. It aims, or should aim, at civilizing what lies beneath politics.

(Since this writing the following texts have come to my attention: Alfarabi 1962, 43–47, 92–93; and Lerner and Mahdi 1963. In the latter volume, consider Roger Bacon's discussion on 376–88.) Cf. also Nietzsche, *Die fröhliche Wissenschaft,* Erstes Buch, No. 1.

20. Cf. Thomas Aquinas, *Summa Theologiae* I-II Q.5 A.4 *ad* 4, I-II Q.27 A.1 *ad* 3. Cf. Also II-II Q.145 A.2 and II-II Q.180 A.2 *ad* 3.
21. Cf. *Nicomachean Ethics* 1140a18 ff., *Metaphysics* 1027a14, 1032a20–23, 1036a9.
22. Lessing 1962, no. 32.
23. Also cf. *Poetics* 1460b33–1461a1.
24. Butcher 1951, 267.
25. At such a stage uncertainty, hope, fear, and pity would be completely purged. Cf. John Milton, *Paradise Regained* III, 206. Cf. Thomas Aquinas, *Summa Theologiae* I-II Q.61 A.5.
26. Cited by Butcher 1951, 217–18. Cf. Aristotle, *Metaphysics* 982b11–983a21, and Aquinas's commentary on the passage.

    Thus the *Poetics* would appear to be that book of Aristotle's which comes closest to dealing with one of the key questions of Martin Heidegger's thought: the question, stated in non-Heideggerian terms, of how fear, tragedy, and natural piety contribute to the establishment of the mood, or disposition, out of which philosophy develops.
27. Cf. Thomas Aquinas, *Summa Theologiae* II-II Q.182 A.2.
28. Jaffa 1964.
29. *King Lear* V.iii.170–75.
30. See Kitto 1958.
31. See Kitto 1954, 124–29 and 1960, ch. 6. R. C. Jebb offers a part "historical" explanation and part apology in his Introduction to the *Ajax* (Jebb 1896, 28–45).

32. Consider also Theseus in *Oedipus at Colonus*. The counterpart to Odysseus and Theseus in *King Lear* would appear to be Edgar. Cf. Plato, *Republic* 604e.

Chapter Three · Gratitude, Nature, and Piety in *King Lear*

1. Oedipus in a questionable way assumes his father's position through violence. Shakespeare's Edgar behaves as a father to his father with perfect justice. Compare the beginning of this scene, IV.vi, with Matthew 4.5–11, and with Prospero's "miracles" in *The Tempest*.
2. Cf. Aristotle, *Nicomachean Ethics* 1161a20 and 1163b12–29.
3. Cf. II.iv.179 ff. and 252, III.iv.20, and Regan's (!) morally indignant words to Gloucester, "Ingrateful fox" (III.vii.28). She probably means that he is ungrateful to his country: he is referred to as a traitor twelve times. All line numbers are from Muir 1959.
4. Cf. Aristotle, *Rhetoric* 1385a16–b11, Cope 1977, Vol. II, 87–93.
5. Cf. Aristotle, *Physics* 192b7–23. Cf. 215a1–5, 230a19 ff., and 254b12 ff.
6. Xenophon's Socrates defines ingratitude as a certain kind of pure injustice: *Memorabilia* 2.2.3. See also *King Lear* I.i.183.
7. Cf. Aristotle, *Nicomachean Ethics* 1163a10–24.
8. In circumstances where either rejection or acceptance is possible, acceptance could in some contexts be understood as implying such a promise.
9. Cf. Aristotle, *Nicomachean Ethics* 1160b23–1162a9, 1163a24–1163b27, 1167a15–22, 1167b16–1168a27. The subject abounds in difficulties. Cp., for example, 1161a20–23 and 1162a4–9 (where it is shown why, in accordance with justice, children, like subjects in relation to their kings, should love parents more than parents should love children), with 1161b18–30 and 1167b16–1168a27 (where it is shown why, generally speaking, parents love children more than children love parents). Cf. *Eudemian Ethics* 1241a35–b11; and Thomas Aquinas, *Summa Theologiae* I-II Q.100, A.5 *ad* 4. Cf. also Plato, *Republic* 330c, 457c end–458b, 462a–e, 463c–465c, 472b3–6.
10. Compare Kent's love for Lear with Cordelia's. The love between Kent and Lear seems inseparable from "service." Cf. I.iv.4–7 and I.iv.92–93.
11. The last line is difficult. Nature here could refer to filial or to paternal affection; merit correspondingly could refer to good deeds, that is, obedience and conformity in ratification of the settlement Lear here proclaims, or simply love of Lear. According to Muir, nature

means "'paternal affection' and *merit,* in the context, means 'filial affection'" (Muir 1959, 6).

12. I.i.3–7. Cordelia and her consort, with Lear so long as he is alive, are to occupy the larger strategic center, balancing Goneril and Albany on the north and Regan and Cornwall on the south. Cf. Jaffa 1964, 118 ff. The present essay is, in a number of important respects, an attempt to develop points first stated by Harry Jaffa.
13. In Cordelia's speech (I.i.248) respect probably means "looking again" or "looking back," *respectare,* to something else beside herself, to her fortune, that is, comparison and calculation. In France's speech (I.i.255) the word means honoring or esteem, but also involves an element of "looking," of calculation, or estimation, of personal worth. The sense of distance suggested by the admiration, estimation, and deference usually associated with "respect" makes the unusual conjunction with "inflam'd" all the more poignant. Cf. also II.iv.24.
14. Cf. IV.i.19–21, and Muir 1959, note to i.20.
15. See notes 5 and 9 above. Cf. Immanuel Kant, "The End of All Things," in Kant 1963, 81–84; Kant 1965, 89–92. (The end of the second paragraph, Kant 1963, 82, should read: "for it is a contradiction to command someone not just to do something but also that he should like to do it" [*auch gern tun soll*].) Should not the "love" referred to by Kant 1963, 84, line 5, be, more strictly, gratitude?
16. There is great division among the commentators. We may distinguish four alternatives:

    1) Lear is a weak, senile, old man in his dotage. Can this be reconciled with the deep and powerful Lear of the rest of the play, with the man whose favorites had been Kent and Cordelia, who wisely favored Albany over Cornwall, who killed the man (probably a captain, V.iii.27) hanging Cordelia?

    2) Lear is a sagacious, though not a wise, king. He is not altogether incognizant of his elder daughters' characters and hypocrisy; he never accuses them of violating their love oaths. He could have regarded the love test at first as primarily a ceremony to ratify and to sanctify the succession; but being particularly vulnerable in relation to Cordelia, he allowed "her most small fault" to wrench his "frame of nature from the fixed place." It was this vulnerability, he rebukes himself, "that let thy folly in, and thy dear judgment out." Why then did Lear in Act II seem to think that he could rely on his elder daughters?

    3) Shakespeare simply took over the old story and did not concern himself with consistency here.

4) There is no inconsistency: A man can be a weak, foolish dotard and under great suffering reveal heretofore untapped great depths of passion and powers of insight.

The argument of this essay is most compatible with the second of these alternatives.

17. It may be that her fault is "small" only when compared with ingratitude, for, as Don Quixote says, "There are those who will tell you that one of the greatest sins man can commit is pride, but I maintain that ingratitude is worse." Part 2, ch. 58. Translation from Cervantes Saavedra 1949, 889. See also Ulrici, quoted in Furness 1880, 456.
18. Cf. Aristotle, *Nicomachean Ethics* 1159a22–25, 1167a11–21, 1170b8–14, 1172a10–14.
19. Cf. *Don Quixote* Part 1, ch. 14.
20. Aristotle, *Nicomachean Ethics* 1177a12–1179a32; and Jaffa 1964,133 ff.
21. Jaffa suggests that "In proclaiming love of himself as the principle of distributive justice," Lear was "pretending to the attributes of divinity" (Jaffa 1964, 132 and 133). Cf. Anastaplo 1971, 791; and II.iv.252.
22. Muir 1959, xliii, n. 1.
23. Cf. III.iv.6–25.
24. Cf. IV.i.27–28.
25. Cf. Hobbes 1950, ch. 8, 59, and *Elements of Law* 1.10.9–11; and Hegel, *Enzyklopädie der philosophischen Wissenschaften, III, Die Philosophie des Geistes,* sect. 408, Zusatz, *ββ*), *"die eigentliche Narrheit."* Cf. *inter alia,* Sophocles, *Ajax,* and Euripides, *Herakles.*
26. The word "heart" occurs rather often in *King Lear* (about fifty times). In general it seems to refer to what is responsible for coordinating men's appetites, passions, desires, thoughts and wills, their loves and hates. Compare Dante's *"animo"* in *Purgatorio,* Canto 17. The word "heart" enters into Thomas Aquinas' discussion in the *Summa Theologiae,* usually when citations from the Bible or Church authorities need explication. Sometimes he interprets it as practical reason or conscience (e.g., II–I Q.94 A.6. Cf. A.5 *ad* 1, A.2, and I Q.24 A.1) and frequently as will (e.g., I-II Q.4 A.4, Q.6 A.4 *ad* 1, Q.19 A.8 *ad* 1, A.10 *sed contra* with *ad* 1, Q.24 A.3). Nonmetaphorically he speaks of the heart as that organ that initiates all bodily, all vital movement, the "instrument of the soul's passions" (e.g., I Q.20 A.1 *ad* 1, I-II Q.17 A.9 *ad* 2, Q.37 A.4, Q.38 A.5 *ad* 3, Q.40 A.6, Q.44 A.1 *ad* 1, Q.48 A.2–4). Cf. Plato, *Republic,* the discussion of θυμός at 439e–442d; and *Timaeus* 69d end–72c1.
27. Cf. Heilman 1963, 72–74. Cf. chapter two, above, 35.

28. Cf. Kent's speech preceding and Mark 13, esp. 13:12; see Furness 1903, 339; cf. Sophocles, *Oedipus at Colonus* 266–67.
29. Cf. I.v.47–48, II.iv.192, and II.iv.273–80.
30. "And show the Heavens more just" is the last line Lear speaks before madness overcomes him. See III.iv.48. In Aristotelian terms this is the point at which the reversal, or peripety, occurs in *King Lear*; *Poetics* 1452a21–b13. Cf. chapter two, above, 25 and 35.
31. The extreme must include madness.
32. Cf. II.iii.7–9.
33. Tom's replacement of the Fifth Commandment's "*Honor* thy father and thy mother" by "Obey" corresponds to a replacement of gratitude by fear.
34. See I.iv.134–39, I.i.90, and I.ii.31–35. Shakespeare's presentation of the "*Angstphänomen*," Lear's "eye of anguish" (IV.iv.15), seems to have been unnoticed by Heidegger 1957, 190; cf. 199 n. 1.
35. Exodus 20.1–17, Deuteronomy 5.6–21, and *King Lear* III.iv.80–83. The statement following the Second Commandment tells of God visiting the iniquity of fathers upon their children; Shakespeare, less mysteriously with a view to considerations of justice, visits the iniquity of children upon fathers. See III.iv.74–75. Cf. Bradley 1961, 222 ff.
36. Cf. III.vi.4–5. Edith Sitwell suggests that these lines were written under the influence of Plato's *Phaedo* 64d–e1 (Sitwell 1965, 75–76).
37. Nineteen times. Gloucester is next with nine times. ("Unnaturalness" occurs once.)
38. Cf. Wilson 1963, 179; Chambers 1925, 240 ff. and esp. 215–16; Traversi 1938, 185; Danby 1949, 15–19; and esp. Heilman 1963, ch. 4 and 5, and 115, 133–34, and 179–81.

    Heilman's careful work is a fundamental book, perhaps *the* fundamental book, for any serious study of *King Lear*. By carefully and searchingly tracing out and relating the amazingly intricate patterns of imagery in the play, Heilman lets Shakespeare's philosophy speak for itself. The book's deficiencies, deficiencies generally shared by critics of pre-nineteenth-century literature, stem from an insufficient understanding of certain key notions of classical philosophy, especially the notion of natural right (see Strauss 1953, ch. 3 and 4) and the notion of "intuitive reason," that is, *nous* (see Klein 1964). Thus Heilman tends to identify "reason" with calculation, so that insight and the perception of "value," that is, the good according to nature, are attributed to a "non-rational" imaginative awareness. See 161, 170, and *King Lear* IV.vi.132–33, Muir 1959, 177 n. 13, and this chapter, 42–43.

39. H. Granville-Barker, *Prefaces to Shakespeare,* quoted in Sitwell 1965, 47. In later editions Granville-Barker has apparently substituted, less aptly in our view, "despot" for "wilful man."
40. Cf. IV.vi.115–16.
41. Leviticus 20:10. He "pardons" an adulterer rather than an adulteress. Cf. II.iv.129–33 and 233–35.
42. Romans 3:1–18; compare 3:10–12 with Psalm 14; and Matthew 7:1–5. Lear is open to the charge the Apostle Paul said was made against himself, Romans 3:8.
43. Cf. chapter two, above, 25–27.
44. For another approach to the problem see *1 Henry IV* I.ii and III.ii; and *Henry V* IV.i.
45. Cf. n. 10 above.
46. Cf. also IV.vi.33–80.
47. See Muir 1959, lv ff.; Everett 1969, 184 ff.; Knight 1963, 187 ff.; and Snyder 1966.
48. Muir 1959, lix.
49. Cf. Heilman 1963, 78; 309 n. 11; and esp. 331 n. 1.
50. *Iliad* XII 176.
51. Aristotle, *Nicomachean Ethics* 1134b18–35. Cf. Leo Strauss, "The Law of Reason in the Kuzari," in Strauss 1952, 95–98; A. Bloom 1964; and White 1970.
52. Cf. Romans 1:20, 2:14–15; and I Corinthians 2:14.
53. Heilman 1963, 155–56. Cf. *King Lear* V.iii.189–90 and I.i.56.
54. I Corinthians 2.20 and Heilman 1963, ch. 1–4. But compare *A Midsummer Night's Dream* IV.i.10–26: and cf. *idem* IV.i.218–21 with I Corinthians 2:9: I.ii.22–99 with I Corinthians 9:22; I.ii.8, 15; III.i.1–81; IV.ii.30–end with Galatians 2:11 ff.: also V.i.195–96, 311, and 360–62.
55. Cf. section II above.
56. J.C. Maxwell, quoted in Muir 1959, lvi.
57. Does this indicate that ingratitude more than prideful disobedience is chiefly responsible for the "general curse"? See n. 17 above.
58. Cf. Ulrici in Furness 1880, 456–57. See also Gervinus on 459–60, on the significance of her leadership of the invading army for the question of her death. Cf. Granville-Barker 1970, 23–24 (277–78) and 51 (305) on Cordelia's silence.
59. Cf. Immanuel Kant, *Critique of Pure Reason* A 829–30 / B 857–58.
60. All the world's a stage in Shakespeare for him who, like Lear, Jaques, and Antonio, is coming to feel himself to be an "exile in 'this' world." Macbeth (V.v.25) is a special case.

61. I am indebted for this observation to Hilail Gildin of Queens College, N.Y.
62. Cf. Bradley 1961, 118 ff.; Heilman 1963, 32 and 298–99 n. 28; and Heilman 1969, 169 ff.
63. Cf. Jaffa 1964, 131.
64. The control is, of course, guided by other natural powers, such as reason and judgment. France, the king, acknowledges the law's authority even over his noble love for Cordelia (I.i.253).
65. Cf. Plato, *Meno*, esp. beginning; and Aristotle, *Nicomachean Ethics* 2.1. [Berns went on to write an essay connecting these passages. See the appendix.—*AP*]
66. Cf. Strauss 1997, 475–76.
67. Cf. Aristotle, *Physics* 2.
68. This is not contradicted by the fact that Edgar is the only major character in the play who never uses the word "nature" or any word with nature as its root. Cf. note 1, above.

Chapter Four · Francis Bacon and the Conquest of Nature

1. Speech at the Massachusetts Institute of Technology, April 1, 1949. Cf. Churchill 1948, 38–42; "Mass Effects in Modern Life" and "Fifty Years Hence" in Churchill 1932.
2. The common, Socratic element in the philosophies of Plato and Aristotle is discussed in chapter fourteen.
3. Unfortunately, in the most widely read English translation, Spedding's, among other inaccuracies, *vincitur,* "conquered," is usually translated as "commanded." Spedding was probably misled by the *imperatur* of I.129. See Anderson 1960, 19, lines 18 and 19; 29, line 8; and 39, I.3.
4. *Novum Organum* I.98.
5. The refutation, or rejection of the natural human understanding has been tried in different ways. Cf. Descartes' "*genium aliquem malignum*" in Meditation I and Meditation VI, 76 and 77; Hobbes's "feigning the world to be annhiliated" in *De Corpore* ch. 7; and *Leviathan* ch. 13, where it is shown why the "condition of nature" is intolerable; John Locke, *Essay Concerning Human Understanding* Book I; and *Essay Concerning Civil Government* ch. v, where the part which nature (compared with labor) contributes to the value of things shifts from 1/10th to 1/100th to 1/1000th to "the almost worthless materials"; Spinoza, *Ethics* Part I, Appendix; and Hegel, *Phänomenologie des Geistes, "Einleitung"* (Hoffmeister 1952, 66–68); Baillie 1910, 135–37. Cf. Klein 1968, 72–74 and 117–21; Strauss 1959,

"Political Philosophy and History" and "On Classical Political Philosophy"; and chapter one, above.

6. Aphorisms, Bacon wrote in *De Augmentis Scientiarum* VI.2, represent knowledge as fragmentary and incomplete, thereby inviting the reader to contribute and supply what is missing.
7. *The Great Instauration*, Preface; and *Novum Organum* I.70.
8. Cf. "Truth and Utility in the Science of Francis Bacon" in Rossi 1970, 146–73; and "The Practical Uses of Theory" in Jonas 1966, 188–210, esp. section v.
9. Bacon's usual term for Aristotelian logic is dialectic, usually rendered by Spedding as "logic."
10. Spedding et al. 1875, 4:412.
11. *Novum Organum* II.16–17.
12. In aphorisms 60 and 15 Bacon condemns the use of certain generally accepted names and notions. He seems to have Aristotle's categories in mind. But names and notions from the category of quantity are not among those condemned.
13. Cf. Plutarch's *Lives*, Nicias XXIII.
14. In *De Augmentis Scientiarum* III.4, and *Novum Organum* II.48. These aphorisms dealing with superstitious philosophy and the failure to search out the moving principles of things are at the center of *Novum Organum* I.
15. In the *Valerius Terminus*, which was never published by Bacon, but evidently circulated privately, the equivalent, or corresponding term is "direction." Spedding et al. 1875, 3:235–41. Cf. Ellis' Preface in Spedding et al. 1875, 201–5. This may be the best place to study what Bacon means by the remark "that which in contemplation is as the cause is in operation as the rule" (*Novum Organum* I.3). Cf. Rossi 1968, 193–201; and Hesse 1964.
16. *Nobum Organum* II.2.
17. Cf. on "simple natures," *Novum Organum* II.5 and Descartes, *Rules for the Direction of the Mind* (*Ingenii*) Rule 12. For Bacon's influence on Descartes, see Lalande 1911, 1996.
18. Cf. *De Augmentis Scientiarum* III.4, on "Abstract Physics." Cf. L. Berns 1957, Appendix, 175–78, 193–94. Cf. Rossi 1968, 202.
19. *De Augmentis Scientiarum* III.4, and IV, end; in Spedding et al. 1875, 4:347 and 404.
20. I.104.
21. Cf. Klein 1968, Part I, Introduction, and Part II.
22. But cf. Lalande 1911, 309–11; 1996, 68–70, where Lalande speaks of Descartes' announcement (in *Rules . . .*, no. 12) of the method of geometrical interpretation of sensible phenomena in words which

"reproduce nearly word for word a passage from the *Valerius Terminus*."

23. *Novum Organum* II.8, 45, 46, and esp. 47; I.96 and 98; and *Preparative [Parasceve] to a Natural and Experimental History* aph. vii. Cf. Hans Jonas, "The Scientific and Technological Revolution," in Jonas 1974, 63–65. Cf. Pemberton 1728 (editor of the third edition of Newton's *Principia* . . .), Introduction, where the importance for Newtonian science of Bacon's critique of the prejudices and obstructions impeding knowledge and his treatment of induction are stressed.
24. *Novum Organum* I.96 and 80; and *De Augmentis Scientiarum* III.6.
25. See *De Augmentis Scientiarum* III.6, and Ellis' notes to the same in Spedding et al. 1875, 1:577.
26. *Novum Organum* I.113.
27. *Nobum Organum* I.91.
28. *Thoughts and Observations* (*Cogitata et Visa*), translated in Montagu 1855, 1:434; original in Spedding et al. 1875, 3:589 ff. Cf. Anderson 1948, 38. The translation in Montagu is more literal than the recent translation in Farrington 1964, which also contains translations of "The Masculine Birth of Time" and "Refutation of the Philosophies."
29. See Swift 1965, 156. Although Swift is, in general, a partisan of the ancients, he seems to have accepted, in this book at least, Bacon's characterization of Aristotle's philosophy as "contentious." Swift may have regarded Bacon as "valiant" because he dared to challenge the ruling "despot" of philosophy, Aristotle, who, according to Swift, had usurped (Swift 1965, 144) Plato's place as "Prince of Philosophers" (*Gulliver's Travels* Part IV, ch. 8; cf. also Part III, ch. 8).
30. *Novum Organum* I.128.
31. Cowley 1721, 2:560.
32. *Valerius Terminus* ch. 26 in Spedding et al. 1875, 3:252: and *Novum Organum* I.90. Cf. Aristotle's *Politics* 2.8; Thomas Aquinas, *Summa Theologiae* I-II Q.97 A.2; and Strauss 1959, 221–22; *et al.* from note 5.
33. See L. Berns 1957; and White 1968.
34. *Discourses* I.44. Cf. Rossi 1968, 109–16.
35. Cf. White 1968, the chapters entitled "Of Island Utopias," esp. for the comparison with *The Tempest*, and "The Old and the New Atlantis"; see also White 1987.
36. Is it in contrast to Hierusalem (the way Jerusalem is spelled in the *New Atlantis*), the good-peace in contrast to the holy-peace (from the Greek *hieros*)?
37. These things are said explicitly only of the Jews.
38. *Novum Organum* I.89.

39. More than 350 years after the publication of the *Novum Organum*, Maxwell's and Rutherford's successor, the Cavendish Professor of Physics, writes, "Physics, indeed, should recognize that it is not in any useful sense the fundamental science, since that peculiarity which makes it fundamental, the fact that its laws are, we believe, applicable in principle to the systems which other sciences investigate, is achieved by adopting an attitude of exclusive concentration on certain approved aspects of the phenomena, such as prevents the development of a scheme by which principle can be translated into practice." Indeed, the claim of fundamental physics that it is "seeking out the Basic Truth of the Universe" is found to be "slightly pretentious." See Pippard 1972, 35 and 37.

    Old questions seem to be opening again. Is the very quest for a fundamental science now even more than "slightly pretentious"? (Cf. Nietzsche, *Beyond Good and Evil* aph. 205.) Or is the way opening for new and, perhaps, even old contenders?
40. Cf. Strauss 1959, 23–25 and "An Epilogue" in Strauss 1968.
41. Cf. Bacon's use of the ambiguity of the word fortune in his "architecture of fortune," (*Advancement of Learning* II), and his attack on the classical subordination of art to nature, its breeding a "premature despair in human enterprises." Spedding et al. 1875, 4:294–95. Cf. also *Novum Organum* I.75 and 78.
42. Cf. also *De Augmentis Scientiarum* IV.1.
43. *Advancement of Learning* II.
44. Spedding et al. 1875, 1:758.
45. See Bacon, *Wisdom of the Ancients* no. 26.
46. See notes 5 and 40, above.

Chapter Five · Thomas Hobbes: A Founding Father of Modern Social Science

1. Thomas Hobbes, *Leviathan* ch. 11, Hobbes 1950, 79. Spelling has been modernized in quotations in this chapter.
2. See, *e.g.*, *Leviathan* ch. 21, end, and *The Elements of Law* 1.17.1 (Hobbes 1928).
3. *De Corpore*, ch. i and ii, esp. vi.7, in Calkins 1948; *Leviathan* ch. 34, Hobbes 1950, 339–41, ch. 46, The Introduction, 4–5; A Review, and Conclusion, 627. It is difficult to determine whether Hobbes conceived of his materialism as simply true, i.e., as "metaphysical," or as "methodological," i.e., an assumption required for proceeding scientifically.
4. *Leviathan* ch. 6. Cf. *Elements* 1.7.1–1.10.11.

5. *Leviathan* ch. 6, Hobbes 1950, 41; ch. 8, Hobbes 1950, 59.
6. *De Cive* (*The Citizen*) in Molesworth 1839–45, 2: ch. i.2; see especially the note.
7. *Leviathan* ch. 11, Hobbes 1950, 79–80.
8. *Leviathan* ch. 13, Hobbes 1950, 103–4.
9. *Leviathan* ch. 13.
10. *Elements* 1.14.6.
11. *Elements* 1.16.2; *De Cive* ch. iii.3.
12. *Leviathan* ch. 14, Hobbes 1950, 107–8; ch. 15, 128, 130–31; ch. 27, 251; ch. 42, 435–36; ch. 26, 231–32.
13. *Elements* 1.17.14 and 1.13.3.
14. *Leviathan* ch. 14, Hobbes 1950, 117.
15. *Leviathan* ch. 21, Hobbes 1950, 183.
16. *Leviathan* ch. 15, Hobbes 1950, 128–30; ch. 21; ch. 38, 258–59; *De Cive* ch. vi.13.
17. *Leviathan* ch. 21, Hobbes 1950, 187.
18. *De Cive* ch. x.2 and x.16.
19. *De Cive*, ch. x, esp. x.7, x.8, and x.15.
20. *De Cive* ch. vi.20.
21. For a confrontation of Hobbesian with premodern traditional jurisprudence, compare ch. 26, "Of Civil Laws," of the *Leviathan* with Thomas Aquinas' *Summa Theologiae* I-II QQ.90–97 (published as *Treatise on Law* in Aquinas 1948), in opposition to which Hobbes's chapter may have been written. See also his *A Dialogue between a Philosopher and a Student of the Common Laws of England*, Molesworth 1839–45, vol. 6.
22. *Leviathan* ch. 29, Hobbes 1950, 275–76.
23. *Leviathan* ch. 29.
24. *Leviathan* ch. 30, Hobbes 1950, 288–96; *De Cive*, xiii.9.
25. *Leviathan* ch. 30, Hobbes 1950, 296 ff. and *De Cive* ch. xiii, esp. xiii.14.
26. *Leviathan* dedicatory epistle; ch. 15, end; ch. 38, beginning; *De Cive* ch. xvii.27.
27. *Leviathan* ch. 40–43. Cf. ch. 22, Hobbes 1950, 189–90 and 200.
28. *Leviathan*, ch. 38 and 44.
29. *Leviathan* ch. 31, Hobbes 1950, 312; ch. 45, 570; ch. 12; ch. 45; cf. ch. 27, 249–50; ch. 44, 558–59; and ch. 13, 104; ch. 39, 406; ch. 42, 435; ch. 40, 417; ch. 46, 591–92.
30. [In Cropsey and Strauss 1987, each chapter focused on a particular thinker, closing with some suggested readings. These readings were broken into an A group and B group, the first more essential than the second. At the end of Berns's chapter on Hobbes, the fol-

lowing readings were proposed: "A. Hobbes, Thomas. *Leviathan*. Ch. 13–15, 17–18, 21, 24, 26–30, 46" and "B. Hobbes, Thomas. *Leviathan*. Ch. 6, 10–12, 16, 19, 20, 21–23, 25, 31–32, 35, 43."—*AP*]

Chapter Six · Putting Things Back Together Again in Kant

1. Citations in this chapter to the standard text of Kant 1902 are as follows: e.g., "AK IX, 94–95" refers to volume IX, pages 94–95. Standard page citations to Kant 1781 are preceded by the letter A, e.g., "A 79." The second edition was published in 1787; standard page citations to it are preceded by the letter B, e.g., "B 105."

Chapter Seven · Radical Historicism and the Attempt to Transcend Philosophy: Some Reflections on Strauss, Heidegger, and Husserl

1. For good recent discussions of those explicit arguments, see Hilail Gilden, "Introduction," in Strauss 1989a, vii–xxiv; Miller 1975; Norton 1981; Kennington 1982, 57–86; Gourevitch 1987, 30–33.
2. See Heidegger 1957, secs. 54–60, and especially n. 1 on 199; and Heidegger 1969, 80.
3. Löwith 1960, 111. Emphasis in original. Cf. "Die religiöse Dimension," in Gadamer 1983, 140–151.
4. Strauss 1964, 240–41. Aristotle's treatment of piety and religion, in addition to scattered remarks in the *Politics, Ethics, Rhetoric,* and *Metaphysics,* is to be found, I have argued, implicit in his discussion of tragic pity and fear: Cf. chapter two, above, 26–29 and 33–34. The first seven books of Plato's *Laws,* it might be argued, should be exempted from this criticism.
5. Chapter three of Strauss 1953.
6. Emphasis added. This last point and its significance seem to be overlooked by Hwa Yol Jung in his discussion of these passages, Jung 1967, 506.
7. Klein and Strauss 1970.
8. Cf. Aristotle, *History of Animals* 1.1 487b33–488a13; and Moses Maimonides, *Guide of the Perplexed* II.40; trans. Maimonides 1963, 2:381–85.
9. This last remark requires qualification, cf. L. Berns 1981, 48–49.
10. Especially 129 and 169 of Heidegger 1957. See 130, sect. 27, next to last paragraph, for what in Heidegger corresponds to an account of man's being "by nature a political animal."

11. Gadamer 1967–1972, 3:200; cf. also 1:84–85; and *Wahrheit und Methode* Part Two, II.2.b. Emphasis supplied. A less literal translation can be found in Gadamer 1976, 196; cf. also 201–202.
12. *Sein und Zeit* Part I, V. A; secs. 29–34.
13. *Befindlichkeit*, the "state in which one may be found," should not be translated "state-of-mind" (as Macquarrie and Robinson do). The emphasis is on mood rather than mind.
14. Simon 1967, 51–54. Simon, of course, implies that it can also be predicted of the whole development embracing both opposites.
15. The sense of the word *Eigentlichkeit* might be conveyed in English more clearly by an Anglo-Saxon cognate with the German, i.e., "ownliness." English-to-German dictionaries render the Greek-rooted "authenticity" by *Echtheit*, "genuineness," not *Eigentlichkeit*. Authentic, in the sense of genuine, slightly raises the moral tone of *eigentlich*, "truly, or really, one's own."
16. Cf. chapter nine, above. Chaninah Maschler has observed that Heidegger's resolute man seems to approach Aristotle's *spoudaios*, the serious, earnest, or seriously good man.
17. This threefold distinction, with order reversed, may be the original source of Heidegger's scheme of fundamental *existentialia*. See text at note 12, above.
18. It is important for the study of the essentially human, Aristotle suggests, to determine what natural powers belong exclusively to human beings in comparison with the other animals. Many of the other animals have spiritedness in abundance, none of them has intellectual intuition, *nous*. The possession of this power is said to be the ground of the possibility of genuine theory, the ground of the most important human peculiarity, the peculiar possibility of being open to the being of things as they are—if this is a possibility.

    Is the rejection of the possibility of *nous*, especially by Kant, and its modern replacements (e.g., transcendental subjectivity) any less problematic? Is the way human beings think, even in philosophy and science, essentially different from the cognition of other animals? If so, what is the best way to account for it? Cf. chapter nine, below, 196, esp. 327–28 n. 15.
19. This is not to deny that spiritedness and its care are operative in theory. *Philosophia* means love and care of the unchanging truth. Knowledge is not knowledge until it becomes one's own. The question is, however, which power of the soul dominates the soul? Aristotle's remarks about philosophic piety indicate that intellect so dominates for the philosopher as to enable him to sacrifice the more commonly "primordial" objects of care to his care for the dis-

covery of truth. Spiritedness in the proper sense of the word, for Aristotle, is aroused by objects of our own that are in some way endangered, that might in some way be protected by ourselves. This would apply only to particular objects, especially objects of practice. This ultimate objects of theory, for Aristotle, cannot be endangered. The objects of spiritedness in practice are usually in some way exclusive. One loses no part of the truth by sharing it with others.

The "care" of theory, then, is not care in the ordinary sense of the word. The endangered object here is the carer's own soul, or being, his or her concern for the possible loss of the greatest of all goods, understanding. Care here revolves around the relation of mortal beings to immortal truths. There is some important common ground in the Aristotelian account of philosophic wisdom and Heidegger's account of authentic conscience. The account needs to be supplemented by an account of pleasures, especially "pure," or philosophic pleasure, the kind of account that Aristotle, but not Heidegger, supplies. Cf. "Religiöse Dimension," Gadamer 1983, 144.

20. Cf. chapter one, above, 7–11. "Prephilosophic," of course, does not mean devoid of what could lead to philosophy. Cf., e.g., Deuteronomy 4:19–20; and Genesis 18:11–15.
21. Cf. Strauss 1979.
22. The demonstration includes discoveries about Machiavelli, Hobbes, and Rousseau that prove to be more interesting and important than historicism itself.
23. Cf. Heidegger 1962b, B.I.5., especially e); "Das Wesen des mathematischen Entwurfs . . . ," "The Essence of the Mathematical Project . . ." [This corresponds to part "e" of sect. 18 in the newer, Niemeyer edition of *Die Frage nach dem Ding.—AP*]; and Jacob Klein, "On the Difference Between Ancient and Modern Conceptualization," in Klein 1968, 117 ff. (It may be advisable to read 3–9 first, and if possible, ch. 6–8.) Cf. also "Political Philosophy and History" in Strauss 1959, 74–77.
24. See especially 154–58 of Strauss 1952.
25. Klein, "On the Difference," Klein 1968, 118–119. Cf. Judah Halevi, *Kuzari* I.63 with Genesis 9:27.
26. Despite his insistence that what he is doing should not be called philosophy, Heidegger's intrepid questioning, his revivification of the problem of being, etc., make it difficult not to see him as being in and of the tradition of (Western) philosophy.
27. Translated by Quentin Lauer, with "Philosophy and the Crisis of European Man," the Vienna Lecture, in Husserl 1965.

28. Strauss's translation in Strauss 1971, emphasis added.
29. Cf. L. Berns 1978, 231 ff., especially note 13. For the preparatory development in Russia, consider, in this order, Turgenev's *Fathers and Sons* and *Virgin Soil* (frustrated populism turns to terrorism), Dostoyevsky's *The Possessed*, and Alexander Herzen's *Memoirs*, especially his account of his time at the university.
30. Strauss 1971, 9.

Chapter Eight · The Relation Between Philosophy and Religion: Three Fundamental Alternatives

1. Heidegger has been discussed in greater detail with a brief discussion of the relation of modern scientific philosophy (Husserl) to religion in the last chapter. The religious character of Nietzsche's thought is exhibited most conspicuously by his Zarathustra, less conspicuously in his extensive critiques of other religions.
2. The reference to God as Creator follows closely on the reference to "the laws of nature and of nature's God," suggesting that the Creation is carried on in accordance with those natural laws.
3. Cf. "What is Equity? The Declaration of Independence Revisited," in Jaffa 1975, 149–60; and Anastaplo 1965, 390.
4. Aristotle, *Metaphysics* 981b27–29, 982b11–983a11, 983b7–984a2, 1014b16–1015a19, 1074b1–14, 1091a29–1091b20. In Homer the word nature occurs only once, in the *Odyssey* (X 303). The first and only man to use the word is Odysseus, who had seen the cities and learned the minds of many men, who had learned how men's thoughts differ from place to place and from tribe to tribe. He uses the divinely given gift of natural knowledge to defeat the baneful magic of a goddess.
5. Aristotle, *Physics* 2; Strauss 1953, 78–97; Burnet 1892, Introduction.
6. Heidegger 1950, 325.
7. Heidegger 1954, 6–7.
8. *Summa Theologiae* I-II Q.40 A.3. Cf. also I-II Q.1 A.2 and I Q.2 A.3, the fifth way.
9. Strauss 1959, 36.
10. Alfarabi 1962, Part I, sect. 55. Cf. Aristotle, *Politics* 1252b24–27.
11. Chapter two, above, 24–29, and 33–34.
12. See Bohm 1957, 1.
13. Cf. the argument of Courant and Robbins that only by a (Cauchy's) *static* definition of limit is it possible to have "a precise mathematical analysis of continuous motion in time." Courant and Robbins, 1941, 303–7, with Plato, *Republic* 508a–511e.

14. Aristotle, *De Caelo* 298b14–25; Thomas Aquinas, *Summa Theologiae* I Q.46 A.2.
15. Thomas Aquinas, *Summa Theologiae* II-II Q.1 AA.4 and 5; Q.2 AA.1, 2, and 9; Q.4 AA.1 and 8. The will, in turn, is moved by hope and charity: hope of attaining the ultimate happiness of a supernatural vision of God, and charity (friendship for God) in the desire to honor God by the acceptance of his authority. Thomas Aquinas, *Summa Theologiae* II-II Q.2 A.3, A.9 *ad* 2, A.10; Q.4, AA.3 and 7; Q.23, AA.1 and 6.
16. Aristotle, *Topics* 100a30–b23 and especially 101a36–b4. Strauss 1981; Strauss 1979. This present essay is the latest version of my attempt to come to grips with what was first brought to my attention in those lectures of 1952 [Berns once remarked to me that, after hearing "Progress or Return" (Strauss 1981), he wandered the streets for three days—*AP*].
17. Strauss 1935, Einleitung and especially 21; translation in Strauss 1987, Introduction and especially 13 (corrected version used here); Strauss 1965, Preface to the English Translation, 28–31; Strauss 1946, 338–39; Cropsey and Strauss 1987, 296 and 297. It is worth noting that in this relatively late writing, on 297, Strauss does not say modern *political* philosophy.
18. *Novum Organum* I.3 (Spedding mistranslates "conquered" as "commanded"); Descartes, *Discourse on Method* Part VI.
19. Cf. Sophocles, *Antigone* 821.
20. Strauss 1953, 172–75; Kant 1781, A125–28, B294–315, B740 ff.; Hobbes, *Leviathan* ch. 46, beginning; *De Corpore* ch. 1, sect. 2, ch. 6, sect. 1, 6, 7, 13; and ch. 25, sect. 1; "Six Lessons to the Professors of the Mathematics . . . ," Molesworth 1839–45, 7:212; Newton, *Principia* Preface to the First Edition; "On the Quadrature of Curves," beginning. Hobbes, Newton, and Kant all, in contrast to Euclid, define the geometric elements operationally, or in terms of their generation. Cf. as an introduction to his book, *Greek Mathematical Thought and the Origin of Algebra* (Klein 1968), "The World of Physics and the 'Natural' World" in Klein 1985, 1–34; and Lachterman 1989.
21. *Enzyklopädie* I, sections 160 and 163; translated by Wallace 1892.
22. Strauss 1953, 178–83; chapter ten, below, 208–11.
23. Strauss 1981, 32–33. For a discussion of the most conspicuous omission from this sketch, see Strauss 1965; for Spinoza and German Idealism, see Strauss 1965, the Preface, 15–17; and Strauss 1952, ch. 5; Kennington 1980; Wolfson 1934.
24. *Die Religion innerhalb der Grenzen der blossen Vernunft*, Kant 1902, 6:104; *Religion within the Limits of Reason Alone*, translated in Kant

1960, 95; *Der Streit der Fakultäten*, Kant 1902, 7:67; *The Conflict of the Faculties*, translated in Kant 1979, 123.

25. Kant 1902, 7:63 (German); Kant 1979, 115 (English). Cf. Fackenheim 1980, ch. 2, "Abraham and the Kantians: Moral Duties and Divine Commandments."
26. Cf. Fackenheim 1970, 15–23.
27. Hegel 1970, beginning; translated in Hegel 1977, 55.
28. Kant 1902, 7:39 (German); Kant 1979 (English), 67; Hegel 1970, 292 (German); Hegel 1977, 59 (English); Hegel 1971, I, 95; *The History of Philosophy*, Introduction; Matthew 12:31–32.
29. Strauss 1946, 358.
30. Heisenberg, "Planck's Discovery and the Philosophical Problems of Atomic Physics," Lecture, September 4, 1958, in Auger et al., 1962.

Chapter Nine · Spiritedness in Ethics and Politics: A Study in Aristotelian Psychology

1. *Advancement of Learning* II. Emphasis supplied.
2. 1252a26–34.
3. *Leviathan* ch. 15.
4. *Phenomenology of Spirit* Ch. IV, A.
5. This solution was first suggested to me by Hilail Gildin
6. *Nicomachean Ethics* 6.2 1139a31–32.
7. *Orektikos nous* or *orexis dianētikē*, *Nicomachean Ethics* 1139b5–6.
8. More precisely, there are two questions raised. (1) Which of the two actually moves? and (2) Which of the two most determines the character of practical action? I have discussed these matters in an unpublished essay, "The Natural Basis of What Is Not by Nature in Ethics." For the first question, as Thomas puts it, the "more true" alternative is intelligent appetite. Cf. Aristotle *Metaphysics* 9.5; *De Anima* 433a31–32.
9. *De Anima* 414b3; *De Motu Animalium* 700b22–23.
10. *De Anima* 432b5–7 and *Metaphysics* 1072a26–28; *Nicomachean Ethics* 1149b1. Cf. *Politics* 1334b17–28 where *boulēsis* is included in the irrational part. Wish in infants is clearly irrational and dominated by desire and spiritedness. It is, however, that part of appetite that is most susceptible to, or transformable by, reason and intellect. The different powers of the soul, then, are not to be understood as spatially separated "parts," but as interpenetrating powers.
11. *Metaphysics* 1072a27–28.
12. *De Anima* 3.10 433a10 ff.; *Nicomachean Ethics* 6.2 1139a32–33; *De Motu Animalium* 6–8 700b4 ff., esp. 702a17–19; Aristotle 1900, 255–

56. Nussbaum 1978, 333–36. Strictly speaking, the second major factor, that *by which* movement takes place, the instrument, should include an account of what Aristotle calls "connate pneuma," that bodily element closest to the psychic or divine. See A. L. Peck's Appendix B, in Aristotle 1942, 576 ff., esp., 578, and lxviii and lix; and *De Motu Animalium* 10 703a4–28. (The analogue to the connate pneuma in contemporary physiology would appear to be the neuron.)

13. 1253a7–18.
14. *History of Animals* 8.1 588a18 ff.
15. Thomas Aquinas speaks of a "cognitive power," or "particular reason," a reason directed to particulars. Cf. *Summa Theologiae* I Q.78 A.1 *ad* 3, A.3, A.4 and *ad* 5; Q.81 A.3; II-II Q.74 A.3 and *ad* 1. Cf. Aristotle, *De Anima* 2.6 418a7–26, and 428b18–26, which establishes that some power of judgement is operative in the perception of accidental and common sensibles. Cf. also *Nicomachean Ethics* 6.10 and 11 1142b end to 1143b14; *History of Animals* 8.1 588a16–588b3; and *Politics* 1291a27–28. (Aristotle's *sunesis* and Thomas's *collatio* are very close in meaning, i.e., "a bringing together.") The power of judgment in animals that operates on sensible particulars, or correlates individualized notions, Thomas calls the estimative power. It operates by natural instinct, e.g., when an antelope flees a lion, or a bird takes a piece of straw for nest building. In man it is called cogitative power, because, although it is a power of sensitivity, it is joined to universal intellect. The cogitative power "apprehends the individual thing as existing in a common nature, and this because it is united to intellect in one and the same subject. Hence it is aware of a man as this *man*, and a tree as this *tree*; whereas instinct is not aware of an individual thing as in common nature, but only in so far as this individual thing is the term or principle of some action or passion." The antelope knows the lion not as this lion, but as something to flee; the bird knows the straw not as this straw, but as something to put in the nest. Aquinas 1951, sections 395–98. This uniting of intellect and sensation that allows the object of sense to be sensed as an object of a certain kind, is evidently what constitutes the *phantasia logistikē*, the calculative imagination, for Aristotle. Cf. *De Anima* 420b29–34, 433b30–434a10; *De Motu Animalium* 700b4–702a21.

This power of judgment in its deliberative mode, because it is connected to reason and "reason in contingent matters may follow opposite courses," is "free judgment," and is the basis, according to Thomas, of the Aristotelian doctrine of free will. Thomas Aquinas,

Summa Theologiae I Q.83 A.1 and *ad* 5. Thomas may have in mind, among other places, the arguments in 9.2 1046a36 ff. of the *Metaphysics*, about reason being a faculty of contraries.

16. *Metaphysics* 1.1 980a1–981b10.
17. *Rhetoric* 1389b end.
18. *De Sensu* 437a4–17, *De Interpretatione* 16a9–11.
19. *Politics* 1282b16–18, 1279a17–1279b10; *Nicomachean Ethics* 1129b15, 1160a14; Plato, *Sophist* 263e; Aristotle, *Rhetoric* 1.6 1362b.
20. Cf. Maimonides, *Guide of the Perplexed* II.40
21. *History of Animals* 1.1 487b33–488a13.
22. Cf. G. Berns 1973, 172–73.
23. *De Anima* 3.8 431b20–432a4; *De Motu Animalium* 701b18–22. Cf. chapter one, above.
24. *Politics* 1334a21–23. Cf. 1283a16–23.
25. This, I believe, more than anything else accounts for the proliferation of commentaries on Aristotle's works: namely, the prospect of coming to understand the very inner, or natural, articulation of the subject one is interested in.
26. Cf. Husserl, 1970, section 44, beginning; Heidegger 1962a, 96–97 (Heidegger 1957, 68); and Strauss 1971, 8–9.
27. Cf. Strauss, "On Classical Political Philosophy," in Strauss 1959, 78 ff.; and in Strauss 1975, 59 ff. These remarks require at least one important qualification, which cannot be discussed here: see Strauss 1964, 240–41. Cf. chapter two, above, 26–29, and 33–34.
28. *Nicomachean Ethics* 1094b12–28, 1139b18–19, 1141a9–20; *Metaphysics* 982a12–18.
29. *Nicomachean Ethics* 1123b15–1124a20, and 1169b8–10.
30. Cf. the Dauphin in Shakespeare's *Henry V*, and Abraham Lincoln, Speech of December 26, 1839, Basler 1953, 1:177–79.
31. Cf. Plato, *Republic* 429e–430c; and *Phaedo* 67b–69e. See Thomas Aquinas, *Summa Theologiae* I-II Q.61 A.5. The standard translation is particularly misleading here: (*virtutes*) *politicas* is rendered "social," *purgatorias* "perfecting," and *purgati animi* [not *animas*] "perfect." Cf. *Nicomachean Ethics* 6.13.
32. On the difference between shame-respect, *aidōs, verecundia,* as used here, and shame-disgrace, *aischunē, turpitudo,* cf. Riezler 1950, ch. 8. Cf. Thomas Aquinas, *Summa Theologiae* II-II Q.144 A.2, near the end.
33. *Nicomachean Ethics* 1108a31–32, and 1128b10–16; cf. Aquinas, *Summa Theologiae* I-II Q.61 A.1.
34. *Nicomachean Ethics* 1106b36–1107a6; cf. *Physics* 246a10–248a9.

35. The "mistaken" attribution of Agamemnon's words to Hector at 1116a32–35 may be connected with Aristotle's sense of what is more appropriate for easterners. Cf. *Politics* 1285a10–14, where the attribution is correct, and the aforecited 7.7. Cf. Benardete 1963, esp. 5–12.
36. The word for spiritedness, *thumos,* is often used colloquially for anger.
37. Emphasis supplied.
38. Some translators might render the "is" in the last clause as "seems to be."
39. There is such a treatment in Thomas Aquinas's *Summa Theologiae* I Q.81, and I-II QQ.23, 25, 40–48, on the irascible faculty.
40. *Republic* 374b–376c, 411a–e, 429a–430c, 435c–441d; cf. Allan Bloom in his translation of the *Republic* in Plato 1968, 353–58, 375–78 and 436; *Laws* 731b–d, and 963e; Strauss 1964, 110–13.
41. The rational control and ordination of anger is treated as the virtue of gentleness, or good temper, in *Nicomachean Ethics* 4.5. Gentleness is treated as a passion in *Rhetoric* 2.3. It has been aptly called "the domestic side of courage" by Ken Masugi. Aristotle argues that ferocity does not go along with courage (*Politics* 1338b17–24; cf. *History of Animals* 629b8), with one possible exception "in relation to those who act unjustly" (*Politics* 1328a7–11).
42. Cf. note 15, above.
43. *Eudemian Ethics* 1234a24–34; Thomas Aquinas, *Summa Theologiae* II-II Q.144 A.4 *ad* 4; G. Berns 1973, 165 ff.
44. *Politics* 1287a30–32. Cf. Shakespeare's Angelo in *Measure for Measure,* esp. IV.ii.80 ff. I have discussed these lines in L. Berns 1981, 47–48.
45. *Politics* 1269b27–29.
46. Cf. Riezler 1950, Part Four, ch. 2 and 3 ("Care"); ch. 4, on humor and play, is entitled "Carefreeness."
47. *Politics* 1262b22–23.
48. Seen from the Platonic-Aristotelian point of view, Heidegger's "thinking" and "authenticity" (one's-owness) with their emphasis on "Being-in-the-World," "the ready-to-hand" (*das Zuhandene*), "mineness" (*Jemeinigkeit*), and care (*Sorge*), appear to be a reevaluation and exaltation of spiritedness in human behavior and cognition. This might provide an interesting perspective on the question of the connection between Heidegger's "existential analytic" and his politics. Historicism in all its forms would seem to entail an elevation of the love of one's own, of spiritedness. I have treated these question more fully in a paper, "The Prescientific World and His-

toricism: Some Reflections on Strauss, Heidegger and Husserl," delivered at the Annual Meeting of the American Political Science Association, September, 1983, under the auspices of the Claremont Institute for the Study of Statesmanship and Political Philosophy. [This paper eventually became the immediately preceding chapter.—*AP*]

49. Cf. *Republic* 330a–c; and *Laws* 963e; and Strauss and Bloom, *loc. cit.*, note 40, above. See also Strauss 1963, 202–26. Jaffa 1978, 169, quotes 208, but see 209, and especially 210. Cf. Aristotle, *Nicomachean Ethics* 1096a11–18.
50. Cf. Shakespeare, *King Lear* I.ii.1–22.
51. 206a.
52. Cf., for example, 178d–180b, 194b, 196d, 203d, 207b, 208c–e, *et al.*, where one might expect references to *thumos.*
53. *Nicomachean Ethics* 1166a13–15.
54. *Nicomachean Ethics* 1170b8–10.

Chapter Ten · Aristotle and the Moderns on Freedom and Equality

1. *The Social Contract* I.8
2. Hobbes 1950, ch. 21, 183
3. Hobbes 1950, ch. 14, 108–9
4. *Leviathan* ch. 15.
5. *Second Treatise of Government* sect. 54. Cf. Diamond 1976, 328–31. Cf. the Aristotelian critique of Locke by Gillies 1894, introduction, xxxi–xxxix.
6. Letter to Henri Grégoire, 25 February 1809. Would the political bearing of Jefferson's remark be as compelling if Newton's superiority were a superiority in "wisdom to discern," coupled with "virtue to pursue, the common good of . . . society?"
7. I.6.
8. Thus, Rosseau could conclude that direct democracy is the only truly legitimate form of government.
9. Strauss 1975, 91–92.
10. *Grundlegung zur Metaphysik der Sitten*; *Foundations of the Metaphysics of Morals*, sect. one. Meiklejohn 1980 makes the interesting argument that "rigidity" is precluded from the Kantian doctrine on lying by taking into account the empirical question as to whether in any particular case rational or some other kind of communication is taking place. Lying is prohibited when "communicating rationally with another moral being." When dealing with drunks,

the insane, would-be murderers et al., other principles properly come into play. Meiklejohn's reformulation of Kantian doctrine does not yet address the question of how to deal with those who are both rational and evilly inclined. Pisanio and Cornelius in Shakespeare's *Cymbeline* avert gross injustice and tragedy by, as they put it, being false (to the bad) in order to be true (to the good) (I.v.43–44 and IV.iii.42). (One may sophisticate or avoid facing the problem by departing from the generally accepted understanding of rational and defining rational and evil as mutually exclusive.)

11. Strauss 1964, 38.
12. The other eye is directed inward to the *ego cogitans.* See Swift's Laputans in *Gulliver's Travels.*
13. Francis Bacon, *Novum Organum* I.3; Descartes, *Discourse on Method* VI; cf. chapter four, above; and Kennington 1978.
14. *Essay Concerning Human Understanding* Bk. II, ch. xx, esp. no. 6, and xxi.
15. Strauss 1953, 250–51.
16. See *Idee zu einer allgemeinen Geschichte in weltbürgerlicher Absicht,* "Idea of a Universal History with Cosmopolitan Intent."
17. Strauss argued that the hard core of these modern doctrinal "secularizations" of Biblical faith is to be found in the development of modern political philosophy, more than in the Bible itself. Cf. Strauss 1975, 82–83 and 95, and Strauss 1953, 60–61 n. 22.
18. Strauss 1981, 32–33. This was understood by Strauss as the linkage between the first and second "waves of modernity" in Strauss 1975, 89–90.
19. Kant's separation of "self" (autonomy = self-legislation) from nature appears paradoxical. The "self" referred to here is not the whole person or soul of the individual, which includes "nature," but the will or the pure practical reason itself: "It is heteronomy ('another's legislation') because the will does not give itself the law." Kant 1956, 32–35, 41–42.
20. The return to nature and natural science as a possible source of ethical and political standards by biologists like Konrad Lorenz, Adolph Portmann, and E. O. Wilson should be noted. Wilson (a prodigious synthesizer with a gift for clear exposition) looks forward to a "genetically accurate and hence completely fair code of ethics." Although he has not yet considered Aristotle's *Physics 2, De Anima,* and the *Nicomachean Ethics,* he seems to be groping towards a framework for synthesis something like what might be provided by the Aristotelian scheme of four causes and the distinction between potency and act. Wilson 1975, 575; Wilson 1978, 58

and 67. In application to human affairs, the scheme could be understood as follows: Nature (Evolution) provides the material (Material Cause), the potencies ("genotype"): Every potency is a potency for something. The potencies point to the purposes and ends (Final Cause) that would actualize and fulfill the potencies. On the basis of the conditions provided by nature and chance or circumstance, man, (Efficient Cause) the habit- and ("culture-") convention-forming animal, through habitation, training, custom, law, art, and education forms the given materials and powers into behavior (Formal Cause) ("phenotype") that either fulfills, perverts, frustrates, or corrupts (or some combination of thereof) those powers and materials. (This is not to minimize fundamental differences between Aristotelian and modern biological sciences. See, for example, Grene 1974, 74–76; see also the very helpful article on Portmann, 254–93; and Kass 1985, 247 ff.) The poverty of most inferences from animal behavior for substantive questions of ethics and politics—Portmann conspicuously expected—is striking for students reasonably acquainted with classical ethical or political philosophy. The combination of the study of modern biology with serious study of the ethical and philosophical tradition seems to be required; for example, Grene and Kass, above; Jonas 1966); Straus 1966, esp. the celebrated article "The Upright Posture," 137–65; et al.

21. *Politics* 6.2 1317a40 ff.
22. Cf. also *Politics* 5 1310a26–35
23. Cf. Simon 1969, esp. 158.
24. Cf. *Politics* 1325b5 ff. and 1333a30–1334a10.
25. *Politics* 1253a1–18. Cf. chapter one, above, 3–4.
26. *Politics* 1278b3 ff., 1289a13–20, 1295a40–b1.
27. Strauss 1968, 16.
28. No. 57. Cf. nos. 63 and 71. Cf. Diamond 1976, 320–22, and especially 1977.
29. *Nicomachean Ethics* 2.4 1105a17 ff.; 1.8 1099a4 ff. et al.
30. This classification of democracy overlaps with "polity." Cf. the elaborate discussion in Eidelberg 1968. I regret that this important book, arguing that the American Constitution establishes and was intended to establish a "mixed regime," came to my attention too late to be reviewed here.
31. *Politics* 6.4 1318b6 ff., especially 1318b28–1319a6; cf. 3.11 1281a39 ff.
32. *Politics* 4.11 1296a7 ff. Cf. Licht 1980.
33. In Jaffa 1975, 149–60. I shall not discuss here Jaffa's remarkable book on Lincoln, *The Crisis of the House Divided*. For a criticism and appreciation of Jaffa's Lincoln book, which moves on a philosophi-

cal plane commensurate with Jaffa's plane, see Anastaplo 1976, 165–68 n. 64.

34. Anastaplo 1965, 390.
35. Strauss 1968, 11–16. Cf. Jaffa 1965, 50–52. Cp. Hamilton's arguments against ancient political thought and practice in Flaumenhaft 1976.
36. Anastaplo 1975, essay V. Cf. also Anastaplo 1971, ch. 8.
37. See Anastaplo 1971, ch. 8, sect. ix, and Thomas Jefferson's letter to John Adams, 28 October 1813.
38. Anastaplo 1975, 139; Jaffa 1959, 227, 232, and 239.
39. Anastaplo 1975, essays III, X, and XVI.
40. See Anastaplo 1983, 279–83; and Strauss 1953, ch. 4.
41. Anastaplo 1980, 439. In the context of a discussion of the right and the wrong way to argue against censorship, Anastaplo gives voice to what has become a growing concern in his recent writings: "Indeed, we may have more to fear from a lack of concern about abuses of our considerable liberties than we have from threats of immediate restrictions upon them." Anastaplo 1979, 746. Cf. Anastaplo 1985.
42. "Heaven grant that it may be the glory of the United States to have established two great truths, of the highest importance to the whole human race; first that an enlightened community *is* capable of self-government; and, second, that the toleration of all sects does *not* necessarily produce indifference to religion." Daniel Webster, speech, reception at Pittsburg, 8 July 1833. Cf. Tocqueville, *Democracy in America* II, Bk. 2, ch. 15, and Xenophon, *Memorabilia* 4.3.1 and 2. See also the remarkable biologist's account of "the distress of the modern soul" by Monod 1972, 164–173.
43. *The Federalist* No. 55, end.
44. Strauss 1975, 98.
45. Adapted from L. Berns 1978. (Correction to 231, line 6 from bottom should read: "And even those causes which are neither judgments nor reasons, like appetites, passions and desires, are rarely unmixed with judgments or reasons.")
46. Large middle classes were rarities in premodern times. Large, even more so very large, middle classes presuppose widespread affluence. The existence of these conditions in the modern world evidently depend on the prodigious productivity unleashed by the technological powers discovered in association with modern natural science and its "conquest of nature." We cannot here discuss the unprecedented dangers, now journalistic commonplaces, brought about by the technological development. Modern science, we have argued, following Leo Strauss, has proved inadequate for the articulation of the meaning of human life. Despite this opposition,

Strauss did not simply reject the science upon which the conditions for modern liberal democracy depend. Science, "man's attempt to understand the whole to which he belongs," incorporates what is true in modern as well as ancient science. Strauss looks forward to "the true universal science into which modern science will have to be integrated eventually." From "Social Science and Humanism," Strauss 1989b, 3–12.

47. See Licht 1980; and chapter twelve, below, 255–56.

Chapter Eleven · Aristotle and Adam Smith on Justice: Cooperation Between Ancients and Moderns?

1. Smith 1982b, 9, 14. References in the text will be to parts, sections, chapters, and paragraphs as given in this edition.
2. Smith 1981, 25, 341, 343, 345, 540. Both books are treated in careful analysis by Cropsey 1977, 53–89.
3. All translations from the Greek are mine, unless otherwise designated.
4. Hume 1978, 2.1.2.
5. According to Smith, Sir Isaac Newton has made "the greatest and most admirable improvement that was ever made in philosophy." His system exercises "the most universal empire that was ever established in philosophy. His principles . . . have a degree of firmness and solidity that we should in vain look for in any other system"; Smith 1982a, 98, 104–5. Smith was especially impressed by so much being explained by the single principle of universal attraction. He seems to have regarded his "sympathy" similarly as "the principle of connection" in morality. Aristotle's method of didactical delivery is compared unfavorably with Newton's. In natural philosophy or any other science "we may either like Aristotle go over the Different branches in the order they happen to cast up to us, giving a principle commonly a new one for every phaenomenon; or in the manner of Sir Isaac Newton we may lay down certain principles known or proved in the beginning, from whence we account for the severall Phaenomena, connecting all together by the same Chain.—This Latter which we may call the Newtonian method is undoubtedly the most Philosophical. . . . [It is] vastly more ingenious and for that reason more engaging"; Smith 1985, 145–46. This criticism of Aristotle (which calls to mind Kant's criticism of Aristotle's categories as an unsystematic "rhapsody"), it seems to me, points to one of the cardinal excellences of Aristotle's way of inquiry: the way he describes things as they naturally pres-

ent themselves, while he makes his way towards uncovering their own inner articulation. The general scheme of act and potency is a most unintrusive general scheme.

6. Cf. Edmund Burke's letter to Adam Smith concerning *The Theory of Moral Sentiments,* Smith 1987, nos. 38, 46.
7. All citations of Aristotle in this chapter are of the *Nicomachean Ethics,* unless noted otherwise.
8. See Aquinas 1949, 323.
9. Cf. Leo Strauss, "What is Liberal Education?" in Strauss 1968, 5–8; and Strauss 1952, 25; and the famous letter of Machiavelli to Vettori, December 10, 1513.
10. Cf. Aristotle, *Eudemian Ethics* 1220b35.
11. Emphasis added.
12. The mean of distributive justice can be represented as follows, letting capital letters stand for persons, lower case letters things or shares distributed. Aristotle begins with A : B = c : d (A|B = c|d). The final formulation is A+c : B+d = A : B (A+c/B+d = A|B). That is, A plus his or her share is to B plus his or her share as A is to B. This is a mean between A+c : B+d > A : B (A+c/B+d > A/B), where A gets more than he or she deserves and B less, and A+c : B+d < A : B (A+c/B+d < A/B), where A gets less than he or she deserves and B more. (Euclid defines proportion, *analogia,* as same [::], not equal [=], ratio. Cf. Lachterman 1989, 29–49.)
13. Cf. *Politics* 7.7 1327b8–1328a8, where spiritedness is shown to be the psychic material for freedom. See also chapter nine, above; and Umphrey 1982.
14. Cf. 8.13 1162b31–1163a24.
15. Emphasis added.
16. On "vicegerent" see also 3.5.6. Cf. John Milton, *Paradise Lost* 5.609, 10.56.
17. Smith's teleology of nature, like that of Thomas Aquinas and Kant, culminates in theology. Cf. chapter eight, above, sect. II, 171–74. The question of the relations between teleology, nature, and theology in Smith (and Hume) is highly complex and cannot here be treated with the elaboration it requires. The compatibility of Smith's teleology with his Newtonianism (note 5 above) is one highly complicated question. (Cf. Cropsey 1977, 87–88.) The consideration with which one perhaps might begin is that for Smith the fact that we are induced by nature to hold certain beliefs is not in itself a warrant for the truth of those beliefs.

    The naturalness of ethical behavior as understood by Smith, Hume, and Aristotle is explicated, and reconciled with natural selection theory, by Wilson 1993, on the basis of a prodigious survey of recent social science research. Wilson quotes the crucial Aristotelian text (here translated literally): "Therefore, neither by nature nor against nature are the virtues engendered in us, but [they are engendered] *by our being natured to receive them and by our being completed [or perfected] by habit*" (II.1 1103a24–6). Nature provides the capacities to receive the virtues with indications of the ends implicit in those capacities. Human beings by their habits fulfill, corrupt, or pervert those capacities. The locus of what others might call moral freedom, from this point of view, lies primarily in the management of habit.

18. See Homer, *Odyssey* IX 473–536. Cf. XVII 284 and XX 1–24. On the tendency of spiritedness to personify, see chapter three, above, 46–47. Classical philology notes the kinship between the Greek words *mēnis,* wrath; *mania,* madness; and *mantikē,* divination.
19. There are a number of words in Aristotle's Greek that are usually referred to in English as powers of judgment. *Dokein* and *doxazein,* opining, refer to the conjoining of notions that issue in complete sentences. *Hupolēpsis,* "taking, or receiving under," subsumption, is the most general (*De Anima* 427b25–7). *Hupolēpsis* and *to kritikon* seem to be the powers implied in the constitution of what Aristotle calls accidental sensibles, what comes to be present in rational *phantasia,* where *what* the sensible is is apprehended along with its purely sensible qualities. Cf. chapter nine, above, 327–28 n. 15.
20. Aquinas 1951, 395–98.
21. Cf. Hume 1989, 1.1.6–7 and 1.4.2, especially 211. On reason and passion see 2.3.3, especially 415.
22. Letter from Adam Smith to William Strahan, November 9, 1776. Smith could respond to my final remark—to put it in dialogue form—as follows: "What I emphasized was not Hume's philosophizing, but his beautiful and most rare joining of amiable and awesome virtues."

    "But the awesome component of that joining was inextricably connected with his philosophizing. Furthermore, what is implied by your remarks that, 'To a real wise man the judicious and well-weighed approbation of a single wise man, gives more heartfelt satisfaction than all the noisy applause of ten thousand ignorant though enthusiastic admirers' (6.3.31, 7.2.4.10); and your extensive descriptions of the higher excellence of the wise and virtuous? Does this not presuppose possession by the wise of a power of intellectual perception that your and Mr. Hume's epistemology does not support?"

"There is more than one basis for connecting the highest human excellence to philosophy. I praised Mr. Hume's most comprehensive capacity. Could it not be that he deserves the highest praise not primarily for what he 'saw,' but for what he did to liberate humankind from centuries-old shackles of prejudice and superstition, to guide the human race as a whole toward genuine and, one might hope, future happiness?"

"But if he did what you think he did, was it not on the basis of what he 'saw'?"

For a more comprehensive treatment of the questions raised by this unfinished dialogue from a modern point of view, namely Francis Bacon's, see chapter four, above, 91–95. Smith's ending of this letter seems to echo the end of Plato's *Phaedo,* with the addition of a delicate Biblical touch.

Chapter Twelve · Classical Prudence and the Declaration's Right to Revolution: Two Old Conservatives Discuss the Anastaplo Case (A Dialogue)

1. Xenophon, *Memorabilia* 1.2. See chapter thirteen, below.
2. Classical tragedy seems to have concentrated more on the second of these two questions, modern drama on the first. This difference seems to depend on a more fundamental difference of opinion about how much rationality it is reasonable to expect in political and social life. Cf. Thomas Aquinas, *Treatise on Law,* in *Summa Theologiae* I-II Q.97 A.2, esp. 1st objection and answer; and Strauss 1964, 21–22. See also chapter two, above.
3. *In re* Anastaplo, 3 Ill. 2d 471, 121 N.E.2d 826 (1954), 348 U.S. 446, 349 U.S. 908 (1955) (Justices Black and Douglas, dissenting), 18 Ill. 2d 182, 163 N.E.2d 429 (1959) (Justices Bristow, Shaefer, and Davis, dissenting), 366 U.S. 82, (Justices Black, Douglas, and Brennan and Warren, C.J., dissenting), *rehearing denied,* 368 US. 869 (1961).

   This bar admission case began in November, 1950, before the Committee on Character and Fitness sitting in Chicago. See Weissman, *Heresy and the Bar: The Cases of Leo Sheiner and George Anastaplo,* 19 *Lawyers Guild Rev.* 64, 65 (1959); Weissman, *The Case of George Anastaplo, id.* 126, 143.

   Anastaplo, born in St. Louis in 1925, an American Air Force volunteer, served as a flying officer during the Second World War. He received his J.D. (1951) and Ph.D. (1964) from the University of Chicago. He is currently Lecturer in the Liberal Arts, The University of Chicago; Professor and Chairman in the Political Science

Department, Rosary College; and Professor of Politics and Literature, The University of Dallas. [This chapter was originally published in 1969. Anastaplo passed away in 2014.—*AP*]

For the standard that seems to have guided his conduct as counsel *pro se* see Anastaplo 1974, 39–40 note 26.

4. *The Constitution of the United States of America: Analysis and Interpretation* 908–09 (1964).

   The "public interest" in the last sentence quoted is balanced against the applicant's "desire," not (as Anastaplo saw it) against his "right and duty," and not even (as the opinion itself has it) against his "private interest."
5. See, in Anastaplo's *Petition for Rehearing,* Supreme Court of the United States, October Term, 1960, No. 58 (1961), his moving farewell to the legal profession. See also Anastaplo, *The Declaration of Independence,* 9 ST. Louis U.L.J. 390, 399 n. 20 (1965); "Thus the Court was moved to repudiate the primary cause of the applicant's exclusion, without correcting the exclusion itself: the Declaration of Independence finally came into its own, but not its stubborn defender. . . ." See also Berns, *In re* Anastaplo, *Transcript of the Record.* Supreme Court, October Term, 1960, No. 58, at 493–97.
6. See G. Anastaplo, *The Constitutionalist: Notes on the First Amendment* (to be published in 1969 by the Southern Methodist University Press, Dallas, Texas); Anastaplo, *supra* note 5, at 390; Anastaplo, Book Review, Jaffa, *Equality and Liberty: Theory and Practice in American Politics,* 41 N.Y.U.L. Rev. 644 (1966); and especially Anastaplo, *Freedom of Speech and the First Amendment,* 42 U. Det. L.J. 55 (1964).

   See also Anastaplo 1964, 16; Anastaplo, Book Review, Levy, *Legacy of Suppression—Freedom of Speech and Press in Early American History,* 39 N.Y.U.L. Rev. 735 (1964); Anastaplo, *On Civil Disobedience: Thoreau and Socrates,* S.W. Rev. 203 (Spring 1969).
7. Dennis v. United States, 341 U.S. 494, 508 (1951).

Chapter Thirteen · Xenophon's Alcibiades and Pericles on the Question of Law, with Applications to the Polity of the United States

1. *The Constitution of the United States* Article 3, section 1.
2. Anastaplo 1989, Lectures 10, 11, 124–48; *Swift v. Tyson,* 41 U.S. (16 Pet.) 1 (1842), *Erie R.R. v. Tompkins,* 304 U.S. 64 (1938). This distortion, Anastaplo suggests, should be connected with the Court's conducting itself as a "super legislature." "[M]uch of what the United States

Supreme Court has been doing, with the Fourteenth Amendment and perhaps with other constitutional provisions, may be somewhat similar to what English common-law courts did in the seventeenth and eighteenth Centuries in building up the great body of common-law privileges and immunities recognized under the British constitution" (Anastaplo 1989, 69). Insufficiently active in its proper sphere, the Court opens itself to charges of too much activism by an improper extension of that sphere.

3. Thomas Aquinas, *Summa Theologiae* I-II Q.90 A.4; Hobbes, *Leviathan* ch. 26. Anastaplo's American "Hobbes" is, of course, Justice Oliver Wendell Holmes, Jr.
4. *Summa Theologiae* I-II Q.90 A.3; Q.92; Q.95 A.1; II-II Q.25 A.6 *ad* 2; Q.64 A.3. Thomas, as well as Hobbes, distinguishes between command and counsel. I-II Q.92 A.2; II-II Q.51 A.2; and *Leviathan* ch. 26.
5. Cf. *Summa Theologiae* I-II Q.97 A.3.
6. In *Summa Theologiae* Q.90 A.3, the word "people" is used to translate Thomas's *multitudo*. Cf. Benardete 1965, 294: "Pericles first used *to plēthos* [the multitude] as equivalent to the city as a *koinon* [commonalty], and not as another name for the *demos* (cf. 4.4.13), but that Alcibiades shifts and brings out its meaning by opposing it to oligarchs and tyrants."
7. The word justly is used once, somewhat unusually, in Alcibiades's early sentence about rendering praise.
8. By "superficial" I don't mean unimportant. Clarity about the superficial, or surface, is indispensable for any understanding that seeks to go beneath the surface.
9. *Memorabilia* 4.4.12–25; *The Education of Cyrus* 1.3.16–17.
10. See the last sentence of Leo Strauss's commentary on *Memorabilia* 4.4, Strauss 1973, 114.
11. Cf. *Memorabilia* 1.2.49–50; for a blend of the Alcibiadean with the Catonic, cf. Anastaplo 1971, 361–62, 336, 337–40.
12. One might, for example, come up with different laws if one were to replace Cyrus's teacher's notion of rightful property with the notion "to each according to his needs, from each according to his ability."
13. Consider the ambiguity of the term "legislator: in philosophers from Plato and Aristotle to Montesquieu and Rousseau, and Strauss 1964, 22.
14. Aristotle, *Nicomachean Ethics* 5.7 1334b20 and 1335a5.
15. The criterion of persuasiveness as Alcibiades formulates it in his fifth question—whatever the stronger without having persuaded the weaker compels the weaker to do is violent and lawless—is a

democratic criterion, another side of what we call the consent of the governed. If with Hobbes, however, we concentrate on the generative or "operational" causes, the makers and masters of persuasion, democracy reveals itself as an unacknowledged aristocracy or oligarchy of orators. *The Elements of Law, Natural and Politic* 2.2.5. Cf. Tacitus, *Dialogue on Oratory* sections 36 and 41.

16. Eidelberg 1968.
17. Elliot 1836, 2:418–34; this claim is reached, as a conclusion, on 434.
18. Elliot 1836, 2:433–34; emphasis added to "opportunities . . ." etc.
19. Elliot 1836, 2:434; emphasis added.
20. Elliot 1836, 2:434.
21. Cf. chapter ten, above, esp. 216–26.
22. Farrand 1966, 1:605 (13 July).
23. Elliot 1836, 2:527, 529. Cf. 524.
24. Basler 1953, 4:268, 270–71 (emphasis added). Cf. *The Federalist* Nos. 63 and 71.

Chapter Fourteen · Madmen and Philosophers: A Note on Xenophon's *Memorabilia* 1.1.13 and 14

1. This, at 1.2.19, is the first occurrence of any word cognate with "philosophy" in the *Memorabilia.*
2. Cf. Plato, *Phaedo* 96 ff.
3. Cf. 253b1, 29. Cf. also Plato, *Sophist* 251c–252e.
4. In 1.1.16 it is the opposite of *sōphrosunē.*
5. Or "he looked down on [despised] all human things in comparison with counsel from the gods."

Appendix · Plato's *Meno* and Aristotle's *Nicomachean Ethics*

I am grateful to George Anastaplo, Gisela Berns, and Joseph Cohen for helpful comments on earlier drafts of this essay.

1. *Phronēsis* is the virtue of practical thoughtfulness, good practical judgment, practical intelligence, practical wisdom. "Prudence" comes from the Latin *prudens,* a contraction for *providens,* "looking ahead." In the preceding chapter prudence is distinguished from cleverness, that is, prudence presupposes good natural predispositions for virtue, its more specialized work is discerning and choosing the right means for achieving those good ends.
2. Plato 2004. The numbers in brackets are speech numbers. All speeches are numbered in this edition. See 87c–89a [356 (end)–396].

3. Cf. Aristotle, *Nicomachean Ethics* 1094b18–19 and 1144b8–9.
4. *Nicomachean Ethics* 1143a35–1143b6. *Nous* opens us to the ultimate units of intelligibility contained in the particulars of sense perception, as well as in the ultimate terms of philosophical and scientific demonstrations. The intellectual power that is most visible in practical reasoning is *dianoia*, linking thought (often translated understanding). *Dia-* is a linking prefix: consider dialogue and dialectic. (*Dianoia*, linking thought, in a negative sentence, links subjects and predicates by unlinking their meanings.) For the units to be linked meaningfully they must at the same time be distinguished, i.e., their differences recognized. The activity of *dianoia* combines the intelligible and sensible units into the meaningful conceptions and judgments of rational discourse, e.g., "That [unit 1] is a dog [unit 2]." Cf. the account of "dianoetic eikasia" in Klein 1965, 115–25.
5. *Nicomachean Ethics* 3.6 1115a25–35.
6. Aristotle's treatment of courage in Book 3 is discussed in greater detail in chapter nine, above, 200–3.
7. This ending of chapter eight returns to and calls into question chapter six's beginning in common opinion, for the "courage" discussed in chapter six is now listed as first among the *likenesses* of courage.
8. *Meno* 72a–72d [12–18], 86c–86e [354–356 beginning], 100b [564]. The fact that Socrates is never able to arrive at a solution with Meno, as he could in his "exhibition" inquiry with the Slave-boy, could suggest that the most fundamental problem of the *Meno* is the problem of inquiry itself. Consider the two occasions that move the Slave-boy to swear oaths. (Plato 2004, Appendix A "Oaths in the *Meno*," 77.)
9. 72a–72d [12–16]. We note that Socrates' statement about the *eidos* presents one and the same *eidos* as constituting the being of the things of which it is the *eidos* and as functioning as a cognitive principle for the percipient of the *eidos*. That which the knower knows is in some way the same as that which constitutes the object known, that is, if there is genuine knowledge of that object.
10. "Piece" translates *morion*, derived from the word *meros*, part, and *-ion*, a diminutive suffix, meaning then "small part," or "small portion," or "piece of." There is more on the language of this section in Plato 2004, note on 79a [170], 59.
11. 77a [112], 79b–d [172, 176].
12. Mollin and Williamson 1997, 339. This volume contains the Greek text of the *Meno* with extensive grammatical and interpretive annotation.

13. I am grateful to Eva Brann for encouraging me to pursue this line of inquiry.
14. Strictly speaking, Aristotle refers to it as a special kind of equivocal term which points to one primary meaning, among others. See *Metaphysics* 6.2 1003a32–b6.
15. Socrates' "model" in the Slave-boy scene is a mathematical model. In more complicated subject matters we may have to reconcile ourselves to the fullest possible clarity about serious alternative solutions.
16. *Hairesis* is simple choosing, which all animals, including irrational animals, engage in. It is also the political term for election. The *pro-* in Aristotle's *prohairesis* points to the engagement of intellect in deliberate or rational choice. Someone can have a right opinion about something and yet choose wrongly: the opinion did not form or shape the choice. See 1112a10–11 and 1113a17–20, where choice is not made correctly and the *pro-* disappears. But see 1151a5–7, where choice is deliberate, but wrong. (A very old translation nicely translates *prohairetikē* as pre-elective.) Cf. *Nicomachean Ethics* 1139b4–5: "*Prohairesis*, therefore, is either appetitive *nous* or dianoetic appetite"—or, we note, both. See note 4, above.
17. Joe Sachs (Aristotle 2002) joins Burnet (Aristotle 1900) and Bywater (Aristotle 1949) in accepting the emendation (*hōi*) "by the means by which" for the manuscripts' (*hōs*) "as," and in translating *logōi* as "proportion." I do not disagree with the interpretation conveyed by Sachs's and Burnet's moves, but find it implicit in the manuscripts' more natural language. Sachs's translation of *phronēsis*, "practical judgment," is easily understandable as good practical judgment, but, Aristotle cautions us (*Nicomachean Ethics* 1179b8–21), much, if not most, "practical judgment" is bad practical judgment. Cf. note 1, above.
18. This is not to argue that general rules are altogether useless, but that if, in any particular situation, rules are to be used, the question becomes what rule, or principle, is appropriate? This depends upon a correct assessment of the situation, an assessment "as the prudent man would determine it."
19. *Kalon*, beauty; the word noble focuses on that special form of beauty that is ethical beauty. (There is another word in Greek for what is called nobility of birth, *gennaion*.) Joe Sachs, who consistently translates the word as beautiful, argues (Aristotle 2002, Introduction, xxi) that "noble" probably first brings to mind a kind of hopelessly impractical high-minded naiveté. This was also Shakespeare's Edmund's view in *King Lear*, "a brother noble, /

Whose nature is so far from doing harms / That he suspects none; on whose foolish honesty / My practices ride easy" (I.ii.186–87). This was always the view of the more cynically minded. But by the end of the play Edmund is killed and his noble brother prevails. It seems to me that in the context of current talk "beautiful" is subject to even more corruption than "noble." The advantage of translating *kalon* as "beautiful" is connecting the word with the other associations beauty has. But that advantage does not overweigh the loss of the grand old word that especially distinguishes the kind of ethical beauty that Aristotle and Shakespeare talk about. (See the four-and-one-half pages of small print under "nobility" and "noble" in Bartlett's *Complete Concordance to Shakespeare's Dramatic Works.*)

20. 1113a29–33, see also 1176a16–23.
21. The "other way" will be discussed below in Section VI.
22. Burnet notes that here Aristotle relies on his understanding that "nature" has both its "principle of motion," potency, or capacity, and its "principle of rest [or standstill]," goal, or end, in itself (Aristotle 1900, 76 n. 17). See Aristotle, *Physics* 192b8–193a2. Despite common usage, it is not difficult for thoughtful readers of English to see the "act" in "actuality." "Actuality," based on the Latin adjective for being in activity and, in Aristotle, keyed to a specific capacity or potency, has, with reference to its potency, a sense of "fulfilling activity," pointing to the more explicit Aristotelian word *entelecheia,* holding on in fulfillment, or in completion (*Metaphysics* 1015a11–19). Concerning habit in *Meno,* see 70b [2], 75a [70], 76d [106], 82a [197], and 86d [356].
23. By disposition I mean tendency to act. Sachs (Aristotle 2002, 17) translates *hexis* as active condition, getting the "holding" in *hex-* (from *echō*) with condition and the action in *-sis* with active. I think of the "holding" in the disposing and the action in the -tion (*-sis*) suffix. The differences, it seems to me, concern how the English words will be understood: both disposition and condition could, mistakenly in these cases, be understood as implying passivity. Cf. John Burnet on *Phaedo* 99b3 (Plato 1956, 106).
24. "The *mesotēs* [mean state] is 'rationally determined,' or 'determined according to the proper ratio or proportion.'" Stewart 1892, I:200. The word *logos,* which means reason, meaning, argument, speech, and selection, is also a mathematical term meaning ratio or proportion. The *logos* in our definition can properly be rendered reason, or ratio or proportion, or, perhaps, rationally proportioned.
25. 73d–e [45–49].

26. See Aristotle, *Politics* 1322b12–37 and 1328b11–13. These passages are discussed by Strauss 1964, 32–34. See also 22–23. Religion, Thomas Aquinas argues, is attached (*adjungitur*) to justice. See *Summa Theologiae* II-II Q.80; Q.81 A.2; see also Q.94 A.1.
27. In the *Politics*, Aristotle, conceiving of the most perfect form of law, says, "The law is intellect (*nous*) without appetite." But this has been qualified: "He that orders the law to rule seems to be ordering god and intellect alone to rule, but he that orders man to rule also adds a beast: for such is desire (*epithumia*), and spiritedness too perverts rulers, even the best men (*andras*)" (1287a16–32).
28. See *Nicomachean Ethics* 1180b3–13.
29. Shame-respect is praiseworthy and usually operates preventively against vice. There is another word for shame in Greek connected with the word for ugly, shame-disgrace (*aischunē*), that is felt when one is caught in some disgraceful action.
30. *Nemesis* is from the same verbal root as the Greek word for law, *nomos*, namely *nemō*, to distribute or to deal out. It is aroused by the presence of something that is "not right!" In the middle or reflexive voice of its verbal form (*nemessōmai*) where its meaning is referred to the subject of the sentence, or to the speaker him- or herself, it can convey the dissatisfaction or displeasure with oneself that we tend to speak of as "conscience."
31. See Plato, *Laws* 731d–732a.
32. Stewart 1892, I:200–204.
33. Again, for Aristotle, nature is not only the primitive beginnings *out of which* a natural being develops, but even more the *active fulfillment* of what the natural being is meant to develop into. Cf. note 23, above. For this linking of nature and soul, see Joe Sachs' Introduction, especially 8–10, in Aristotle 2001, and Kass 1994, chapter 1. Both of these recent essays present the fundamental evidence for the scientific and philosophical conception of the soul with more than competent critical analysis of the philosophic and scientific objections to that conception.
34. Abstraction, *aphairesis*, "taking away," according to Aristotle, is used only by mathematicians to take away or to neglect all perceptible qualities in natural bodies in order to theorize solely about the numerical and continuous geometrical quantities found in them (*Metaphysics* 1061a28–b3). In Plato's *Crito* (46c6), the word is used for *confiscations* of money. See also Aristotle, *Politics* 1281a26.
35. Aristotle 2002, 108 n. 155. See also note 9 and accompanying text, above. Sachs avoids the usual misconceptions by translating *epagōgē* as "example." See the glossary in his translation of Aris-

totle's *On the Soul,* Aristotle 2001, 192–93. See also in his *Nicomachean Ethics* translation the remarkable note 168 (Aristotle 2002, 114). The prospect held out in the penultimate sentence of that note is amply clarified by 31–38 of his Introduction to *On the Soul* (Aristotle 2001).

36. See the text quoted at note 20, above.
37. *De Motu Animalium* 702a15–21.
38. See Sachs's glossaries under "abstraction" in his translations of Aristotle's *Physics, Metaphysics,* or *On the Soul.*
39. Aquinas 1951, §§ 395–98. Controversies in connection with such distinctions are still very much alive. See, for example, P. Bloom 2004, 1605–6; and Coppinger and Coppinger 2001, 217–20 (a new border collie mother retrieves a tape recorder sending out a puppy's 'I am lost' signal and puts it in the nest with her puppies).
40. 72c [16], 78c [150], 80d [184], 81b [194], 82c [212], 82e [226], 82e [232], 84c [288], 86d [356], 86e [356], 87b [356], 87c [362], 87d [363] (Meno speaking), 87e [374], 88a [378], 88a [380], 88b [382], 89d [408], 90b [412], 91a [422], 93b [440] (4x), 94a [452], 94a [454], 96d [489] (Meno speaking), 96e [490].
41. 80a [179]. The word is used three times by Socrates between 72c and 72e, speeches 16, 18, and 20.
42. This requires qualification. The inquiry is a model for Meno: to show him how the careful exposure of one's own ignorance furthers inquiry and benefits him who is so exposed. But in itself it is perhaps rather a model prelude to inquiry, for in that whole Slave-boy scene the "What is . . . ?" question is never raised.
43. 75b [78]. The word for color, *chrōma,* also means visible surface. Edmund Husserl, it seems, would have appreciated Socrates's definition. See Husserl 1976, II, §9, c), 32–36: Husserl 1970, Part II, §9, c., 34–37.
44. E.g., 89e [412]. See the end of note 22, above.
45. See Plato, *Phaedo* 99b2–4. See also the reference to *Nicomachean Ethics,* note 62, below.
46. The words for "foot" and "feet" in classical Greek can be used to measure both lines and areas, that is, both linear units and area units. They know the difference, but (certainly in the *Meno*) they do not say "square feet" (*Meno* 82b–e [204–225]).
47. Numbers in classical times are restricted to what modern mathematicians call positive whole numbers, they are always numbers of things, either perceptible things or the pure monads or units of arithmetical science. Euclid, *Elements* VII, definition 2, defines number as a multitude composed of units, which means that the

first number is two, although the unit, "1," is perfectly usable in arithmetic calculations.

48. 84e–85a [302]. See Plato 2004, Appendix B, Geometrical Diagrams, Figures 47–50 and 64, on 84–85. Socrates does not mention the Pythagorean Theorem, but his diagrams and the argument he makes to show that the line he constructed is indeed the sought-for line could be used to explicate the Pythagorean Theorem.
49. Plato 2004, note on [274] 83e–84a, 63. Theaetetus calls these lines which we might call square root lines, "powers (*dunameis*)," meaning straight lines capable of allowing certain specified squares to be constructed on them. Euclid says that, while the diagonal of a square is incommensurable in length with the side of its own square, those lines are "commensurable in square." In *Theaetetus* 147d Theodorus probably used the Pythagorean Theorem and an isosceles right triangle with sides equal to one to derive the square root of two line, then a right triangle with one side equal to one and the other equal to the square root of two line to derive the square root of three line, the square root of two line and the square root of three line to derive the square root of five line, etc.
50. Aristotle 2002, 83. Other translations are "corrective" or "commutative" justice.
51. Aristotle does begin this discussion by reference to that steady disposition of the soul from which people are apt to seek, to do and to want just things. The "mean" for the truly just *human being* does fit the general definition despite its difference from the mean of the just distribution.
52. Cf. Plato, *Republic* 545d–547a.
53. See, for example, *Nicomachean Ethics* 1132b34–1135a5. These two paragraphs are taken from chapter eleven, above.
54. How these arguments about comparability and equality apply to political functions is discussed in Aristotle, *Politics* 3.12 1282b14–1283a22.
55. What seems to be behind Aristotle's gentle but potent "somehows" is the fact, soon to be made explicit, that the intrinsic commensurability between persons, work, and products that the standard of absolutely perfect justice would require does not exist.
56. Cf. Plato, *Republic* 369a–372a.
57. Stewart 1892, I:463.
58. G. Berns 1973, 186. See Aristotle, *De Anima* 415a16–22; Strauss 1953, 145–46; and chapter one. The distinction between natural and unnatural exchange is developed in Aristotle's *Politics* 1256b27–1257b5.

59. "Everything is measured by money" seems to have been set down here as a generally accepted opinion expressing what is said about money. "Everything" seems to mean here every good, evil, or service for which equal exchange of external goods is expected.
60. For the first alternative, consider 99a [548] to the end of the dialogue; for the second alternative, consider, among other places, 88a–d [380–388].
61. Meno never objects to these arguments. Anytus gets angry; perhaps he sensed the anti-democratic implications of an argument based on natural inequalities (he may well fancy himself to be the successor of one or more of those famous statesmen).
62. Cf. Aristotle, *Nicomachean Ethics* 1180b28–1181a13.
63. Socrates speaks here as if they were living in the city in speech of Plato's *Republic.*
64. Plato 1961, 28–29 and 395.
65. In Plato's *Timaeus* (71a–72c) the diviner (*mantis*) "who utters oracles while not in his right mind but in a state of divine frenzy" is distinguished by Timaeus from the prophet (*prophētēs*) who in his right mind judges and interprets such oracles. The word *mantis,* but not *prophētēs,* does occur in the *Meno.*

    George Anastaplo suggests that the fact that this is an "opposition" is indicated very early in the dialogue, 71b [2], where Socrates imitates Meno's disjoining of conjoined powers in his opening speech by asking whether "someone who has no cognizance of Meno at all, who he is, could know whether he is handsome *or* rich *or* well-born *or* the opposite of these." (Emphasis added.) We learn, he argues, "in the course of the dialogue that Meno himself is indeed handsome *and* rich *and* well-born (in the conventional sense of these terms), not 'the opposite of these'" (Anastaplo 2004, 138).
66. See Plato 1961, 394.
67. Burnet 1900, 468. Aristotle adds "justly" to "bear off" in the otherwise common then-clause.
68. There is a distinction between habit as understood here in relation to incomplete childlike or youthful souls, and the completing or perfecting habits that persons of more advanced understanding need in order to bring their actions in line with what they are capable of understanding. See, above, the text of Aristotle containing note 22. In regard to childlike or youthful souls, consider *Nicomachean Ethics* 1094a6–13: "And it makes no difference whether one is young in age or immature in character, for the defect is not a matter of time, but of living and pursuing each thing according to feeling. . . ."

69 See 70b–71d [2–10], 95b–c [462–469].

70. Meno, Callicles (of the *Gorgias*), and Hippocrates (of the *Protagoras*) all seem to be primarily practical men who have been impressed by and attracted to the intellectual fireworks of the sophists in a much more powerful way than they were ever attracted to Socrates' dialectical arts. They might be called intellectuals, even somewhat educated men (e.g., Meno's knowledge of geometry), but not scholars. Why did Plato devote a good-sized dialogue to the ways and ideas of each of them, to Protagoras and to Gorgias? They might be brought to function in ways uncongenial to Socrates himself as intermediaries between Socratic philosophy and practical life, between philosophy and spirited and intellectual men like Meno, Callicles, and Hippocrates.
71. See 1181a12–b11 and *Metaphysics* 981a12–b9.
72. See *Nicomachean Ethics* 1099a30–1099b25.
73. See *Meno* 78c–d [148–156], and Aristotle, *Politics* 1260a25–28.
74. In the *Politics* too the opening of the *Meno* is reflected in Aristotle's introduction to his extended discussion of education where (1332a38–b11) he asserts, "But surely men become good [*agathoi*] and seriously good [*spoudaioi*] through three things, and these three are nature, habit, and rational speech [*logos*]." In the sequel he makes clear that his *logos* embraces Meno's teaching and learning, and that "these [nature, habit, and *logos*] are required to harmonize [*symphōnein*] with one another."
75. 1252b27–31.

Bibliography

Alfarabi. 1962. *The Philosophy of Plato and Aristotle.* Trans. Muhsin Mahdi. Glencoe, IL: Free Press.

Allison, Henry E. 1973. *The Kant-Eberhard Controversy.* Baltimore: The Johns Hopkins University Press.

de Alvarez, Leo S. (ed.). 1976. *Abraham Lincoln, the Gettysburg Address and American Constitutionalism.* Irving, TX: University of Dallas Press.

Anastaplo, George. 1964 "Human Being and Citizen: A Beginning to the Study of Plato's *Apology of Socrates*" in Cropsey 1964, 16–49.

——. 1965. "The Declaration of Independence," *St. Louis University Law Journal* 9, 390–415.

——. 1971. *The Constitutionalist: Notes on the First Amendment.* Dallas, TX: Southern Methodist University Press.

——. 1975. *Human Being and Citizen: Essays on Virtue, Freedom, and the Common Good.* Chicago, IL: Swallow Press.

——. 1976. "American Constitutionalism and the Virtue of Prudence: Philadelphia, Paris, Washington, Gettysburg" in de Alvarez 1976, 77–170.

——. 1979. "Human Nature and the First Amendment," *University of Pittsburg Law Review* 40, 661–778.

——. 1980. "Abraham Lincoln's Emancipation Proclamation" in Collins 1980, 421–46.

——. 1983. *The Artist as Thinker.* Chicago, IL: Swallow Press.

——. 1985. "Censorship." *Encyclopaedia Britannica, Macropaedia.* 15th ed. 3:634–41.

——. 1989. *The Constitution of 1787: A Commentary.* Baltimore, MD: The Johns Hopkins University Press.

——. 2004. *On Trial: From Adam and Eve to O. J. Simpson.* Lanham, MD: Lexington Books.

Anderson. F. H. 1960. *Francis Bacon: The New Organon, and Related Writings.* New York, NY: Liberal Arts Press.

Aquinas, Thomas. 1948. *Treatise on Law.* Chicago: Henry Regnery Co.

——. 1949. *In decem libros Ethicorum Aristotelia ad Nichomachum Exposito.* Raymond Spiazzi, ed. Turin and Rome: Marietti.

——. 1951. *Commentary on Aristotle's De Anima.* Kenelm Foster and Sylvester Humphries, trans. New Haven, CT: Yale University Press.

——. 1970. *Commentary on the Posterior Analytics of Aristotle.* Albany, NY: Magi Books.

Aristotle. 1900. *The Ethics.* Ed. John Burnet. London: Methuen & Co.

——. 1942. *Generation of Animals.* A.L. Peck, trans. Cambridge, MA: Harvard University Press.

——. 1949. *Ethica Nicomachea.* Oxford: Oxford University Press.

——. 1999. *Metaphysics.* Joe Sachs, trans. Santa Fe, NM: Green Lion Press.

——. 2001. *On the Soul.* Trans. Joe Sachs. Santa Fe, NM: Green Lion Press.

——. 2002. *Nicomachean Ethics.* Trans. Joe Sachs. Newburyport, MA: Focus Publishing/R. Pullins Co.

Auger, P., Born, M., Heisenberg, W., and Schrödinger, E. 1962. *On Modern Physics.* New York, NY: Collier Books.

Baillie, J. B. (trans.). 1910. *G. W. F. Hegel: Phenomenology of Mind.* London: Macmillan.

Basler, Roy P. (ed.). 1953. *The Collected Works of Abraham Lincoln.* 9 vols. New Brunswick, NJ: Rutgers University Press.

Benardete, Seth. 1963. "Achilles and the *Iliad*," *Hermes* 91, 1–16.

——. 1965. "XPH and DEI in Plato and Others," *Glossa* 43, 285–98.

Benveniste, Emile. 1971. *Problems in General Linguistics.* Coral Gables, FL: University of Miami Press.

Berns, Gisela. 1973. "*Nomos* and *Physis* (An Interpretation of Euripides' *Hippolytus*)," *Hermes* 2, 165–87.

Berns, Laurence. 1957. *An Introduction to the Political Philosophy of Francis Bacon with Special Attention to the Principles of Foreign Policy.* Ph.D. Dissertation, University of Chicago.

——. 1978. "Speculations on Liberal and Illiberal Politics," *The Review of Politics* 40, 231–54.

——. 1981. "Transcendence and Equivocation: Some Political, Theological, and Philosophic Themes in Shakespeare" in Alvis and West 1981, 41–49.

——. 2007. "Plato's *Meno* and Aristotle's *Nicomachean Ethics*" in Kalkavage and Salem 2007, 1–26.

Bloom, Allan. 1964. "Introduction," in Bloom and Jaffa 1964, 1–12.

Bloom, Allan and Jaffa, Harry V. 1964. *Shakespeare's Politics.* New York, NY: Basic Books.

Bloom, Paul. 2004. "Can a Dog Learn a Word?" *SCIENCE* 304 (11 June): 1605–06.

Boggess, William F. 1970. "Alfarabi and the Rhetoric: The Cave Revisited." *Phronesis* 15, 86–90.

Bohm, David. 1957. *Causality and Chance in Modern Physics*. Philadelphia, PA: University of Pennsylvania Press.

Bradley, A. C. 1961. *Shakespearean Tragedy*. London: Macmillan.

Brann, Eva T. H. 1991. *The World of the Imagination: Sum and Substance*. Savage, MD: Rowman and Littlefield.

Burnet, John. 1892. *Early Greek Philosophy*. London: Adam and Charles Black.

Butcher, Samuel. 1951. *Aristotle's Theory of Poetry and Fine Art*. London: Dover.

Calkins, Mary W. (ed.). 1948. *The Metaphysical System of Hobbes*. Chicago: Open Court.

Cassirer, Ernst. 1963. *Rousseau, Kant and Goethe*. New York: Harper and Row, 1963.

Cervantes Saavedra, Miguel de. 1949. *The Ingenious Gentleman Don Quixote de la Mancha*. Trans. Samuel Putnam. New York, NY: Viking.

Chambers, E. K. 1925. *Shakespeare: A Survey*. New York, NY: Hill and Wang.

Churchill, Winston. 1932. *Thoughts and Adventures*. London: Thornton Butterworth Limited.

———. 1948. *The Gathering Storm*. Boston, MA: Houghton Mifflin Co.

Collins, Ronald K. L. (ed.). 1980. *Constitutional Government in America*. Durham, NC: Carolina Academic Press.

Cope, Edward Meredith. 1877. *Aristotle: Rhetoric*. Cambridge: Cambridge University Press.

Coppinger, Raymond and Coppinger, Laura. 2001. *Dogs: A New Understanding of Canine Origin, Behavior, and Evolution*. Chicago: University of Chicago Press.

Courant, Richard, and Robbins, Herbert. 1941. *What is Mathematics?* London: Oxford University Press.

Cowley, Abraham. 1721. *The Works of Mr. Abraham Cowley*. 3 vols. London: W. Taylor.

de Crespigny, Anthony, and Minogue, Kenneth (eds.). 1975. *Contemporary Political Philosophers*. New York, NY: Dodd Mead.

Cropsey, Joseph (ed.). 1964. *Ancient and Moderns: Essays on the Tradition of Political Philosophy in Honor of Leo Strauss*. New York, NY: Basic Books.

———. 1977. *Political Philosophy and the Issues of Politics*. Chicago: The University of Chicago Press.

Cropsey, Joseph and Strauss, Leo. 1987. *The History of Political Philosophy*. Third Edition. Chicago: University of Chicago Press.

Crowley, Abraham. 1721. *The Works of Mr. Abraham Crowley*. London: B. Tooke.

Danby, John F. 1949. *Shakespeare's Doctrine of Nature, A Study of King Lear*. London: Faber & Faber.

Deutsch, Kenneth, and Soffer, Walter (eds.). 1987. *The Crisis of Liberal Democracy: A Straussian Perspective*. Corrected Edition. Albany, NY: SUNY Press, 1987).

Diamond, Martin. 1976. "The American Idea of Equality: The View from the Founding," *The Review of Politics* 38, 313–31.

——. 1977. "Ethics and Politics: The American Way" in Horwitz 1977, 39–72.

Eidelberg, Paul. 1968. *The Philosophy of the American Constitution*. New York, NY: Free Press.

Elliot, Jonathan. 1836. *The Debates in the Several State Conventions on the Adoption of the Federal Constitution*. 5 vols. Philadelphia, PA.

Else, Gerald F. 1957. *Aristotle's Poetics: The Argument*. Cambridge, MA: Harvard University Press.

Everett, Barbara. 1969. "The New *King Lear*" in Kermode 1969, 184–202.

Fackenheim, Emil L. 1970. *The Religious Dimension in Hegel's Thought*. Boston, MA: Beacon Press.

——. 1980. *Encounters between Judaism and Modern Philosophy*. New York, NY: Schocken.

Farrington, Benjamin. 1964. *The Philosophy of Francis Bacon: An Essay on its Development from 1603 to 1609*. Liverpool: Liverpool University Press.

Flaumenhaft, Harvey. 1976. "Alexander Hamilton on the Foundation of Good Government," *The Political Science Reviewer* 6, 143–214

Furness, Horace. 1880. *A New Variorem Edition of Shakespeare: King Lear*. Philadelphia, PA: J. B. Lippincott Company.

——. 1903. *A New Variorem Edition of Shakespeare: Macbeth*. Revised edition by Horace Furness Jr. Philadelphia, PA: J. B. Lippincott Company.

Gadamer, Hans-Georg. 1967–1972. *Kleine Schriften*. 4 vols. Tübingen: Mohr.

——. 1976. *Philosophical Hermeneutics*. David E. Linge, ed. Berkeley, CA: University of California Press.

——. 1983. *Heideggers Wege*. Tübingen: Mohr.

Gillies, John. 1894. *The Politics and Economics of Aristotle*. London: George Bell and Sons.

Goldwin, Robert A. (ed.). 1980. *Political Parties in the Eighties*. Washington, DC: American Enterprise Institute for Public Policy Research.

Gourevitch, Victor. 1987. "The Problems of Natural Right and the Fundamental Alternatives in *Natural Right and History*," in Deutsch and Soffer 1987, 30–47.

Granville-Barker, Harley. 1970. *Prefaces to Shakespeare*. Vol. 2. London: B. T. Batsford.

Grene, Marjorie. 1974. *The Understanding of Nature: Essays in the Philosophy of Biology*. Dordrecht, Holland: D. Reidel.

Hazlitt, W. H. 1817a. *Characters of Shakespear's Plays*. London: C. H. Reynell.

———. 1817b. *The Round Table: A Collection of Essays on Literature, Men, and Manners*. Vol. 2. Edinburgh: Archibald Constable and Co.

Hegel, G.W.F. 1970. *Glauben und Wissen (Jenaer Schriften)*. Frankfurt am Main: Suhrkamp.

———. 1971. *Vorlesungen über die Geschichte der Philosophie*. Frankfurt am Main: Suhrkamp.

———. 1977. *Faith and Knowledge*. Walter Cerf and H.S. Harris, trans. Albany, NY: State University of New York Press.

Heidegger, Martin. 1950. *Holzwege*. Frankfurt am Main: Vittorio Klostermann.

———. 1954. *Was Heisst Denken?* Tübingen: Max Niemeyer Verlag.

———. 1957. *Sein und Zeit*. Tübingen: Max Niemeyer Verlag.

———. 1962a. *Being and Time*. John Macquarrie and Edward Robinson, trans. New York, NY: Harper & Row.

———. 1962b. *Die Frage nach dem Ding*. Tübingen: Niemeyer.

———. 1969. *Zur Sache des Denkens*. Tübingen: Max Niemeyer Verlag.

Heilman, Robert B. 1963. *This Great Stage, Image and Structure in King Lear*. Seattle, WA: University of Washington Press.

———. 1969. "The Unity of *King Lear*," in Kermode 1969, 169–78.

Hesse, Mary B. 1964. "Francis Bacon," in O'Conner 1964, 141–52.

Hobbes, Thomas. 1928. *The Elements of Law, Natural and Politic*. Ferdinand Toennies, ed. Cambridge: Cambridge University Press.

———. 1950. *Leviathan*. New York, NY: Dutton.

Hoffmeister, Johannes (ed.). 1952. *G. W. F. Hegel: Phänomenologie des Geistes*. Hamburg: Felix Meiner.

Horwitz, Robert H. (ed.). 1977. *The Moral Foundations of the American Republic*. Charlottesville, VA: University of Virginia Press.

Hume, David. 1989. *A Treatise of Human Nature*. L. A. Selby-Bigge and P. H. Nidditch, eds. Oxford: Oxford University Press.

Husserl, Edmund. 1962. *Phenomenology and the Crisis of Philosophy*. Quentin Lauer, trans. New York, NY: Harper & Row.

——. 1970. *The Crisis of the European Sciences and Transcendental Phenomenology*. David Carr, trans. Evanston, IL: Northwestern University Press.

——. 1976. *Die Krisis der Europäischen Wissenschaften und die Transzendentale Phänomenologie*. Ed. Walter Biemel. The Hague, Netherlands: Martinus Nijhof.

Jaffa, Harry V. 1959. *Crisis of the House Divided: An Interpretation of the Issues in the Lincoln-Douglas Debates*. New York, NY: Doubleday.

——. 1964. "The Limits of Politics: *King Lear*, Act One, Scene One," in Bloom and Jaffa 1964, 113–45.

——. 1965. *Equality and Liberty*. Oxford: Oxford University Press.

——. 1975. *The Conditions of Freedom: Essays in Political Philosophy*. Baltimore, MD: The Johns Hopkins University Press.

——. 1978. *How to Think about the American Revolution*. Durham, NC: Carolina Academic Press.

Jebb, R. C. (ed.). 1896. *Sophocles, the Ajax*. Cambridge: Cambridge University Press.

Jonas, Hans. 1966. *The Phenomenon of Life: Toward a Philosophical Biology*. New York, NY: Harper & Row.

——. 1974. *Philosophical Essays: From Ancient Creed to Technological Man*. Englewood Cliffs, NJ.

Jung, Hwa Yol. 1967. "Leo Strauss's Conception of Political Philosophy: A Critique," *Review of Politics* 29, 492–517.

Kalkavage, Peter and Salem, Eric. 2007. *The Envisioned Life: Essays in Honor of Eva Brann*. Philadelphia, PA: Paul Dry Books.

Kant, Immanuel. 1781. *Kritik der reinen Vernunft*. Riga: Johann Friedrich Hartknoch.

——. 1790. *Kritik der Urtheilskraft*. Berlin: Lagarde and Friedrich.

——. 1902. *Kant's Werke, Akademie-Textausgabe*. Berlin: Preussische Akademie der Wissenschaften.

——. 1956. *Critique of Practical Reason*. Lewis White Beck, trans. New York, NY: Liberal Arts Press.

——. 1960. *Religion within the Limits of Reason Alone*. Theodore M. Greene and Hoyt H. Hudson, trans. New York, NY: Harper and Brothers.

——. 1963. *On History*. New York, NY: Liberal Arts Press.

——. 1964. *The Groundwork of the Metaphysics of Morals*. H. J. Paton, trans. New York, NY: Harper and Row.

——. 1965. *Ausgewählte kleine Schriften*. Hamburg: Meiner.

——. 1974. *Logic*. Hardman and Schwarz, trans. Indianapolis: Bobbs-Merrill.

———. 1979. *The Conflict of the Faculties*. Mary J. Gregor, trans. New York, NY: Abaris.

———. 1987. *Critique of Judgment*. Werner Pluhar, trans. Indianapolis, IN: Hackett Publishing.

———. 1996a. *Critique of Pure Reason*. Werner Pluhar, trans. Indianapolis, IN: Hackett Publishing.

———. 1996b. *The Metaphysics of Morals*. Mary J. Gregor, trans. Cambridge: Cambridge University Press.

Kass, Leon. 1985. *Toward a More Natural Science: Biology and Human Affairs*. New York, NY: Free Press.

———. 1994. *The Hungry Soul: Eating and the Perfecting of Our Nature*. New York, NY: The Free Press.

Kennington, Richard. 1978. "Descartes and Mastery of Nature" in Spicker 1978, 201–23.

———. (ed.). 1980. *The Philosophy of Baruch Spinoza*. Washington, DC: The Catholic University of America Press.

———. 1982. "Strauss's *Natural Right and History*," *The Review of Metaphysics* 35, 57–86.

Kermode, Frank (ed.). 1969. *Shakespeare: King Lear*. London: Palgrave Macmillan.

Kitto, H. D. F. 1954. *Greek Tragedy*. New York: Anchor.

———. 1958. *Sophocles—Dramatist and Philosopher*. London: Oxford University Press.

———. 1960. *Form and Meaning in Drama*. New York, NY: Barnes and Noble.

Klein, Jacob. 1964. "Aristotle: An Introduction" in Cropsey 1964, 50–69.

———. 1965. *A Commentary on Plato's* Meno. Chapel Hill, NC: University of North Carolina Press.

———. 1968. *Greek Mathematical Thought and the Origin of Algebra*. Cambridge, MA: M.I.T. Press.

———. 1985. *Lectures and Essays*. Robert B. Williamson and Elliott Zuckerman, eds. Annapolis, MD: St. John's College Press.

Klein, Jacob, and Strauss, Leo. 1970. "A Giving of Accounts," *The College* (April), 1–5.

Knight, G. Wilson. 1963. *The Wheel of Fire: Interpretations of Shakespearean Tragedy*. New York, NY: Meridian.

Lachterman, David. 1989. *The Ethics of Geometry: A Genealogy of Modernity*. London: Routledge.

Lalande, André. 1911. "Sur quelques textes de Bacon et de Descartes," *Revue de Metaphysique et de Morale* 19.3, 296–311.

———. 1996. "On Some Texts of Bacon and Descartes." Translated by Pamela Kraus. *St. John's Review* 43.3, 51–72.

Lerner, Ralph and Mahdi, Muhsin (eds.). 1963. *Medieval Political Philosophy: A Sourcebook*. Glencoe, IL: Free Press.

Lessing, Gotthold Ephraim. 1962. *Hamburg Dramaturgy*. London: Dover.

Licht, Robert. 1980. "On the Three Parties of America" in Goldwin 1980, 67–96.

Löwith, Karl. 1960. *Heidegger: Denker in dürftiger Zeit*. Göttingen: Vandenhoeck & Ruprecht.

Maimonides, Moses. 1963. *Guide of the Perplexed*. 2 vols. Chicago: University of Chicago Press.

Marx, Karl. 1953. *Die Früschriften*. Stuttgart: Kröner.

Meiklejohn, Donald. 1980. "Review of Sissela Bok, *Lying: Moral Choice in Public and Private Life*," *Ethics* 90, 296–300.

Miller, Eugene F. 1975. "Leo Strauss: The Recovery of Political Philosophy," in de Crespigny and Minogue 1975, 67–99.

Molesworth, William (ed.). 1839–45. *The English Works of Thomas Hobbes of Malmesbury*. 11 Vols. London: John Bohn (vols. 1–6, 8–9) and Longman, Brown, Green, and Longmans (vols. 7, 10–11).

Mollin, Alfred and Williamson, Robert. *An Introduction to Ancient Greek*. 3rd ed. Lanham, MD: University Press of America, 1997.

Monod, Jacques. 1972. *Chance and Necessity*. New York, NY: Vintage Books.

Montagu, Basil (ed.). 1855. *The Works of Francis Bacon*. 3 vols. Philadelphia, PA: Parry Macmillan.

Muir, Kenneth (ed.). 1959. *The Arden Shakespeare: King Lear*. Cambridge, MA: Harvard University Press.

Murray, A. T. (ed. and trans.). 1919. *Homer: The Odyssey*. 2 vols. Cambridge, MA: Harvard University Press.

Norton, Paul. 1981. "Leo Strauss: His Critique of Historicism," *Modern Age* 25,143–54.

Nussbaum, Martha. 1978. *Aristotle's* De Motu Animalium*: Text with Translation, Commentary, and Interpretive Essays*. Princeton, NJ: Princeton University Press.

O'Connor, D. J. (ed.). 1964. *A Critical History of Western Philosophy*. Glencoe, IL: Free Press.

Oesterle, Jean T. 1962. *Aristotle: On Interpretation, Commentary by St. Thomas and Cajetan*. Milwaukee, WI: Marquette University Press.

Pemberton, Henry. 1728. *A View of Sir Isaac Newton's Philosophy*. London: S. Palmer.

Pippard, A. B. 1972. *Reconciling Physics with Reality, An Inaugural Lecture*. Cambridge: Cambridge University Press.

Plato. 1956. *Phaedo*. Ed. John Burnet. Oxford: Clarendon Press.

——. 1961. *Meno*. Ed. R. S. Bluck. Cambridge: Cambridge University Press.

——. 1968. *The Republic*. Allan Bloom, trans. New York, NY: Basic Books.

——. 2004. *Meno*. Trans. Geoarge Anastaplo and Laurence Berns. Newburyport, MA: Focus Publishing/R. Pullins Co., 2004.

Riezler, Kurt. 1950. *Man, Mutable and Immutable: The Fundamental Structure of Social Life*. Chicago, IL: Henry Regnery.

Rossi, Paolo. 1968. *Francis Bacon, from Magic to Science*. London: Routledge and Kegan Paul.

——. 1970. *Philosophy, Technology, and the Arts in the Early Modern Era*. New York, NY: Harper & Row.

Simon, Yves. 1967. *The Tradition of Natural Law: A Philosopher's Reflections*. Vukan Kuic, ed. New York, NY: Fordham University Press.

——. 1969. *Freedom of Choice*. New York NY: Fordham University Press.

——. 1970. *The Great Dialogue of Nature and Space*. Albany, NY: Magi Books.

Sitwell, Edith. 1965. *A Notebook on William Shakespeare*. London: Macmillan.

Smith, Adam. 1981. *An Inquiry into the Nature and Causes of the Wealth of Nations*. R. H. Campbell, A. S. Skinner, and W. B. Todd, eds. Glasgow Edition. Indianapolis, IN: Liberty Press.

——. 1982a. *Essays on Philosophical Subjects*. W. P. D. Wightman and J. C. Bryce, eds. Glasgow Edition. Indianapolis, IN: Liberty Press.

——. 1982b. *The Theory of Moral Sentiments*. D. D. Raphael and A. L. Macfie, eds. Glasgow Edition. Indianapolis, IN: Liberty Press.

——. 1985. *Lectures on Rhetoric and Belles Lettres*. J. C. Bryce, ed. Glasgow Edition. Indianapolis: Liberty Press.

——. 1987. *Correspondence of Adam Smith*. Ernest Campbell Mossner and Ian Simpson Ross, eds. Glasgow Edition. Indianapolis: Liberty Press.

Snyder, Susan. 1966. "King Lear and the Prodigal Son." *Shakespeare Quarterly* 17.4, 361–69.

Spedding, James; Ellis, Robert Leslie; and Heath, Douglas Denon (eds.). 1875. *The Works of Francis Bacon*. 7 vols. London: Longmans.

Spicker, S.F. (ed.). 1978. *Organism, Medicine, and Metaphysics*. Dordrecht, Holland: D. Reidel.

Stewart, John A. 1892. *Notes on the Nicomachean Ethics of Aristotle*. 2 vols. Oxford: Clarendon Press.

Straus, Erwin. 1966. *Phenomenological Psychology*. New York, NY: Basic Books.

Strauss, Leo. 1935. *Philosophie und Gesetz: Beiträge zum Verständnis Maimunis und Seiner Vorläufer.* Berlin: Schocken.

——. 1946. "On a New Interpretation of Plato's Political Philosophy," *Social Research* 13, 326–67.

——. 1952. *Persecution and the Art of Writing.* Glencoe, IL: Free Press.

——. 1953. *Natural Right and History.* Chicago, IL: University of Chicago Press.

——. 1959. *What is Political Philosophy? And Other Studies.* Glencoe, IL: Free Press.

——. 1963. *On Tyranny.* Revised and enlarged ed. Glencoe, IL: Free Press.

——. 1964. *The City and Man.* Chicago, IL: University of Chicago Press.

——. 1965. *Spinoza's Critique of Religion.* New York, NY: Schocken Books.

——. 1968. *Liberalism Ancient and Modern.* New York, NY: Basic Books.

——. 1971. "Philosophy as Rigorous Science and Political Philosophy," *Interpretation* 2, 1–9.

——. 1972. *Xenophon's Socrates.* Ithaca, NY: Cornell University Press.

——. 1975. *Political Philosophy: Six Essays by Leo Strauss.* Hilail Gildin, ed. Indianapolis, IN: Pegasus-Bobbs-Merrill.

——. 1979. "The Mutual Influence of Theology and Philosophy," *The Independent Journal of Philosophy* 3, 111–18

——. 1981. "Progress or Return? The Contemporary Crisis in Western Civilization," *Modern Judaism* 1, 17–45.

——. 1987. *Philosophy and Law: Essays Toward the Understanding of Maimonides and his Predecessors.* Trans. Fred Baumann. Philadelphia, PA: The Jewish Publication Society.

——. 1989a. *An Introduction to Political Philosophy: Ten Essays by Leo Strauss.* Hilail Gildin, ed. Detroit, MI: Wayne State University Press.

——. 1989b. *The Rebirth of Classical Political Rationalism.* Thomas Pangle, ed. Chicago, IL: University of Chicago Press.

——. 1997. *Jewish Philosophy and the Crisis of Modernity: Essays and Lectures in Modern Jewish Thought.* Edited by Kenneth Hart Green. Albany, NY: State University of New York Press.

Swift, Jonathan. 1965. *A Tale of a Tub, With Other Early Works, 1696–1707.* Oxford: Basil Blackwell.

Telford, Kenneth A. 1961. *Aristotle's Poetics: Translation and Analysis.* Chicago, IL: Gateway.

Traversi, Derek A. 1938. *An Approach to Shakespeare*. London: The Paladin Press.
Umphrey, Stewart. 1982. "Erōs and Thumos," *Interpretation* 10, 353–422.
Wallace, William (trans.). 1892. *The Logic of Hegel*. London: Oxford University Press.
White, Howard B. 1968. *Peace Among the Willows: The Political Philosophy of Francis Bacon*. The Hague: Martinus Nijhoff.
———. 1970. *Copp'd Hills Towards Heaven: Shakespeare's Classical Polity*. The Hague: Martinus Nijhoff.
———. 1987. "Francis Bacon" in Cropsey and Strauss 1987, 366–85.
Wiesheipl, J. A. 1955. *Nature and Gravitation*. Rivert Forest, IL:: Albertus Magnus Lyceum.
Wilson, E.O. 1975. *Sociobiology: The New Synthesis*. Cambridge, MA: Harvard University Press.
———. 1978. *On Human Nature*. New York, NY: Bantam Books.
Wilson, James Q. 1993. *The Moral Sense*. New York, NY: Free Press.
Wolfson, Harry A. 1934. *The Philosophy of Spinoza*. 2 vols. Cambridge, MA: Harvard University Press.
Young, Robert. 1955. *Young's Analytical Concordance to the Bible*. Grand Rapids, MI: Eerdmans.